AUTONOMY

AUTONOMY

Edited by
**Ellen Frankel Paul, Fred D. Miller, Jr.,
and Jeffrey Paul**

CAMBRIDGE
UNIVERSITY PRESS

CAMBRIDGE
UNIVERSITY PRESS

32 Avenue of the Americas, New York NY 10013-2473, USA

Cambridge University Press is part of the University of Cambridge.

It furthers the University's mission by disseminating knowledge in the pursuit of education, learning and research at the highest international levels of excellence.

www.cambridge.org
Information on this title: www.cambridge.org/9780521534994

Copyright © 2003 Social Philosophy and Policy Foundation

First published 2003

A catalogue record for this publication is available from the British Library

Library of Congress Cataloguing in Publication data

Autonomy / edited by Ellen Frankel Paul,
Fred D. Miller, Jr., and Jeffrey Paul.   p.   cm.
Includes bibliographical references and index.
ISBN 0-521-53499-2
1. Autonomy (Philosophy)–History.
I. Paul, Ellen Frankel.   II. Miller, Fred Dycus, 1944-   III. Paul, Jeffrey.
B105.A84A88   2003
126–dc21   2003043769
CIP

ISBN 978-0-521-53499-4 Paperback

The essays in this book have also been published,
without introduction and index, in the semiannual journal
Social Philosophy & Policy, Volume 20, Number 2,
which is available by subscription.

CONTENTS

INTRODUCTION

Autonomy is often recognized as a central value in moral and political philosophy. There are, however, fundamental disagreements over how autonomy should be understood, what its implications are for public policy, and even whether the concept itself is theoretically defensible.

Autonomy is generally understood as some form of self-regulation, self-governance, or self-direction. As some of the essays in this volume show, great philosophers of the past have shed valuable light on the subject of autonomy: including the ancient Stoics, modern philosophers such as Spinoza, and most importantly, Immanuel Kant. Theorists have disputed whether such a view can be reconciled with the most plausible accounts of human motivation. Some have tried to analyze autonomy in terms of the self being fueled by its higher-order desires, passions, or commitments. Others have argued that autonomy must be understood in terms of acting from reason or a sense of moral duty independent of the passions. Theorists have also questioned whether the ideal of autonomy presupposes a metaphysical theory of free will, or whether it is consistent with some version of determinism. The difficult question of whether the concept of autonomy can be reconciled with empirical scientific theories of human psychology is also a pressing concern.

The role of autonomy in moral and political theory is controversial too. Some theorists argue that human rights are essentially rights to autonomy, whereas others treat the right to welfare as fundamental and autonomy as derivative. Still others maintain that individual autonomy should be subordinated to often conflicting values, for example, those centering on race, class, gender, or local community. Autonomy seems to be closely related to the notion of freedom, but what sense of "freedom" is involved: freedom from coercion, from psychological constraints, or from material necessity? Some theorists have argued that autonomy and freedom should, after all, be sharply distinguished.

These various interpretations seem to have very different implications for public policy, that is, for how laws, customs, and social institutions should protect individual autonomy. For example, what role should legal institutions play in safeguarding autonomy? Is any particular economic system—capitalism, social democracy, or socialism—more favorable to autonomy? What is the relation between individual autonomy and autonomy viewed as a property of political systems?

The contributors to this volume explore these and other important questions regarding the concept of autonomy.

The first three essays in this collection take a historical approach to autonomy. In his essay, "Stoic Autonomy," John M. Cooper points out that the ancient Stoics did not use the term "autonomy." (He does, however, identify one exception: Dio of Prusa, a first-century C.E. writer under Stoic influence, did use the term "autonomy.") Nonetheless, the notion did play a central and crucial role in the Stoics' conception of human nature, human rationality, and the basis of morality. On the Stoic view, perfected human beings live according to Zeus's or nature's law, and that law is also their own law, *qua* rational beings. In living in agreement with nature they live according to their own law, that is, they live autonomously. The similarities of autonomy as the Stoics conceived it to Kant's much more familiar conception make the Stoics important forerunners of Kant—neglected though they are in this capacity. The Stoic conception presents interesting and important differences from Kant's and, therefore, deserves attention in its own right, not just in comparison to Kant and the moderns.

"Autonomous Autonomy: Spinoza on Autonomy, Perfectionism, and Politics" engages in something of a quixotic enterprise, as Douglas Den Uyl points out at the outset of his article. Since the concept of autonomy was only developed in its modern form by Kant in the eighteenth century, the century after Spinoza's death, treating *autonomy* in Spinoza is anachronistic. Complicating Den Uyl's project, too, is Spinoza's lack of a concept of metaphysical freedom, except for God/Substance/Nature. In addition to these historical and metaphysical hurdles to accepting Spinoza as a political philosopher with valuable insights on autonomy, Spinoza disassociates freedom (or autonomy, which Den Uyl argues is linked to freedom) from politics. This disassociation is unfashionable in modern political thought, Den Uyl maintains, yet he finds in Spinoza a self-perfectionist meaning of autonomy that is designedly in conflict with politics. Rather than politics being about autonomy, even as an aspiration, for Spinoza it is about securing peace and stability by appealing to the emotive side of human nature. Thus, Spinoza's project is very different from the three leading Western political theories of modern times, which Den Uyl identifies as communitarian, liberal, and welfarist. Proponents of each of these views value autonomy for different but, in some cases, overlapping reasons: respectively, a concern that autonomy not be roped off from the political realm; that autonomy is necessary for politics or people might be treated as means to the ends of those in power; and that since autonomy is good for everyone it is the role of politics to promote this good. A modern Spinozist might use the language of autonomy employed by any of these three viewpoints, but he would be using it only as an instrument for promoting peace and security. The Spinozist, in other words, would use the language of autonomy for political purposes only if it served as an effective emotive device for persuading people to understand and perform their civic "duties."

Paul Guyer's essay, "Kant on the Theory and Practice of Autonomy," offers an exegesis of Kant's thought on autonomy, focusing on the seminal role of Kant's analysis in shaping future treatment of this concept to the present day. The first part of this essay analyzes Kant's concept of autonomy and argues for its independence from his transcendental theory of free will. The second part canvasses some of Kant's arguments for the value of autonomy that are suppressed in his published works, and shows how autonomy remains as a presupposition of moral imputation in Kant's mature works. The third part examines Kant's recommendation of methods by which persons may attain autonomy in the actual circumstances of human life.

Marina Oshana's "How Much Should We Value Autonomy?" grapples with the intriguing question: "What happens if we value autonomy too much?" She identifies three possible outcomes of such an overvaluation. First, we may believe that all persons deserve to have their autonomy respected, which may lead us to think that no incursions on autonomy are ever justified. This problem can be obviated, she argues, by modifying a negative test for desert based on John Stuart Mill's harm principle. Second, events in the world, such as the September 11, 2001, attacks on New York City and Washington, may test our commitment to autonomy by underscoring the susceptibility of the freedom and independence that autonomy fosters to dangerous forces in the world that do not share this basic value with us. Thus, in dangerous times, autonomy may have to be weighed in the balance against security, for the two will be in constant tension. Third, and both more difficult to resolve and more pernicious than the first two, an overvaluation of autonomy may lead us to intervene paternalistically in the lives of persons whom we consider insufficiently autonomous. That is, we might attempt to force them to be free, to borrow Rousseau's locution. Oshana wrestles with these three dangers, through a series of devices, including such intriguing examples as the "Taliban woman" and the "schizophrenic artist." She concludes that autonomy—as individual freedom—"is not sacrosanct." Although she is not prepared to offer a definitive, bright line to distinguish between permissible and impermissible interferences with autonomy, she offers much that is illuminating on the quandary of balancing autonomy and other important values.

James Stacey Taylor writes, in his essay entitled "Autonomy, Duress, and Coercion," that contemporary discussions of both personal autonomy and what it is for a person to "identify" with his or her desires are dominated by the "hierarchical"analyses of Gerald Dworkin and Harry Frankfurt. At the core of these analyses is the claim that it is a necessary condition for a person to be autonomous with respect to (that is, to identify with) a desire that moves her to act that she desires that this desire so move her. Irving Thalberg argues that these analyses should be rejected. This is because, he contends, a person who is forced to perform an action through being subjected to duress will desire to be moved by her desire to submit, and so the proponents of these analyses will be forced to hold that such a person did not suffer from any impairment in her autonomy. And this is highly counterintuitive. Taylor evaluates and ultimately rejects Thalberg's critique, finding that his objections are based on a fundamental misunderstanding of the hierarchical analyses. Unfortunately, Taylor concludes, even when the hierarchical analyses are properly understood they *still* have counterintuitive implications when they are applied to a situation in which a person acts under duress. Thus, even though these analyses are flawed, they can still provide the key to answering one of the perennial questions in the philosophy of action: Does a person who is forced to perform an action solely in order to avoid a threatened penalty thereby suffer from impaired autonomy?

Michael E. Bratman, in "Autonomy and Hierarchy," locates the central feature of autonomous action in *agential direction*. In agential direction there is sufficient unity and organization of the motives of action for their functioning to constitute direction by the agent. *Agential governance* is agential direction that appropriately involves the agent's treatment of certain considerations as reasons. Bratman defends a model of agential governance—and so of autonomous agency—that highlights higher-order policies about the role of one's desires in one's motivationally effective practical reasoning. He calls such policies "self-governing policies" and argues also that they are an important kind of valuing, a kind of valuing that is responsive both to our need for management of our motivation and to our need to shape our own lives in the face of multiple values. His discussion constitutes a defense of the *autonomy-hierarchy thesis*, the thesis (roughly) that there is a close connection between autonomous agency and motivational hierarchy.

In Keith Lehrer's essay, "Reason and Autonomy," he states that philosophers have often thought that governing your life by reason or being responsive to reason is the source of autonomy. This leads to a paradox, however: *the paradox of reason*. It is that if we are governed by reason in what we choose, then we are in bondage to reason in what we choose and we are not autonomous, but if we are not governed by reason, then we do not govern ourselves in what we choose, and again we are not autonomous. The resolution of the paradox requires that whether we are governed by reason must itself be an autonomous choice. Which comes first, the choice to be governed by reason, or the governance of reason in the choice? The answer is to be found in a higher-order account of autonomous preferences that involves a power preference that loops back onto itself, thus avoiding a regress. The power preference is, then, the keystone of autonomy.

"Identification, the Self, and Autonomy" is the title of Bernard Berofsky's essay. He argues that the idea of personal autonomy would appear to be that of regulation or direction by the self, an idea that he distinguishes from self-expression or self-fulfillment. Although we also suppose that this direction must be undertaken for the most part through conscious decision-making, different conceptions of the self abound. Close examination of a prominent theory—the *Self-Constituting Decision Theory*—is undertaken. The central concept of the theory is an act of identification, which he analyzes in order to see whether it can bear the required weight. He concludes that autonomy cannot be understood in this way insofar as identification is conceived as overly abstracted from a psychic system that must play a more significant role in self-characterization. A surprising consequence of this result is his abandonment of the driving conception of autonomy as self-direction. For the self may direct action in a way that the agent repudiates when that repudiation is informed, uncoerced, rational, and healthy, that is, autonomous. Such an agent cannot be thought of as autonomous.

Jonathan Jacobs, in his essay entitled "Some Tensions between Autonomy and Self-Governance," writes that it is a crucial part of a great deal of moral theorizing that rational agents have a distinctive moral status and are owed a distinctive kind of respect on account of being autonomous. At the same time, our estimations of agents and the regard we have for them depend upon their characters and the extent of their responsibility for their characters. While autonomy *demands* respect, the ways in which agents are self-governing *merits* certain sorts of regard; and these can be at odds with each other. This is particularly evident in the context of blame and punishment. Some agents, while rational and responsible, may have such vicious characters that they seem to merit loathing in a way that threatens the respect owed to agents. Jacob's discussion explores the moral psychology and normative issues associated with this tension.

Howard Rachlin's essay, "Autonomy from the Viewpoint of Teleological Behaviorism," argues that the social purpose of classifying some subset of a person's particular acts as autonomous is to give society a basis for attributing responsibility for those acts to the person. Responsibility, in turn, is the rationale for society allocating rewards and punishments to its members. Consistent with this purpose, the degree of autonomy of an act depends not only on the characteristics of the act itself but also on the characteristics of the more abstract pattern of acts of which this act is a part. Acts performed not for their own sake but for the sake of a more abstract pattern are defined as autonomous. For example, refusal of a drink by an alcoholic is an autonomous act, whereas indulging in the drink is nonautonomous. Rachlin's concept of autonomy is, therefore, congruent with that of self-control.

Christopher Heath Wellman's essay on "The Paradox of Group Autonomy" explores the prospects of developing a satisfying account of group autonomy without rejecting value-individualism. That is, he examines whether one can adequately explain the moral reasons to respect a group's claim to self-determination while insisting that only individual persons are of ultimate moral value. In this quest, he reviews three possible accounts of group autonomy: (1) value-collectivism, (2) individual autonomy, and (3) individual well-being. In the end he finds none of these approaches fully adequate, concluding with what he terms the "Paradox of Group Autonomy."

In "Abortion, Autonomy, and Control over One's Body," John Martin Fischer explores implications of autonomy for an important and controversial political issue. The core of his article is a critique of Judith Jarvis Thomson's famous essay, "A Defense of Abortion." In her essay, Thomson argues that it is perfectly permissible for you to unplug yourself from a severely ill violinist to whom you have been connected without your permission, even if the violinist's survival depends upon remaining plugged into your body. Using the violinist case as an analogy to abortion, she concludes that abortion is permissible, even if the fetus is assumed to be a person from the beginning. Fischer takes up the violinist case, arguing that, despite the conventional wisdom, it is morally *impermissible* for you to unplug yourself from the violinist. This is because the violinist case is indistinguishable from various cases in which you do need to provide assistance to another person. But, disaggregating the violinist from a case of pregnancy due to rape, Fischer contends that it need not follow from his position on the violinist case that abortion is impermissible in a case of rape. He argues that there are important asymmetries between the violinist example and the context of rape.

Steven Wall's piece, "Freedom as a Political Ideal," treats the political aspects of freedom (or autonomy) and identifies the kind of freedom that the state ought to promote. The ideal that Wall endorses holds that the state ought to promote and sustain an environment in which its subjects are best able to carry out their plans and form new ones. More precisely, he argues that a freedom-supportive state will sustain a legal and economic structure that allows its subjects to coordinate their activities and plan efficiently. Furthermore, such a state will ensure that all of its subjects have access to a wide range of valuable options, and it will minimize the interference and domination that frustrate the plans of those who are subject to its authority. After describing this ideal and arguing that it is superior to its main rivals, Wall defends his freedom-supportive state from a number of objections and discusses implications for institutional design.

The essays in this collection complement each other and represent the many different approaches that are taken to the concept of autonomy among political philosophers.

ACKNOWLEDGMENTS

The editors gratefully acknowledge several individuals at the Social Philosophy and Policy Center, Bowling Green State University, who provided invaluable assistance in the preparation of this volume. They include Mary Dilsaver, Terrie Weaver, and Assistant Director Travis S. Cook.

We especially wish to thank Publication Specialist Tamara Sharp for her very efficient and patient help throughout the production process, Editorial Assistant Carrie-Ann Khan for her meticulous attention to detail, and Managing Editor Teresa Donovan.

CONTRIBUTORS

John M. Cooper is Stuart Professor of Philosophy at Princeton University. He is the author of *Reason and Human Good in Aristotle* (1975), which was awarded the American Philosophical Association's Franklin Matchette prize, and *Reason and Emotion: Essays on Ancient Moral Psychology and Ethical Theory* (1999). He is co-editor of *Seneca: Moral and Political Essays* (with J. F. Procope, 1995), and editor of *Plato: Complete Works* (1997). He is a past President of the American Philosophical Association, Eastern Division, and has held research fellowships from the National Endowment for the Humanities, the John Simon Guggenheim Foundation, the American Council of Learned Societies, and the Center for Advanced Study in the Behavioral Sciences.

Douglas Den Uyl is Vice President of Education at Liberty Fund, Inc. He taught Philosophy and served as Department Chair at Bellarmine College (now Bellarmine University). He co-founded the American Association for the Philosophic Study of Society, the North American Spinoza Society, and the International Adam Smith Society. Interested in the history of ideas, as well as moral and political theory, he has published articles and books on Spinoza, Smith, Shaftesbury, and Mandeville, among others.

Paul D. Guyer is Professor of Philosophy and Florence R. C. Murray Professor in the Humanities at the University of Pennsylvania. He is the author of four books on Kant, covering Kant's aesthetics, theoretical philosophy, and moral and political philosophy: *Kant and the Claims of Knowledge* (1987), *Kant and the Experience of Freedom: Essays on Aesthetics and Morality* (1996), *Kant and the Claims of Taste* (1997), and *Kant on Freedom, Law, and Happiness* (2000). He is the editor of four anthologies, including an anthology of critical essays on Kant's *Groundwork for the Metaphysics of Morals* (1998), and is a co-translator of new editions of Kant's *Critique of Pure Reason* (1998) and *Critique of the Power of Judgment* (2000). He has recently been editing Kant's *Notes* and *Fragments*, and continuing work on many aspects of Kant's philosophy.

Marina Oshana is Associate Professor of Philosophy, Bowling Green State University, and a Senior Research Fellow at the Social Philosophy and Policy Center, Bowling Green State University. Her interests include normative ethics, moral psychology, and the relationship between autonomy, responsibility, and rationality. She has written for such journals as *Journal of Social Philosophy*, *American Philosophical Quarterly*, *Midwest Studies in Philosophy*, and *The Journal of Ethics*.

James Stacey Taylor is Assistant Professor of Philosophy at Louisiana State University. His teaching and research interests focus on both normative and applied ethics and theories of personal autonomy. He has been working on a book that develops a cognitivist analysis of personal autonomy and its applications to a variety of issues in both applied ethics and social philosophy. He has published reviews and articles in *Journal of Value Inquiry*, *Philosophical Quarterly*, and *Eidos*.

Michael E. Bratman is U. G. and Abbie Birch Durfee Professor in the School of Humanities and Sciences and Professor of Philosophy at Stanford University. He is the author of *Intention, Plans, and Practical Reason* (1987), *Faces of Intention: Selected Essays on Intention and Agency* (1999), and various articles on philosophy of action and related fields.

Keith Lehrer is Regents Professor of Philosophy at the University of Arizona. He has published numerous works, including books on epistemology, rational consensus, and Thomas Reid. He recently authored *Self-Trust: A Study of Reason, Knowledge, and Autonomy* (1997). He has been awarded fellowships from the National Science Foundation, the National Endowment for the Humanities, the American Council of Learned Societies, the John Simon Guggenheim Foundation, the Center for Advanced Study in the Behavioral Sciences at Stanford University, and, most recently, the Research School of the Australian National University and the School for Advanced Study, University of London. He received an honorary doctoral degree from the University of Graz, Austria, where he is also an honorary professor.

Bernard Berofsky is Professor of Philosophy at Columbia University. He has taught at Vassar College and the University of Michigan, and has been a Fellow of the American Council of Learned Societies and a Fulbright Research Scholar at the Hebrew University of Jerusalem. He has written extensively on free will, responsibility, and autonomy, and is the author of *Freedom from Necessity* (1987) and *Liberation from Self* (1995). He is a member of the Executive Committee of the Editorial Board of *Journal of Philosophy*.

Jonathan Jacobs is Professor of Philosophy and Chair of the Department of Philosophy and Religion at Colgate University. His recent books are *Dimensions of Moral Theory* (2002) and *Choosing Character: Responsibility for Virtue and Vice* (2001). He has published widely in metaethics and moral psychology, and also on Maimonides and Aquinas, in journals such as *Review of Metaphysics*, *Monist*, *Philosophy*, and *Ratio*, among others. He has been a Visiting Professor at the University of Edinburgh, and a Research Fellow at the Center for Philosophy and Public Affairs at the University of St. Andrews.

Howard Rachlin is Distinguished Professor of Psychology at the State University of New York at Stony Brook. He is the author most recently of *The Science of Self-Control* (2000). His research interests include human and animal decision-making, temporal and probabilistic discounting, self-control, addiction, gambling, and social cooperation.

Christopher Heath Wellman directs the Jean Beer Blumenfeld Center for Ethics and is Associate Professor of Philosophy at Georgia State University. His work is primarily in ethics, specializing in political and legal philosophy. He co-edited, with R. G. Frey, *A Companion to Applied Ethics* (2002). He has published in such journals as *Political Theory, American Philosophical Quarterly, Philosophy and Public Affairs, Law and Philosophy, Social Theory and Practice,* and *Ethics.*

John Martin Fischer is Professor of Philosophy at the University of California, Riverside. He is the author of *The Metaphysics of Free Will: An Essay on Control* (1994) and *Responsibility and Control: A Theory of Moral Responsibility* (with Mark Ravizza, 1998). His research interests include free will and moral responsibility, philosophy of religion, topics in normative and applied ethics, and the metaphysics of death.

Steven Wall is Associate Professor of Philosophy at Bowling Green State University and previously taught at Kansas State University. He is currently on leave as a Laurence S. Rockefeller Visiting Fellow at The University Center for Human Values at Princeton University. His dissertation, *Liberalism, Perfection, and Restraint,* won the 1997 Sir Ernest Barker Prize for Best Dissertation in Political Philosophy from the Political Studies Association. He is the author of *Liberalism, Perfectionism, and Restraint* (1998) and co-editor, with George Klosko, of *Perfectionism and Neutrality: Essays in Liberal Theory* (2003).

STOIC AUTONOMY

By John M. Cooper

I. Introduction

As it is currently understood, the notion of autonomy, both as something that belongs to human beings and human nature, as such, and also as the source or basis of morality (that is, duty), is bound up inextricably with the philosophy of Kant. The term "autonomy" itself derives from classical Greek, where (at least in surviving texts) it was applied primarily or even exclusively in a political context, to civic communities possessing independent legislative and self-governing authority.[1] The term was taken up again in Renaissance and early modern times with similar political applications, but was applied also in ecclesiastical disputes about the independence of reformed churches from the former authority in religious matters of the church of the Roman popes.[2] Kant's innovation consisted in conceiving of (finite) individual rational persons, as such, as lawgivers or legislators to themselves, and to all rational beings (or rather to all that are not perfect and holy wills), for their individual modes of behavior. For Kant, rational beings possess a power of legislating for themselves individually, according to which they each set their own personal ends and subject that selection, and their pursuit of the ends in question, to a universal principle, which is expressed in Kant's *categorical imperative*. The categorical imperative requires that one set one's own ends only within a framework that would warrant acceptance by all other such beings. For Kant, autonomy accompanies individual (finite) rationality, and has nothing to do with the political (or other organizational) circumstances of any specific community of agents, even though it un-

---

[1] See H. G. Liddell, Robert Scott, and H. S. Jones, *A Greek-English Lexicon* (Oxford: Clarendon Press, 1940), s.vv. αὐτονομία, αὐτόνομος. See also Martin Ostwald, *Autonomia: Its Genesis and Early History*, American Philological Association *American Classical Studies* 11 (Chico, CA: Scholars Press, 1982). Ostwald, building upon E. J. Bickerman's demonstration ("Autonomia: Sur un passage de Thucydide [1,144,2]," *Revue Internationale des Droits de l'Antiquité* 5 [1958]: 313–44) that the term belongs to the vocabulary of interstate relations, argues persuasively that it was coined in order to help weaker states drawn into an orbit of dependence on a stronger one to assert and preserve their limited independence. (Such states included especially Athens' allies in the Delian League, which was initially established to combat the Persians, in 478–77 B.C.E.) The term was not applied in classical times to the stronger states themselves.

[2] Here I follow the summary provided in J. B. Schneewind, *The Invention of Autonomy: A History of Modern Moral Philosophy* (New York: Cambridge University Press, 1998), 3 n. 2, and the full account in R. Pohlmann, "Autonomie," in J. Ritter, ed., *Historisches Wörterbuch der Philosophie* (Basel: Schwabe, 1971), 1:701–19, to which Schneewind refers.

1

derstandably gave rise to the conception of a "kingdom" or "realm" of ends in which each (fully) rational end-setter would cooperate with, and support, all other end-setters in a harmonious pursuit by all of their individual self-set ends, under the umbrella of the commonly legislated categorical imperative.

Without making any reference to possible influences of Stoic ideas upon Kant—that would be beyond my competence, and anyhow would be work for a subsequent study—I shall explore here what I think are related ideas in ancient Stoicism. Before doing so, however, it might be both interesting and helpful to review the early history of the term "autonomy," particularly as it was applied to individuals.

So far as I have been able to determine, there are just three places in surviving classical Greek literature (i.e., down to Roman imperial times) where the term is applied to individuals, as such, and without immediate reference to political autonomy, so understood. In one passage of Sophocles' *Antigone* (821, referred to in Liddell-Scott-Jones) the chorus, in a lyric exchange with Antigone about her already decreed punishment, by being deposited alive in a blocked-off cavern to make her own way to Hades, speaks of her as the only mortal to descend to Hades alive and "of her own law" (αὐτόνομος). The unusual choice of word here (where the basic meaning intended seems to be "of her own free will"—ἑκών—and the word is applied not in virtue of any political autonomy) must, however, have something to do with Antigone's own tragic insistence, which has led to her predicament, on following the higher religious law that requires burial for her traitorous brother in the face of directives of King Cleon forbidding it. If she does go down to Hades while still alive, and by her own act of defiance, that, too, will be a case of her following her own ideas of what law itself—religious and civic—requires in a case of such conflict with civic authority. In going down to Hades "of her own law," she is deciding for herself which law (or directive) to follow—with this consequence. So, even here the context of political independence for the use of this term is not lacking, although it is a highly unusual case of it; there is no hint here of Kantian self-legislation of ends or of principles of self-criticism.

Somewhat similar is a passage of Xenophon's *Constitution of the Lacedaemonians* (3.1), where he praises Lycurgus's Spartan arrangements for teenage boys, contrasting them with customs in other cities, where boys upon reaching that age are freed from daily oversight by tutors (παιδαγωγοί) and left "to be their own law" (αὐτονόμους): the implied contrast here is with the laws (νόμοι) of Lycurgus (see the reference to those in 1.2, 8). Teenagers in other cities are not under special laws of good and modest behavior at all, of the sort that Xenophon goes on to detail that were in force in Sparta (3.2–4); hence, they can be described as being "their own law"—they are allowed to do what they please (this is the meaning), since they are *not* subject to "youth laws" at all. In the "epilogue" of the *Panathenaic Oration* (215), Isocrates turns the tables on Xenophon (whether the correction is intended or not) in seeking to draw favorable attention to his own allegedly balanced account, earlier in the speech, of Sparta's contributions to the values of Hellenism, alongside those of Athens. He puts into the mouth of an unnamed former pupil, described as well known for his praise of Spartan practices, the word αὐτονομία, with strongly negative connotation, to describe one of the practices that Xenophon had praised so highly himself (2.6–9): that of encouraging young Spartans to steal food and other supplies from the non-Spartan country dwellers, provided that they could do so undetected. Thus, Isocrates seems to be saying, Xenophon was not right to count other Greeks' failure to have "youth laws" as granting the youths reckless "autonomy"; on the contrary, the Spartans are the ones who are guilty in this instance of making the boys and youths behave in recklessly "autonomous" ways that everyone else knows are disgraceful, despite their being demanded by Lycurgan laws.

Thus, even in these three apparently anomalous passages, personal "autonomy" carries with it a clear contrast to some existing legal provision with which it conflicts. As we shall see in the next section, it is only with Dio Chrysostom's *80th Discourse* (end of the first century C.E.), that we first find the terms αὐτόνομος and αὐτονομία used for personal autonomy understood in approximately Kant's way.

II. DIO CHRYSOSTOM ON THE "AUTONOMOUS" LIVES OF PHILOSOPHERS

In speaking of ideas related to Kant's in ancient Stoicism, I have primarily in mind the work of the original Stoics of the third century B.C.E. and especially that of the great philosopher Chrysippus. However, in order to introduce the themes I want to discuss in this essay, I begin by citing a fascinating and, in this context, apparently overlooked oration of the late first century C.E. popular philosopher, Dio of Prusa (who is also called Dio Chrysostom, "of the golden mouth," in recognition of his powerfully inspiring speechifying). Dio was not strictly a Stoic philosopher—he apparently did not teach or hold forth in any "school"—but he did study at Rome with the important Roman Stoic, Musonius Rufus (who taught in Greek, and who had among his other pupils Epictetus). During the middle decades of his life, Dio was a wandering orator, in forced exile from both Rome and his home in Bithynia, in northwest Asia Minor. He was a popular proponent of salvation through "the philosophical life." His conception of what that life is like and the source of its value owes a very great deal to Stoic theory and example. The discourse that I have in mind is the eightieth and last in the standard order, and bears the title *On Freedom* (Περὶ ἐλευθερίας).[3]

[3] *Dio Chrysostom*, V, trans. H. Lamar Crosby, Loeb Classical Library (Cambridge, MA: Harvard University Press, 1951).

Dio opens the discourse with a conceit. He attributes to his audience bafflement at, and dismissal of, the odd behavior of self-professed philosophers, who wander around the town, sporting beards, wearing torn cloaks reminiscent of Socrates, preferably walking barefoot, with no remunerative occupation or ordinary social connections, and paying no attention to the theatrical or other spectacles of Greek city-life. Rather, they attend individually to passersby on the street and engage them in conversation, or else just stand there in the middle of things, thinking (80.2). Dio then turns the tables, by declaring that only such philosophers are, in fact, in the condition, which was highly prized by all ordinary Greeks, of freedom (ἐλευθερία). Ordinary people, these critics of philosophers, are definitely not free; they are actually slaves. Indeed, Dio insists, only the philosopher is αὐτόνομος, living under his own law (another, related, condition that was highly prized in the Greek cities). In contrast, all ordinary people are subject to direction by outside forces (80.3); they are not under their own law. Money, fame, or pleasures with their alluring appeal are their self-imposed mistresses; they are in fact, Dio says, their self-imposed fetters and enslavement (80.7–14).

Dio goes on to explain (80.3–6) that the *political* autonomy that the cities and tribes have constantly fought for, from time immemorial, is worthless if (as, in fact, is the case) the people possessing it are themselves, individually, merely slaves. Indeed, even the great lawgivers of the politically autonomous cities, for example, Solon in Athens, were not personally autonomous themselves (τούτων οὐδενὶ μετῆν αὐτονομίας), since the laws that they gave were not actually the laws that would have satisfied themselves, but rather, only less satisfactory (indeed, bad) laws that were the best that their fellow citizens could be persuaded to accept (80.4). Thus the lawgivers lacked autonomy, because the laws that they were famous for establishing were not ones that, if the lawgivers were left to themselves, they would have laid down for everyone, including themselves, to obey. The actual laws were not really *their* laws at all. In fact, autonomy — self-rule, living under one's own laws—only comes when one obeys the law of nature (ὁ τῆς φύσεως νόμος), that is to say, the ordinance of Zeus (τὸν τοῦ Διὸς θεσμόν). This is the only law that is true, and that has any valid authority. Although it is open to view, people do not see it, and do not make *it* the leader of their lives.[4] This, however, is precisely what the philosopher does see, and what he does do. In living by the law of nature, the law of Zeus, he also lives by his *own* law—and so obtains true autonomy, the only autonomy worth having.

In this short discourse, Dio uses the Greek words for "autonomous" or "autonomy" repeatedly (four times in all),[5] always in a usage that he

---

[4] νόμον δὲ τὸν ἀληθῆ καὶ κύριον καὶ φανερὸν οὔτε ὁρῶσιν οὔτε ἡγεμόνα ποιοῦνται τοῦ βίου (80.5).
[5] Five, if one counts, as well, the very striking phrase that he substitutes once in explication or variation: τοῖς αὐτὸς αὑτοῦ χρῆσθαι νόμοις (80.3), "to use oneself one's own laws."

himself clearly grasps and, indeed, clearly explains, but in which the terms do not appear, except, at best, in very undeveloped form (see n. 1), in Greek of the classical period. Classical Greek refers only glancingly to persons governing themselves individually on the basis of their own "laws" (i.e., laws that are, if not necessarily self-imposed, then at least self-chosen or self-recognized). One striking feature of the text is that Dio first uses this terminology (80.3) before he introduces (in 80.5) any reference to laws of nature or of Zeus, which, as I mentioned, he eventually equates with the "laws" that a philosopher, in living according to his own laws, will obey. The idea of autonomy, as Dio uses the term from the outset, is simply that of living according to one's own "laws" of personal behavior. But what laws could these be? What justifies any claim, of the sort that Dio makes from the very beginning, and before making any reference to nature's law, that what the philosophers live according to are entitled to the name of *laws*? How is this to be understood?

It helps that Dio couples the term autonomy with freedom (ἐλευθερία) at its first occurrence, and slavery (ἐν οἰκέταις 80.3; cf. δουλεία 80.4) with the lack of autonomy, both in the personal and in the political spheres. It was a commonplace of Stoic theory, which Dio could confidently expect his readers to recall immediately upon hearing philosophers described as the only free persons, that only perfected human beings, or "wise" people in Stoic terminology,[6] are free, while everyone else is both a fool and (therefore) a slave.[7] As Cicero explains the Stoic view (*Stoic Paradoxes* 5, sec. 34), if freedom is the power to live as you will (*potestas vivendi ut velis*), then, in fact, only the wise are free.[8] Only the wise have a clearly conceived plan of life which they unwaveringly also follow; only they never do anything from fear, or through any threat or coercion; only they never regret anything that they have to do, or anything that they have done. Everyone else acts in obedience to circumstances, acting as *circumstances* direct, so as to avoid pain, or monetary loss, or the like, and following opportunities for pleasure or gain as circumstances dictate. Such a person acts in the abject and broken spirit of a slave, as Cicero puts it, ordered about willy-nilly—as a person that has no will of its own (*arbitrio carentis suo*) (sec. 35). Only wise people live as they themselves will. Even if they, too, vary their behavior to suit their circumstances, as everyone must, they do this not in pursuance of any fundamental attachment to anything that circumstances can control—that is, any external

---

[6] Σοφοί, traditionally rendered in English by "sages"—but it is better to avoid that term nowadays, since it smacks of pretentiousness and obscurantism, and it was no part of Stoic theory that a wise person would have either of those qualities.

[7] See Diogenes Laertius, *Lives of Eminent Philosophers*, trans. R. D. Hicks, Loeb Classical Library, two volumes (Cambridge, MA: Harvard University Press, 1925), 7.121. For evidence that these claims were already, and offensively, made by Zeno, the Stoic founder, in his *Republic*, see 7.32–33.

[8] In H. Rackham, ed. and trans., *Cicero IV*, Loeb Classical Library (Cambridge, MA: Harvard University Press, 1942).

object or condition, whether pleasant, or painful, or possessed of any
other concrete characteristics. They act only out of a single, consistent
desire, in every circumstance, simply to "follow nature." (And, of course,
their wisdom consists centrally in knowing what following nature means,
in each circumstance that may arise.) Thus the wise, and only the wise,
are free, according to well-known Stoic principles, because only they, in
consistently "following nature" in all their actions, are acting on their *own*
will—their will to follow nature. They are never led by the nose by
particular, concretely characterized events that occur or that are in prospect. Diogenes Laertius, in setting out the Stoic view, speaks of this freedom as the "power of 'self-action,'" the power to do one's own actions
(ἐξουσίαν αὐτοπραγίας, 7.121).[9]

Still, it is quite a step from freedom as self-action and acting according
to one's own will (αὐτοπραγία), to autonomy or living according to one's
own laws (αὐτονομία). As if to distract the listener from recoiling at his
novel conception of autonomy as something that belongs to individuals
as such (without reference to their political circumstances), Dio immediately follows up by leaving aside freedom understood in Cicero's way, as
an individual's "self-action," and pursues, instead, the implications of
political freedom, and the autonomy that goes with that. It was for that
sort of autonomy, he says, instead of this philosophical independence,
that tribes and cities have always fought[10]—fruitlessly, he says, as the
history of Solon's legislation shows. The laws of Athens that we know as
Solon's were not "his own" laws: as Solon himself confessed in a famous
poem, he was not (as Dio puts it) "autonomous" in laying down the
political laws and social practices that he devised and imposed on everyone, himself included (once he returned from a voluntary, ten-year-long
exile). He imposed not the laws that he would have preferred, but the
ones that he thought the citizens would accept. Under those laws, the
Athenians continued to be slaves in their dependence on external circumstances, even after achieving political self-rule under Solon's laws. Political autonomy was therefore useless to them, and so it is to all of us, as
well. By contrast, Dio suggests, philosophers, however bizarre they might
appear in the eyes of ordinary people and however unconventional their
way of life may be, have not only freedom but *true autonomy*—a life truly
under their own rule, under their own laws.

---

[9] Plutarch quotes a passage of Chrysippus's lost work *On Lives*, where Chrysippus equated
the Platonic phrase, familiar from the *Republic* (and the *Charmides*), "to do one's own" (τὰ
αὐτοῦ πράττειν, which is characteristic of virtuous people, for example, just or temperate
ones), with αὐτοπραγία or "self-action": *Plutarch: Moralia*, XIII, ed. and trans. H. C. Cherniss,
Loeb Classical Library (Cambridge, MA: Harvard University Press, 1976), pt. 2, *Stoic Self-
Contradictions* 1043b.
[10] There is a problem with the text at this point; the MSS read in 80.3 something ungram-
matical and unintelligible, ἀνόητοι εἴδους αὐτονομίας ἔρωτι ἐρῶτες. I am not satisfied with
the emendations that have been proposed by Post (printed, e.g., in the Loeb text and
translated there) and others, but I believe that this issue does not affect what I say in my text.

It is only at this point (80.5–6), when he goes on to speak of the laws of nature and the laws of Zeus, that we hear from Dio any reason at all for thinking of the philosopher's or the wise person's life in that way, as one under "his own laws." Now we can see, but not before, that for the philosopher, living by his own will (freedom) is living by his own laws (autonomy), because his consistent will is not only to follow nature, or Zeus, but also in doing so, to obey nature's and Zeus's *law*. As Dio, and his audience, too, knew very well, it was a central tenet of Stoicism that this is what following nature means. As we hear from Diogenes Laertius (7.88), the Stoic "end," which is understood as living following nature (τὸ ἀκολούθως τῇ φύσει ζῆν), involves not doing anything that "the law common to all things" (ὁ νόμος ὁ κοινός) normally forbids; and, as Diogenes tells us, this law is equated with the correct reason (λόγος) that runs through everything and is the same as Zeus. So, in living following nature — that is, as we have seen from Cicero's explication, in living freely and by his own will — the Stoic philosopher also lives by Zeus's or nature's law, which thereby becomes his own law for himself.

It seems, then, that Dio felt the need to draw upon both the Greeks' overriding goal of political autonomy and his claim that it fails to make people truly free (by the stringent, but well and forcefully articulated, standards of Stoic philosophy), in order to prepare the way for, and to validate retrospectively, this conception of philosophical freedom as a more important, indeed, the only true kind of, "autonomy." This seems to me to be some indication that the idea of personal, as against political, autonomy, which he introduces in this roundabout way, may have been Dio's invention. At the least, it does not seem that such use of the term was common coin by his time. (As I mentioned above, no earlier ancient author whose works have come down to us presents any such idea.) Thus, it seems that Dio juxtaposed, for the first time, the standard Stoic idea of the philosopher's (or, rather, the wise person's) freedom with another standard Stoic idea, that the philosopher (or the wise person) always obeys nature's and Zeus's law. The result is a conception of the philosopher or the wise person as the only one who truly lives autonomously, that is, by his own law.

III. Rationality as the Ground of Autonomy

Although they seem never to have used the term autonomy in this connection, I suggest that the classical Stoics did, in fact, conceive the lives of wise people in just this way — as lives lived autonomously, under each individual's own law, where that law is also, and indeed by its origin, Zeus's or nature's law. The implication here — since the wise person is simply the perfected human being — is that Zeus's or nature's law is our law too, the law of human beings as such. So, it is only through

accepting and implementing in one's life Zeus's law, that is, Stoic morality, that any human being achieves autonomy and lives autonomously.
What in Stoic theory grounds this idea? This question is the focus of my
discussion in the following sections of this essay.

The key point here is that, for the Stoics, human beings, and, out of all
of nature's creations,[11] only human beings, are rational—only they possess the power of reasoning. It is important, though, to attend closely to
what this power consists in, for the Stoics. We, with modern understandings of reason, might be inclined to think that it is simply the ability to tell
what follows from what, or, in general, to deal with given data so as to form
some reasoned opinion about what to think on the basis of them about some
question that might be asked. But that is not how the Stoics, or indeed ancient philosophers, in general, think about rationality.[12] Rather, for them,
reason is constituted, in the first instance (subject to further developments
and perfections), by (the possession of) a somewhat open-ended set of particular *concepts*, which are themselves regarded as a body of basic knowledge, rationally articulated. Human beings are not born rational, and no
child before "the age of reason" has any effective rational capacities at all.[13]
As children we follow natural instincts, aided, of course, by parental guidance, in seeking our growth and survival in our environments. In doing
so, we come, through naturally imbued procedures, to form original, "natural" concepts of all sorts of objects, and their properties, that we confront
in our experience. We only become rational, or possessed of reason, when,
after a long period of such exposure to the world around us, we have ac-
cumulated this basic set of concepts. Thus, as we develop, we get an idea,
or a concept, of human beings themselves (what it is to be a human being),
of males and females, of mothers and fathers, of trees and plants that are
of interest to us, of animals, such as dogs, or cats, or cows, or mice, that are
found in our environments and that make a difference to us. As we seek
to grow and survive, we also form concepts of various foods, of utensils,
and, of course, of all the colors and tastes, and sounds and textures, that
matter to us in our daily lives. In addition to accumulating such basic knowledge as children, as we develop we also get the concepts of good and bad,
and certain other evaluative notions.

To say that we get these concepts "naturally" is to say that (still on the
Stoic theory) we do not reach them by calculating or inferring anything in
any way, for example from our experiences; we just naturally, given our
experiences of, and with, the world around us, form the relevant con-

[11] That is, its creations on or in the vicinity of the earth. The exception implied here is
meant to cover the sun and moon and stars, which, according to the Stoics, were rational
beings, too—I do not mean to suggest that the Stoics envisaged or accepted any such
nonhuman rational beings as, e.g., creatures on alien planets, or creatures flying through the
air as angels.

[12] On what follows see M. Frede, "The Stoic Conception of Reason," in K. J. Boudouris,
ed., *Hellenistic Philosophy*, vol. 2 (Athens: International Association for Greek Philosophy,
1994), 50–61.

[13] What I mean here by "effective" will become clear below.

cepts. You could say that this is how we are made, how we are constituted by nature when we are born into the world. We are born so as to develop in this way, and we do so develop unless some untoward circumstance prevents it. In fact, because we do not reach our first and basic concepts by any sort of reasoning, but simply by a natural process of development, the Stoics think that these are guaranteed to be correct concepts: concepts such that their content is guaranteed to apply to, to be true of, some of what the world itself contains. The world contains things of which our basic, natural concepts are true, just because those concepts have been reached in our development by these natural, noninferential, and on our part, totally nonvoluntary routes. We (our minds) have contributed nothing to the concepts' formation, so there is no possibility of distortion or mistake in them from our own minds. And what other source of mistake should anyone imagine there might be?

For a human to be a rational being, then, is, in the first instance, to possess this basic stock of totally natural, well-grounded and correct, concepts. These are concepts that all human beings, as such, will have, wherever and whenever they live, if they have not been specially prevented or deprived.[14] Thus, to be rational, for the Stoics, is first of all to possess a certain stock of basic knowledge: knowledge about the objects that a human being deals with in the ordinary course of living, and of the properties of those objects on the basis of which this ordinary interaction takes place. These objects and properties really are such as we conceive them, through our "natural" concepts. (Below, I will consider some of the implications of this.) So far, I have said nothing about reasoning itself, that is, the power to draw inferences, to recognize logical consequence and incompatibility. These powers, it appears, are thought by the Stoics to be implicated in the possession of all concepts, including, of course, the concepts that constitute this basic stock.[15] To have the concept of a dog, for example, is (in part) to know that anything that *is* a dog has four legs (unless one has been removed, or the animal has suffered some horrendous birth defect), and that if a thing is not alive at all, or not made of flesh and hair (but rather, say, of metal) it is not a dog. Thus, the Stoic conception of reason does include the capacity to think logically (using, e.g., as in these illustrations, *modus ponens* and *modus tollens*), but in their view, that capacity is conceived as a component of "natural" conceptual knowledge, in the possession of which rationality basically consists. This is not some further capacity on its own, and, of course, it is not, by itself, the whole of rationality or even rationality's basic element.

Being rational does not, however, mean simply that one possesses basic knowledge and basic thinking capacities. When we reach "the age of

---

[14] So the Stoics seem to have thought. But maybe this was intended to be subject to a certain amount of local or even temporal variation—the "natural" concepts for one group of humans living in one environment might differ in some particulars from the "natural" ones for another group.

[15] See the discussion by Frede, "The Stoic Conception of Reason," 54–55.

reason" and become rational beings, instead of the nonrational, brute animal-like beings that children are, even while undergoing the experiences from which they are arriving at the basic concepts, our nature now becomes such that we *use* our rationality in all of our perceptual experiences, in everything we think, and in everything we do. Plutarch, in his essay *On Moral Virtue* (450d), quotes Chrysippus clearly to this effect: "[T]he rational animal is disposed naturally to use reason in all things and to be governed by it."[16] Before achieving the "age of reason," we may, and will as we progress, have a limited ability to use such concepts as we have begun to acquire, and so to reason in ways that belong to them, but that is an on-and-off affair. Its results do not determine what we think or what we do; natural instincts and inclinations continue to prevail with us, regardless. However, after we reach the "age of reason," we use reason in all of our perceptions, all of our thoughts, and all of our actions, by a necessity of our nature. This means that when we see, say, a dog, and it looks to us like a dog, we are using our relevant concepts—thinking that, according to what we know a dog to be, this thing that we see *looks like that*, that is, it looks like it has the properties that are contained in our dog-concept. And we must either accept this impression, and judge that it *is* a dog (i.e., that it actually instantiates the characteristics contained in the concept); or we must reject this impression (holding that, despite appearances, the thing that is seen does not instantiate those characteristics); or else we must suspend judgment either way, withholding any claim that it does, or that it does not, have the included properties. (I do not mean to say that any discursive process to such conclusions necessarily takes place, only that such is the content of the thought that one thinks.) Being rational means operating in this way, by a necessity of one's nature.

Now, in these acceptances and rejections truth and falsehood play a directive role, again by virtue of what a rational nature itself includes. What one holds to be true is what one accepts (and to accept something is to accept that it is true), and what one holds to be false is what one rejects (and to reject it is to declare that it is false). Thus, Epictetus says (*Discourses* 3.3.2), "It is the nature of every soul [he means, every rational one] to nod yes to the true [i.e., what one takes to be true], to nod no to the false, and to suspend on the unclear."[17] Rational nature, simply being what it is, pursues the true and flees from the false. But equally, as Epictetus in this passage goes on to say, it also pursues the good (i.e., what it takes to be good) and avoids the bad. The rational soul's nature

[16] *Plutarch: Moralia*, VI, ed. and trans. W. C. Helmbold, Loeb Classical Library (Cambridge, MA: Harvard University Press, 1939). The Greek text of the passage here translated is: τοῦ λογικοῦ ζῴου φύσιν ἔχοντος προσχρῆσθαι εἰς ἕκαστα τῷ λόγῳ καὶ ὑπὸ τούτου κυβερνᾶσθαι.

[17] Epictetus, *The Discourses, as Reported by Arrian, the Manual and Fragments*, bks. 3–4, ed. and trans. W. A. Oldfather, Vol. 2, Loeb Classical Library (Cambridge, MA: Harvard University Press, 1928). The Greek text of the passage here translated is: πέφυκεν δὲ πᾶσα ψυχὴ ὥσπερ τῷ ἀληθεῖ ἐπινεύειν, πρὸς τὸ ψεῦδος ἀνανεύειν, πρὸς τὸ ἄδηλον ἐπέχειν.

is "to be moved with desire for the good, with aversion from the bad, and in neither way to what is neither bad nor good."[18] Here we should recall that the concept of good (with, as its correlative, that of bad) is among the basic pieces of knowledge that Stoic theory claims all human beings acquire, by natural means, by the "age of reason." Thus, once we are at, and past, that point in our lives, we are, as part of being rational, only ever moved toward action by the idea that something that is to be obtained (or avoided) by acting is either good or bad (and the rational desire for the good and aversion from the bad are what always motivate us).[19] In contrast, anything that we take to be neither good nor bad leaves us completely unmoved. It is, of course, quite possible, indeed quite normal, even virtually universal, for human beings frequently to mistake what is false or unclear for what is true, and vice versa, or to be moved to desire something that is not, in fact, good at all, or to be averse from something that is not bad at all. Indeed, most human beings desire as good, and are repelled from as bad, only things that are actually neither bad nor good, according to Stoic theory. But in both sorts of cases, human beings are wielding correct concepts of the true and false, of good and bad; that is, they have an adequate basic knowledge of what it is to be true and what it is to be good (no doubt, however, it is not a completely developed knowledge). Their error lies in thinking that things that do not, in fact, instantiate the characteristics that are included in those concepts do instantiate them.

In fact, in rational nature itself, according to the Stoics, there are certain inherent standards for judging what is true, or false, or simply unclear. The rules of logic are among these. So, if you accept some propositions as true, and they together imply some other proposition, then you ought to accept the latter as true, as well (if you think of it at all), on the ground of that implication. Your rationality commits you to this, whether or not, in particular cases, you follow this rule when it applies. This rule is a norm of rational behavior, inherent in rationality itself. In a similar way, Chrysippus notoriously insisted that some sensory impressions are such that when you experience them, as some later Stoics put it, they "all but seize you by the hair and drag you to assent."[20] These sensory impressions are so very obviously, manifestly, indisputably true that it would be deeply

[18] πρὸς μὲν τὸ ἀγαθὸν ὀρεκτικῶς κινεῖσθαι, πρὸς δὲ τὸ κακὸν ἐκκλιτικῶς, πρὸς δὲ τὸ μήτε κακὸν μήτε ἀγαθὸν οὐδετέρως.

[19] Here we should recall that, for Stoics, even misguided and emotional desires, "appetites" and anger, and so on, are functions of our reason. These may be irrational in the sense of being contrary to reason's proper standards for what should be desired, for what should be thought good or bad, or in what way one should desire something. But these desires and so forth are not irrational in the sense of being nonrational, that is, having some origin or seat in the human soul other than its rational nature. See, e.g., Plutarch, *On Moral Virtue*, 446f–447a, and the section "The Stoic Theory of the Emotions" in my introduction to Seneca's *On Anger*, John M. Cooper and J. F. Procopé, *Seneca: Moral and Political Essays* (Cambridge: Cambridge University Press, 1995), 5–10.

[20] As Sextus Empiricus reports (*Against the Theoreticians* [M.], 7.257). See *Sextus Empiricus*, II, trans. R. G. Bury, Loeb Classical Library (Cambridge, MA: Harvard University Press,

irrational not to accept them as such. The Stoics are not speaking here of any external compulsion, or any internal, merely psychological one, either, but, rather, of what you necessarily do simply because you are rational. You can see so *clearly*, when you have an impression of this kind, that the impression is true, that it could not possibly *not* be true. Your rational commitment to seeking the truth demands that you accept such an impression. While we do not find in our sources any special elaboration of such "rules" or "standards" of right reason, it is clear that the Stoics do suppose that rational nature presents itself to itself as answerable to such standards, even in cases where one might, in fact, be violating them. No doubt it is the task of philosophy to articulate the original and basic standards, and to expand their range by formulating new ones. But, in principle, all of these are standards to which rational beings, as such, are committed simply by their nature as rational. All anyone needs to do in order to recognize these standards is to think enough so as to see, on the basis of their own thought, that they are committed to them.

IV. ZEUS'S OR NATURE'S RATIONALITY

In the preceding section I discussed what, according to Stoic theory, the power or capacity of reason (or reasoning) consists in. Now we need to take into account the fact that, for Stoics, the natural world as a whole, including not only our bodies but also our minds, is animated by a single mind, a single rational being and rational nature—Zeus. The natural world is a material world. Everywhere in it there is matter, of one formation and complexity or another, and there are no gaps of emptiness.[21] However, Zeus is also everywhere in the world, and Zeus, although he is a single body spread out everywhere, is not at all a *material* body.[22] Material bodies reduce ultimately to four basic material elements: fire, air, water, and earth.[23] But the body that Zeus is is not made of any of these elements, not even of elemental fire taken on its own.[24] (Indeed, although

---

1935), 7.257. The Greek text of the passage here translated is: αὕτη γὰρ ἐναργὴς οὖσα καὶ πληκτικὴ μόνον οὐχὶ τῶν τριχῶν, φασί, λαμβάνεται, κατασπῶσα ἡμᾶς εἰς συγκατάθεσιν.

[21] See, for example, Galen, *On the Differences in Pulses*, quoted in J. von Arnim, *Stoicorum Veterum Fragmenta* (Leipzig: Teubner, 1903-1924), 2:139-40 (= *SVF* 2.424), translated, in part, in A. A. Long and D. N. Sedley, *The Hellenistic Philosophers* (Cambridge: Cambridge University Press, 1987), 1:293 (= *LS* 49D).

[22] Zeus is everywhere in the world: see Alexander of Aphrodisias, *On Mixture*, ed., I. Bruns, *Supplementum Aristotelicum* (Berlin: Reimer, 1892), II.ii.225, 1-2 (trans. in *LS* 45H). Zeus is not a material body: see, in addition to Alexander, Diogenes Laertius 7.134 (trans. in *LS* 44B, first part) together with Cicero, *Academica*, 1.39 (trans. in *LS* 45A).

[23] See Diogenes Laertius, 7.135-36 and 7.142 (trans. in *LS* 46B and 46C).

[24] See Stobaeus, *Selections*, ed. C. Wachsmuth and O. Hense (Berlin: Weidmann, 1884), 1:129-30 (= *SVF* 2.413, trans., in part, in *LS* 47A). Note that on the account that Stobaeus provides here (attributing it to Chrysippus), god is the "element" of all things in a very special sense. God is what causes generation out of itself in a methodical way from a first beginning of generation up to an end, in which everything previously generated is resolved finally back into god. Fire is the basic element in a further special sense, as the first of the material elements to come into being by generation from god, while the other three elements

this interpretation is controversial, I think that Zeus's body, as understood, at least, by Chrysippus, is not any form of fire at all, however "pure": Zeus is a body *sui generis*.)[25] It is Zeus's body's presence everywhere (as a body, but no material body), completely intermixed with matter, that makes possible the differentiations that he has imposed upon matter, through his contact everywhere, all the way down, so to speak, with matter. (Action from a distance is ruled out on Stoic physical principles.) By these means Zeus constitutes and sustains: first, the material elements themselves (with their specific differences); then particular, more complex types of different material stuffs; and, finally, the differentially organized bodies of the different kinds of material objects, including the plants, animals, and human beings, that the world-order contains.[26]

---

are generated by god from that fire, by condensation of it first into air and then successively into water and earth. Thus, god, on Chrysippus's account, is not to be identified in any way or sense with the material element fire. (Most commentators, including Long and Sedley, *The Hellenistic Philosophers*, in their comments on the passages collected in chaps. 46 and 47, fail to see this.)

[25] See Philo, *On the Eternity [Indestructibility] of the World*, 90 (*SVF* 1.511, *LS* 46M): "[W]hen the world has been conflagrated (τὸν κόσμον ἐκπυρωθέντα) . . . it must change either into a flame (φλόξ) as Cleanthes thought, or into a flash of light (αὐγή), as did Chrysippus." On Philo's account, both Cleanthes and Chrysippus thought it necessary to avoid saying that the world was consumed *into* a fire (as Zeno seems to have done), since no fire survives the loss of its fuel, whereas, *ex hypothesi*, at the conflagration all fuel (in fact all other bodies besides Zeus) is done away with. See the whole context, secs. 85–93, *Philo*, trans. F. H. Colson, IX, Loeb Classical Library (Cambridge, MA: Harvard University Press, 1941). Philo goes on to argue against both of these views, more successfully against Cleanthes' suggestion than against Chrysippus's. A flash of light may last for only a second, but it does not simply cease once its source goes out, and it is not located simply at that source. If at (or rather, after) the conflagration, when he is by himself (see n. 27), Zeus is, or is like, a flash of light — in effect a concentration of energy — then, even when he is spread through all matter, it is as that concentration of energy that he is spread. Chrysippus's idea that Zeus is, or is like, a flash of light is quite a compelling way of developing the original Zenonian theory of the conflagration (and correcting it, though Chrysippus would never have admitted that).

[26] In doing all this, Zeus first has to constitute a special basic sort of material stuff, called by the Stoics "breath" or *pneuma*. This is made of fire *and* air (the hot and the cold elements, respectively), with the result that *pneuma*'s nature is simultaneously to contract (as cold) and to expand (as hot). It is thus suited to work upon grosser kinds of material in such a way as to hold them together (by exercising its contractive, inward-turning power). At the same time (by exercising its expansive, outward-reaching power), it makes these materials capable of affecting other material bodies through contact with them. And, depending upon the degree of "tensility" in *pneuma* in its different locations, it can imbue things with their specific qualitative differentiations. Thus *pneuma* plays a very special role throughout Zeus's creative activity. It is important, however, not to confuse *pneuma* with Zeus himself. *Pneuma* is Zeus's essential, indispensable material tool. He remains a distinct body from, while spreading through, his tool, *pneuma*. Zeus and *pneuma* are both of them everywhere in the world, but only Zeus is the (ultimate) agent of what happens in the world. See the passages collected in Long and Sedley, *The Hellenistic Philosophers*, 47B, D–I, O–Q. The Stoic theory of "through and through" mixture of distinct bodies (see Long and Sedley, chap. 48) was worked out so as to show how a body, such as Zeus, can be spread everywhere in some matter (in fact, in Zeus's case, in all of it), while *pneuma*, his material instrument, is equally spread everywhere through all the other forms of matter (and all material things). Since bodies are, all of them, divisible, all the way down, there can be in every portion of any material body some of god's body, as well as some *pneuma* (indeed *pneuma* in any number of different degrees and kinds of tension, so as to enable the composition and different characteristics of the bodily thing in question). Note that Aetius, in H. Diels, *Doxographi*

As a rational being or rational nature, this nonmaterial body, Zeus, is a reasoned understanding of, and basis for, everything that it creates and sustains. A particular plant is what it is, and bears all the conceptual and other relations that it bears to other things of its own, and of other types, because of Zeus's thought in constituting it. Likewise for everything else that the world contains—stuffs, individual objects, whatever. I said above that the Stoics claim that human beings develop to maturity through their experience with the objects around them, and with those objects' properties, in such a way as to form, by natural, automatic, and nonvoluntary processes, concepts of those objects and properties. We can now see that the natural concepts that humans acquire through this process are simply crude, basic versions of those with which Zeus has worked in forming the relevant objects and properties in the first place. That is why these natural concepts are correct concepts, why they constitute knowledge, albeit of a crude and rough-and-ready kind. To have these concepts is to possess a share of Zeus's own concepts, the ones that he used, and uses, in creating, constituting, and sustaining the world in which human beings live and operate. Zeus, of course, has a vaster conception of what he is doing in creating and sustaining these objects and properties than we have when we acquire our basic concepts of them. His conception is even vaster than the more sophisticated knowledge that we could develop by further investigation and thought of our own. He understands each thing, and each kind of thing, and each property of a thing, in relation to every other thing, and every other kind of thing, and every other property. As a single mind that is responsible for the *whole* world, Zeus understands everything he does at any one place, and over any one period of time, in relation to everything else that he does everywhere else and in all other periods.

Because Zeus is a rational being, he does everything that he does for the sake of the good (and/or to avoid the bad) precisely like adult humans. According to Stoic theory, our good is *in fact* (whatever most people may misguidedly think) entirely a matter of how our minds are conditioned and how, as a result, they work. All externals are neither good nor bad, but at best preferable or not. So, also, for Zeus. The good that he is constantly seeking in everything he does is the good that consists in the thoughts that he thinks in doing it, and in their relations both to the other thoughts that he is thinking at the same time and to the thoughts that preceded and those that are to follow. It is a mistake to think, as perhaps readers of the Stoics have sometimes thought, that this good is the beauty and order of the resulting *material* world, or of its progress through time.

Graeci (Berlin: Reimer, 1879), 310, = *SVF* 2.340, trans. in Long and Sedley, *The Hellenistic Philosophers*, 55G, says that for the Stoics, *all* causes are in fact "breaths" or *pneumata*. Thus, causal agency is always exercised through some *pneuma* belonging in one way or another to an agent.

Zeus's thoughts are, indeed, all of them, thoughts about how to constitute and sustain, alter over time, destroy, and create material things of an enormous and interlocking variety. But the *good* that is constantly aimed at in this process is the goodness of the ordered thoughts—absolutely nothing else. Ultimately, this good is the totality of the history of Zeus's thoughts in governing the world from its first formation right through to its final dénouement in the so-called *conflagration*, when all matter is reabsorbed into Zeus's mind, and it, or he, is "all by himself"[27]—only then to restart the whole process, exactly as it happened before.

V. Zeus's Thoughts, Human Thoughts, and the Law of Nature

According to the Stoic theory, then, there are two kinds of rational beings—humans, and Zeus or nature—each constituted, *qua* rational, in exactly the same way.[28] Zeus thinks at each moment one huge, single thought: a thought about everything that he is doing then everywhere in the material world in constituting, sustaining, changing, moving from place to place, creating, or destroying things. Moreover, this thought is thought explicitly in relation to the preceding thoughts that he has thought in progression, all the way from the beginning. It is also thought in relation to all of the succeeding thoughts that he is going to think in succession right up to the conflagration. So, in another way, this single thought, the overall thought that Zeus thinks at each moment, is much more immense than even that first hugeness might seem to imply. It is, all at once, the whole succession of thoughts that constitute Zeus's life-history. The current thought (so to speak) is simply highlighted as the currently active and effective one in that series. Thus, Zeus's thought contains a correct, fully worked out concept of each and every kind of thing and each and every individual thing in the world. His thought also contains not only a correct account of what happens anywhere and to

---

[27] See Diogenes Laertius 7.136: κατ' ἀρχὰς μὲν οὖν καθ' αὑτὸν ὄντα. It should be observed that this passage, taken together with the Philo passage cited above in n. 25, shows that it is a mistake to say, as commentators often do (see, e.g., Long and Sedley, *The Hellenistic Philosophers*, 1:278–79), that, for the Stoics, Zeus cannot in fact be "abstracted" from matter, but always exists as an internal principle within matter, forming it into material bodies. The sort of intelligent energy that Zeus is, in fact, is quite clearly conceived as being abstracted at the conflagration, or rather during the time between a conflagration (the end of the world) and the world's rebeginning. See also Diogenes Laertius 7.137: "god . . . at certain cycles of time absorbing into himself the whole of material substance and again generating it from himself" (θεόν . . . ὃς . . . κατὰ χρόνων ποιὰς περιόδους ἀναλίσκων εἰς ἑαυτὸν τὴν ἅπασαν οὐσίαν καὶ πάλιν ἐξ ἑαυτοῦ γεννῶν).

[28] I leave out of the account here and in what follows the important difference between human and Zeus's or nature's rationality, that (see the previous note) Zeus brings matter into existence, and does not merely, with his thoughts, shape, characterize, move, and change it. However, this power of initial creation (and destruction) of matter aside, Zeus's rationality is, as I say in the text, constituted exactly in the same way as human rationality.

anything at any time in the world's history, but also a full knowledge of *why* it happens. The thought of whatever happens happening is needed as part of the overall history of thoughts constituting Zeus's history. The thought of it happening as and when it does has its point in, and explanation by, that thought's relation to prior thoughts and subsequent ones, as well as to other thoughts about other things happening at the same time. It is the overwhelmingly good order of the whole series, in all its internal relationships, that on Stoic theory, is identical with the good, so this current thought's place in the series is explained by its contribution to that overall good. Thus, Zeus's thought constitutes the totality of truth, as well as the good. Anything true is true because it (or the concept or thought of it) has its place in Zeus's mind, in his mental history; and that history is the embodiment of goodness.

Human beings, however, think special and different thoughts, depending upon the location of each one of them in the world, their particular experiences at the moment and before, or their expectations. Whereas Zeus's thought is the thought of the whole, any human being's thought is always a local thought. It is sometimes a thought about or toward the whole world, perhaps, but it is always from a single, localized point of view. What is any such individual to think, at any point in his or her history? Human thinking begins with an "impression" (a rational one, since we are rational minds) to some effect: that so and so.[29] We are constantly bombarded with such impressions, not only through and from the senses, but also from memory, anticipation, habits of past thinking, and built-up concepts (whether they are concepts arrived at naturally or through voluntary thought). No doubt, we are bombarded from other sources, too. Upon receiving these impressions, it is then up to each individual mind to exercise its judgment as to which of them to accept, to "assent" to, and which to reject, or, to suspend judgment over. Some of these will be impressions about some apparent matter of fact (perhaps something theoretical or, as we would say, something directly empirical). Others will be about what is good or bad to pursue or to do. Because of reason's inherent natural inclination to seek what is true and to avoid anything false, and to pursue what is good and to avoid everything bad, the two key questions for judgment are as follows. Is this *in fact* true (as it appears to be, as I am inclined to think)? Or is this *in fact* good (as it appears to be, as I am inclined to think)? I mentioned above (at the end of Section III) that there are standards and rules of "right reason" that we can invoke to help decide these questions. Ultimately, however, the standard is what Zeus himself thinks; he and the processes of his thought are definitive of what it is rational (i.e., correct by the standards of reason

---

[29] See Diogenes Laertius 7.49 (last sentence), 51 (last three sentences); Origen, *On Principles*, 3.1.3 (= *SVF* 2.988), trans. in part in *LS* 53A(4–5); and, in general, the materials collected in Long and Sedley, *The Hellenistic Philosophers*, chaps. 39 and 53.

itself) to think. As Diogenes Laertius tells us (7.88), Zeus *is* right reason (ὁ ὀρθὸς λόγος).

In the passage where Diogenes Laertius tells us that Zeus is right reason, he also tells us that Zeus is "the law that is common to all things" (ὁ νόμος ὁ κοινός). Right reason, Diogenes says, is the same thing as this common law, Zeus being the "leader of the government of the things that have being" (καθηγεμόνι τούτῳ τῆς τῶν ὄντων διοικήσεως ὄντι), and the "things that have being" being all the bodies, material and nonmaterial, that make up the world. The law of Zeus, however, does not govern all of these bodies in exactly the same ways. Rational beings and their minds are governed by Zeus differently from the way in which he governs everything else. Plants, nonrational animals, and all material stuffs, whether existing on their own or constituting a living thing, are wholly and directly governed by Zeus's own thoughts. He has a "plan," as we have seen, consisting in an ordered series of thoughts that he thinks (and is going to think), and these thoughts produce and sustain all of the characteristics of all those things, bring them into existence, remove them from it, alter and develop them, and move them from place to place, in ways that we can observe happening, as well as in ways that we cannot. We can observe the effects of Zeus's "law," or nature's "law," in the behavior of the material bodies themselves. The nature of wood is such that when it comes into contact with a hot fire it burns, invariably, while the nature of stone is such that when it comes into contact with fire it merely (and invariably) heats up, even to a very high degree. The nature of the different metals is such that, depending on the specific metal and the size and intensity of the fire, in some cases a metal gets soft, or even actually melts. Similarly, mutatis mutandis, nature's "law" governs the behavior of the different nonrational animals: but in these cases the relevant "laws" are vastly more complex, encompassing as they do a variety of different behaviors, species by species, in response to different stimuli.

Nowadays, when we speak of laws of nature, we do so with reference to empirical generalizations like those about wood, stone, and metals that I have just mentioned, backed up, no doubt, by much theory about the behavior of molecules and particles; but that theory is itself based on further empirically supported hypotheses about how molecules and particles behave under varying conditions. It is of crucial importance in understanding the Stoic theory of natural law to realize that, for the Stoics, the law or laws of nature consist not in such empirical generalizations, but rather in the thoughts of Zeus which lie behind and cause the behaviors of material things. It may be, and presumably is the case, that the best that we humans can do in order to grasp Zeus's law, so far as it applies to the things that I have so far been talking about, is by way of observation of the behavior of material bodies and the derivation, by that means, of empirical generalizations. However, even so, no statement about how material bodies behave, drawn up in that empirical way, in itself expresses any part of Zeus's or nature's law for them. His (or nature's) law consists in the rational determination to think whatever thought he (or nature) is going to think in causing the bodies to behave in the ways that we may (or may not) observe them to behave. And that determination is grounded in Zeus's (or nature's) conception of what thoughts, and what combination of thoughts, will constitute the best and most beautiful rational order of thoughts over the whole period of the world-order's existence and development. The fact that, as it seems, we can observe many differences in the behavior of different sorts of things, and invariances in those behaviors, shows that one part of this self-determination on Zeus's part is a determination to operate in a vast and interlocking set of widely differentiated, but in each case universally applied and invariant, ways. To operate in this way is part of the rational order that he (or nature) achieves, or, rather, it is its direct effect.

How, then, does Zeus's law govern rational beings and their minds? The first thing to notice is that in many respects the behaviors of our bodies (in the use of the term "body" that contrasts with "mind") are governed no differently from that of other material bodies. If rain falls on my head, then my hair and skin are affected in relevantly precisely similar ways to that of any animal or any nonanimate thing that is also rained on. Similarly, if I eat something, what then follows in my body proceeds in ways similar to what follows when a nonrational animal eats something. Zeus's thought is just as directly responsible for all of such processes in the human case as in the nonhuman, and in just the same ways. However, the second example, that of eating something, differs in the human case in one very important respect from the case of the nonrational animal: with the animal, Zeus's thought is just as directly the cause, and in precisely the same way, both of the animal's getting the sense-impressions that it gets (that lead it to obtain the item) and of its then eating it, as it is in causing the consequences in the animal's body. As the Stoics put it, the animal's "impulse" to eat, which is triggered by the impression (together with its soul's nature and condition), is caused by Zeus having a thought, following in due order on the thoughts of his that were involved in giving the animal the particular impression that it got. (So, too, and in exactly the same way, the impression itself, the nature of the animal's soul, and its condition at the time, are caused by Zeus's thoughts.) The "impulse" that is the animal's response to the impression and the immediate cause of the animal's action of eating, follows automatically upon the receipt of the impression.[30] The human case is different.

---

[30] The sources leave it rather unclear in just what way an animal impulse does follow automatically upon receipt of the impression. Some sources speak of some counterpart in animals (at least some animals), of that "assent" which is necessary before a rational impulse (i.e., an adult human being's impulse) can be formed. See R. W. Sharples, *Alexander of Aphrodisias On Fate* (London: Duckworth, 1983), chaps. 13–14 (relevant passages are collected in *SVF* 2.979–81, esp. 285 lines 37–38, 286 lines 7–8); see also Nemesius *De natura*

Human beings, when they act (act voluntarily, I mean), do so because of reasons that they see for doing so. They may reach out and start to eat something immediately upon getting the impression of it as a good thing to eat, and without any apparent process of thinking and deciding whether to eat it, or what else to do instead. But, nonetheless, it simply belongs to their nature as *rational* beings that they always act—even in such cases of unreflective, virtually "automatic," action—for what they take, at the time of acting, to be good reasons for doing what they do. It belongs to their nature to act always and only on some thought of their own (when they do really *act*, i.e., act voluntarily), to the effect that this act is a good thing to do, that there is good reason to do it. Human beings cannot *not* do this, if they act in any way at all (even if they simply refrain from acting). If and when they have no thought at all of any reason to do anything, they merely stay inertly where they are, or get moved about by outside forces (or internal ones)—in either case, forces coming from Zeus's thoughts. Their thought is the direct cause of their action, just as Zeus's thoughts are the direct cause of the corresponding happenings in those other cases. So, one way that Zeus governs human beings is by sustaining them in existence as rational beings, as beings that produce some of their behavior (that which is, as we put it, voluntary) from their *own* thoughts about what is best to do—not from *his*, as is the case with the behavior of animals and every other thing that the world contains. In fact, as I will explain (or, at least, maintain), this is the only way, the only respect at all, in which Zeus directly governs this part of any human being's behavior. (A human's self-governance by calling upon standards of rational behavior that derive ultimately from Zeus's thought is another matter altogether. On this point see Section VI, which follows.) Zeus's thought or intention in making rational beings part of his world—the world that he animates—is to make there be beings who are located in specific places and times and who possess a localized outlook on the rest of the world, which will then act in accordance with their own reasoned views (not necessarily with Zeus's). Accordingly, the causality of Zeus's thought in relation to them (insofar as they are behaving *qua* rational beings) is limited simply to making and sustaining them in existence as rational beings of this sort. Beyond that, they exercise the causality of their own thought through the power of that thought itself, exactly as Zeus causes everything that he causes through the power of his own much more powerful thought. (I leave aside here, as before, the important difference

---

hominis, cited in *SVF* 2.991 and *LS* 53 passage O. This does seem to make sense of the fact that animals can learn to double-check something before proceeding to action; they do not always act immediately upon becoming aware of something that is apparently tasty to eat and that is within their range. In any case, with nonrational animals the Stoics seem to have thought that, even if something like an assent to an impression is needed before an impulse can take shape in the animal's soul, the assent, too, is generated automatically upon receipt of (the right sort of) impression. This is not so with rational animals, i.e., humans.

between Zeus's and our causality, namely, that Zeus's includes the power
to bring matter into existence and to destroy it by absorbing it into himself at the conflagration.)

VI. How Rational Beings, as Such, Follow Zeus's Law

It is by Zeus's (nature's) law that we are created and sustained as
rational beings, with this particular set of natural powers and under these
particular constraints. This is one aspect of how Zeus's (nature's) law
applies to human beings, *qua* rational. However, Zeus's law applies in a
second way as well. In deciding what to think, and especially in deciding
how to behave (voluntarily), as our nature compels us to do, Zeus's law
is authoritative for human beings in a second, purely normative way.
Since the law in question applies specifically to our voluntary behavior,
we need to take into account Stoic views on the scope and limitations of
that behavior, before we can turn to see what the content of this law might
be, and how we can come to know it, as well as from what its authority
for us derives.

Since any human being's reason is, of course, located entirely within
his or her own body,[31] we can exercise our mind's powers, in the first
instance and directly, only on our own bodies. Our mind has direct
contact only with our own body, and for anything to affect anything
else, according to Stoic theory, direct contact is required.[32] In fact, strictly
speaking, according to Chrysippus, the whole of any action (even one
like walking) consists simply and entirely in that certain condition of
the so-called "leading" or "commanding part" of the soul, the ἡγεμονικόν,
that is, the mind, which results when one decides to walk, or, rather,
which is constituted by that decision.[33] What follows upon the decision

---

[31] For Chrysippus and other Stoics, the human soul is a sort of high-quality breath spread
throughout the body. Impulse, the direct cause of action, takes place in the "commanding
part" of the soul, the part where reason is lodged or, anyhow, where acts of reasoning take
place, i.e., in the heart. From there the breath that is the first and immediate material body
that reason uses as its tool spreads throughout the body—to all the sense organs, nerves, and
muscles. (See Calcidius, *Commentary on the Timaeus*, cited in *SVF* 2.879 and trans., in part, in
LS 53G, quoting Chrysippus in Latin.) Thus, our reason can have its effects everywhere in
us, even though it is concentrated in the "commanding part" residing in the heart.

[32] See Simplicius, *Commentary on Aristotle's Categories*, ed. K. Kalbfleisch, *Commentaria in
Aristotelem Graeca*, vol. 8 (Berlin: Reimer, 1907), 302.29–35 (= *SVF* 2.342, in part).

[33] See *Seneca VI, Epistles 93–124*, ed. and trans. R. M. Gummere, Loeb Classical Library
(Cambridge, MA: Harvard University Press, 1925), 113.23. Seneca reports that Cleanthes
held a different view, viz., that the action, e.g., of walking was the soul-breath extending
from the commanding part out to where the bodily movement itself would begin, when that
breath is in the condition for initiating that movement. It seems that Chrysippus intended
to correct Cleanthes, in adopting the position that an action is strictly the commanding part
itself, when in the relevant condition. Presumably, his reason was that our mind does not
even control directly and without possibility of slip-up or interference the state of the breath
extending out from itself to the muscles and limbs. The commanding part, like all the parts
of the soul, is indeed a material body, some breath stationed in the heart, but our reason
(itself a body, as noted above, but not a material one) is lodged in the breath of the com-

then, if conditions are normal—for example, the flexing of muscles and all the rest that goes on inside the body, and then the motions of the limbs and the progress of the whole body across some space—are not part of the action itself. They are its consequences and effects (wholly intended, of course). For those things to take place, the body itself must be of a certain nature and condition; and for that Zeus is, at least primarily, responsible. (Some aspects of one's relevant bodily condition could, of course, have resulted from prior voluntary decisions and actions of one's own, not from Zeus's thoughts in constituting our bodies and in maintaining them, or causing them gradually to change, or even to deteriorate. But, obviously, Zeus's direct causality is paramount, so far as the required condition of the relevant parts of our bodies is concerned.) This means that, in principle, I can only have any effects in the outer world, and indeed within my own body (except in my mind), provided that Zeus does not block me. He could block me by changing my muscles and limbs, so that when I decide to walk (and, according to Chrysippus' stipulation, do walk), the muscles do not flex, or the limbs do not move, or whatever. In that case, my intentions would only get carried out so far as the action that consists in that decision itself goes, and no movement across space takes place. However, we know that Zeus cannot cause any such failure by any kind of simple fiat or miracle: the orderliness of his thought requires a regularity and invariance that would be grossly violated by any such interference on his part. So, normally, and absent some unexpected, but ultimately perfectly natural, sudden disability, I *can* control my muscles and limbs at will, and I *can* get myself to where I want to go (provided, again, that no outside force, whether another person's action and its consequences, or external natural events under the direct control of Zeus's lawlike thought, blocks me). Thus, it is part of what Zeus has done in creating us as rational animals that this degree of control normally does hold for us. His plan was to make there be rational beings who would take care of their own lives and their own affairs on the basis of their own rational understandings.[34]

---

manding part in such a way as always to be able, immediately and without slip or any possible interference, to have the necessary effects on that breath for its decisions to count as precisely the decisions that they are (and not just some free-floating phantasies, unconnected to any possible results). For your reason *not* to be able to cause at least these effects, perhaps because of some sudden defect in the breath of the commanding part, is for you literally to lose your mind.

[34] See Diogenes Laertius 7.86: nature regulates (οἰκονομεῖ) the lives of plants, the other animals, and human beings as well, but in different ways. Animals have "impulse" added to plants' vegetative capacities, so as to be able to go on their own toward things that suit them (food, for example), while "reason is given to rational animals by way of a more perfect kind of management ... ; for reason is added as the craftsman of impulse" (τοῦ δὲ λόγου τοῖς λογικοῖς κατὰ τελειοτέραν προστασίαν δεδομένου ... τεχνίτης γὰρ οὗτος ἐπιγίνεται τῆς ὁρμῆς).

In order to make possible such rational beings, it was necessary for Zeus to arrange the order of his own thoughts in such a way that this degree of control by agents on the relevant movements of their internal organs and their outer limbs, is maintained (for the most part, in any event). It is at this point in our analysis that the second, or normative, aspect of Zeus's or nature's law for rational beings, which I mentioned at the beginning of this section, comes in. What does reason demand, or permit, of us in developing our own rational understandings of what to do, and in conducting our individual (and our communal) lives on that basis? As I mentioned above (Section V, first two paragraphs), the standards and norms of reason are directly exhibited in, indeed, are ultimately constituted by, Zeus's or nature's own thinking. Zeus and nature *are* "right reason." One way of posing the question that I just asked, therefore, is to ask, What does Zeus, or universal reason, think that we should do—what, in other words, does it wish us to do? This is what it is right for us to do, what reason (in us, too) declares that we ought to do, and what it is best for us to do. In general terms the answer is clear. Zeus and nature wish us to think, in each circumstance, whatever thought on our part would most perfectly cohere with all of the prior and all of the future thoughts that constitute the (rest of the) history of thoughts that is universal reason's, or Zeus's, own life. But these terms are too general for them to be of any use to us.[35]

More concretely—and this seems to be how the Stoics went about answering this question[36]—we can bear in mind that we are individual animals, living a special sort of life for an animal (one directed by our own individual powers of reasoning), but, nonetheless, an *animal's* life. So we can examine how nature, or Zeus, directly governs the lives of all of the vastly diverse creatures who, not being rational themselves, live by such direct governance. If, once we reach the "age of reason," we are now to take over, with our own minds, our own governance, then surely we ought to follow the patterns of life that we see the nonrational animals following, so far as, given our other differences from them, these patterns apply rel-

---

[35] Indeed, understood one way, this turns out to be a trivial and totally useless answer. If one takes into account (see Section VII below) that human decisions and other thoughts are actually part of the history of Zeus's mind (since human minds are "disjoined portions" of Zeus's), whatever decision or other thought a person, in fact, does have at any moment is the one that most perfectly coheres with the rest of the series. Recall that, in Stoic theory, the total history of Zeus's thoughts is the most perfectly ordered one imaginable, or even conceivable. Understood in this way, this answer, therefore, would tell us simply to decide, do, and think on any occasion whatever we are, in fact, going to decide, do, or think. I intend the answer differently. We are to understand it as directing us to consider what action of our own would fit in best with the ways that Zeus or nature itself, in directing the progress of the parts of the world that are under its direct control (i.e., everything that is not the direct consequence of any human decision), does direct. We look to patterns or norms of rationality that are found in nature's own actions to discover norms for our own human decision-making.

[36] See my exposition in Cooper and Procopé, *Seneca: Moral and Political Essays*, xxi–xxiv.

evantly to us. Zeus's or nature's law for us must be some parallel to, or reasonable extension from, what we can observe as his (or its) law for other animals' lives. Consistency and coherence in Zeus's thinking about us, as animals, seems clearly to require this. In this way, the Stoics think, we can arrive at a large set of conditions and outcomes for ourselves that we can declare "preferred" ones, in that they give us good reason to pursue them, or to seek to maintain them so far as we can, and to avoid their "rejected" opposites. These preferred conditions and outcomes (or values) include health, continued life, all the attributes of a well-developed physical condition, warm and supportive relations in family life and with friends, loyalty, supportive social relations with all with whom we come in contact, the improvement of our own intellectual capacities generally, and the sense of ourselves as part of local, as well as wider, human communities, whose needs and interests thereby become needs and interests of our own. It will be rational, as we are struck by various "impulsive" impressions during our daily lives, to evaluate these impressions, in deciding what to do, by appeal to these preferred values. In general, if you pursued these values, then the sort of life that you would want to, and try to, live would be a well-balanced and well-integrated one, with a full involvement in the life of the community and some appropriate productive work. So part of Zeus's law for us is to live that way, to the extent that external circumstances can be made to permit us to do it.

Additional guides toward what it is rational to think and to do can be derived from the stock of natural concepts that all of us obtain during the time when we are growing up, as part of our natural endowment as rational beings, and that are available to us once we reach the "age of reason" (see Section III above). Most important, here, is the concept of goodness, since, as I mentioned (end of Section III), every action expresses an implicit or explicit decision to act that way, grounded in some thought that something or other is good, either to do or to get, or is bad and so is to be avoided. As I mentioned (Section III, next to last paragraph), most people spend their entire lives constantly misapplying and really grossly misunderstanding their own concept of the good, since according to that concept, what it is to be good is to be rationally well-ordered—something that ultimately can only apply to acts of thinking, or rather, to trains of thought. Nonetheless, unless one does come to understand explicitly and self-consciously that this in fact is what goodness consists in, then one is failing to use one's naturally acquired rationality in a way that conforms correctly to its own inherent standards of thought. Thus, it is part of nature's or Zeus's law that we should understand goodness in this way, and, therefore, should never regard mere conditions of our bodies, passive states of our minds, or any external condition or outcome, whether of our action or produced in some other way, as either good or bad for us. Only our own thoughts, when they are appropriately well ordered—and of course Zeus's thought, always and in general—are good things.

Now, according to Stoic theory, if we accept the norms for decision-making and behavior adumbrated in the previous two paragraphs, and live fully according to them, then we will not only be living fully rationally, we will also be living as fully virtuous persons. We will govern our lives by the concrete values that were partially listed above: our own health, physical well-being, continued life, productive work, warm and supportive relations in family life and with friends, loyalty, cooperative social relations with all with whom we come in contact, a sense for the values of community, both immediate and wider, and so on. We will do so with the full recognition that none of these values can correctly be thought of as anything good, nor are their opposites bad. The only good that is available in human life is the orderly thinking and deciding that occur in the assiduous pursuit and maintenance of these values, while recognizing that their attainment, always and inevitably, also depends partly on what happens outside oneself and outside one's own control. In particular, their attainment depends upon Zeus's own decisions in maintaining a course of external events (and, for that matter, events internal to our own bodies too) into which our own efforts fit, so as to lead to our desired outcomes. These outcomes may be, and are, authorized by universal reason as the appropriate and correct ones for us to pursue, but this does not mean—and if we are virtuous we will always bear this vividly in mind—that Zeus's actual thoughts, in determining actual outcomes, will necessarily, on any particular occasion, lead to their fruition. If they do not eventuate, then we know (retrospectively, in the only way that we with our limited knowledge *can* know) not only that it was not meant to be, but also that it is in fact better that it did not happen. Its not happening was in fact the direct result of Zeus's maximally well-ordered, fully coherent thought-history—the very embodiment of goodness. The Stoics argue, with considerable plausibility, that if we live like this, then we will be exhibiting, in our ways of thought and in our behavior, justice, temperance, loyalty, honesty, courage, industriousness, love and respect for humanity, and all the rest of those socially approved traits of character that are traditionally regarded as human virtues (however limited and inadequate traditional conceptions of their nature and requirements might be).

VII. AUTONOMY AND FREEDOM OF CHOICE: CONCLUSION

In sum, if we live in consistency with nature, that is to say, fully rationally, we will be living in accordance with norms, established by nature's or Zeus's law, of "preferability" and "rejectability," on the one hand, and goodness on the other. As a result, we will be living fully virtuous lives. I take it that when Dio of Prusa says in his oration *On Freedom* (sec. 5, cited above, Section II), that the law of nature or Zeus's law, though open to view (φανεϱόν), is neither seen by most people nor made by them the leader of their lives (οὔτε ὁϱῶσιν οὔτε ἡγεμόνα ποιοῦνται τοῦ βίου), it is this second aspect of Zeus's law that Dio has in mind. This aspect concerns, specifically, the norms established in nature for our own decisions and actions, as I just explained. My analysis has now put us in a position to see why he is correct, as a matter of Stoic theory, even if not of standard or official Stoic terminology, to describe this law as *our* law—our law for ourselves, as well as Zeus's law for us. Hence, by following this law we achieve autonomy. This law is Zeus's law for us only because it is reason's law: Zeus's lawgiving authority is, or derives from, the authority of reason, which is identical, according to Stoic theory, to Zeus. And because, as I have explained, our own being as agents is wholly constituted by our rationality, this same law is thereby our own law, delivered by our own rational nature—by ourselves as we are in our essence—to ourselves as agents. Only if we live in full accordance with this law do we measure up to the law to which our own nature, as rational, makes us answerable. To the extent that we fail to measure up in our lives to this law—however much we are ourselves, and necessarily, the source of our interest in the modes of behavior or objects of pursuit that we adopt for ourselves in lieu of the law's authority—we are living, as Dio puts it, in a self-inflicted, grievous slavery that is forbidden by the law (τῆς χαλεπῆς καὶ παρανόμου δουλείας ἐν ᾗ ζεύξαντες αὑτοὺς ἔχετε, sec. 7). In this slavery, we misguidedly, arbitrarily, and pointlessly set up for ourselves interests and desires, and whole ways of life, that then dominate *us*—when we could and ought to be ruling ourselves by our own law.

It is obvious that this ancient conception of autonomy differs greatly from the familiar Kantian conception that has been, and still is, so influential in modern and contemporary thinking. The self-imposed law of Stoic autonomy is much more comprehensive in its requirements than the Kantian categorical imperative. The Stoic law gives directives for all kinds of personal and private matters, as well as for more public and communal ones. Furthermore, it makes no provision for finite rational beings as possessing the dignity of authoritative setters of their own ends (and derivatively also for others), within the limits of this basic categorical law. Under Stoic autonomy, ends are set for us by (universal) reason itself, never by the arbitrary pleasures and preferences of individuals among us. These and other differences, I think, all stem directly from the difference between Kant's and the Stoics' conceptions of the nature of reason and rationality itself. For Kant, reason is essentially something formal, a matter of logical consistency in one's reasoning from given premises to appropriate conclusions, and of the most abstract, universal principles for the organization of experience. For the Stoics, as I explained (Section III), reason's formal aspects are, at most, the outer surface of something with a rich and deep substance of its own—it is a whole system of concepts that constitute a basic knowledge of the world and our place in it. This difference in the understanding of reason and rationality is, in fact, a central and fundamental difference between the whole tradition of ancient philosophy and that of modern, post-Renaissance thought.

Nonetheless, there are important resemblances and, no doubt, also historical connections between the two conceptions of autonomy, Kantian and Stoic. (As I indicated at the outset of this essay, however, I make no claims about, and will not explore here, any of the history that might connect them.) First of all, unlike many current conceptions of autonomy, both Kant and Dio (on behalf of the Stoics) understand autonomy in strict accordance with its etymology, as involving being subject to and consistently following *law(s)* (νόμοι) of one's own making. For Kant and Dio, autonomy is not mere self-direction or self-governance, which might, of course, be quite arbitrary, unprincipled, and inconsistent. Secondly, in both theories the inner source of this law is conceived of as reason itself—in particular, reason as something with universal or universalizing scope. And thirdly, the law of autonomy, in both cases, is centrally conceived as the basis of morality (duty, virtue). To be sure, within each of these three common aspects of Stoic and Kantian autonomy there are very important differences, as I indicated above, but these broad similarities are very striking.

I conclude with some brief comments on one difficulty that the Stoics faced if they were to develop and defend their conception of autonomy adequately—a difficulty with which, though again in different ways, Kant had to contend as well. In both theories, the freedom given by autonomy is not at all the same as the mere freedom of free choice—the freedom required by agents' responsibility for their choices and actions. But it does seem to be a requirement on any acceptable conception of autonomy that autonomous agents also possess, and exercise in their autonomous acts, that lesser freedom. As is well known, Kant struggled mightily in his works of moral philosophy subsequent to the *Groundwork of the Metaphysics of Morals* (1785) to work out theories of these two sorts of freedom which would allow not only autonomous agents, but also those who live "heteronomously" and flout the moral law, to retain the freedom of free choice and responsibility.[37] For the Stoics, the difficulty arose immediately and in a very severe form because of their doctrine of Fate. This is the doctrine, roughly, that everything that happens at any time anywhere in the world happens through the determination of Zeus's thought, as part of his overall plan, and conceived in some way or sense in advance of the coming to be of the world-order—a plan that extends into the smallest detail, however trivial, of every circumstance and event.[38] The Stoic theory of human action seems vulnerable, or worse, because of the way that it at-

---

[37] There are many translations of the *Groundwork*; it is conveniently available in the volume *Immanuel Kant's Writings on Practical Philosophy* in the Cambridge Edition of the Works of Immanuel Kant, trans. and ed. Mary J. Gregor, with a general introduction by Allen Wood (Cambridge: Cambridge University Press, 1996). In his effort in the *Groundwork*, chap. III, to establish the authority for us of the categorical imperative, Kant developed an argument that had the implication that free will itself was only exercisable if one followed that imperative.

[38] Some of the most important ancient reports on this Stoic doctrine are collected in Long and Sedley, *The Hellenistic Philosophers*, chap. 55 (see especially the passages at 55J through 55S).

tempts to combine freedom, and, thus, responsibility, with a global determinism by Fate. Critics of the Stoics, from ancient times onward, have found this a particularly difficult combination to sustain.[39] If Fate (equivalent to Zeus's thought) determines everything, does it not then determine our own thinking too, in some way, however much the Stoics might have tried to deny it, in maintaining our own responsibility for what we think and what we decide to do? In that case, how can we be meaningfully held to be responsible for our own thought and action—to think and act freely, even if and when we act (allegedly) autonomously?

In the debates over the relationship between Fate and individuals' responsibility for their own thought and action, one crucial point seems to me to be overlooked, or, at least, its significance is missed. It is here, as it seems to me, that the best Stoic response—an entirely adequate one—is to be found to these difficult questions: according to Stoic theory, our individual minds are held to be actual, disjoined *portions* of Zeus's mind.[40] So when the Stoics speak of Zeus's universal causality (i.e., Fate), this cannot threaten to remove the possibility of our own causality, or our own responsibility. Our causality is part of Zeus's. This causality is simply that which belongs to mind or minds as such. Minds just *do* have the power to act upon (suitable) materials with which they come into contact, and, ultimately, as we have seen, only minds, through the *pneuma* with which they are mixed, have this power. It is our privilege, as rational animals whose minds are portions of Zeus's, to share with Zeus in the government of the world. Most of what happens, he (or nature) causes directly through his (its) own rational substance, or rather, through the part of it that is not separated off in the form of human minds. But the rest of what happens is caused by our own thoughts and decisions. As I explained

---

[39] Thus, in introducing Chrysippus's effort to "mediate" between the old determinists who simply, on the basis of fate, declared human actions to be necessitated and so not "free," and those who (like Epicurus) exempted movements of the mind from control by fate in order to preserve freedom, Cicero says that, although Chrysippus *wanted* to establish a view of human freedom that would make it compatible with universal determinism, he employed terminology of his own devising that got him into such difficulty that, against his will, he actually ended up lending support to the old determinists' position: see *De Fato*, trans. H. Rackham, Loeb Classical Library (Cambridge, MA: Harvard University Press, 1942), sec. 39; see also sec. 20. Alexander of Aphrodisias (in his treatise *On Fate*, ed. Sharples, chap. 27), argues at length that, in fact, people can be legitimately subject to praise or blame for their actions (i.e., are responsible for them) only if—as the Stoics deny—they had the "liberty of indifference" in deciding to do them. In other words, they can be held responsible only if at that time they could either do or not do what they did.

[40] "Disjoined portion" here translates ἀπόσπασμα, D. L. 7.143; see also Epictetus, *Discourses* (trans. W. A. Oldfather, 1.1.12): speaking in Zeus's voice, Epictetus says that Zeus gives each of us μέρος τι ἡμέτερον, a part of himself. This Greek word is often translated, e.g., by Long and Sedley, *The Hellenistic Philosophers*, 1:319 (53 X), as "offshoot." But in the literal sense an offshoot can be a branch running off from a main stem to which it remains connected, while the Greek verb from which the noun is derived means to tear off or away, to detach. If we think of ourselves as "offshoots," it must be in the other meaning of the literal sense of this word, where "offshoots" refers to something cut off from a stem and planted on its own. Hence, to render this Stoic idea, I prefer the less elegant "disjoined portion" to the potentially misleading "offshoot."

above (Section V), it is entirely up to us what we shall think in reaction to the impressions that we receive; what we will think depends entirely upon what we find it reasonable to think in the light of our impressions. Nor does Zeus play any role in determining what we *will* find reasonable to think; he gives us minds that are adequate to the task of figuring out correctly what really *is* most reasonable, but it is then up to us to use that power as we think best.

Thus, since our minds are portions of Zeus's, the total history of the world's thoughts, which is the history of Zeus's thoughts, actually includes our thoughts, and thereby, of course, their effects, as part of its own course. The amazing thing is that even with all of our individual errors, the total ordered sequence of thoughts (our thoughts, plus Zeus's on his own) that cause all of the objects and happenings in the course of world history displays the most perfect rational order that there could possibly be. (Part, of course, of the beautiful orderliness of that history is due to, or consists in, the fact that it is the result of the contributions of a huge number of distinct minds, Zeus's plus each of our own. Each of us thinks according to our own ideas of what is best in light of the impressions that we receive.) This most perfect rational order happens, however, hardly at all through human effort to bring it about—most of us have no such intention, even no such idea at all. The rational order is brought about almost entirely by the power that Zeus has on his own, apart from human minds, to anticipate and plan the whole course of his own life, while allowing each of us at each moment to make up our own minds about what to think and what to do, and, thus, allowing us to contribute those parts of the sequence of his ideas. In planning his total life, he anticipates what each of us will think and decide at every moment in relation to the impressions that we will experience then, and, in advance as it were (from the very beginning), he adjusts the rest of his thoughts to accommodate our own into an overall magnificently well-ordered total history of thought—a history that is inconceivably beautiful and good. In this way, whether or not in our own decisions we do follow Zeus's (or nature's) law, and so whether or not we live autonomously, we nonetheless live with full personal responsibility for all of our own thoughts and all of our actions. We are exactly as responsible for our thoughts, and in exactly the same way, as Zeus himself is responsible for his own thoughts (or rather, for that part of his thoughts that he thinks in separation from us).[41]

[41] Here again I leave aside, as irrelevant to what I am saying, the fact that Zeus, in the portion of his thought that lies apart from what human minds contribute, possesses the power actually to bring matter into existence. Zeus's mind is, indeed, in this way as in others, vastly more powerful than our minds are, but in thinking whatever thoughts we do think, we are just as free, in the sense of responsible, for what we do as Zeus is in thinking his own thoughts.

My remarks in this paragraph are the briefest sketch of part of what, I recognize, is a controversial interpretation of the Stoic theory of Fate and human beings' individual responsibility for their actions—an extraordinarily complex and difficult topic. I hope to present and argue fully for that interpretation on another occasion.

Stoic autonomy, then, is a complex and, I think, deeply interesting conception of human nature, human rationality, and the basis of morality. In the similarities of autonomy, as they conceive it, to Kant's much more familiar conception, the Stoics deserve to be considered important forerunners of Kant, neglected though they are in this capacity. But, independently of historical comparison, the Stoic theory deserves to be studied and appreciated in its own right.

Philosophy, Princeton University

AUTONOMOUS AUTONOMY: SPINOZA ON AUTONOMY, PERFECTIONISM, AND POLITICS*

By Douglas Den Uyl

> The fundamental assumption of moral philosophy is that men are responsible for their actions. From this assumption it necessarily follows ... that men are metaphysically free.
> —Robert Paul Wolff, *In Defense of Anarchism*

> A man can be free in any kind of state.
> —Spinoza, *Tractatus Theologico-Politicus*

I. INTRODUCTION

These epigraphs present us with part of the problem that is to be discussed in this essay. For Spinoza (1632–1677) there is no metaphysical freedom, except for God/Substance/Nature. The behavior of individual things, or *modes*, is completely a function of causes that bring about the behavior. This might suggest that there can be no *autonomy* in any meaningful sense either, thus aborting at the outset any talk of autonomy in Spinoza. To add to this problem, "autonomy" is somewhat anachronistic when applied to Spinoza.[1] The philosophical theory surrounding the concept of autonomy seems to have developed later, perhaps mostly from Kant (1724–1804),[2] which is not to say that it did not have parallels earlier.[3] Kantian metaphysics is certainly different from Spinozistic metaphysics in allowing for freedom, if nothing else. But even if we ignore the metaphysics, the structure of a Kantian ethics is different from a Spinozistic one in its focus on duty and imperatives.

---

* I wish to thank Lee C. Rice for very helpful comments on an earlier draft of this essay.
[1] The Oxford English dictionary recognizes the term "autonomy" in a political sense in English into the seventeenth century, but the term does not seem to have had much currency at that time.
[2] See J. B. Schneewind, *The Invention of Autonomy: A History of Modern Moral Philosophy* (New York: Cambridge University Press, 1998), 3–13, 533–54.
[3] Though there are earlier parallels, David A. J. Richards suggests that we find the beginnings of the use of the term "autonomy" around the time of the English Civil War (1642–1645). David. A. J. Richards, "Rights and Autonomy," *Ethics* 92, no. 1 (1981): 3–20. Still, the term's philosophical usage stems largely from Rousseau and Kant. Of course, even the early usage postdates Spinoza to some extent.

One finds little of that in Spinoza. Consequently, on both metaphysical and historical grounds, it seems somewhat problematic to speak of Kantian autonomy in Spinoza.

Subsequent versions of autonomy, such as that which might be connected to J. S. Mill (1806–1873), serve us no better. Though there are both utilitarian and perfectionistic elements in Spinoza, they are grounded in rather different foundations than those of Mill, as we shall see presently. There is, for example, no general hedonic calculus with normative bite for Spinoza, and perfectionism is rooted in something metaphysically more expansive than pleasure and pain.

The problem of discussing "autonomy" in Spinoza is only compounded if we take into account Spinoza's statement that "a man can be free in any kind of state." For if freedom can be linked with autonomy in some way—and I shall argue that it can—his statement suggests that it would be quite irrelevant to politics. This, at least for much of post-Kantian Western political theory, would seem to give us further cause to dismiss Spinoza. One reason for dismissal might be because making such a case for the dissociation of autonomy from politics would likely depend on "outmoded" distinctions, such as that between the state and society or between the individual and community. On this view, any concept with morally normative characteristics must, ipso facto, be connected to the political in some way. I shall call this the *communitarian* perspective. Another reason for dismissing someone who dissociates autonomy from politics might be because, without some notion of autonomy, respect for persons would be impossible; and without respect for persons, we would have no impediments to treating people as objects and thus using them as we see fit. I shall call this the *liberal* perspective on the necessary link between autonomy and politics. Finally among various possible reasons for dismissing Spinoza, there is the objection that we will fail to protect something of importance or of central value to human living if we dissociate autonomy from politics. Politics is nothing if it is not at least in the service of fending off encroachments to what is most valuable to human life. More generally, politics from this perspective is viewed as having some role to play in the *promotion* of the principal goods or values of human existence. If we know something to be truly and universally good for persons, we should encourage its presence. I shall call this the *welfare* perspective. The three perspectives are not mutually exclusive of one another. In the minds of many people, they are mutually supportive. Yet they all seem to suggest that it is both undesirable and mistaken to believe that questions of autonomy could be separate from political questions.

Of course, the dissociation of autonomy from politics depends upon being clear about what autonomy is, not to mention being clear about politics. There is a vast array of accounts about what autonomy means

and its implications for moral and political philosophy.[4] Though we may
feel that we have a good intuitive sense of the meaning of autonomy, we
are probably left with Joel Feinberg's position that "our conception of
autonomy as an actual condition is sufficiently vague and uncertain to
allow us considerable flexibility."[5] As Feinberg notes, we can think of
autonomy as a capacity, a condition, an ideal, and a right, and as inte-
grally bound up with such notions as self-possession, self-identity, self-
selection, self-determinism, self-legislation, moral authenticity, moral
independence, self-fidelity, self-discipline, self-reliance, self-generation (ini-
tiative), and personal responsibility.[6] Trying to keep all such notions before us is daunting, if not impossible, so the easiest course would be to
assume that there must be some connection somewhere between autonomy and politics, given the vast scope of the concept.

The dissociation of autonomy from politics, then, may apply to some
types of autonomy and not to others. To better grasp the problem, I have
found David Johnston's tripartite division helpful in sorting the basic
categories into which discussions of autonomy can be relegated.[7] To over-
simplify somewhat, discussions of autonomy are either about *agency*,
morality, or *self-perfection*. In the first category, we are speaking of the
conditions necessary for holding someone responsible for his or her actions; in the second, we are examining the sorts of moral and political
principles that are required once we recognize each other as agents; and
in the third we are looking into the conditions that obtain when one
achieves some state of self-sufficiency and independence. These three
levels are generally meant to diffuse into one another—at least with respect to the first two levels, and into the third, if one is a perfectionist
liberal. The third level, however, which may be most closely linked to
what I have called the welfare argument, is also the one where autonomy
seems most easily dissociated from politics. For if the condition of autonomy as self-sufficiency is rare, it might be said that it could have little

[4] While ignoring major thinkers such as Rousseau, Kant, and Mill, I have included the
following sources in this obviously incomplete sampling of some of the secondary literature
(most of which have discussions of autonomy embedded in larger discussions): Horacio
Spector, *Autonomy and Rights* (Oxford: Clarendon Press, 1992), 90–100, 161–64; Gerald Dwor-
kin, *The Theory and Practice of Autonomy* (New York: Cambridge University Press, 1988);
Schneewind, *The Invention of Autonomy*; Attracta Ingram, *A Political Theory of Rights* (Oxford:
Clarendon Press, 1994), chap. 5; David Johnston, *The Idea of Liberal Theory: A Critique and
Reconstruction* (Princeton, NJ: Princeton University Press, 1994), chap. 3; S. I. Benn and R. S.
Peters, *The Principles of Political Thought* (New York: The Free Press, 1965), 49–58; Alan S.
Rosenbaum, *Coercion and Autonomy: Philosophical Foundations, Issues, and Practices* (Westport,
CT: Greenwood Press, 1986), 122–33; David Shapiro, *Autonomy and Rigid Character* (New
York: Basic Books, 1981), chaps. 1–2; Joel Feinberg, *Harm to Self* (New York: Oxford Univer-
sity Press, 1986), chap. 18; John Christman, "Constructing the Inner Citadel: Recent Work on
Autonomy," *Ethics* 99, no. 1 (1988): 109–24.
[5] Feinberg, *Harm to Self*, 44.
[6] Ibid., 31–44. Feinberg lists these under the category of autonomy as "condition," but
most seem applicable to all of the types of autonomy that he mentions.
[7] Johnston, *The Idea of Liberal Theory*, 71ff.

bearing on politics, which is hardly rare. Still, it might be argued that politics exists to make possible the finest of human endeavors, however rare they might be.

As we shall see, Spinoza does seem to say things that are very much connected to the self-perfectionist meaning of freedom and thus autonomy. Perhaps, then, if this does allow for the easy separation of autonomy from politics, the issue of this connection is trivial. I want to go further, however, and suggest that Spinoza's view is that autonomy and politics are in actual conflict, and attempts to attach them are misguided. Making this case would depend on showing that the nature of each is quite different and incompatible, such that the attempt to bring one into the other is a confusion of some consequence. In order to make this case, we will need to get some idea of what counts as autonomy in Spinoza, how that notion functions in his ethics, and the implications of it for political theory.

Proceeding with the question of the relationship (or lack thereof) between autonomy and politics leaves open the deeper metaphysical question of free will and responsibility. I could demur, in standard academic fashion, by saying that this deeper issue is outside the scope of this essay and much too difficult, anyway, to be handled in a few pages. All that would be true, but, putting aside the bigger issues would leave me vulnerable to the charge by advocates of both free will and determinism (or compatibilism) alike that I have failed to establish the metaphysical status of autonomy, and thus inferentially undermined the rest of the project. Perhaps one can only plead guilty to such a charge; yet, it is not uncharacteristic of Spinoza to recognize the value of exploring smaller perspectives as a way of seeing the nature of a larger issue.[8] Furthermore, while the political writings of Spinoza may point to deeper metaphysical issues, they are themselves focused primarily upon ordinary human circumstances, and even give primacy of place to the individual, rather than to the God/Substance/Nature concept that is so central in the early part of Spinoza's *Ethica*.[9] Finally, it is possible, I believe, to make sense of much of what Spinoza has to say about freedom and bondage without either solving the free will debate or ignoring Spinoza's stand on it. We shall see how well this approach serves us in what follows.

---

[8] Spinoza's example of a "worm in the bloodstream" is a good parallel. We are taking the worm's perspective. It is not a false perspective—it is just not the broadest or most complete. See Spinoza's *Letter* 15 (32) to Henry Oldenburg. Numbering of Spinoza's letters is standard across editions of Spinoza's writings.

[9] For example, consider Chapter XVI of Spinoza's *Tractatus Theologico-Politicus* (TTP). See also Douglas Den Uyl and Lee C. Rice, "Spinoza and Hume on Individuals," *Reason Papers* 15 (1990): 91–117. One might do well in this connection to consider Edwin Curley's "The *TTP* as a Prolegomenon to the *Ethics*," in J. A. Cover and Mark Kulstadt, eds., *Central Themes in Early Modern Philosophy* (Indianapolis, IN: Hackett, 1990).

II. Autonomy and Activity

Since autonomy is a post-Spinozistic term, it is perhaps best to begin with how it might relate to concepts that Spinoza does use, such as human "freedom" (*libertatas humana*) or "activity" (*agere*). The central core of the concept of autonomy as it is currently used by most philosophers includes some idea of self-governance and self-directedness. In the Kantian tradition, self-governance is the dominant modality for autonomy, and it gets translated almost immediately into willing universal maxims of conduct, which one (having willed them) acts upon out of self-acceptance of those maxims. The value of autonomy, not to mention its self-directedness, is bound up in the fact that we can formulate universal principles, understand and appreciate their meaning, and choose to follow them. From this we must come to recognize that each and every being who is capable of doing the same thing possesses worth or dignity. Mixed together here are notions of self-directedness as acts of agency, and self-governance as notions of living according to rules that we have prescribed for ourselves. Although there is an argument in Kant about the necessary connection between agency and morality, these two forms should be kept distinct (following our opening schema), because the moral notion of autonomy—understood as the ability to formulate and follow universalizable rules—is not much found in Spinoza. However, I believe that the agency notion is.

The other "classic" tradition of autonomy is the one found in Mill, and it might be thought of as the self-development tradition. At first, this view looks like the self-perfectionist level mentioned in my opening comments. Individuals ground their choices in the most complete set of relevant information and choose only after critical, rational reflection upon the options available. They are self-governing because their choices stem from their own considerations, rather than from another's, and they are sufficiently well developed to be able to formulate decisions that are not fundamentally a function of another person's decisions, views, or interests. Moreover, their decisions are not simply the uncritical expression of their own desires. In the Millean tradition, autonomy seems more closely linked to agency than to morality; but the moral level is connected to agency, as well as to self-development, by the fact that fully considering an action means taking into account its effects upon all agents (oneself included). Though Mill often suggests that self-development is in some important way intrinsically valuable,[10] whether it is, in the end, subsumed by the moral perspective is open to question. For the intrinsicist Mill, agency seems to be a function of self-development rather than the other way around—that is, the degree to which one qualifies as an agent

---

[10] This seems to be the import of at least some of the "higher pleasures" argument in Chapter 2 of J. S. Mill's *Utilitarianism*.

is a function of one's self-development. Such an approach looks like it is immune from the utilitarian calculus, because it is self-focused, and its value is said to come from the intrinsically humanizing character of self-development. But with pleasure and pain as the root source of value in Mill, it might ultimately be impossible to give *self*-development any standing independent of the utilitarian calculus, precisely because of the lack of special status the self has in such a framework. Nevertheless, Mill's notion of self-developed agency informs our understanding of autonomy just as much as does Kant's notion of self-legislation. While Spinoza and Mill seem to me different in a number of significant respects, their self-developmental aspects share at least a prima facie similarity.

Self-governance, or self-directedness, or autonomy, in the authors just described, incorporates acting on decisions that are made by us through some process of reflection, critical examination, and self-directed, rational deliberation. It also means that our actions are essentially the product of our own wills, rather than someone else's or some other factor outside of us. Thus, the extent to which one is autonomous is a function of how authentically self-directed one is, in just these ways. Spinoza has no language of autonomy, but, rather, a language of activity (*agere*) and passivity (*pati*). These terms are defined early on in the third book of Spinoza's *Ethica*:

> I say that we are active when something takes place, in us or externally to us, of which we are the adequate cause; that is, ... when from our nature there follows in us or externally to us something which can be clearly and distinctly understood through our nature alone. On the other hand, I say that we are passive when something takes place in us, or flows from our nature, of which we are only the partial cause. (E3Def.2)[11]

Just prior to this, Spinoza gives us his definitions of *adequate cause* and *inadequate cause*:

> I call that an adequate cause whose effect can be clearly and distinctly perceived through the said cause. I call that an inadequate or partial cause whose effect cannot be understood through the said cause alone. (E3Def.1)

---

[11] The standard practice for referencing Spinoza's main treatise—his *Ethica*—is to have "E" represent the work, have the first number represent the book within the *Ethica*, and then "P" for "proposition," "C" for "corollary," "Def." for "definition," "App." for "appendix," and "Schol." for "scholium," all followed by the appropriate numeral. In this case, then, we are referring to the second definition of the third book of the *Ethica*. I have used primarily the Edwin Curley translation of the *Ethica*: See *The Collected Works of Spinoza*, ed. [trans.] Edwin Curley (Princeton, NJ: Princeton University Press, 1985), vol. I.

For our purposes, what is important here is the connection that Spinoza makes between these definitions and the "emotions" or affects that move us. This is important, because the idea of freedom (and thus "autonomy") will be found herein. Typically, being governed by one's emotions is not a sign of "autonomy." Yet given Spinoza's somewhat specialized understanding of "emotion," we need to follow his definitions closely because there are exceptions. In the end, as we shall now start to see, he does not deviate that much from the tradition of seeing emotions as an impediment to "autonomy."

> By emotions (*affectus*) I understand the affections of the body by which the body's power of activity is increased or diminished, assisted or checked, together with the ideas of these affections. Thus if we can be the adequate cause of one of these affections, then by emotion I understand activity, otherwise passivity. (E3Def.3)

Spinoza's famous *doctrine of parallelism*, which holds that mind and body have corresponding but distinct descriptions for all events, indicates that we must pay some attention to both sides of the equation.[12] Hence, he tells us that, on the one hand, "the more the mind has inadequate ideas, the more it is subject to passive states; and on the other hand, it is more active in proportion as it has a great number of adequate ideas" (E3P1Cor.). In these descriptions or definitions, we see that activity has both a mental and physical dimension. The two are related through the concept of *conatus* and finally *appetite*. *Conatus* is a kind of persistence or endeavoring, true of both mind and body (E3P7). *Conatus* is thereby expressed through our essence, which turns out to be appetite.

> When this conatus is related to the mind alone, it is called Will; when it is related to mind and body together, it is called Appetite, which is therefore nothing else but man's essence (*ipsa hominis essentia*), from the nature of which there necessarily follow those things that tend to his preservation, and which man is thus determined to perform. Further, there is no difference between appetite and Desire except that desire is usually related to men in so far as they are conscious of their appetite. (E3P9Schol.)

The endeavor of mind and body exerting itself through and into the world is the base from which we can describe what we do as being either essentially active or passive. Heightened exertion is not, however, equivalent to activity.

---

[12] We learn earlier that "nothing can happen in the body without its being perceived by the mind" (E2P12), and, moreover, that "the object of the idea constituting the human mind is the body" (E2P13).

[T]he mind can undergo considerable changes, and can pass now to a state of greater perfection, now to one of less perfection, and it is these passive transitions [*passions*] that explicate for us the emotions of Pleasure [*laetitia*] and Pain [*tristitia*]. So in what follows I shall understand by pleasure *the passive transition of the mind to a state of greater perfection* and by pain *the passive transition of the mind to a state of less perfection.* (E3P11Schol.)

Perfection and *reality* mean the same thing for Spinoza (E2Def.6).

Though hardly adequate or complete, what I have discussed thus far provides us with a sufficient foundation to begin to add some of the value elements to the theory of activity and passivity. In general, activity is better than passivity because it carries with it more perfection or "reality." Perfection and reality are themselves understood in terms of power and virtue. How this might look in practice I shall try to clarify in a moment, but we can begin by noting the following:

By virtue and power I mean the same thing; that is virtue, in so far as it is related to man, is man's very essence (E3P7),[13] or nature, in so far as he has power to bring about that which can be understood solely through the laws of his own nature. (E4Def.8)

We are passive to the extent to which we need to explain our actions by what is "outside" of us. Of course, we can never attain complete activity according to Spinoza (E4P4), so the issue of passivity and activity is a relative one. But given that general caveat, we can move forward in discussing activity, passivity, freedom, and bondage.[14]

The key to Spinoza on the issues that concern us here is provided in the opening line of the Preface to Part IV of the *Ethica*: "I assign the term 'bondage' (*servitutem*) to man's lack of power to control and check the emotions (*affectibus*)." Our passivity or bondage is a function of the degree to which we lack adequate ideas (E5P3), and the more adequate our ideas, the more active and free we become (E5P10 and Schol., E5P40). Our adequate ideas, as modes of reason, turn out to be a way of controlling our passive emotions (E5P7), which put us into bondage. In the scholium to E5P20, for example, we get a brief summary account of how the mind might control the passive emotions so that we are able to move toward more freedom and activity. We can add to this the value component by noting that "our active emotions, that is, those desires that are defined by

---

[13] "The *conatus* with which each thing endeavors to persist in its own being is nothing but the actual essence of the thing itself."

[14] Incidentally, this is a reason why not everything one discusses in Spinoza has to be discussed *sub specie aeternitatis* (under the aspect of eternity) all the time. Spinoza is perfectly willing to discuss human freedom even though, even by his standards, there is no possibility of complete freedom.

man's power, that is, by reason, are always good; the other desires can be either good or evil" (E4App.3). This statement shows both that there can be active emotions and that passive ones are not necessarily bad, though active ones are always good.

To the uninitiated reader, unpacking a paragraph like the foregoing one seems to be a necessity. To the initiated, doing so is nothing less than daunting! A full unpacking would require a survey of almost the whole collection of secondary literature on Spinoza, since this topic is so fundamental to his *Ethica*.[15] Short of such a survey, however, perhaps a few (and, I hope, salient) observations are in order. In general, I would like to borrow a metaphor from economics as a guide here. Economists will sometimes speak of "internalizing the externalities" when referring to problems of market failure. For them, if costs are distributed widely but benefits are captured by a few, then the incentive to manage costs is weakened and inefficiencies result. The idea is to get the costs to be carried by those who will be reaping the benefits. Now it is not costs and benefits that concern us, but the phraseology of internalizing what is external. For Spinoza, to be active is to be the source of our own actions and not to be impelled by forces that are external to us. We will always be impelled by some force in this system, but if what we are impelled by stems from us, rather than something outside of us, then we are active and free. In this case, our endeavors are internal when they "follow from the necessity of our nature," which means that we are the adequate cause of them in Spinoza's special sense of adequate cause. What we generally do not want is to be impelled by what is external to us, that is, by what does not follow from our nature alone and of which we are only the partial cause. What is outside of us is what we do not understand, so if we do understand something it could be said that we have internalized it.

What may seem puzzling at first is to think of our emotions as being "external" to us. This is not so strange as first appearances might suggest, though, because we are accustomed to speaking of being "taken over" by our emotions, as if they were outside of us in some way (see E4P20Schol.). In Spinoza, since appetite is our essence, and mind and body are in tandem in any appetite (by definition), our appetites only become our own, so to speak, when we are clear about what they are, what has given rise to them, and how they are functioning in the current situation. That is to say, we can be the adequate cause of what we do (our "effects") if we are clear about the sources of our actions and their impact upon the

---

[15] There are a number of good, general introductions to Spinoza that discuss these themes. For example, see Henry Allison, *Benedict de Spinoza: An Introduction* (New Haven, CT: Yale University Press, 1987); Stuart Hampshire, *Spinoza* (Harmondsworth, UK: Penguin Classics, 1993); and Genevieve Lloyd, *Spinoza and the* Ethics (London: Routledge, 1996). For a more detailed analysis consider Jonathan Bennett, *A Study of Spinoza's Ethics* (Cambridge: Cambridge University Press, 1984), chap. 11. Especially influential on my own perspective is Lee C. Rice, "Emotion, Appetition, and *Conatus* in Spinoza," *Revue Internationale de Philosophie* 31 (1977): 101–16.

environment in which they are undertaken. If we do not understand what we are doing, or do so only partially and inadequately, then it seems perfectly plausible to suggest that we are being moved by forces that are in some way not us—however much those forces may be located within our own bodies. For whether I have a pain that is causing me to squirm in my chair because I am sitting on something that I do not see and am not aware is present, or because there is some neural malfunction inside my body, seems to have little to do with *me* being the cause of my squirming. If, however, I squirm because I understand that my discomfort is being caused by something sticking through the bottom of the chair, and I will be able to displace it in such a way that I am no longer affected, then my squirming would seem to be an action of mine rather than something that I am noticing about myself.

Emotions are a certain type of reaction to stimuli given to us physically by our environment. That environment could be "inside" of us or "outside." As we saw above, there can be active emotions, but for Spinoza these are rather rare in most people, most of the time. For an emotion to be active, it would have to stem from the presence of adequate ideas (E3P58), but this is not likely to be our ordinary state (E4P4–6). Passive emotions are by far the most common ones, and are seen by Spinoza as being in a significant way "external" to us (E4P5). The project of freedom, then, is one of internalizing our emotions, that is, making them a function of adequate, rather than inadequate, ideas. We succeed in this project either by checking or by replacing our passive emotions with more active ones (E4P7, 14, 59, 61), thus harnessing their power in ways that are clear to us. But we should not expect passive emotions to disappear, and they are quite capable of ruling us entirely (E4P6). This is why freedom is an achievement that draws us out of our ordinary state of passivity. Our very finitude, and the limited character of our power relative to the universe around us, indicate not only why our freedom can never be complete, but also how difficult and fragile is its achievement.

Already we see from Spinoza's concepts of activity and freedom some parallels to ideas that are connected to autonomy. Activity is a kind of self-causation, which links up nicely with notions of self-determination, self-government, and agency. We are the authors and sources of our actions, because we are the cause of them. Furthermore, with activity being a function of adequate ideas, we are reminded of the requirements of rationality that are built into many notions of autonomy, since the adequacy of our ideas is, more often than not, provided by reason.[16] To have a clear understanding about our motivations and what we are doing would certainly seem to parallel some of the requirements for considered

---

[16] Not exclusively or even most importantly, however. There is a "third kind of knowledge" (*scientia intuitiva*) that is the highest and deepest for Spinoza and is not the usual sort of discursive reasoning (E5P25).

rationality that are common in many notions of autonomy. Indeed, the call for activity over passivity rules out impulsive or passionate behavior. These terms which we have been discussing deal more with agency and self-perfectionist forms of autonomy than with moral forms, but we shall have a brief word to say about that in a moment. The point at this stage, however, is to suggest that Spinoza's philosophy—however different in structure it may be from other forms where "autonomy" is explicitly mentioned—nevertheless accords an important place to drawing a distinction between self-governed and self-directed conduct, on the one hand, and the sort of conduct where one is pushed and pulled by forces outside of oneself, on the other hand.

What is missing from this account, so far, is a certain distinctive tone to the argument that comes from Spinoza's use of terms such as power and virtue. First of all, we might remind ourselves of Spinoza's doctrine of parallelism as mentioned in E3P11: "whatsoever increases or diminishes, assists or checks, the power of activity of our body, the idea of the said thing increases or diminishes, assists or checks the power of thought of our mind." This proposition is followed by his definitions of pleasure and pain, already mentioned above. With this in mind, perhaps the distinctive tone between what we have been saying and what is unique to Spinoza, as well as the more normative side of our issue, is conveyed in the following passage:

> True virtue is nothing other than to live only by the guidance of reason, and so weakness consists solely in this, that a man suffers himself to be led by things external to himself, and is determined by them to act in a way required by the general state of external circumstances, not by his own nature considered only in itself. (E4P37Schol. 1)

Recall that, for Spinoza, power and virtue are the same; so by this account, reason gives us power, and weakness is a function of inadequate ideas about ourselves and the environment in which we act. Recall also that power and perfection are the same, and that pleasure increases our perfection, while pain diminishes it. From this we can see that virtue and *conatus* are intimately connected in a way that makes "autonomy" significantly more connected with successful self-extension and efficacy of action than what might be found in typical responsibility-based conceptions of autonomy. Consider in this regard the following:

> The more every man endeavors and is able to seek his own advantage, that is, to preserve his own being, the more he is endowed with virtue. On the other hand, in so far as he neglects to preserve what is to his advantage, that is, his own being, to that extent he is weak. (E4P20)

Furthermore, Spinoza writes:

> To act in absolute conformity with virtue is nothing else in us but to act, to live, to preserve one's own being (these three mean the same) under the guidance of reason, on the basis of seeking one's own advantage. (E4P24)

With these passages in mind, it is not off the mark to say that one's "autonomy," for Spinoza, can be measured by one's success in extending one's power in, through, and over one's environment. Thus the approach is not one of determining the degree of autonomy by measuring the extent to which one lives up to certain criteria of responsible conduct. Instead, virtually the reverse is true in Spinoza: successful living just *is* the standard of "autonomy" for Spinoza, and our notions of what it may mean to be responsible for what we do may be better understood in light of success, rather than in light of prior conceptions of responsibility.[17]

I shall conclude this section on autonomy and activity with an example to help illustrate some of what I have been discussing. Imagine a situation in which a person is driving along, let us say in a hurry to arrive somewhere, and his car suddenly and unexpectedly stalls out and will not restart by turning the key. We can easily imagine how a person who knows nothing about cars might act and feel in this situation. We might expect the driver to exhibit, apart from the frustration that comes from the inevitable delay, a certain amount of anger. We can imagine him swearing, looking under the hood to no effect, perhaps kicking the car, or throwing up his hands, and so forth. The point is, having no ideas, the driver is completely at the mercy of his circumstances and emotions. The driver would be, to say the least, completely passive. The "pain" and frustration that he experiences would perhaps only add to his ineptitude and ineffectiveness, for his thinking is likely to become even more clouded and less focused in such a situation. Notice in this scenario another possibility: in the driver's frustration and anger, he begins to poke randomly and pull at some of the wires under the hood of the car. Suppose that, in doing so, there is some indication that the car might start again (e.g., the driver gets back in and turns the key and the engine makes some sort of sound). Now the pleasure that comes from this consequence will move him to a "higher state of perfection"—that is, he will likely continue to adjust those

---

[17] This again may lead us toward the "free will" issue, which I want to skirt around as much as possible. However, I think that the question of "holding people accountable" for their actions would be a separate one from full-blown responsibility in Spinoza's sense. For simply telling someone that if he does X then he will suffer certain consequences might itself be causally significant for actors who do not act from adequate ideas.

wires to start the car. But the man is still completely passive: since he has no real understanding of how the automobile works, the noise that he heard may or may not be connected to his movement of the wires. From this example, we can see that a person's endeavoring may be increased in a certain direction, but that he is still not "active" in Spinoza's sense and, thus, not "autonomous."

Contrast the foregoing scenario with one in which the person driving is quite knowledgeable about cars—let us say he is an automobile mechanic. The frustration at the delay is likely to be the same, but there the similarity to the other case ends. This person might know by the particular sound that the car made as it stalled out where the problem is likely to be found. When he opens the hood, it is with an understanding of what he is looking at and how the various parts of the engine function and are connected together. Attitudinally, the driver will not be bombarded by various emotions, but will instead have emotions that would be closer to the attitude of confidence. The driver will understand that there is a reason for the problem, he will understand what the likely alternatives are, and he will approach the situation with a belief that he can at least plan what to do, if not solve the problem right then and there. The feelings of confidence, efficacy, and focus all stem from the driver's possession of adequate ideas. He will not dwell on confused, negative, and unhelpful emotions such as anger. Indeed those will soon get displaced, if they were present at all, by the more active emotions connected to knowing what one is doing and doing it.

Of course, most of us are neither as knowledgeable as the mechanic nor as ignorant as the first driver. We may have some knowledge of cars, but not an extensive amount. Yet our case is instructive, too. Suppose that we are passive and sitting by the roadside, wallowing in the pain of our misfortune. Imagine what happens to us when we think of an idea, or even a set of ideas or plan, for solving our car problem. Our ineffective, negative emotions start to get displaced, and we begin to act on the idea or plan. Having an idea or a plan is not the same as having an *adequate* idea or plan. But if the particular ideas that make up a plan are good ones, then the endeavoring thus created will reinforce itself through success, and we will persevere until the problem is solved. Emotionally we are focused on what increases our control and our extension into, and over, our environment. The less passive we are, the less our emotions impede our progress; rather, they give us increased motivation. This is why terms such as "perfection," "reality," "activity," and "virtue" are virtually synonymous for Spinoza. They all refer, in some way, to the power of something to exert itself efficaciously into its environment. And if we are allowed to speak of death as a terminal extreme of what is inefficacious, weak, and passive, we can see why Spinoza would say that "the free man thinks of death least of all things, and his wisdom is a meditation of life, not of death" (E4P67).

III. Autonomy and Morality

Spinoza's ethics is not easily described. Don Garrett tells us that "Spinoza is both a consequentialist and a virtue ethicist."[18] In a connected vein, Lee C. Rice claims that we should describe Spinoza as a "classical" moralist.[19] The essential element in Spinoza's classicism is described by Rice as follows:

> [Spinoza's] ethical theory is classical in structure. It is not, like contemporary metaethical theories, an account of normative predication and the function of normative discourse in language, but rather a first-order normative theory which purports to outline and argue the prospects for human well-being (Aristotle's *eudaimonia*, Spinoza's *beatitudo*) in a system of nature viewed as largely amoral.[20]

Another way to say that Spinoza's ethics is classical in nature is to note that it is unlike most modern ethical theories, which are centrally concerned with questions of obligation, duty, or one's social roles with respect to others. Instead, Spinoza's approach would be typically described as one that is focused on the good, but for reasons that are somewhat peculiar to Spinoza.[21] It is best to think in terms of an orientation toward well-being or "perfection." Spinoza's ethics is thus consequentialist in looking to the effects of action upon well-being. It is virtue-oriented in that well-being resides mostly in developed qualities of character and mind.

Rice also claims that for Spinoza we must draw a strong distinction between ethics on the one hand and morality on the other.[22] The quotation above explains one reason for drawing this distinction, namely, that morality concerns the application of such normative predicates as *right* or *wrong, just* or *unjust, virtuous* or *vicious,* and the like, and not how to live a life. There is another reason, however, for drawing a distinction between ethics and morality: ethics concerns human activity, whereas morality

---

[18] Don Garrett, "Spinoza's Ethical Theory," in Don Garrett, ed., *The Cambridge Companion to Spinoza* (New York: Cambridge University Press, 1996), 297. Garrett notes later (p. 313 n. 35) that Spinoza bears little resemblance to deontologists by his lack of the use of terms like "duty," "obligation," and, I might add, "autonomy." Still, Garrett notes that Spinoza links ethics to "reason" in a way not totally unlike Kant, and, of course, other similarities that may exist between Spinoza and Kant will be explored in the text.

[19] Rice and I together make the same point. See Den Uyl and Rice, "Spinoza and Hume on Individuals," 102ff.

[20] Lee C. Rice, "Spinoza's Notion of 'Tenere' in His Moral and Political Thought," in *Ethik, Recht und Politik bei Spinoza,* Vorträge gehalten anlasslich des 6. Internationalen Kongresses der Spinoza-Gesellschaft vom 5. bis. 7. Oktober 2000 an der Universität Zürick, 150.

[21] "Good" and "evil" are terms related to our limitedness, partiality, and inadequacy. I cannot avoid using them entirely, but this caveat about their use should be noted.

[22] Rice, "Spinoza's Notion of 'Tenere' in His Moral and Political Thought," 150. For further elaboration, see also Rice, "Spinoza's Ethical Project," forthcoming in *Agora.*

concerns itself either with what is passive or with forms of passivity that would receive endorsement by reason, were the conduct to spring from adequate ideas.[23] In both cases, factors that contribute to human well-being are the foundation for any descriptions of normative value; but as we saw when we examined the notion of pleasure, something may contribute to human well-being that is not in itself active.

Spinoza indicates the difference between morality and ethics when he tells us that, "if men were born free, they would form no conception of good and evil so long as they were free" (E4P68). The meaning of this proposition is connected to the general thesis that nature acts neither for us nor against us (and thus contains no good or evil in itself), but follows its own inexorable laws. Within this framework, this proposition is a way of saying that good and evil, as terms of ordinary moral discourse, reflect the inadequacy of our ideas. We are passive when our ideas are inadequate. If passive, we are moved by things "outside" of ourselves, which we do not fully understand and do not know how to internalize within our active conduct. On the one hand, we would, under such conditions, come to see things in the world as being either for us (good) or against us (evil). If, on the other hand, we had adequate ideas, we would know that nothing in the world is, in itself, for or against us; we would know that what is happening is the result of intelligible causes, and that we are doing all that can be done, and only what can be done, to expand our power into the environment. We cannot suppose that the active person could do something differently, because that would be to suppose that she or he could recognize the "correct" course, but not undertake it. For Spinoza, will and intellect are the same (E2P49Cor.), so understanding what to do is already to be doing it. Acts of prior deliberation about what to do and which course or action is better or worse are, to some extent, expressions of mental confusion. To know what is right is not to then do the right but to *be doing* the right, for the knowing and the doing would be simultaneous and coextensive, with no reflections on "good" or "evil." That the right action is the only action does have some resemblance to Kant's claim that acting from duty is both autonomous and the only thing a rational being could choose to do. In Spinoza's case, however, one does not first become rational and then will that rationality into practice. Rather, rationality is expressed. It is not a detached conclusion waiting to be engaged with the world, but the activity of engagement itself.[24] The notion that we cannot have adequate ideas about our actions that are waiting to be engaged explains why Spinoza is more comfortable with an exemplar model of ethics than with models that articulate principles or

---

[23] I am not completely satisfied with the locution of "ethics" versus "morality," though it does capture something of what I am saying here, and no better distinction comes to mind.

[24] Spinoza tells us exactly this when he says, "if it *were* as much in our power to live by the precept of reason as it is to be led by blind desire, all men *would* be guided by reason, and *would* order their lives wisely." Spinoza, *Tractatus Politicus* II, 6.

rules of conduct, which are themselves the product of discursive rationality (E5P10Schol.). An exemplar, being a model of an agent in action, is
closer to the very doing of the action than is a set of principles that are to
be followed.[25]

The psychological disposition we are exploring here is not foreign to
ethical theory and might be suggested in the difference between the attitude of the "Rescuers" during World War II and that of most other
people at that time (or of us imagining ourselves as part of the scene).
Virtually everyone would agree that the Jews who were pursued by Nazi
forces were being victimized. The Rescuer, however, offered help and did
so without a sense that there was anything else to be done under the
circumstances. One might expect that most other people, by contrast,
were likely to have wondered about the extent and meaning of their
"obligation" to provide aid under such circumstances, and whether their
own interests outweighed those of endangered Jews, and whether avoiding risk to others was a stronger obligation than the contemplated aid,
and so forth. As this example makes clear, morality, as it is normally
conceived and practiced, is a sign of our passivity and uncertainty, and
Spinoza tells us

> "The best thing, then, that we can do, so long as we do not have
> perfect knowledge of our affects, is to conceive a correct principle of
> living, *or* sure maxims of life, to commit them to memory, and to
> apply them constantly to the particular cases frequently encountered
> in life." (E5P10Schol.)

Spinoza points out in the scholium to E4P68 (that is, the proposition
that we would form no conception of good or evil if we were born free)
that we are definitely not born free, nor do we ever achieve freedom fully.
We are limited creatures of very finite dimensions and abilities, and we
are often subject to forces well beyond our control. The whole proposition
(E4P68 and Schol.) is therefore illustrative, not descriptive. We see from it
just how distinct human freedom is from the forces that usually govern
us. We should also see why it is likely that morality constitutes a necessary feature of human life; for, given our inadequate ideas and this
passivity, we need various aids in overcoming our passivity. In this regard I want to claim that morality, while passive in itself, is nevertheless
the bridge to the active and may possess active elements under some
circumstances.

Spinoza's ethics takes place on three levels: pleasure and pain, the
socially useful, and self-perfection or "blessedness." Rice and I have else-

---

[25] Another reason the exemplar works well for Spinoza has to do with the third level of
the good and the third level of knowledge discussed below.

where described these levels as "three levels of the good."[26] The first level is simply the level of individual pleasure and pain (E3P39Schol.). Here the individual is considered more or less in isolation, with pleasure and pain either encouraging or discouraging his endeavors. Of course, as Spinoza points out (E3P11Schol., P28–29), the basis for the next level is provided in the first. The second level could be called the "socially useful," which originates in pleasure and pain as they are transformed into the various emotions that ground our relationships with one another (e.g., E3P30ff.). Spinoza uses the word "useful" (*utile*) in his political writings (*Tractatus Theologico-Politicus* [TTP] XX), and he tends to judge the "well being" of social orders in terms of what is useful (TTP XVI, XX; *Tractatus Politicus* [TP] II, 18–20; TP V, 1–3).[27] In any case, the idea here is complicated. The "useful" encompasses custom, law, authority, and culture as they affect us in various ways, as well as utility, which is ordinarily understood as what benefits us. These social settings and forces are among the things that compel us. We are passive with respect to them, but properly ordered, they would be both necessary and beneficial and would tend to benefit most of us, collectively. Spinoza adds:

> The things that beget harmony are those which are related to justice, fairness, and being honorable. For men find it difficult to bear, not only what is unjust and unfair, but also what is *thought* dishonorable, *or* that someone rejects the accepted practices of the state. But especially necessary to bring people together in love, are the things which concern Religion and Morality. (E4App.15)

Here we see affective elements dominating the moral enterprise as it is considered from a social point of view.

Spinoza anticipates here, at least logically, the more systematic accounts of morality that would be developed by thinkers such as David Hume (1711–1776) and Adam Smith (1723–1790). If morality is passive, it would then become a matter of understanding just how the affections can give rise to moral norms and conduct. The working out of the mechanisms for this approach to ethics is a way of seeing how the "sentiments" can fashion our moral universe—a project that extends from Francis Hutcheson (1694–1746) through Adam Smith and beyond. Reason, for the most part, is not the basis of morality. We interact with each other affectively, and the multiplicity and diversity of those interactions across society get gener-

[26] Den Uyl and Rice, "Spinoza and Hume on Individuals." A number of aspects of this present essay are elaborations of themes suggested in that one.

[27] The *Tractatus Theologico-Politicus* was the first and major political work of Spinoza's available in his lifetime. The *Tractatus Politicus* was written toward the end of his life and was never finished or available during his lifetime. The typical way of referencing these works is TTP and TP, respectively, followed by chapter numbers. The TP also has paragraph numbers.

alized and codified into norms of conduct and standards for according merit and demerit, propriety and impropriety, to actions and individuals. There is virtually no fundamental questioning or understanding of these collective norms by the vast majority of individuals who act under them and according to them. Moreover, it is evident that strong sentiments for their adherence and against their violation are attached to the moral sentiments themselves, serving to reinforce the norms as springs of actual conduct.

In the *Ethica*, the passages that provide the transition from morality passively considered to a more active form are found primarily from E4P30 to E4P37, though E4P40 sums up the point most succinctly. Morality might be passive in its origin and general functioning, but it can also accord with what is active, and be a form of conduct that an active person would undertake or presuppose. In this part of the *Ethica*, the language is mixed, alternating between the active and the passive. Perhaps the following passage best indicates the general passivity that pervades morality and its possible connection to activity:

> Every man judges what is good and what is bad, and has regard for his own advantage according to his own way of thinking . . . and seeks revenge . . . and endeavors to preserve what he loves and to destroy what he hates. . . . Now if men lived by the guidance of reason, every man would possess this right of his . . . without any harm to another. But since men are subject to passive emotions . . . which far surpass the power or virtue of men . . . they are therefore often pulled in different directions . . . and are contrary to one another . . . while needing each other's help. . . . It is necessary . . . to create a feeling of mutual confidence that they will refrain from any action that may be harmful to another. The way to bring this about, (that men who are necessarily subject to passive emotions . . . and are inconstant and variable . . . should establish a mutual confidence and should trust one another) is obvious. . . . [I]t was demonstrated that no emotion can be checked except by a stronger emotion contrary to the emotion which is to be checked, and that every man refrains from inflicting injury through fear of greater injury. On these terms, then, society can be established, if it has the power to prescribe common rules of behavior and to pass laws to enforce them, not by reason, which is incapable of checking the emotions . . . but by threats. (E4P37Schol.2)

That human beings should unite and can live in harmony to their mutual advantage according to "common rules" is something suggested by reason, but it is also something that needs to be put in place among beings who are *not* guided by reason. Consequently, however important the common rules may be to a rational consideration of social interaction, the passage shows that they are clearly not effective unless they are affective. The only potentially misleading feature of this passage is its emphasis on threats. While the power to enforce must lie somewhere at the foundation of the social system, it is more accurate to say of Spinoza that he favors inducements and incentives over threats and fear as mechanisms for social control and unity.[28]

As I have suggested, the affective turn in ethics that was so prominent in the eighteenth century might have been a recognition of the truths about human beings that I just mentioned in the previous paragraph. The sophisticated, sympathetic mechanisms of morality described by David Hume and Adam Smith, which indicate the affective qualities of moral norms in practice, are valuable extensions of the Spinozistic project. In the end, however, we are still dealing largely with passivity from a Spinozistic point of view. The recognition of this was certainly, if only tacitly, a motivation for Kant to find some role for reason within this sort of outlook on ethics. Like Kant, Spinoza might be willing to say that the rational man would will the principles for himself, even while others might follow them for other reasons. Unlike Kant, for Spinoza actions that are not taken in a state of activity are not necessarily devoid of moral content. And as we have seen, for Spinoza, one's freedom does not consist in a grasping of generalized principles, but almost the reverse—in the particular form of one's endeavoring. To see this, let us revert for a moment to our previous example.

The person who is merely knowledgeable about automobile mechanics is not thereby free, according to Spinoza, simply in his knowledge of the working of cars, and certainly not in his knowledge of the principles of auto mechanics. It is generally more correct to say that he is free or active to the extent that he has both understood and applied these principles in the past, and most free when he is endeavoring with them in the present. It is the extension of the general into the particular—not simply the possession of general knowledge—that gives us activity. Hence, the person who faces the disruptive breakdown of his car by using knowledge to repair the vehicle's defect is more active than the person with similar knowledge who merely argues well about what ought to be done or who remains in the car for fear of soiling his hands. We cannot make the transition to the required sort of activity without the general principles that reason provides, but these principles are not freedom in themselves. So we make the move to the third and highest level of the good *through*

[28] In TTP XVII, we are told that "he who rules in the hearts of his subjects has the most absolute sovereignty," and that "nothing takes a greater hold on the mind than joy arising from devotion." Unless otherwise noted, when citing the *Tractatus Theologico-Politicus* (TTP) I shall use the A. G. Wernham edition, *The Political Works* (Oxford: Clarendon Press, 1965). These remarks are found on pages 151 and 181, respectively. When citing the *Tractatus Politicus* (TP) I shall cite the Samuel Shirley translation (Indianapolis, IN: Hackett, 2000) and consult Wernham.

the universal, but universal principles do not describe it. That third level, which Spinoza calls "blessedness" in some contexts, but which for us here is "activity," is a form of personal self-perfection through the adequacy of our ideas. We need to explore briefly its distinctiveness from passivity, leaving aside the many dimensions of piety and the intellectual love of God that Spinoza discusses.[29]

I have not yet mentioned Spinoza's theory of the three levels of knowledge, in order to avoid introducing another facet of his philosophy, which may take us too far afield. However, we are now at a stage where mentioning the third level of knowledge can be helpful in understanding the third level of the good. In general, Spinoza describes three levels of knowledge (E2P40Schol.2). The first is a correct, but sensory, grasp of some truth, received by the mind in a "fragmentary and confused manner." This level is what Spinoza calls "imagination." The second level is a form of reason that deals with common properties and general ideas of things. Finally, there is the third level, about which there is considerable unclarity,[30] but which grows out of the second level (E5P28). Spinoza tells us that the "highest conatus of the mind and its highest virtue is to understand things by the third kind of knowledge" (E5P25). When we do this, we "proceed from the adequate idea of certain of God's attributes to the adequate knowledge of the essence of things" (E5P25). In this regard Margaret Wilson notes:

> Spinoza gives us some reason to suppose that what he has in mind is [at least in part] our coming to grasp intuitively the "force to persevere in existence" that defines the essence of singular things as a manifestation and consequence of God's power. Unfortunately — and exasperatingly — he says little else to elucidate this fundamental notion.[31]

Wilson's emphasis is useful to our project here, and without pretending, as she does not, that we are fully clear about the notion of the third kind of knowledge, her insight is worth a moment of our reflection.

We do not live in a world of static Platonic forms or Kantian noumenal objects, which, like furniture in a room, are stationary and aloof. The objects in our environment have powers and forces of their own, which assert themselves against us in ways that are quite independent of their epistemic role in our minds. Whether we grasp these powers and forces or not, they are there pushing at us, aiding our progress or wearing us

---

[29] One might wish to consult Paul J. Bagley, ed., *Piety, Peace, and the Freedom to Philosophize* (Dordrecht: Kluwer, 1999) for essays on this topic, including one of my own.

[30] See, e.g., Bennett, *A Study of Spinoza's Ethics*, 364–69.

[31] Margaret D. Wilson, "Spinoza's Theory of Knowledge," in Don Garrett, ed., *The Cambridge Companion to Spinoza*, 132.

down, providing obstacles or clearing our path. The problem, then, is one of learning how to make their powers our own, thus making *us* the agent pushing against *them*, so to speak. We learn, in other words, how to turn their power into an extension of our own, thus using their powers to expand our own. By doing so, we preserve and extend ourselves more effectively into the environment of objects in which we find ourselves. The problem with Spinoza's second level of knowledge is that it is too universal. Spinoza's nominalism is one that forces us to realize, however, that at least at the modal level (that is, the level of individuals) what is impinging upon us in the world is not a general type or general principle, but particular things and particular actions with particular natures.

Objects and actions cannot be seen merely as instances of some general type, but must be seen as individuals, not exactly like others, however they may be grouped by the same general term. As such, these individuals have their own *conatus*, which, if they are part of what populates the actual environment in which we act, must be understood in their *individual* capacity if their power is to work effectively with ours. So-called "theoretical knowledge" is never sufficient for effective action, because it pays no attention to the *conatus* exhibited by each individual. Learning from experience alone is somewhat more effective in this respect, but it suffers from two main defects: (1) it is limited to cases as experienced and thus does not readily benefit from any commonalities that are helpful when confronting new cases; and (2) it is too conservative, and thus ultimately limiting, since our incentive to learn more and expand our reach is not contained in the cases experienced. Indeed, our tendency is to rest with what we know. The third level of knowledge, then, unites the general and the particular while, at the same time, urging us forward in our expansion of knowledge. "The more capable the mind is of understanding things by the third kind of knowledge, the more it desires to understand things by this same kind of knowledge" (E5P26).

Part V of the *Ethica* develops from this proposition and presents to us a life that seems essentially contemplative and philosophical. Now, whether Spinoza intended to embrace the Aristotelian paradox that what seems least active is actually most active, is open to debate.[32] I suspect that Spinoza is not as quietistic and contemplative as he may appear to be under many readings.[33] Be that as it may, our domain of reference for the moment is ordinary practical action, since we are speaking of moral, political, and personal actions that are taken in the world by individuals. Given this focus—and again in the spirit of Aristotle—we may have to think of Spinozistic activity as a "second best" life, if philosophical con-

[32] Steven B. Smith interprets it exactly this way in his *Spinoza, Liberalism, and the Question of Jewish Identity* (New Haven, CT: Yale University Press, 1997), 138. He then gives this centrality in Spinoza's political philosophy, contra my position as discussed below.
[33] In this connection, for example, see Moira Gatens and Genevieve Lloyd, *Collective Imaginings: Spinoza, Past and Present* (London: Routledge, 1999), chap. 3.

templation is finally the quintessential form of activity for Spinoza. Even so, the practical life is clearly a life from which Spinoza did not mean to *exclude* the third level of knowledge (E4P35Cor.2 and Schol.). In addition, it is important to notice that, although the purging of our passive emotions is a Stoic sort of project and was certainly influenced by them, ultimately Spinoza seeks not to purge our emotions and withdraw us from the world, but exactly the opposite: to induce in us emotions that are effective for action in the world.[34] We know that Spinoza does not want to purge emotions altogether because we have seen him advocate active ones. Moreover, passive emotions are not necessarily contrary to our perfection.

With respect to what is not connected to the body as emotions are — namely, ideas — they carry with them their own forms of perfection, which means their own power of affirmation and negation (E2P49Schol.). A powerful and clear idea is presumably one that leads us on to others. A confused and weak idea is one that leaves us unable to give a precise account of the idea, or that leaves us without an ability to integrate it well with other ideas. Thus, if our essence is appetite, which unites the *conatus* of our ideas with that of our body (pleasure and pain), then ideas about action will only tend to withdraw us from the world if they are in some way defective, inadequate, and painful. Effective, adequate, and pleasurable ideas will only encourage more of the same. The free person thinks of death least of all things. The life of the mind — assuming in this case that the mind's object is action — will not issue in quietistic withdrawal, but in ever more enthusiastic action.

The propositions that are literally central to Part IV of the *Ethica* (EP35–40) — and which I am claiming are transition propositions, from knowledge and good at level two to level three — are essentially about internalizing the powers of others with one's own, for effective flourishing for all. It is here that one might seek to develop a perfectionistic political interpretation of Spinoza, which is an interpretation that I believe to be mistaken, but not implausible. If one wants to argue that Spinozistic "autonomy" has a central place in his politics, one is likely to take one's stand here. For my part, when Spinoza does talk about politics in these propositions, he drops away from reason and back to affection (e.g., E4P37Schol.2), so I believe that the case cannot be made from these pas-

---

[34] Nevertheless, I believe that Spinoza is wrestling with a real problem of modernity, later considered again by Hume and most forcefully by Adam Smith. This is the problem of the role of philosophy in a world moved primarily by sentiment and practical action. How successful Part V of the *Ethica* is in this regard is an important question. On the one hand, I believe that the general framework for a successful answer is better laid out here than in, say, Adam Smith. On the other hand, I also believe that Spinoza is less successful than Adam Smith in understanding the nature of the problem and the sorts of concerns that it contains. For Smith on this issue, see Charles Griswold, *Adam Smith and the Virtues of Enlightenment* (Cambridge: Cambridge University Press, 1999), especially chap. 2; and my review of Griswold's book in *The Journal of the History of the Classical Tradition* (forthcoming).

sages that Spinoza has a perfectionist politics. However, I shall say more on this below.

Clearly, harmonious interaction with others accords with reason, and it would be something "willed" by the active person. "There is no individual thing in the universe more advantageous to man than a man who lives by the guidance of reason" (E4P35Cor.1). We are told that this is so because these individuals "agree in nature" with us. We learn, then, that our power of action is most enhanced by the joint efforts of other human beings, in a social setting in which such individuals understand what they are doing. This is a form of cooperation, in which the parties involved are clear about what they are doing and about their respective roles in the joint enterprise—in other words, the parties are active. We are less effective when we are at odds with one another, and this is an increased possibility when we are passive (E4P34). Obviously, if people are in conflict then they are not engaged in accomplishing some mutually beneficial objective.

The recognition of the mutual "gains from trade" that the active person finds in others of like nature might be seen as the "dignity" component in Spinoza's theory of "autonomy." Other agents are inherently of value, because their value derives from their nature—that is, the value is *inherent* within them and recognized as such by others. Or to put this another way, as active agents they are the adequate causes of their own conduct, and, given that such people are of most value to us, that value is internalized within them and comes completely from them. The inherent character of value within active agency is just as true when speaking of the agent, because passivity can lead to internal conflict, as well. But since most of us are passive most of the time, full activity escapes us. As a consequence, it would be unlikely that this sort of "dignity" can be the basis upon which to build a political philosophy, or even much of a social ethics. For, while the active agent would certainly endorse some of the general rules of ethics, those rules would have little meaning if they depended upon a predominance of active agents. Recognizing this, Kant makes a transcendental turn away from individuals found in experience, to discern the sort of autonomous rationality necessary to ground inherent dignity. For Spinoza, the achievement of inherent value would be an increasing form of *immanent* self-perfection. But our nature as less than fully perfected beings is such that we always have some varying degrees of virtue with respect to each other.

On the basis of the foregoing observations, I want to suggest, then, that there is very little "ethics" in the *Ethica*, at least as we normally understand "ethics." As we have noted, Spinoza says little about our obligations and more about our self-perfection. In addition, it seems that we can say that modes of moral thinking are not likely to be the first, or necessarily a primary, consideration for Spinoza when conceptualizing effective approaches to human interaction. If moral modes of reasoning are attempts to locate cases under their appropriate normative rules, roles, or obligations, then this may be significantly less optimal than the recommendation simply to secure mutual agreement. In other words, rather than looking to a rule or principle that might cover what one should do in a given case, one decides what to do on the basis of what the parties who are involved find mutually advantageous. On this reading, individuals interact largely as individuals, and not as repositories of familial, communal, or other special obligations that they bring to a situation. There would be, of course, limiting conditions to any mutual agreements given by the basic principles of social order that emerge in the formation of political society. But active people know that harming others or breaking promises is not conducive to cooperation and, therefore, to the effective enhancement of their joint power. So, although their actions might be "universalizable" in some way, these active individuals are not looking for principles to guide them in what they do or in how best to exhibit respect for one another, but rather, they are looking for specific ways in which their separate powers might be jointly exercised to achieve maximum effectiveness. The process is much more tailored to the capacities and circumstances of the actors involved, than is action in accordance with universalized rules.

The recognition that others are of highest value to us, and we to them, ensures that we are not engaged in some proto-Nietzschean project of circumventing others, or of seeing concern for others as a sign of a weak character. There is no *übermensch* ("superman") for Spinoza. Quite the contrary is true: cooperation, rather than superiority, is the hallmark of Spinoza's ethics, and the key to enhanced power for the individual. Yet, there remains in Spinoza the distinction between the active and the passive individual. How are they to interact? Do active individuals have more "rights" than passive individuals, and, therefore, can active individuals do as they please with respect to passive individuals? Some aspects of these questions will be addressed in the next section. For now, let us end with a few final reflections on Spinozistic interaction.

It is, first of all, important to remind ourselves that there are not "active people" and "passive people," as the foregoing paragraph might imply. Each of us is a mixture of active and passive in many ways (E3P51). There is, then, a built-in reason to be skeptical of claims to inherent and systematic superiority of some people over others, although, of course, relative superiority of some individuals, at some times, and on some levels is undoubtedly the case. Given this diversity of powers and adequacy, the sensible strategy would be to find ways of effectively utilizing the relative superiorities of individuals to the benefit of all. The second thing to keep in mind here is that passivity is not *necessarily* opposed to activity. Recall that pleasure is passive, but it nevertheless moves us to a state of greater perfection. There is, then, no reason in principle that effective and mutually beneficial interaction cannot take place among those who are passive, or between the active and the passive.

Passive interactions can parallel active ones by being modeled on what is mutually agreeable to the parties involved. If the parties find their association "pleasurable," then they will be moved to pursue it further. Of course, since the relationship is passive, it is subject to all the instabilities to which relations of utility are prone. Nevertheless, passivity can imitate at least the structural characteristics of active relationships by increasing the perfection or endeavoring of the parties who are interacting. And since most people are passive most of the time, the model of human interaction that is most likely to maximize perfection would be one that is grounded in perceived mutual benefit. In the language of economics, all of the parties to the transaction perceive themselves to be better off, and an ideal arrangement would be one in which all the parties *are* better off and none is worse off. Both active and passive individuals can be alike in seeking to cooperate, based upon their own desire, which is a function of their particular form of endeavoring. In both cases, there is an increase in one's own endeavoring when the arrangement accords with interest or desire. Moreover, with desire as a basis for the relationship, the individual is accorded a central focus.

The limitations to what might be mutually agreeable would come from the general rules of reason that must circumscribe the universe of mutually interested interactions and set some limits to allowable forms of interactions. Since human beings can find pleasure in virtually anything (E3P15), there is a need to neutralize or eliminate those agreements that especially undermine the process of forming mutually agreeable associations. Obviously, people cannot be allowed to agree to absolutely anything that might please them. The setting of limitations on mutual agreements is what we examine in discussing below the nature of the political for Spinoza.

With respect to the ethical dimension of Spinoza's thought, we have learned that, although there are a number of parallels with our more familiar conceptions of "autonomy," actual cases of "autonomy" are rare. More importantly, we have learned that "autonomy," for Spinoza, is not going to serve as much of a basis for framing principles or normative imperatives, as it does with Kant. Even in situations where passivity predominates, surrogates for autonomy in the form of cooperation by mutual agreement or enjoyment alone is Spinoza's preferred form of interaction.

IV. AUTONOMY AND POLITICS

Steven B. Smith is one of the few commentators on Spinoza's political theory to give autonomy a central place: "Spinoza endorses the democratic republic because it is the regime most consistent with the autonomous individual or liberated self. Democracy is desirable because it fosters the conditions for reason and the expression of the individual."[35] Smith also tells us, however, that Spinoza's notion of what it means to be active is "deeply antipolitical," looking instead to a "deeply private or solitary idea of the philosophic life, for which the requirements of political rule are inappropriate."[36] These potentially conflicting perspectives bring us to the problem that I noted at the introduction of this essay: namely, if "autonomy" is so deeply antipolitical in Spinoza, then how can it function centrally in politics or in a political theory? One possible interpretation is that if the state can "foster conditions for reason," and if it indeed exists to serve such a purpose, then "autonomy" could be at the very center of Spinoza's political philosophy.

My own view is that autonomy (or activity) is in certain respects deeply antipolitical, as Steven B. Smith says, but not necessarily because it is solitary or contemplative. Rather, and most simply, it is because the political is very limited in scope for Spinoza, and it always and inherently appeals to what is passive in human nature, whatever pretenses and accordances it may have with the rational. Indeed, as we shall see, confusing what accords with reason with what is a direct expression of it is not just a significant error in conceptions of duty as Kant noted, but a recipe for political problems in the Spinozistic framework, as well. Political activity is never active in Spinoza's sense, and the effort to make it such carries with it confusions that can translate into social conflict. Politics for Spinoza has a simple, limited function that, in itself, has nothing to do with perfection, activity, or blessedness. In this respect, the perfectionist politics attributed to Spinoza by Steven B. Smith is, itself, a kind of confusion of reason with what accords with reason. By Smith's own account, the best we could say is that "democracy" does not contradict autonomy—and Smith does say this[37]—and not that it fosters it. For to foster autonomy would mean that we would have some clear conception of how to bring activity about through political means; but that would be odd, since activity is something that comes from within and not from without. Politics is always concerned with what is "outside" of us, in the ordinary sense of always operating in the public forum, and in the technical Spinozistic sense that is connected to passivity. Of course, we can make the case negatively and say that "democracy" leaves those who are active free to *be* active. That is certainly true, and it is certainly something Spinoza, in a normative posture, would advocate. But we must remember that democracy also leaves people free to be passive, and it could be fully functional and successful in the absence of *any* active participants. There-

[35] Smith, *Spinoza, Liberalism, and the Question of Jewish Identity*, 122.
[36] Ibid., 144.
[37] Ibid.

fore, based on the sort of argument that Steven B. Smith uses, we would
be equally entitled to say that democracy encourages passivity; but if it
encourages both activity and passivity, it is either trivial or contradictory.

The problem is that one cannot analyze Spinoza in ways that are traditional to political philosophy, because he does not identify a normative
ideal and then measure the state against it. Spinoza's liberalism, for example, is not the point or purpose of his theory, but the consequence.
Following Spinoza, one does not advocate liberal democracy in order to
protect autonomy, but, rather, in the presence of liberal democracy, autonomy is protected.[38] Like everything else in Spinoza, if something acts
from its nature, then it possesses the most power that it can. When the
state acts in accordance with its political nature, it, too, will maximize its
power and effectiveness. As it turns out, states that act most in accord
with the nature of the political are liberal states; and because the liberal
state is the most effective employment of political power, we may wish to
advocate it. Our advocacy of the liberal state, however, is not a reason for
its superiority or its legitimacy. Rather, its superiority and legitimacy is
our reason for advocating it. But we are beginning to lapse into paradox,
so let us regroup and support some of the foregoing claims.

That Spinoza separates activity from political participation seems
clear enough. We find, for example, statements like the following from the
TTP:

> Simplicity and integrity of spirit are not inspired in men by the
> command of laws or by public authority, and it is quite impossible to
> make anyone blessed by force or legal enactments; the means re-
> quired are pious and brotherly counsel, a good upbringing, and,
> above all, a judgment that is free and independent. (TTP VII)

In the TP Spinoza makes similar remarks:

> Those who believe that a people, or men divided over public busi-
> ness, can be induced to live by reason's dictate alone, are dreaming
> of the poets' golden age. . . . For freedom or strength of mind is a
> private virtue; the virtue of a state is stability. (TP I, 5–6)[39]

The foregoing attitude toward the political is illustrated as well when
we come to the issue of God and religion. In chapter four of the TTP,

[38] Using the word "encouraged" rather than "protected," in my view, makes the proposition false, which would be consistent with my point. Consequently, "protected" begs fewer
questions about what I am saying.
[39] I use these passages to similar effect in Douglas J. Den Uyl, "Liberalism and Virtue," in
T. William Boxx and Gary M. Quinlivan, eds., *Public Morality, Civic Virtue, and the Problem of
Modern Liberalism* (Grand Rapids, MI: William B. Eerdmans Publishing Co., 2000), 58–60.

Spinoza distinguishes human from divine law and tells us that they have different aims. Divine law is the love of God, which stems neither from fear nor from the "love of anything else we desire to enjoy," but from knowledge that is "self-validating and self-evident." In this chapter of the TTP, Spinoza is trying to show that belief in historical narratives is not necessary for our supreme good, but he is demonstrating, at the same time, that fears and rewards do little for that end. Consequently,

> [a]ctions whose only claim to goodness is the fact that they are pre-scribed by convention, or that they symbolize some good, can do nothing to perfect our understanding, but are simply empty forms, and no part of conduct which is the product or fruit of understanding and sound sense. (TTP IV)

Sacred rights, we are told in chapter five of the TTP, have nothing to do with divine law and "consequently nothing to [do with] blessedness and virtue." Sacred rights are, in effect, political forms for Spinoza, since their object is obedience to some prescribed set of norms. This is equivalent to saying that politics—the pattern of stability that is established by obedience—has nothing to do with virtue or moral excellence.

There are, however, passages in Spinoza that seem to lend some support to a strong perfectionist reading. The following is the most compelling one that I can find:

> Thus when I say that the best state [*imperium optimum*] is one in which men live in harmony, I am speaking of a truly human existence, which is characterized, not by the mere circulation of blood and other vital processes common to all animals, but primarily by reason, the true virtue and life of the mind. (TP V, 5)

If the best state were one that exhibits the highest moral excellence, it would seem that such a condition, within practical limitations, would be Spinoza's model for all political orders. Of course, it is logically possible for this passage not to contradict the others mentioned above, if "best state" is interpreted to mean what is desirable for "society at large," and not as a statement about political ends or processes. I believe that this is the interpretation that one must adopt to reconcile all of the passages, and I shall argue for it below. If I am correct, then we have the basis for the standard liberal distinction between state and society.[40] In any case, the

---

[40] In the preceding paragraph of the TP, Spinoza uses "*civitas*" rather than "*imperium*," which may indicate this distinction. I am not convinced, however, that the case can rest on this alone, because I am not confident that the terms have such consistent usage.

passages cited prior to the foregoing one are significantly more representative of Spinoza's political work.

Spinoza's E4P35 and a number of the propositions that directly follow
it also read as though he is recommending a perfectionist politics through
the promotion of reason. (E4P35 states: "In so far only as men live in
obedience to reason, do they always necessarily agree in nature.") The
more reason there is, the more likely we are to live in harmony. Yet even
though an ideal order is envisioned, Spinoza clearly tells us in the scholium to this same proposition that "it is rarely the case that men live by
the guidance of reason." Moreover, two propositions later, in the second
scholium to proposition 37, we are told that "wrong-doing is therefore
nothing other than disobedience ... and obedience is held to be of merit
in a citizen because he is thereby deemed to deserve to enjoy the advantages of the state." Wrongdoing or sin has more to do with social disruption than anything like activity in the ethical sense, and what is "morally"
meritorious seems so because of its contribution to social stability. Furthermore, in E4P40, where reason and harmony are all but equated, "good"
(*bona*) and "bad" (*mala*) are made equivalent to concord and discord,
which are some distance from blessedness in any contemplative sense.
("Whatsoever conduces to man's social life, or causes men to live together
in harmony, is useful, whereas whatsoever brings discord into a state is
bad.") So Spinoza is not at all averse to mixing passivity with what
accords with reason, in such a way that it is difficult to tell when he is
speaking of one or the other. We can see this point to a large extent in
passages like the following:

> It is not, I say, the purpose of the state to change men from rational
> beings into brutes or puppets; but rather to enable them to exercise
> their mental and physical powers in safety and use their reason
> freely, and to prevent them from fighting and quarrelling through
> hatred, anger, bad faith, and mutual malice. Thus the purpose of the
> state is really freedom. (TTP XX)

Here, it not only appears that the state has purposes, but that its main
purpose is to secure freedom. Yet "freedom" at the end of the passage is
little more than the avoidance of physical conflict. I have argued elsewhere[41] that many of Spinoza's key normative terms in his political writings, such as "peace," "freedom," and "reason," all have roughly the
same meaning: namely, cooperative conduct and obedience (to the laws
of the state). They are all, in other words, political synonyms for harmony
and order. These terms, therefore, do not necessarily have the same mean-

---

[41] Douglas J. Den Uyl, *Power, State, and Freedom: An Interpretation of Spinoza's Political
Thought* (Assen, The Netherlands: Van Gorcum, 1983), chap. 5.

ing in the political writings that they have in the *Ethica*.[42] "Freedom" in the political writings, for example, does not refer to "freedom" as activity, found in books 4 and 5 of the *Ethica*. One can therefore be free in the political sense and yet be completely passive (hence, unfree) from an ethical perspective. The state "promotes" freedom when it is orderly and free of discord. Its members need not be free in the ethical sense. The same is to be said about "reason," which gets an exalted rendering in the latter books of the *Ethica*, but takes on its rather mundane meaning of cooperation in the politics. In TTP XX, "reason" *may* refer to actions exhibited by the active person, but it need not, and, in any case, preventing fighting and quarreling, and securing safety, are clearly the main objects of state action.

Although it may be said that politics has no direct connection with the promotion of ethical freedom (and thus "autonomy" as we are using the term here), it may still be possible to assert that Spinoza believes that "participation in political life helps create conditions (i.e., stability) under which the higher goods, such as philosophy, can be realized."[43] Here a kind of indirect perfectionism obtains where the state—unable to directly secure freedom, activity, or autonomy—is set to the task of providing the conditions upon which these goods might flourish. The state has, in other words, a society of fully free and responsible individuals as its object, but it lacks the appropriate tools to achieve that end directly. Of course, this itself is something of an admission, for it gives a significant role to something outside of the realm of the political. Yet even this mitigated indirect claim is, I believe, too much perfectionism for Spinoza.

The basis for my skepticism is found in the TTP, where we are told that the objects of human desire fall into three categories: knowledge of primary causes, control of the passions, and security and physical well-being (*sano corpore*). The objects of desire also seem to be ranked by Spinoza with the highest ranked being knowledge of primary causes, and the lowest ranked being security and physical well-being. Politics is only applicable to the last category.

> The direct means to the first two goods, their proximate and efficient causes if you like, are contained in human nature itself; so that their attainment largely depends on our own unaided power, i.e., on the laws of human nature alone. . . . But the means to security and [con-

---

[42] Rice pointed out to me that terms do not always have consistent meanings in the *Ethica*, either. Some of the remarks that I make about the passages in the *Ethica* on issues related to politics should support this observation. Rice also cautioned that one should not read this statement as meaning that one can avoid reading the *Ethica* and still get Spinoza's views on politics. I would endorse this caution and do not mean this point to imply that one could read one without reading the other.

[43] Michael A. Rosenthal, "Tolerance as a Virtue in Spinoza's *Ethics*," *Journal of the History of Philosophy* 39, no. 4 (2001): 549.

servation of the body (*corpus conservandum*)]⁴⁴ lie mainly in things outside us. Accordingly, these goods are called gifts of fortune. . . . Still, human guidance and vigilance can do a great deal to help men live in safety and avoid injury . . . and the surest means to this end, and the means prescribed by reason and experience, is to form a society with definite laws. . . . (TTP III)

Political life is concerned with security and physical well-being. Even with this limited function, success is not guaranteed, but politics is certainly necessary. Politics is really not concerned with moral and ethical matters, since those fall into the first two categories. In this connection, and keeping in mind what Spinoza calls "fortune" in the above passage, he tells us later in the TTP that "the happiness and peace of the man who cultivates his natural understanding depends mainly on his own inherent virtue . . . and not on the control of fortune" (TTP IV). If the realm of "fortune" is the realm of the political, and is limited to physical security and harmony, in the sense of minimizing or eliminating violence, injury, and social discord, then we have the quintessential minimal liberal state.

Why should politics be limited in this way? Has our case for the minimal liberal state (i.e., one that distances itself from moral matters) really been proved? Is Spinoza's politics really as detached from the development of virtue and the good social consequences that follow from it, as I have suggested? Consider as a possible counterargument the following passage:

He who seeks to determine everything by law will aggravate vices rather than correct them. We must necessarily permit what we cannot prevent, even though it often leads to harm. Things like extravagance, envy, greed, and drunkenness are a source of much evil; yet we put up with them because they cannot be prevented by legal enactment, vices though in fact they are. Much more then must we allow independence of judgment; for it is certainly a virtue, and it cannot be suppressed. Besides, it leads to no trouble which cannot be forestalled by the influence of the magistrates; . . . to say nothing of the fact that it is quite indispensable for the advancement of the arts and sciences, for these are cultivated with success only by men whose judgment is free and unbiased. (TTP XX)

Consider also that when Spinoza discusses sumptuary laws in his later work, he indicates a favorable attitude toward political manipulation for ends other than mere security:

⁴⁴ The brackets indicate that this is my translation of *corpus conservandum* and not that of Wernham, who uses "physical survival" instead. Wernham's rendering actually supports my point more strongly than does my own translation.

I therefore conclude that the common peace-time vices which we are here discussing should be prevented indirectly and never directly; that is, by basing the state on such laws as will cause the majority, not indeed to seek to live wisely—for that is impossible—but at any rate to be governed by those passions which are most useful to the commonwealth. (TP X, 6)

In these passages, Spinoza seems not to reject, and perhaps encourages, the idea of the state using its resources to manipulate people toward "higher ends." In citing such passages, I have tried to indicate where those who wish to offer a more expansive view of the role of politics in Spinoza's political philosophy might find some support in his texts.[45]

For me, however, the passage that probably best expresses Spinoza's normative attitude about politics is the following:

For the state whose sole aim is to govern men by fear will be free from faults rather than possessed of merits. Men should really be governed in such a way that they do not regard themselves as being governed, but as following their own bent and their own free choice in their manner of life; in such a way, then, that they are restrained only by love of freedom, desire to increase their possession, and the hope of obtaining offices of state. (TP X, 8)[46]

I believe that this passage, coupled with some others that I have cited, suggests strongly that some form of what is now called *classical liberalism* is Spinoza's political philosophy, as we ordinarily think of "political philosophy." In no plausible interpretation, then, can there be a *direct* connection between autonomy and politics in Spinoza, for clearly politics is concerned with the passive side of human nature. The issue, as we have seen, becomes one of whether the state should seek to foster autonomy by indirect means, and thus also hold it out as an end to be sought by governments and advocated by political philosophers. But having put the matter in these terms, the Spinozist should begin to feel that there is something wrong with the way that we are now discussing the issue.

As I suggested at the opening of this section, Spinoza finds it mistaken to begin with our preferred normative objectives and then to develop a political philosophy accordingly. The first chapter of the TP is an indictment of this approach. Philosophers "conceive men, not as they are, but

---

[45] Such texts are often "contradicted" by others that refer to the same subjects. One might, for example, take Spinoza's passage about the arts and sciences to mean support for government promotion in that area. Such an interpretation is refuted directly by TP VIII, 49.

[46] Spinoza follows these words by linking equality to freedom, suggesting that he, in a significant way, did not abandon the democratic ideal in this later work, and also suggesting that the nondemocratic regimes that he discusses do work to the extent that they retain some significant element of democracy.

as they would like them to be." The result is that they have "produced either obvious fantasies, or schemes that could only have been put into effect in Utopia, or the poets' golden age" (TP I, 1). The complaint is not just that philosophers are too idealistic and unrealistic. It is, rather, that they misunderstand the nature of the political by failing to understand that politics is either outside the realm of the moral and ethical altogether, or of such a limited connection to it that moral categories have little value when theorizing about it. This last point brings up an issue that we cannot pursue in detail here. Spinoza stands at the threshold of the development of modern social science. Social science seeks to give an impartial, objective account of social institutions, with normative conclusions and recommendations given (if at all) only reluctantly, modestly, and "at the end" of the research. This is a procedural point that Spinoza emphasizes in the first chapter of the *Tractatus Politicus* (e.g., paragraphs 4 and 5). I believe that Spinoza was engaged in an effort to undermine political philosophy as it was traditionally conceived and practiced and, therefore, as it may still be pursued today. But it is outside the scope of this project to pursue that interpretation, or the more interesting questions surrounding the benefits and limits of such an approach.

Returning to the point that philosophers misunderstand the nature of the political, Spinoza tells us that the problem is with those "who believe that sovereigns ought to handle public affairs in accordance with the same moral rules as are binding on private individuals" (TP I, 2). Now this statement brings us to an interpretative fork in the road. On the one hand, given Spinoza's praise of Machiavelli, one could interpret this statement to mean that the moral rules that govern us privately do not apply to the public realm, where violations of those rules might be necessary to maintain a regime. On the other hand, another interpretation is the one to which I subscribe. On this interpretation, the problem is imputing to the sovereign functions that it is not suited to perform: most notably, the moral improvement of its subjects. Although Spinoza admires Machiavelli and his rejection of the utopian character of ancient political philosophy, he is not a Machiavellian in politics, and he does not advocate a two-tier moral universe that allows for the abrogation of ordinary moral principles for the sake of political ends. Indeed, almost the reverse is the case. If the political realm functions within its nature, ordinary moral principles against theft, dishonesty, mutual harm, and so forth are more likely than otherwise to be secure and governing. The problem comes when we ask politics to do more than that to which it is suited, and this is especially the case when we moralize politics beyond what is required for the simple peace and stability of the political order itself (TP I, 5).[47]

---

[47] There may appear to be an ambiguity in Spinoza that could lead one to conclude that Spinoza actually does the opposite of what I have suggested above, namely, that he ends up virtually equating morality and politics. We are told, for example, that "sin is inconceivable

We are told by Spinoza that "the political order is naturally established to remove general fear and to dispel general suffering," and that this is a teaching of "reason" (TP III, 6). He then goes on to tell us:

> Just as in the state of nature the man who is guided by reason is most powerful and most fully possessed of his own right . . . , so also the commonwealth which is based on and directed by reason will be most powerful and most fully possessed of its own right. For the right of a commonwealth is determined by the power of a people guided as if by one mind; but this union of minds is quite inconceivable unless the commonwealth does its best to achieve those conditions which sound reason declares to be for the good of all men. (TP III, 7)

What could sound reason possibly declare to be good for *all* men, unless it is something fairly simple, basic, and general? In answering this question, one must keep in mind both the fact that people are not always guided by reason, and also that "if a state is to be capable of lasting, its administration must be so organized that it does not matter whether its rulers are led by reason or passion. . . . In fact, it makes no difference to the stability of a state what motive leads men to conduct its affairs properly, provided they *are* conducted properly. For freedom or strength of mind is a private virtue; the virtue of the state is stability" (TP I, 6). Indeed, when it comes to politics, "the whole teaching of reason is that men should seek peace" (TP III, 6). So the state most in accord with reason, and thus most possessed of its own power, will be the one that limits itself to the maintenance of peace and stability.

Spinoza makes the point many times about the limited ends of the state being peace and security, but he puts it most succinctly when he states that "the best condition of a commonwealth is easily discovered from the purpose of political order: which is simply peace and security of life" (TP V, 2). This statement not only includes the word "best" (*optimus*), but also comes in a chapter where Spinoza is describing for us his *ideal* state. This strongly suggests that, kept within its proper limits of securing peace, the state so limited will be most fully possessed of its own right and will act according to its own nature. The entire fifth chapter of the TP is consistent

---

except in a state" (TP II, 19), and that the sovereign power of the commonwealth is to decide what is "fair or unfair, moral or immoral" (TP III, 5). Such views are found not only in the TP, but also in the TTP as well, e.g., chap. XVI. In this connection, we do well to keep in mind our distinction between ethics and morality. It should also be noted, I believe, that Spinoza in these contexts is establishing the practical basis for the functioning of morality, namely, the relevant base of power. For a discussion of power in Spinoza, see Steven Barbone, "Power in the *Tractatus Theologico-Politicus*," in Bagley, ed., *Piety, Peace, and the Freedom to Philosophize*, 91–109.

with this principle, except for paragraph 5, where we have the passage (cited earlier in this section) about how the best state is one where there is "true virtue and life of the mind." But since this sort of virtue is a "private virtue" and not a virtue of the state, Spinoza must be telling us that, while it might be most desirable to live among persons of true virtue, this is quite a distinct matter from what is connected to politics.

We must conclude, therefore, by rejecting any sort of moralistic or perfectionist politics when it comes to Spinoza.[48] We cannot, in other words, endorse the indirect perfectionism that I mentioned above, where (as philosopher Michael A. Rosenthal puts it) "participation in political life helps create conditions (i.e., stability) under which the higher goods, such as philosophy, can be realized."[49] Such a statement is either trivially true—stability is necessary for virtually any good to be achieved, including philosophy—or its aspirations clearly go beyond the political. The tools of politics involve appeals to passive emotions, primarily hope and fear (TP V, 6). The "ends" of politics are uniquely and sufficiently served when these tools are used to secure peace and stability. There is nothing more for politics to aim at or encourage. We do not participate in political life in order to have a shot at the philosophical, but, rather, we participate in political life so that we don't get beaten up, cheated, or exploited by our neighbor.

Despite concluding that we must reject any sort of moralistic or perfectionist politics in Spinoza, I have argued elsewhere that the liberal state is also the most powerful one for Spinoza and expected to be such.[50] Here I mean powerful in every sense of the word: economically, culturally, intellectually, and militarily. The temptation is to turn such expressions into a perfectionist political program. We must, however, be careful of our logic here. The fact that obtaining some set of conditions C makes some other set of conditions P possible, is not at all the same as saying that C functions to produce P or that C ought to function to produce P. Even if we expect C to produce P more often than not, it does not follow that C functions to produce P as a sufficient condition for P. And obviously, if C is a necessary condition, then there might be other necessary conditions, as well. Even if C is the only necessary condition, it does not follow that C functions to produce P, since C might also be a necessary condition for Q. So, while I do believe that Spinoza thought that something like the liberal state would be coupled with more perfection (that is, more activity, pleasure, and power) among its citizens than would alternative forms of government, this is not perfectionist politics, because the failure to obtain

[48] The first author to make this point is H. F. Hallet, *Creation, Emanation, and Salvation* (The Hague: Martinus Nijhoff, 1962), esp. chap. 10.
[49] Rosenthal, "Tolerance as a Virtue in Spinoza's *Ethics*," 549.
[50] Den Uyl, *Power, State, and Freedom*, chap. 5.

(positive) state P has no bearing whatsoever on there being something amiss or absent in (conditions) C.[51]

I suspect that the move to say that C exists so that P will obtain in reading Spinoza comes from a false analogy. Individuals can move from conditions of passivity to activity, as we saw earlier. Though the temptation is strong to turn certain expressions into a perfectionist political program,[52] and controversy about it exists in the Spinoza literature,[53] we cannot say the same about the state. The state is not an individual, and it does not have ever higher levels of perfection to attain. Individuals within a state can obtain more or less perfection, and thus make the state a more or less desirable place to be, but beyond peace and security, the state has nowhere else to go. This is why when C obtains, P might not, in fact, do so. Conditions of freedom not only provide the opportunity for self-perfection, but also may offer many incentives for it, such that, if self-perfection is to develop at all or most fully, those sorts of liberal orders are its most fertile soil. But if self-perfection does not develop, it does not follow that the political order in question is acting any less in accord with reason or less in possession of its own right. Nor does it mean that the state has failed to achieve its purpose of moving people along the path of virtue. All it means is that the individuals of that state failed, for some reason, to utilize the opportunities that freedom provides. The most we could say is that the state makes virtue possible, but as we saw in the second epigraph to this essay, the link that Spinoza draws between virtue and statecraft is so minimal that virtually any state could be said to do this.

Continuing with the issue of the state being an individual, the places where Spinoza occasionally mentions unity of mind or purpose are less than convincing. In politics, any unity of mind (or purpose) that we seem to possess can never be anything more than a commonality of passions (TP VI, 1). The passions here are simple, basic ones: "subjects are under the control of the commonwealth . . . only in so far as they fear its power or its threats, or in so far as they love the political order" (TP III, 8). The sense here is that, because we must unify with passions, the simpler and more basic they are, the better they are. Attempts to unify across the wide range of passions would seem to be a recipe for dissolution, rather than for unity. Moreover, no hope is given that we will be unified through

[51] I believe that this is also an adequate response to those who might argue that the "effect" of Spinoza's politics is the same as the "effect" of a politics that is intentionally sought by the same means. The latter would call for additional measures, should the end that is sought fail to be achieved, whereas the former would not.

[52] Rosenthal, for example, succumbs to it when he equates the state to an individual. See Rosenthal, "Tolerance as a Virtue in Spinoza's *Ethics*," 554, n. 29.

[53] The most important scholarly statement to this effect is found in Alexandre Matheron, *Individu et communauté chez Spinoza* (Paris: Les Editions de Minuit, 1969). As a subject of controversy in interpreting Spinoza's political theory Matheron also makes the point in a book review in *Studia Spinozana* (Hannover, FRG: Walther & Walther Verlag, 1985), 1:425.

reason, as an individual might be. So, rather than try to make a case for the state being an individual in Spinoza, it makes more sense to say, as he does, that the state might sometimes act *as if* it were of one mind (*una veluti mente*). See, for example, TP III, 7. What the state is really doing, however, is providing a structure for aggregating individuals, so that conflict and strife among them are avoided. Indeed, if we make the state an individual, we seem to be compelled to try to find its higher levels of perfection, since it would be a human or human-like entity. That project, I submit, has virtually no textual basis to support it and seems prone to speculative absurdities (e.g., is the active state more blessed than the active individual?). Indeed, if the state were an individual, then we would expect the text to go well beyond issues of conflict avoidance, to which Spinoza continually and perpetually returns in both political treatises. When he seems to be making a positive case for some end beyond simple security—as he does, perhaps, in the famous Chapter 20 of the TTP, which I mentioned earlier in this section—he always returns to the main focus. This strongly suggests that any connection between politics and "higher ends" such as autonomy is at best only negative.

V. Conclusion: Whither Autonomy?

I opened this discussion with three main objections to the idea that autonomy can be separated from politics: the communitarian, the liberal, and the welfare (or what could also be labeled "perfectionist") objections. The first holds that since politics cannot be so neatly roped off from the rest of social life, autonomy—if it has meaning or importance elsewhere— would have to have importance for politics. The second objection holds that, without giving people respect as individuals, we would have nothing to say against using people for whatever purposes those who are capable of doing so might wish. Finally, holds the third objection, if autonomy is a good for everyone, then it ought to be promoted by that which is concerned with everyone, namely, politics. Spinoza's response to each of these objections is roughly the same: "autonomy" simply is not a part of politics, however much one may wish it were otherwise. It is either factually mistaken to suppose that "autonomy" is a part of politics, or the desire to make it so does not thereby produce it. Politics, for Spinoza, is not about "autonomy" at all, even as an aspiration, but is about securing peace and stability by appealing to the emotive and affective side of human nature.

In this connection, it would seem that we must separate the rhetoric of autonomy from its philosophical content. There would be nothing inconsistent about a Spinozist using or recommending the language of autonomy, and its cognate terms and formulations, if doing so contributed to peace and cooperation. If, in other words, people become better citizens as a result of the general belief that one's dignity and worthiness of respect is not a wit less than anyone else's, then a Spinozist would not, to that extent, object to speaking of autonomy and politics together. The use of moral terms as affective devices of social control is, as we have seen, within the purview of Spinozistic theorizing about politics. It may indeed be the only, or the best, way people in general can understand and perform their civic "duties." This is quite different from saying that autonomy describes the political landscape, is a general realizable ideal, or functions as a correct foundation for developing political theory. We have seen that, insofar as something like "autonomy" exists in Spinoza's conception of ethics, it has no connection to the political in any of these ways.

Focusing upon Spinoza's version of "autonomy" (activity) undoubtedly highlights the idealistic qualities of other perspectives—qualities to which we may be strongly attached. Consider the following rather typical claim from philosopher David A. J. Richards:

> The central mark of ethics is not respect for what people currently are or for particular ends. Rather, respect is expressed for an idealized capacity which, if appropriately treated, people can realize, namely, the capacity to take responsibility as a free and rational agent for one's system of ends.[54]

Yet why should one approach another in terms of that other person's "idealized capacities," rather than in terms of the other person's actual characteristics and abilities? Is this anything but an idealistic foundation for political theory—the "poet's golden age," as Spinoza calls it? Perhaps by holding to the "myth" that everyone is autonomous, the cause of freedom and peace is better served than by doing without it. That is the salutary benefit to which I referred in the preceding paragraph. But is the myth possibly true of anything in some significant philosophical way? It may be that, at this crossroad, Kant was right: to secure a value such as equality and remove ourselves from the mire of empirical reality where inequality abounds, we must make some sort of transcendental turn; we must see the idealized value as somehow necessary for any concrete expression of it in practice. If we are not willing to make this turn—and I am certainly not advocating that we do so—then perhaps Spinoza looms larger in our horizon as a thinker whom we must confront. At stake, I believe, are very deep and general questions about what a theory like liberalism needs to presuppose in order to get itself off the ground.

It may be that liberalism can move forward quite well without a transcendental turn. Would at least the rhetoric of autonomy be necessary for liberalism to take root? We have been cautioned by Spinoza that the rhetoric of "autonomy" in politics can present dangers. The main danger

---

[54] Richards, "Rights and Autonomy," 16.

is the moralization of politics. Here, too, we face a fork in the road.
Spinoza's realism as indicated in the preceding paragraphs will certainly
be taken by many, not as a refutation of the role of autonomy and morality in politics, but rather as the throwing down of a gauntlet—one that
is to be taken up by political and moral philosophers everywhere. What
they might claim is needed is more, not less, influence by, and reflection
about, morality in politics. While it is clear to me that Spinoza would be
rather skeptical of that perspective, I have in no way intended to convert
those who hold that perspective. Even less have I expected that I could do
so. My intention has been simple: to bring to light some challenges to
orthodox political theory that the reading of Spinoza inevitably engen-
ders. These challenges alone might be worth consideration, whatever
might be one's final conclusions on the place of ethics in politics and
political theory.

But a thinker must be judged not only by the challenges that are posed,
but also by the role that his theories play amid the pantheon of political
philosophers and political philosophies. Consider the following:

> The general view of personal competence of the ancient Greeks
> suggests the fragmented ego, the "divided self"—generally pas-
> sive, with appetites, emotions, and intellect isolated as indepen-
> dent agencies on the battleground of the body, unintegrated by
> any coherent higher-order planner within the self.... Certain ex-
> ceptional people might achieve something close to the contempo-
> rary concept of developed ego strength (i.e., Plato's philosophical
> souls), but they were rare, exceptional, god-like—the natural rulers
> of society. Correlatively, Greek political theory understandably fo-
> cuses on rule by the best.[55]

This passage, also from Richards, is cited at length because of its similarity to a number of the points that we have made about Spinoza. The
classical perspective described here was countered by the modern, where
everyone is supposed to have capacities for autonomy. Rule in the modern framework, then, belongs to no one by nature. Where does Spinoza
stand? Active individuals, who are so rare and are the natural rulers in
this account of classical political thought, are never called upon by Spinoza
to rule. Activity is neither necessary for, nor advocated by, Spinoza as a
criterion for rule. The rulers may be (and are expected to be) as passive as
their subjects. Antiquity seems to hold that perfectionism in ethics leads
naturally to perfectionism in politics. The lack thereof in the egalitarian
foundations of modern ethics tends toward a lack of perfectionism in
politics, or at least toward a level of "perfectionism" that is matched to the
universally shared "capacities" that all people possess. Either way, no one

[55] Ibid., 8.

has the right by nature to rule, because no one is better than anyone else. Spinoza, by contrast, is clear that some people are "better" than others, yet he does not accord them a special right to rule. Perhaps that is because activity is, after all, of little special value to politics. Viewed in this light, what we can say about Spinoza's place in the pantheon is that he takes the road less traveled: perfectionist ethics and nonperfectionist politics.

Philosophy, Liberty Fund, Inc.

KANT ON THE THEORY AND PRACTICE
OF AUTONOMY*

By Paul Guyer

Introduction

We all know what Kant means by autonomy: "the property of the will by which it is a law to itself (independently of any property of the objects of volition)" (*G*, 4:440),[1] or, since any law must be universal, the condition of an agent who is "subject *only to laws given by himself but still universal*" (*G*, 4:432). Or do we know what Kant means by autonomy? There are a number of questions here. First, Kant's initial definition of autonomy itself raises the question of why the property of the will being a law to itself should be equivalent to its independence from any property of objects of volition. It is also natural to ask, how does autonomy as Kant conceives it relate to more familiar notions of

* An earlier version of this essay was presented at the *Collegium transatlanticum philosophicum* at Emory University in January 2002. I thank Jeff Edwards and Laszlo Tengelyi for their comments on that occasion. I also thank Fred D. Miller, Jr., and Ellen Frankel Paul for the valuable comments that they made on this more recent version.
[1] Citations from most of Kant's works will be located by volume and page number of the Academy edition, *Kant's gesammelte Schriften,* edited by the Royal Prussian (successively the German and then Berlin–Brandenburg) Academy of Sciences (Berlin: Georg Reimer, later Walter de Gruyter & Co., 1900-). Citations from the *Critique of Pure Reason* will be located in the traditional manner by the pagination of its first ("A") and second ("B") editions.

Translations of the *Critique of Pure Reason* are from Immanuel Kant, *Critique of Pure Reason,* ed. and trans. Paul Guyer and Allen W. Wood (Cambridge: Cambridge University Press, 1998). Translations of Kant's published works in moral philosophy are from Immanual Kant, *Practical Philosophy,* ed. and trans. Mary J. Gregor (Cambridge: Cambridge University Press, 1996); those of *Religion* are from Immanuel Kant, *Religion and Rational Theology,* ed. and trans. Allen W. Wood and George di Giovanni (Cambridge: Cambridge University Press, 1996); and those of his lectures are from Immanuel Kant, *Lectures on Ethics,* ed. Peter Heath and J. B. Schneewind, trans. Peter Heath (Cambridge: Cambridge University Press, 1997). Since these three volumes reproduce the Academy pagination, separate page references for the translations will be omitted. This is also true of Immanuel Kant, *Anthropology from a Pragmatic Point of View,* trans. Mary J. Gregor (The Hague: Martinus Nijhoff, 1974). Unless otherwise attributed here in note 1, all other translations are my own. The abbreviations used throughout this essay are as follows:

PureR = *Critique of Pure Reason*

G = *Groundwork for the Metaphysics of Morals*

PracR = *Critique of Practical Reason*

TP = "On the Common Saying: That May be Correct in Theory, but it is of No Use in Practice"

MM, DV = *Metaphysics of Morals,* "Doctrine of Virtue"

freedom. For example, consider Locke's conception of freedom as the condition of a person "to think, or not to think; to move, or not to move, according to the preference or direction of his own mind," rather than according to the preference or direction of any other person.[2] What is the relation between autonomy and this traditional conception of freedom as the liberty of an agent? And what is the relation of autonomy to the traditional conception of freedom of the will; that is, the condition that obtains, as G. E. Moore puts it, if, "wherever a voluntary action is right or wrong ... it is true that the agent *could*, in a sense, have done something else instead,"[3] or in Kant's own terms, "*freedom* in the transcendental sense, as a special kind of causality ... namely a faculty of absolutely beginning a state, and hence also a series of its consequences" (*PureR*, A 445/B 473)? Second, we can ask why does Kant think that we have an unconditional obligation to strive to achieve autonomy through a self-given law, or why "the *principle* of every human being as *a will giving universal law through all its maxims* ... would be very well suited to be the categorical imperative" (*G*, 4:432). Third, we can ask how does Kant think that human beings can actually achieve autonomy in the empirical conditions of human life, which include, among other conditions, those of being subject to a wide range of inclinations, and of being able to gain control over those inclinations, if at all, only by a slow process of education and maturation.

As it addresses these questions, this essay accordingly consists of three major parts. Section I makes two claims: First, that Kant sees autonomy, or self-governance by universal law, as the condition that is necessary to achieve and maintain freedom in two ordinary and, as it turns out, related senses—namely, the independence of the choices and actions of a person not only from domination by other persons, but

---

Rel = *Religion within the Boundaries of Mere Reason*

Col = *Moral Philosophy from the Lectures of Professor Kant*, Winter Semester 1784–85, Georg Ludwig Collins

Mrong = *Morality According to Professor Kant: Lectures on Baumgarten's Practical Philosophy*, January 3, 1785, C. C. Mrongovius

Vig = *Notes on the Lectures of Mr. Kant on the Metaphysics of Morals*, begun October 14, 1793, Johann Friedrich Vigilantius

APV = *Anthropology from a Pragmatic Point of View*

Notes = *Notes on the Observations on the Feeling of the Beautiful and Sublime*

R = Reflections from *Kant's Handschriftliche Nachlaß*

Friedländer = Lectures on Anthropology from the Winter Semester 1775–76, according to the manuscript *Friedländer*

Rischmüller = *Notes on the Observations on the Feeling of the Beautiful and Sublime*, ed. Marie Rischmüller (*Kant-Forschungen*, Band 3).

[2] John Locke, *An Essay concerning Human Understanding*, ed. P. H. Nidditch (Oxford: Clarendon Press, 1975), bk. II, chap. XXI, sec. 8.

[3] G. E. Moore, *Ethics* (Oxford: Oxford University Press, 1965), 84. Originally published in 1912.

also from domination by his own inclinations. The second claim of Section I is that autonomy cannot simply be equated with freedom of the will, but must instead be understood as the aim that a person with free will must adopt if he is to preserve and promote his freedom of choice and action in an ordinary sense, which is something such an agent ought to do, and can do, but does not necessarily do. Section II of this essay considers a variety of arguments by means of which Kant attempted, at various points in his career, to ground the assumption that the achievement of autonomy is the fundamental unconditional obligation for human beings, as it is for any finite rational beings who can, but do not automatically, act in accordance with pure practical reason. Sections I and II will thus comprise a study of Kant's theory of autonomy. Section III then examines Kant's conception of the practice of autonomy, first by considering his account of how human beings can actually gain control over their inclinations in the course of their maturation, and then by distinguishing the empirical realization of autonomy from other conditions with which it might be confused.

I. Freedom, Freedom of the Will, and Autonomy

A. Freedom and autonomy

In a number of passages, notably in his lectures on ethics, Kant suggests a bipartite account of freedom in choice and action. On the one hand, freedom consists in a person's ability to determine his ends independently of domination by his own inclinations and desires; on the other hand, freedom consists in a person's ability to select and pursue his own ends independently of domination by other persons. Thus, in his lectures in 1785 on moral philosophy, Kant is reported to have said, first, that a person demonstrates his freedom by "employing the power he has, to rule over his strong inclinations" (*Mrong*, 29:617). Then, a moment later, he reportedly said: "Freedom consists in this, that everyone can act according to his own will, without being necessitated to act according to the will of another" (*Mrong*, 29:618). Eight years later, in the *Vigilantius* lectures on the metaphysics of morals, we likewise find both definitions, although not in such close proximity to one another. On the one hand, Kant states that a person "actually proves himself free, in that he thereby demonstrates an *independentia arbitrii liberi a determinationibus per stimulos*," or an "independence of his free will from determination by stimuli" (*Vig*, 27:520). On the other hand, Kant also states that freedom consists in the independence of one person from domination by another: "Freedom consists only in this, that the agent utilizes his powers at his own choice, in accordance with a principle of reason; now anyone who ceded himself, with all his powers, to the disposition of another, and thus voluntarily enslaved himself, would alienate this freedom" (*Vig*, 27:594). It seems natural to ask what is the relationship between these two conceptions of freedom, before asking what is the relation of either or both to autonomy.

In fact, an account of the relationship between freedom as independence from domination by one's own inclinations and as independence from domination by others will readily emerge if we begin by considering the relationship between the first of these forms of freedom and autonomy. In the *Vigilantius* lectures, some pages prior to his definition of freedom as the independence of the determination of one's will by stimuli or inclinations, Kant had already stated:

> The concept of freedom . . . *negatively* consists in the independence of choice from all determination *per stimulos*; so often, that is, as reason is determined by itself, independently of all sensory drives; *positively*, however, it consists in spontaneity, or the ability to determine oneself by reason, without the need for triggers [*Triebfedern*] from nature. (*Vig*, 27:494)

This passage parallels a familiar one from the *Groundwork*, in the opening of its section III:

> *Will* is a kind of causality of living beings insofar as they are rational, and *freedom* would be the property of such causality independently of alien causes *determining it*, just as *natural necessity* is the property of the causality of all nonrational beings to be determined to activity by the influence of alien causes.
>
> The preceding definition of freedom is *negative* and therefore unfruitful for insight into its essence; but there flows from it a *positive* concept of freedom, which is so much the richer and more fruitful. Since the concept of causality brings with it that of laws in accordance with which, by something that we call a cause, something else, namely an effect, must be posited, so freedom, although it is not a property of the will in accordance with natural laws, is not for that reason lawless but must instead be a causality in accordance with immutable laws but of a special kind. . . . (*G*, 4:446)

Why should the freedom of the determination of the will by one's own inclinations or sensory drives be possible only if the will is instead determined by reason in accordance with its own immutable laws; that is, why should freedom, negatively described, be possible only by the achievement of autonomy?

This question should not be overlooked, because Kant, at least sometimes—and notoriously—makes it sound as if one could obtain freedom from domination by one's own inclinations simply by abolishing those inclinations: "[T]he inclinations themselves, as sources of needs, are so far from having an absolute worth, that it must instead be the universal wish of every rational being to be altogether free from them" (*G*, 4:428). However, it is Kant's considered position not only that our inclinations cannot be abolished because of our finitude or imperfection, but also that, since we can undertake no particular actions without particular ends, and yet particular ends are always suggested, although not determined, only by our natural inclinations, we can have no coherent conception of our own agency, that is, our ability to act, whether in accord with the demands of morality or in violation of them, without inclinations. Thus, freeing the determination of our wills from domination by our own inclinations cannot consist in the abolition of those inclinations, but, rather, only in the regulation of their role in the determination of our ends, a regulation that must consist in the application of principles of pure practical reason to our inclinations.

That particular actions always have particular ends, that particular ends are given empirically (that is, by inclinations or sensory impulse), and that the exercise of pure practical reason must therefore consist in the application of laws of reason to empirical impulses (or the elevation of the objects of some of those inclinations into ends, in light of their permissibility or even necessity in the eyes of reason), are constant principles in Kant's theory of action from early to late. In the mid–1770s, for example, Kant wrote:

> Moral philosophy is the science of ends, so far as they are determined through pure reason. Or of the unity of all ends (where they do not contradict themselves) of rational beings. The matter of the good is given empirically, its form *a priori*.... (*R* 6820, 19:172)

The doctrine that the "form of the good" must be *a priori* was subsequently amplified into the view that not only must the form of the good be given by pure practical reason, in the form of the moral law, but also that this law must itself be the motivation for any morally estimable action. Yet it remained Kant's view that any particular action needs a particular end, so that the moral law, as both form and motive of morally praiseworthy action, must still be applied to particular ends. Thus, almost twenty years after the previous passage, Kant wrote in the 1793 preface to *Religion within the Boundaries of Mere Reason*:

> In the absence of all reference to an end no determination of the will can take place in human beings at all, since no such determination can take place without an effect, and its representation, though not as the determining ground of the power of choice nor as an end that comes first in intention, must nonetheless be admissible as the consequence of that power's determination to an end through the law ... ; without this end, a power of choice which does not add to a

contemplated action the thought of either an objectively or subjectively determined object . . . , instructed indeed as to *how* to operate but not as to the *whither*, can itself obtain no satisfaction. (*Rel*, 6:4; see also *TP*, 8:279–80 n.)

Thus, it is clearly Kant's view that inclinations are to be regulated, not abolished. But what justifies his further claim that freedom from domination by our own inclinations can only be achieved by achieving autonomy, that is, by the subjection of our inclinations to a self-given but universal law in the selection of morally permissible and necessary ends?

Kant never spells out his argument for this claim, but his reasoning must have been something like this: Since all complete actions must seek to realize some end or other originally suggested by inclination, any regulation of the ends of action can be considered as the subordination of some inclinations to one or more other inclinations. Yet, if a person regulates his actions merely by subordinating all of his other inclinations to the pursuit of one or more inclinations, to the satisfaction of which he assigns priority, that would merely represent his domination by these dominant inclinations, unless they themselves have been selected in accordance with some principle other than inclination. What could such a principle be? If the principle is simply that one ought to subordinate the satisfaction of any or all of one's own inclinations to the satisfaction of those of one or more other persons, then that would not constitute an escape from domination by inclination. Indeed, he would still be dominated by inclinations, not only by the inclinations of the other person(s) to whom he would (barring the introduction of any other principle) be subordinating the satisfaction of his own inclinations, but also by his inclination to subordinate himself to the inclinations of others. For, unless some further ground is forthcoming, this would be all that could explain his apparent subordination of his own inclinations to those of other persons. The only way out of this dilemma would be to subordinate the satisfaction of his inclinations to an impartial principle, which privileges no inclination over any other, that is, no inclination of one person over any other of his own inclinations, nor any inclination of one person over that of any other person(s). Instead, an impartial principle would permit, and indeed prescribe, the satisfaction of only an interpersonally consistent set of inclinations. However, this is exactly the principle of autonomy, at least as it is given by the second of our opening definitions, namely, the principle that all of any individual's maxims must be part of a system of universal law (*G*, 4:432).

This argument also connects the two parts of Kant's bipartite characterization of freedom by revealing that the avoidance of domination by one's inclinations and the avoidance of domination by other persons are not two independent goals after all. Allowing oneself to be dominated by the inclinations of others depends upon allowing oneself to be dominated by one's own inclination to be dominated by others, and the principle that will allow one to avoid being dominated by this inclination also requires one to avoid domination by the inclinations of others. Of course, a condition in which no one is dominated, either by his own inclinations or by those of any other individuals, is not a situation in which no one acts to satisfy any of his own inclinations or any of the inclinations of anyone else. Rather, it is a condition in which, under normal circumstances, each person will work to satisfy some of his own inclinations and some of those of others, subject to the impartial principle of intra- and interpersonal consistency or compatibility among inclinations. But such a situation is precisely one in which no one is *dominated* by anyone's inclinations, neither his own nor those of anyone else. Instead, it is a situation in which everyone's pursuit of the satisfaction of inclinations is *regulated* by the principle of autonomy itself.

By means of the foregoing argument, adherence to the principle of autonomy can be shown to be the necessary condition for the realization of freedom from domination by both one's own inclinations and those of others, in the choice and pursuit of ends. At this point, I turn to the relation between Kant's concept of autonomy and his concept of transcendental freedom, which is his version of the traditional concept of freedom of the will.

B. *Freedom of the will and autonomy*

Kant conceives of the freedom of the will as the ability to initiate a series of events, even when that series would appear to differ from what would be entailed by the conjunction of one's own history with the natural laws of human behavior: "a faculty of absolutely beginning a state, and hence also a series of its consequences" (*PureR*, A 445/B 473). In the *Critique of Pure Reason*, Kant wrote that *"freedom in the practical sense,"* that is, "the independence of the power of choice from *necessitation* by impulses of sensibility," which, as we have just seen, can only be achieved by adherence to the same principle that is also necessary and sufficient to establish freedom from domination by others, is "grounded" on "this *transcendental* idea of freedom" (*PureR*, A 533-34/B 561-62). Kant certainly means that transcendental freedom is a necessary condition of practical freedom, or that the ability to free oneself from domination by one's sensory impulses presupposes the ability to initiate new series of actions, independent of natural laws, since he assumes that such laws would grant sensory impulses inexorable sway over our conduct.[4] Of course, he also assumes that the possibility of transcendental freedom

---

[4] See Allen W. Wood, "Kant's Compatibilism," in Allen W. Wood, ed., *Self and Nature in Kant's Philosophy* (Ithaca, NY: Cornell University Press, 1984), 73-101, esp. at 82-83, 85.

can, in turn, be explained only by transcendental idealism, which is the doctrine that the history of our behavior in time, and the natural laws that hold sway there, are all a matter of appearance, and that, as we are in ourselves, we may always be able to initiate any course of action, regardless of the appearance of our histories and the natural laws of behavior. But does Kant also mean that transcendental freedom is a *sufficient* condition for practical freedom, that is, that any agent who is transcendentally free must, in fact, choose to liberate himself from domination by his own sensory impulses in the choice of his ends and actions? One might think that sensory impulses are all a matter of appearance, and thus that an act of choice that takes place outside the order of mere appearance must necessarily be free from domination by sensory impulses. Perhaps this is what Kant means by his statement that "every action, irrespective of the temporal relation in which it stands to other appearances, is the immediate effect of the intelligible character of pure reason; reason therefore acts freely, without being determined dynamically by external or internal grounds temporally preceding it in the chain of natural causes" (*PureR*, A 553/B 581). But Kant does not explicitly commit himself in the first *Critique* to the claim that transcendental freedom is both a necessary and a sufficient condition for practical freedom.

In the *Groundwork*, however, he seems to commit himself precisely to this claim. In this work Kant asks, "What, then, can freedom of the will be other than autonomy, that is, the will's property of being a law to itself?" where the "proposition, the will is in all its actions a law to itself, indicates only the principle, to act on no other maxim than that which can also have as object itself as universal law" (*G*, 4:447). Here, adherence to this principle is sufficient to ensure practical freedom in both its parts. Kant's intended answer to this question is clearly that the freedom of the will cannot be anything other than autonomy. And this indeed follows from Kant's conception, in the *Groundwork*, of transcendental freedom: "although [it is] . . . not a property of the will in accordance with natural laws, [it is] not for that reason lawless but . . . instead . . . a causality in accordance with immutable laws but of a special kind" (*G*, 4:446). His assumption here is that, just as the phenomenal realm of appearances is thoroughly governed by natural laws, the noumenal realm of the real self, where freedom of the will is exercised, must also be thoroughly governed by law, which can be nothing other than the law of pure practical reason itself. So a free will cannot but choose in accordance with the fundamental principle of pure practical reason, and thus, freedom of the will is not only a necessary but also a sufficient condition for the achievement of autonomy, understood as practical freedom, or as freedom from domination by one's own sensory impulses and, therefore, as freedom from domination by others as well.

However, Kant's position in the *Groundwork* is notoriously problematic. He simply appeals to general epistemological considerations for the distinction between the two "standpoints" (*G*, 4:450) of the phenomenal and noumenal, thus presupposing the soundness of his arguments for transcendental idealism in the first *Critique*, without adding anything to them. Worse yet, he justifies his assumption that the principle of pure practical reason is the causal law of the noumenal realm by what appears to be a blatant category mistake. He argues that, because the possession of reason is what distinguishes us from all other things *in the phenomenal realm*, it must also be what distinguishes our *noumenal selves* from our phenomenal selves! But, what is most problematic, as has often been pointed out, perhaps most famously by Henry Sidgwick a century after the publication of the *Groundwork*,[5] is that Kant's assumption that freedom of the will is not only necessary but also sufficient for autonomy would undermine our ordinary belief that we can impute responsibility to individuals for immoral actions (that is, choices that reflect heteronomous submission to impermissible inclinations, rather than the autonomous regulation of our inclinations by means of self-given, but universal, law). If the mere existence of freedom of the will were to entail the existence of autonomy, then, by the logical principle of contraposition, the commission of any immorally heteronomous action, as a failure of autonomy, could only imply the complete absence of freedom of the will. But, if the imputation of responsibility presupposes freedom of the will (that is, the ability to have chosen otherwise than one actually did—as we ordinarily assume), then the agent who fails to be autonomous, that is, to free himself from domination by his own inclinations or those of others, cannot be held responsible for his actions, because he could not in fact have chosen to do otherwise.

Kant was not much inclined to explicitly acknowledge his errors, but he clearly came to retract the thesis that freedom of the will entails autonomy. He is usually thought to have done so in the *Critique of Practical Reason*, which he produced just three years after the *Groundwork*, but the evidence for this view is actually less than decisive. In the second *Critique*, Kant begins by arguing that a will that is determinable by the moral law must be a transcendentally free will, because "the mere form of a law," which is the essence of the moral law, is "not an object of the senses and consequently does not belong among appearances," but can instead be apprehended and acted upon only by a transcendentally free will (*PracR*, 5:28). This clearly implies that freedom of the will is a necessary condition of autonomy, but not that it is a sufficient condition for autonomy or that it necessarily entails it. Kant then claims, however, that the "lawgiving form" of the moral law is "the only thing that can constitute a determining ground of the will." Because "the matter of the will . . . can never be given otherwise than empirically"—that is, as an object of inclination—a

[5] Henry Sidgwick, "The Kantian Conception of Free Will," *Mind* 13 (1888), reprinted in Sidgwick, *The Methods of Ethics*, 7th ed. (London: Macmillan, 1907), 511–16.

free will "must nevertheless be determinable, a free will must find a determining ground in the law but independently of the *matter* of the law" (*PracR*, 5:29). What this means depends on just what Kant means by a "determining ground": On the one hand, if he is assuming that the free will must have a determining ground in order to act rationally (that is, a determining ground that could only be the principle of autonomy), but that it need not act rationally, then he is not committed to the thesis that the free will is necessarily autonomous. On the other hand, if he is assuming that the free will must always have a sufficiently determining ground, which could only be the formal principle that suffices to establish autonomy, then he is assuming that freedom of the will entails autonomy, with all the problems such an assumption involves. So it is not clear whether the *Critique of Practical Reason* actually retracts the problematic claim of the *Groundwork*.

By the time of his *Religion within the Boundaries of Mere Reason*, however, Kant clearly does withdraw the thesis of the *Groundwork*, that the mere existence of freedom of the will is a sufficient condition for autonomy. The thesis of the *Religion* is that we have transcendental freedom to choose between making our fundamental maxim the priority of the moral law over the principle of self-love, or, conversely, making our fundamental maxim the priority of self-love over the moral law. Since, all too obviously, many human beings often choose the latter, we are clearly prone to evil, and since our evil is a reflection of our own choice of our fundamental maxim, when we are evil, our evil is radical. But since our choice of evil is an expression of the same freedom that we could also use to choose the moral law, we have the possibility of being radically good as well as radically evil, and the power of conversion from evil to good is always in our own hands. It does not depend upon the grace of a god or the suffering of a savior, for they are nothing more than symbols of our own capacity for goodness and self-redemption. What is crucial for our present purposes, however, is just Kant's construal of the character of the free choice between good and evil. First, Kant puts it beyond doubt that we must be able to choose either good or evil in order for evil, as well as good, to be imputable to us: The "subjective ground" of "the exercise of the human being's freedom in general" must "itself always be an act [*Actus*] of freedom (for otherwise the use or abuse of the human being's power of choice with respect to the moral law could not be imputed to him, nor could the good or evil in him be called 'moral')" (*Rel*, 6:21). Kant no longer conceives of the moral law as the causal law of the noumenal self, but, rather, conceives of the noumenal self as absolutely free either to affirm or to reject the unconditional priority of the moral law. Second, Kant conceives of the free choice between the priority of the moral law and the priority of self-love precisely as the choice between autonomy, on the one hand, or domination by one's inclinations, that is, heteronomy, on the other. For a human's choice to be evil is simply the choice to be "dependent on the incentives of his sensuous nature," or "according to the subjective principle of self-love" to take "them into his maxim *as of themselves sufficient* for the determination of his power of choice, without minding the moral law" (*Rel*, 6:36). To choose evil is nothing more, and nothing less, than to give one's inclinations free reign over one's choice of ends, or to surrender one's autonomy to self-love. As the second *Critique* had already made clear, self-love is merely another name for the policy of determining one's choices by "material practical principles," or ends that are suggested by inclination alone (*PracR*, 5:22).

So how does Kant ultimately conceive of the relationship between freedom of the will and autonomy? Clearly, he continues to conceive of freedom of the will, in the form of transcendental freedom, as a necessary condition for the achievement of autonomy. Without such freedom, he imagines, we would necessarily be subject to domination by our own inclinations and could not even entertain the possibility of realizing autonomy. But transcendental freedom is not a sufficient condition for, or guarantee of, the realization of autonomy: we can freely choose to give our inclinations free reign over us. So transcendental freedom and practical freedom, that is, freedom of the will and autonomy, are not identical. Rather, autonomy must be conceived of as a condition of mastery over our inclinations in our choice of ends and actions, and for that reason as a condition of cooperation with, but not domination by, others as well, a condition which we can freely choose to maintain, but which we can just as well freely choose to subvert. Autonomy is not identical with a noumenal "act" of freedom. Autonomy is a condition, dependent upon an a priori principle but realized in the empirical world, which we can freely choose to realize and maintain, or to subvert or destroy.

Do we need to accept Kant's theory of freedom of the will as transcendental freedom in order to understand and accept this normative ideal of autonomy? Of course not; we could also explain the possibility of autonomy by dismissing his assumption that the laws of nature, by themselves, would always produce domination by sensuous incentives, and instead allow that self-governance by reason, rather than domination by inclination, is possible within the domain of nature and in accordance with its laws. If we take that route, we are very likely to conclude that the freedom to be autonomous is something that human beings develop only over the course of an extended process of maturation and education, and only to a degree that might well vary over a lifetime and might vary for different people. Perhaps we are even likely to conclude that some human beings cannot and do not get very far in this process at all. I will suggest in the last section of this paper that, when he came to think concretely about the duty of self-development, Kant drew exactly such conclusions. First, however, I will consider the quite different question of how Kant attempted to establish the absolute value of autonomy.

II. The Absolute Value of Autonomy

How does Kant argue for the unconditional obligation to use our freedom of the will in order to attain autonomy? Since the formula of autonomy is one of the "three ways of representing the principle of morality" that "are at bottom only so many formulae of the very same law" (G, 4:436), to ask this question could be to ask, How does Kant argue for the unconditional obligation to act in accordance with the moral law itself? That is, of course, too large a question to be answered in this essay. What I propose to do here is to look at two arguments for the fundamental value of autonomy that Kant tried out in connection with his bipartite conception of autonomy as freedom from domination, both by other persons and by one's own inclinations. I then intend to see what elements of these arguments might have survived in Kant's mature practical philosophy. Of course, the concepts of unconditional obligation and absolute value are not identical to one another, but it would not have been unlike Kant to think that an unconditional obligation could only be grounded in something of absolute value.

A. Psychological arguments for the value of autonomy

Chronologically, Kant's thought about the value of autonomy begins with what we may consider to be empirical, psychological arguments for the value of freedom from domination, by others and by one's own inclinations in the choice of one's ends. The earliest record of Kant's emerging conception of autonomy can be found in the notes that he made in his 1764 work, *Observations on the Feeling of the Beautiful and the Sublime*, shortly after its publication. Here, he remarks on the natural human abhorrence of domination by other people. For example:

> The human being has his own inclinations, and by means of his capacity of choice a clue from nature to conduct his actions in accordance with these. Nothing can be more appalling than that the action of a human stand under the will of another. Hence no abhorrence can be more natural than that which a person has against servitude. On this account a child cries and becomes bitter if it has to do what another wants without one having made an effort to make that pleasing to him. And it wishes only to become a man quickly and to operate in accordance with its own will. (Rischmüller, 60)

A few pages later, Kant adds:

> Find himself in what condition he will, the human being is dependent upon many external objects. He depends on some things because of his needs, on others because of his concupiscence, and because

he is the administrator but not the master of nature, he must often accommodate himself to its compulsion, since he does not find that it will always accommodate itself to his wishes. But what is harder and more unnatural than this yoke of necessity is the subjection of one human being under the will of another. No misfortune can be more terrifying to one who has been accustomed to freedom, who has enjoyed the good of freedom, than to be delivered over to another creature of the same species and to see the latter compel him to do what he will (to give himself over to his will). (Rischmüller, 70–71)

It might be natural to interpret passages such as these as assuming that our happiness lies in the gratification of our own inclinations, and that domination by others is abhorrent to us because it is the chief obstacle to such happiness: Anyone in a position to dominate the choices of another individual would naturally attempt to use that power to gratify his own inclinations, rather than those of the other. But Kant does not explicitly state this, so these passages are at least consistent with a view that there is simply a special satisfaction in making our own choices, free from the interference of others—a satisfaction that is distinct from, and more profound than, the satisfaction of whatever particular inclinations we choose to gratify by means of our actions. This could, in turn, imply that our dissatisfaction at having actions imposed upon us by others is so great that it would outweigh any pleasure we might take even in the satisfaction of our own inclinations if that satisfaction is forced upon us by others. To avoid the frustration of being dominated by others and to experience, instead, the pleasure of making their own choices, human beings who live in circumstances in which they cannot avoid contact with others, or in which they even depend upon interaction with others—that is, all human beings in the empirical conditions of their actual existence—must figure out how to act in accordance with a principle of cooperation but nondomination, which is at least part of a principle of autonomy.

That Kant had recently read Rousseau is evident in these notes, and perhaps this emphasis on our love of freedom from domination by others can be traced to this source. But beginning in these notes, Kant also develops an account of our satisfaction in making choices free from the domination of our own inclinations, which seems original to him and to which he would return in his notes and lectures on both moral philosophy and anthropology for many years to come. At one point in these notes, Kant begins with a passage emphasizing our gratification in making choices freely, which might be read in the same vein as the passages that we have already seen:

We have gratification in certain of our perfections, but much more if we ourselves are the cause. We have the most if we are the freely acting cause. To *subordinate* everything to the free capacity for choice is the greatest perfection. And the perfection of the free capacity for choice as a cause of possibility is far greater than all other causes of good even if they have produced actuality. (Rischmüller, 107–8)

Here, he could be taken to be describing again the pleasure of making one's own choices, rather than having someone else make them for him. But as Kant continues, it becomes clear that he is now talking about a special satisfaction that lies in subordinating our own capacities other than the capacity for free choice to our own capacity of free choice:

Since the greatest inner perfection and the perfection that arises from that consists in the subordination of all of our capacities and receptivities to the free capacity for choice, the feeling for the *goodness* of the capacity of choice must be immediately much different and also greater than all the consequences that can thereby be actualized. (Rischmüller, 108–9)

During the 1770s, Kant would develop this thought into a fuller account of our satisfaction in regulating, rather than being dominated by, our own inclinations.

Here is Kant's idea as he further developed it. The fullest expression of life, and therefore the deepest source of our satisfaction, lies in free and unhindered activity. Such free activity precludes being ruled by inclination, both because we are, in principle, passive rather than active with respect to the occurrence of our inclinations, and also because, in practice, our inclinations can always come into conflict with one another, thus exposing the freedom of any activity that would be based on any particular inclination to limitation by another inclination at any time. In order to preserve and promote our full freedom of activity, we must, therefore, govern our activity by laws of reason, rather than being pushed around by whatever inclination happens to be strongest in us at any given time. Laws of reason, unlike particular inclinations, are impersonal and interpersonally valid, so to govern ourselves by reason, rather than by inclination, is necessarily to govern ourselves by universally valid laws. Yet to govern ourselves by reason cannot mean simply to eliminate all inclinations, for without inclinations suggesting desirable courses of action to us, we would have nothing to do, nothing for reason to govern. Rather, what the full enjoyment of our freedom requires is that we subject both our own inclinations and those of others to the regulation of reason in a way that, while respecting the freedom of all, leads to the pursuit of the satisfaction of an intersubjectively compatible set of inclinations, representing the union of the free choices of all who are involved.

This argument is briefly suggested in Kant's lectures on ethics, when he equates "the greatest use of freedom" with the "highest *principium* of life" itself, and then proposes that the conditions under which freedom can "be consistent with itself," rather than those under which "it comes into collision with itself," are precisely the conditions that must be satisfied in order to realize this "highest *principium* of life" (*Col*, 27:346). The argument is spelled out in a little more detail in Kant's notes and anthropology lectures from the 1770s. The first step in this argument is the premise that our deepest satisfaction lies in the promotion of life, which, in turn, consists in the maximally unhindered activity of all of our powers and capacities. Here is a representative statement from Kant's anthropology lectures from 1775–76:

> The feeling of the promotion of life is gratification or pleasure. Life is the consciousness of a free and regular [*regelmäßigen*] play of all of the powers and faculties of the human being. The feeling of the promotion of life is that which is pleasure and the feeling of the hindrance of life is displeasure. (*Friedländer*, 25:559)

One page later Kant reiterates the point that what we enjoy in life is the exercise of our own activity, while he also introduces the second step in the argument, that the maximization of our activity requires our self-regulation by rules of reason:

> The play of the mental powers [*Gemüths Kräfte*] must be strongly lively and free if it is to animate. Intellectual pleasure consists in the consciousness of the use of freedom in accordance with rules. Freedom is the greatest life of the human being, whereby he exercises his activity without hindrance. Through some hindrance of freedom life is restricted, since [then] freedom does not stand under the coercion of a rule. If this were the case, then it [our activity] would not be free, but since this introduces a lack of rule if the understanding does not direct it, while this lack of rule hinders itself, thus no freedom can please us except that which stands under the rule of the understanding. This is the intellectual pleasure, which leads to the moral. (*Friedländer*, 25:560)

A note from the beginning of the 1770s also quickly states the first two steps in Kant's argument:

> Feeling is the sensation of life. The complete use of life is freedom. The formal condition of freedom as a use that is in complete concordance with life is regularity [*Regelmäßigkeit*]. (*R* 6870, 19:187)

Our deepest pleasure in life is activity itself, and freedom is equivalent to activity, but in order to maximize the use of our freedom, we must subject it to regulation by law.

As I mentioned above, each of these two steps in Kant's argument can also be found in Kant's notes on ethics from the 1770s. Several notes from the crucial period 1769–70 make the first step by contrasting the distinctive and superior quality of our pleasure in activity, rather than passivity, and explicitly associate the latter with the determination of our will by inclination. Kant's second claim, that the enjoyment of our free activity depends upon the subordination of that activity to rules rather than inclination, is made in a number of notes. He argues that it is only by the use of rules that the *unity* of our actions can be maintained, or conflicts avoided among actions inspired by competing inclinations, which would otherwise have the effect of restricting or reducing the scope of our free activity. The following note, probably from 1776–78, reiterates Kant's first claim and then makes the second in the form that I have just suggested:

> In the end everything comes down to life; what animates (or the feeling of the promotion of life) is agreeable. Life is unity; hence all taste has as its *principio* the unity of the animating sensations.
>
> Freedom is the original life and in its connection [*Zusammenhang*] the condition of the coherence [*Übereinstimmung*] of all life; hence that which promotes the feeling of universal life or the feeling of the promotion of universal life causes a pleasure. Do we feel good in universal life? The universality makes all our feelings agree with one another, although prior to this universality there is no special kind of sensation. It is the form of *consensus*. (*R* 6862, 19:183)

Here two thoughts are interwoven. Kant is assuming, first, that the primary source of satisfaction in life is the gratification of particular inclinations, but that the use of free choice is necessary to maximize such satisfaction by selecting a coherent set of inclinations as the object of our actions. He also assumes, second, that there is a "special kind" of satisfaction associated with the exercise of free choice, one that is connected with activity or life itself. This special satisfaction is the source of the priority that we give to the freedom of choice from domination by any particular inclination over the satisfaction of any particular inclination.

Kant's argument is thus that the deep satisfaction that we take in maximally free activity—a satisfaction that he equates with the feeling of life itself—is incompatible with simply acting on whatever inclinations present themselves to us. This is, in the first instance, because he takes the mere occurrence of inclination to be something with respect to which we are passive rather than active, and in the second instance, because he assumes that any of one's own inclinations can always conflict either with other inclinations of one's own or with those of other persons in such a way as to reduce the sphere of our free activity, or even to undercut any possibility of coherent activity at all. The only way to avoid this conflict is to govern our actions by rules of reason.

Of course, there is an obvious problem with Kant's observation that humans abhor being dominated by each other, and with his more elaborate argument that humans take a deep and distinct satisfaction in freely choosing which of their inclinations to satisfy, rather than simply being pushed to act by whatever inclinations happen to be strongest at any moment. The problem is simply that, first of all, these psychological claims are empirical and, thus, as far as we can tell, contingent, so they would not seem to be adequate premises for what the mature Kant demands, namely, a moral law that would "hold for all rational beings and *only because of this* be also a law for all human wills"—a law that states an unconditional obligation. These claims could yield only what he rejects, namely, a principle "derived from the special natural constitution of humanity—what is derived from certain feelings and propensities and even, if possible, from a special tendency that would be peculiar to human reason and would not have to hold necessarily for the will of every rational being" (G, 4:425). Second, it should worry not only Kant but also anyone that these claims might not be true even of all human beings. To state it mildly, there is much in modern psychology and modern history to suggest that many human beings are happy to be dominated by whatever inclinations they happen to have, and are all too ready to allow themselves to be dominated by other people and their inclinations. If not for this second reason, then certainly for the first, the project of providing a psychological foundation for the value of autonomy, and thus for our obligation to achieve it, disappears from Kant's mature writings in moral philosophy. But Kant's early thoughts about our love of the two forms of freedom hardly disappear without a trace. In one of his last publications, his 1798 textbook for the anthropology lectures that he had ceased to give the year before, Kant preserves the love of freedom from domination by others in its original form as the passion for "outer freedom," while suggesting that the love of freedom from domination by one's own inclinations is the basis for moral feeling itself: "It is not only the concept of freedom under moral laws that arouses an affect, which is called enthusiasm; the mere sensuous idea of outer freedom, by analogy with the concept of law, raises the inclination to continue in it or extend it to the point of vehement passion" (APV, sec. 82; 7:269).

B. A metaphysical basis for the value of autonomy

If Kant cannot use his psychological observations on our love of the two forms of freedom that comprise the practice of autonomy in order to ground its value and our obligation to achieve it, then what else can he try? Other passages from his writings suggest that at various times he was tempted by a metaphysical argument. In the following note from 1769–70, Kant grounds his view that the value of freedom is the source of the unconditional validity of the moral law in a metaphysical conception of the essence, and thus the perfection, of the will:

> There is a free capacity for choice, which has no proper happiness as its aim, but rather presupposes one. The essential perfection of a freely acting being rests on this, that this freedom is not subjected to inclination or to any foreign cause at all. The primary rule of externally good actions is not that of agreement with the happiness of others but that of agreement with their capacity for choice, and just as the *perfection* of a subject does not rest on its being happy but on its *subordinating its state to freedom*, likewise the universally valid perfection rests on actions standing under universal laws of freedom. (*R* 6605, 19:105–6)

This form of argument does not depend upon empirical claims about human beings that must ultimately be confined to anthropology, and it could be true of other forms of rational beings, not just human beings. This form of argumentation may also be present in the *Groundwork*'s conception of a "metaphysics of morals" that can derive a proper formulation of the moral law from the mere analysis of the concept of a rational will (*G*, 4:426–27). But as the *Groundwork* itself makes clear, the analytic derivation of the correct formulation of the moral law is not yet the necessary but synthetic proof of its validity (*G*, 4:444–45). At least in Section II of the *Groundwork*, Kant seems to be aware of Hume's prohibition of deriving a moral "ought" from a metaphysical "is"; thus, the strategy of deriving the obligation to achieve autonomy from a metaphysical conception of the perfection of the human will, or of rational wills in general, does not seem to be one that Kant can maintain. So, if he can appeal neither to psychology nor to metaphysics to demonstrate the absolute value of autonomy, then what is left?

C. Respect for autonomy

Kant's early arguments for the value of autonomy turn on the psychological and metaphysical superiority of activity over passivity. In his mature practical philosophy, I suggest, this fascination with the ideal of pure activity is transmuted into the normative premise that only what is the product of an agent's activity is suitable for moral evaluation, *a fortiori* for esteem or respect. Coupling this normative assumption with the theoretical premise that inclinations simply happen to us, and that we remain passive if we are dominated by them, but that we can be active in regulating them in accordance with the principle of autonomy, Kant reaches this conclusion: Only an agent's self-regulation of inclinations in accordance with the principle of autonomy, which entails freedom from domination by his own inclinations and those of others, is worthy of respect.

Thus, only the achievement of such autonomy itself can be the source of all our unconditional obligations.

Kant's most famous assertion of the unique dignity of autonomy in the *Groundwork* makes explicit that acting in accordance with universal laws of reason is the only way to free oneself from subjection to mere laws of nature, and he suggests, for this reason, that lawgiving has unique dignity:

> And what is it, then, that justifies a morally good disposition, or virtue, in making such high claims? It is nothing less than the *share* it affords a rational being *in the giving of universal laws*, by which it makes him fit to be a member of a possible realm of ends, which he was already destined to be by his own nature as an end in itself and, for that very reason, as lawgiving in the realm of ends—*as free with respect to all laws of nature* [emphasis added], obeying only those which he himself gives and in accordance with which his maxims can belong to a giving of universal law (io which he at the same time subjects himself).... *Autonomy* is therefore the ground of the dignity of human nature and of every rational nature. (*G*, 4:435-36)[6]

What the foregoing passage does not make explicit, however, is what the value of freeing oneself from subjection to mere laws of nature is. But much earlier in the *Groundwork*, Kant has revealed what I take to be the missing premise of the present argument and the underlying assumption of his entire view:

> For an object as the effect of my proposed action I can indeed have *inclination* but *never respect*, just because it is merely an effect and not an activity of the will. In the same way I cannot have respect for inclination as such, whether it is mine or that of another; I can at most in the first case approve it and in the second sometimes even love it, that is, regard it as favorable to my own advantage. Only what is

---

[6] At the elision, I have omitted Kant's statement that "For, nothing can have a worth other than that which the law determines for it. But the lawgiving itself, which determines all worth, must for that very reason have a dignity, that is, an unconditional, incomparable worth; and the word *respect* alone provides a becoming expression for the assessment of it that a rational being must give." This passage suggests the interpretation, advocated by Christine Korsgaard and Allen Wood, that Kant argues for the value of autonomy by inferring from the objective value of particular objects of choice to the absolute value of the act of choice that confers the first sort of value; see Christine Korsgaard, "Kant's Formula of Humanity," in Korsgaard, *Creating the Kingdom of Ends* (Cambridge: Cambridge University Press, 1996), 106–32, and Allen W. Wood, *Kant's Ethical Thought* (Cambridge: Cambridge University Press, 1999), chap. 4, sec. 5, 124–32. (However, neither author actually cites this passage from Kant in the locations that I have cited.) But since this argument presupposes that we assign objective value to particular objects before recognizing the value of free choice itself, it would seem to run afoul of the *Groundwork*'s opening argument that nothing has unconditional value except the good will itself: the unconditional value of free choice could not, it seems, be inferred from the merely conditional value of any particular objects of the will.

connected with my will merely as ground and never as effect, what does not serve my inclination but outweighs it or at least excludes it altogether from calculations in making a choice—hence the mere law for itself—can be an object of respect and so a command. (*G*, 4:400)

This passage alludes to the two forms of domination with which Kant had been concerned since the 1760s—domination by one's own inclinations and by those of others—and states that there can never be respect for either, because neither is an "activity of the will." Only what is an activity of the will is even a candidate for respect, and the only form of pure activity of the will is making choices in accordance with "the mere law for itself," rather than by mere inclination. Thus, acting in accordance with the principle of autonomy is the only way to express the activity of the will and the only possible candidate for respect.

Now it might well seem as if the normative premise that a genuine action of the will is a necessary condition for moral evaluation or imputation is not sufficient to establish that activity of the will is sufficient for the positive evaluation of esteem; after all, heteronomy or evil-doing is also, by Kant's account of radical evil, a genuine expression of an action of the free will. So it might seem as if an additional normative premise must underlie the claim that autonomy is the proper object of moral esteem. However, although it is true that any evil act, considered by itself, is just as much an expression of the freedom of the will as is a good action, we have also seen that the condition of autonomy is precisely that in which a free action of the will preserves and promotes free activity itself, in the sense of preserving the possibility of further free acts on the part of both the agent of the particular act concerned, as well as other agents who might be affected by his actions. Compliance with the principle of autonomy is the only form of free action that preserves the possibility of further exercises of freedom. Thus, while the normative premise that a genuine activity of the free will is a necessary condition for imputation or moral assessment of a single action considered by itself does not seem to be sufficient to determine the character of actions that should be esteemed rather than reviled, reflection on the fact that only autonomous actions *preserve* the possibility of further free actions seems to point directly to autonomy as the necessary object of respect.

However, it might still seem natural to ask whether such an argument for autonomy as the basis of the normative theory of the *Groundwork* is consistent with Kant's insistence in the *Religion* that not only goodness or autonomy but also evil or heteronomy must be imputed to free choice. Kant's argument will be inconsistent with this premise if the activity that can only be expressed by adherence to the principle of autonomy is simply equated with the act of choosing a maxim for a single action. The activity of the will that necessarily deserves esteem, rather than blame, must be understood as the free choice of continuing freedom in the setting and pursuit of particular ends on the part of both oneself and others, which is a form of freedom in real time, so to speak, and which can be achieved and preserved only by adherence to the principle of autonomy, that is, a principle that can, in turn, be affirmed or rejected by an act of the transcendentally free will. In other words, Kant's notion of activity needs to become as complex as his notion of the will in order to preserve his conception of the value of autonomy.

III. THE PRACTICE OF AUTONOMY

A. Autarky, autocracy, and autonomy

What is it like to practice autonomy in the empirical conditions of human life? Kant's remark that "[o]nly . . . what does not serve my inclination but outweighs it or at least excludes it altogether from my calculations . . . can be an object of respect" (*G*, 4:400) might suggest that to be autonomous simply requires that we must exclude inclinations and the attempt to satisfy them from our lives altogether. As we have already seen, a few other comments in the *Groundwork* also suggest as much, such as Kant's statement that "the inclinations themselves, as sources of needs, are so far from having an absolute worth, as to make one wish to have them, that it must instead be the universal wish of every rational being to be altogether free from them" (*G*, 4:428). The complete elimination of inclinations as sources of needs would represent the extreme case of what Kant calls, in his lectures on ethics, *autarky* (*autarchia*), the "capacity to master oneself, to possess oneself, to be sufficient to oneself," giving rise to the "duty of being able to do without" (*Vig*, 27:653), or to "[s]eek independence from all things of nature, as needs, and likewise from other people" (*Vig*, 27:651).[7] Complete autarky might seem to guarantee the preservation of our autonomy, because it would remove every inclination that might tempt us to surrender our autonomy to ourselves or to others. But Kant could not have thought that complete autarky should be the moral ideal for human beings, because, as we have seen, he had made it plain, from early on in his lectures and notes, that human action requires a matter as well as a form: particular human actions always attempt to fulfill particular human needs, which are suggested by inclinations, although *which* inclinations are to be gratified must be regulated by reason. As he said in the mid-1770s, "The matter of the good is given empirically,

---

[7] In spite of its spelling, Kant's Latin term *"autarchia"* would have to be derived from the classical Greek *autarkeia*, meaning self-sufficiency, rather than from the later term *autarchia*, meaning politically self-governing. In his *Ethica Philosophica*, the textbook for Kant's lectures on ethics, Alexander Baumgarten had correctly used the former Greek term to connote the "status of a man . . . in which he is the sole and sufficient ground of his own felicity" (Baumgarten, *Ethica Philosophica*, sec. 277; in the Academy edition of Kant's lectures on ethics, 27:948–49). The misspelling in Kant's lectures could be due, of course, either to Kant's own error or to the student transcriber of the notes.

its form *a priori*" (*R* 6820, 19:172). Complete autarky cannot be a goal for human conduct, because it would leave us with nothing whatever to do, and thus with no way in which to express our activity. And this conclusion is actually consistent with Kant's statement that it must be "the universal wish of every rational being to be altogether free from" inclinations, for a *wish* is not a *will*, and differs from the latter precisely in that we can wish for what is impossible, but we cannot will it.[8] Kant does not, in fact, suggest that we strive to realize autonomy by realizing complete autarky or the elimination of inclinations. Rather, he urges that we put the ideal of autonomy into practice by developing what he calls *autocracy* or "self-mastery," "the authority to compel the mind, despite all the impediments to doing so," involving "mastery over oneself, and not merely the power to direct" (*Col*, 27:363).

Kant describes the principle of self-mastery in bold terms:

> The rule is this: Seek to maintain command over yourself, for under this condition you are capable of performing the self-regarding duties. There is in man a certain rabble element which must be subject to control, and which a vigilant government must keep under regulation, and where there must even be force to compel this rabble under the rule in accordance with ordinance and regulation. (*Col*, 27:360)

Kant does not suggest that this form of self-government can be achieved all at once by a single action. Instead, he clearly regards it as a condition that must be achieved and maintained by the cultivation and discipline of a number of capacities and practices, guided by the ideal of the moral law, that is, by the ideal of autonomy. This process of achieving autocracy, as the empirical realization of autonomy in the actual circumstances of human existence, is not only temporally extended, but also complex, for it requires, apparently, both that we directly strengthen the efficacy of the moral law on our conduct, and also that we learn techniques that indirectly support the reign of the moral law, by removing or diminishing impediments to its rule.

These two aspects of the cultivation of self-mastery are evident in Kant's initial discussion of moral feeling in his lectures. In his major published works, Kant often makes it sound as if moral feeling, in the form of the feeling of respect, is the immediate and automatic consequence of consciousness of the moral law (See *G*, 4:401 n. and *PracR*, 5:75). But in his lectures he makes it clear that, while it is moral feeling that gives "executive authority" to the moral law, that is, makes it

---

[8] See *Critique of the Power of Judgment*, "Introduction," sec. III, 5:177-78 n., in Immanuel Kant, *Critique of the Power of Judgment*, ed. Paul Guyer, trans. Paul Guyer and Eric Matthews (Cambridge: Cambridge University Press, 2000), 65.

empirically efficacious in the etiology of our actions, this feeling must be "cultivated," and this requires two different things. First, competing incentives to action coming from sensibility must simply be "weakened and overcome"; "we first have to discipline ourselves, i.e., to root out, in regard to ourselves, by repeated actions, the tendency that arises from the sensory motive." This can be understood simply as removing impediments to the efficacy of moral feeling. But second, "He who would discipline himself morally must pay great attention to himself, and often give an account of his actions before the inner judge, since then, by long practice, he will have given strength to the moral motivating grounds, and acquired, by cultivation, a habit of desire or aversion in regard to moral good or evil" (*Col*, 27:361). These two statements together suggest that humans have a natural disposition to moral feeling, which can make the moral law efficacious in the regulation of our conduct, but that we must do two things to make this disposition effective: we must practice, by repeated actions, the suppression of competing incentives, for they are not simply eliminated by a single act of the will, at least in actual experience; and we must repeatedly attend to the voice of moral feeling, or the inner judge within us, for to hear it once is not enough to make it effective. Both the moral feeling and the suppression of alternatives to moral feeling must be cultivated by attention and vigilance over time.

Beyond these general requirements for the development of self-mastery, Kant also recommends a number of particular techniques for the realization of autocracy. His discussion aims to show how we can gain autocracy over "the mental powers, insofar as they have a bearing on morality," or develop "a capacity [*Vermögen*] for keeping them under free choice and observation." The division of the mental powers on which his discussion is based is not explicit, but can be understood thus: since we are concerned with how the cultivation and discipline of other mental powers bears on the use of the faculty of choice or desire for the determination of conduct, it is these other mental powers, rather than the faculty of desire itself, which is to be discussed. Using the tripartite scheme that Kant accepted throughout his anthropology lectures, and that would ultimately dictate his system of three critiques, the mental powers other than the faculty of desire can be divided into the cognitive powers and the capacity for feeling. Among the cognitive powers, pure reason is excluded from the discussion, since its role is to provide the principle of autonomy, the implementation of which is to be facilitated by the use of the other mental powers. This leaves the cognitive powers of imagination, understanding, and judgment, and Kant then advises how best to cultivate each of these in order to achieve self-mastery.

First, since the imagination—which is the general power to have images, thus including the senses—is a source of images of "sensual pleasures" that can tempt us to "vices that run contrary to nature, and extreme

violations of the self-regarding duties," then "[a]utocracy should consist
... in the person banishing his imaginings from his mind, so that the
imagination does not work its spell of presenting objects that are unob-
tainable" or impermissible. But since the imagination, like the senses in
general, tends to "dupe and also outwit the understanding," this can best
be accomplished by our learning to "outwit them in turn, by trying to
furnish the mind with another form of sustenance than that offered by the
senses, and seeking to occupy it with ideal diversions, comprising all
refined forms of knowledge" (*Col*, 27:364). In other words, in order to
keep the imagination from presenting us with inappropriate temptations,
we must occupy it with other things. This is a discipline that both can and
must be learned. As Kant also stresses a few pages later in the same
lecture notes, the trick is not simply to learn how to substitute morally
appropriate for morally inappropriate images, but also to cultivate appropriate activities: "[W]e display autocracy by keeping our mind active
and effective under the burden of work. . . . We must therefore have the
resolve to stick firmly to what we have undertaken, and to carry it through
regardless of the arguments for procrastination." To gain control over the
imagination, we must not only develop alternative habits of imagination,
but also develop the discipline to keep ourselves fully involved in meaningful activity. We must cultivate "the union and harmony of the mental
powers evinced in carrying out our business. This is not, indeed, a thing
for everyone, but depends upon talent. Yet it can be strengthened by
practice" (*Col*, 27:366).

Second, we must apply the understanding in "the observation of oneself," not "eavesdropping on oneself," but learning "to observe ourselves
through actions, and to pay attention to them." By this Kant seems to
mean not the more general point that he has already made, that we must
learn to be aware of the presence of moral feeling and the promptings of
conscience in us, but, rather, that we must learn to pay attention to our
particular tendencies to action, that is, "to examine our actions to see if
they are good or bad," and thus to learn in which arenas of conduct we
need to make special efforts in order to act in accordance with the general
principle of autonomy. This, too, is not an ability that is simply given, but
one that must be cultivated: a "person always has to get to know himself
in a gradual way" (*Col*, 27:365).

Finally, autocracy "includes *suspensio judicii*," or the ability to defer
decision on a proposed course of action until we have had time to consider it and its moral status fully. "In such judgment we must have enough
autocracy to be able to defer it if we will, and not be moved to declare our
judgment on [merely] persuasive grounds." For example, "if I receive a
letter, and it has aroused anger in me on the spot; if I answer right away,
I let my anger be very plain; but if I can put it off until the following day,
I will see the matter from a very different standpoint" (*Col*, 27:365–66). In
this case, Kant does not explicitly assert that the discipline to suspend

judgment on a fraught matter is one that must be learned and cultivated over time, but perhaps that is too evident to need saying. Like the ability to control and divert the imagination, and like the practice of carefully attending to one's actions and motives in order to see where one needs to apply the greatest effort to comply with the demands of autonomy, the practice of not making hasty judgments is clearly something that both can and must be learned and strengthened over time.

After describing the techniques that we can and must use in order to develop autocracy in the use of our cognitive powers, Kant comments more briefly on how we must cultivate, for the sake of self-mastery, the faculty of feeling. Here, he first observes that there is a difference between "feelings and inclinations" [*Empfindungen und Neigungen*], on the one hand, and "emotions and passions" [*Affecten und Leidenschaften*] on the other—the former being natural and unavoidable states of mind that can be regulated, while the latter are momentary or enduring conditions that interfere with sound judgment and reasoning (see *APV*, secs. 73–74, 7:251–52). He then merely says: "In duty to ourselves, and for the dignity of mankind, the demand upon a person is that he have no emotions and passions at all; such is the rule, although it is another matter whether people can actually get as far as that." The suggestion is not that we have a duty to try to eradicate feelings and inclinations, but that we must try to prevent them from developing into emotions and passions. But Kant does not have very much to say about how we can actually do that; he merely says that a person "should be brave, orderly, and steadfast in his work, and guard against falling into the fever-heat of passions" (*Col*, 27:368). Apparently, each person will have to work out for himself what he needs to do in order to keep his feelings and inclinations from degenerating into emotions and passions, and thereby undermining his autonomy. But presumably, in whatever way people develop such discipline, it will take time for them to do so; and Kant's remark that it is a question how far anyone can get in this process surely presupposes that the development of such discipline is a temporally extended process.

Indeed, not one of Kant's recommendations for the development of autocracy is terribly specific, but they all clearly evince the recognition that, in the actual circumstances of human life, the moral ideal of autonomy is not something that can be achieved by a single act of the will, but something that can be implemented only over time, only with effort and discipline, and only to a certain degree. Autonomy is the goal, but a certain degree of autocracy is the most for which we can actually hope.

B. Fallback or usual and customary means?

How should we appraise the moral merit of such practices of autocracy as learning how to divert our imaginations from unsuitable objects, or learning how to suspend judgment until a cooler moment? Should we regard such practices as ways of getting ourselves to comply with the demands of duty that are alternatives to acting directly from respect for the moral law, that is, as techniques for acting in conformity with duty but not out of duty, which should as such be praised and encouraged, but which have no "true moral worth" and merit no real "esteem"? (See *G*, 4:398.) Or should we regard them as the usual means to the end of acting from duty, that is, the characteristic ways in which human beings, when motivated by respect for the moral law, can implement that respect, and thus as fully worthy of true esteem? Kant does not raise this question in his discussion of autocracy, but his comments in another context suggest his answer to it. In the "Doctrine of Virtue" of the late *Metaphysics of Morals*, Kant mentions two kinds of naturally occurring feelings that we have a moral duty to preserve and cultivate. The first kind are natural inclinations toward the beauty of nonhuman nature, and the second kind are natural feelings of sympathy toward other human beings. In light of Kant's apparent insistence that there is no moral merit in any actions, even actions in outward conformity to the requirements of duty, that are motivated by mere feelings (see, most famously, *G*, 4:398–99), it would seem as if such natural inclinations could at best be morally irrelevant. But Kant insists, with regard to the first of these natural feelings, that we have a duty to preserve and cultivate "a natural predisposition that is very serviceable to morality in one's relation with other people" (*MM*, DV sec. 17, 6:443). Here his assumption is that how we treat nonhuman beings—"humanely" or "inhumanely," as we say—will affect how we treat human beings. With regard to the second—natural feelings of sympathy—he makes the following statements: "Nature has already implanted in human beings receptivity to these feelings. But to use this as a means to promoting active and rational benevolence is still a particular, though only a conditional, duty" (*MM*, DV sec. 34, 6:456), and

> While it is not in itself a duty to share the sufferings (as well as the joys) of others, it is a duty to sympathize actively in their fate; and to this end it is therefore an indirect duty to cultivate the compassionate natural (aesthetic) feelings in us, and to make use of them as so many means to sympathy based on moral principles and the feelings appropriate to them.—It is therefore a duty not to avoid the places where the poor who lack the most basic necessities are to be found but rather to seek them out, and not to shun sickrooms or debtors' prisons and so forth in order to avoid sharing painful feelings one many not be able to resist. For this is still one of the impulses that nature has implanted in us to do what the representation of duty alone [*für sich allein*] might not accomplish. (*MM*, DV sec. 35, 6:457)

It might seem natural to read the last sentence of this citation as saying that feelings of sympathy should be cultivated so that we will have a fallback when the representation of duty alone is insufficient to get us to do for others who are in need what we ought to do for them. In such a case, the performance of beneficent deeds would seem to be in conformity *with* duty, and therefore worthy of encouragement, but not to be *from* duty, and therefore not worthy of esteem. However, I do not think that such an interpretation is consistent with the rest of what Kant says here, for what his other statements suggest is that nature has implanted certain feelings in us as the means to execute the ends that duty requires of us. It is by cultivating these feelings and then acting on them in appropriate circumstances that we, constituted as we are, can do what respect for duty requires of us. The duty to cultivate such feelings is, as Kant says, indirect, because it cannot be a duty simply to have feelings that we do not naturally have (see *MM*, DV sec. 25, 6:449), but it can be a duty to preserve and cultivate tendencies to feeling that we do have, for such preservation and cultivation call for actions that are under the control of our wills. And the duty to use naturally occurring feelings as a "means to promoting active and rational benevolence" is a conditional duty, because we must only act on such feelings when the actions they would prompt are indeed actions called for by duty. The objects of our benevolence must be appropriate candidates for our help, and the occasion must be suitable, that is, we must not, in the particular circumstances at hand, have other, more pressing duties that need to be satisfied (for example, we cannot give to charity money that we need to repay a debt). But once these conditions are satisfied, then it is our duty to cultivate natural feelings that prompt us to perform beneficent or other acts that are required by duty, for it is through feelings that we human beings can act, and those feelings are the means that nature has granted us to fulfill the ends that duty imposes on us. On this account, that the representation of duty alone is insufficient for the fulfillment of our duties should not be taken to mean that the motive of duty is *sometimes too weak* to get us to do what we ought to do, but, rather, that it is *always incomplete*: it specifies the end, but not the means. We have to look to our nature to find what means we have available to realize this end.[9]

I suggest that the same analysis should be applied to the cultivation of techniques for self-mastery. Developing control over our imagination,

---

[9] I would also argue that the idea that natural feelings should be cultivated as a fallback to substitute for weak moral motivation, which is worthy of encouragement but not esteem, is actually incoherent. If these feelings are intentionally cultivated, so as to enable us to perform our duty regardless of other circumstances, then they are, presumably, cultivated out of recognition of the need always to be able to do what duty demands, that is, out of respect for duty itself. The very fact that such feelings have been cultivated is, therefore, itself worthy of esteem.

using our understanding to comprehend our own proclivities, learning how to defer judgment, figuring out how to prevent our feelings from degenerating into irrational passions—these are not alternatives to willing to be autonomous out of respect for morality itself, but are simply the means by which human beings can implement the ideal of autonomy in the empirical circumstances of human life. Whether we think of the decision to make the cultivation of such forms of discipline our maxim and end, as the product of a free choice outside of time, as Kant does, or as the products of choice within time, with whatever sort of freedom is possible within time, as most of us now do, it remains the case that the cultivation of such forms of discipline over time, by the variety of techniques to which Kant alludes, is the naturally available means that we have to implement such a maxim and end. The achievement of autocracy by such means is thus not a fallback to genuine autonomy, worthy of grudging encouragement but not true esteem. Rather, it is the only means that human beings have to implement the ideal of autonomy, and thus it is fully worthy of genuine esteem.

There might seem to be a risk of a vicious regress here: namely, that if the motive to perform our duty out of respect for the moral law itself is always incomplete, requiring for its implementation particular feelings to which we are naturally disposed, but which need cultivation, then we will not have a complete motive to cultivate these feelings themselves. It is perhaps in order to avoid such a regress that Kant himself distinguishes between a general "moral feeling," that is, "the susceptibility to feel pleasure or displeasure merely from being aware that our actions are consistent with or contrary to the law of duty" (*MM*, DV, Introduction, sec. XII, 6:399), and particular feelings of "[l]ove of human beings" (6:401). The former is the expression of our susceptibility to be moved by the moral law itself, while the latter, like aesthetic feelings of disinterested love toward nonhuman nature, are naturally occurring means that can be cultivated for the implementation of the general demands of morality, given that we are, in fact, motivated to fulfill these demands. However, it must also be noted that Kant explicitly says that our "obligation with regard to [general] moral feeling can only be to *cultivate* it and to strengthen it through wonder at its inscrutable source" (6:399). He clearly supposes that both general and particular moral feelings can and must be cultivated. Perhaps he thus imagines that our natural disposition to take pleasure in doing as morality commands us to do is strong enough to get us going on the project of cultivating that feeling, in order to make it strong enough to be efficacious in particular circumstances in which our commitment to morality will be put to the test, and then that our general commitment to morality, strengthened in that way, will also lead us to cultivate particular sorts of feeling, such as feelings of benevolence and sympathy, that can be useful in the implementation of the general demands of morality in the normal course of affairs. This does not seem to me to be an implausible moral psychology.

Conclusion

In Section I of this essay, I argued that Kant's principle of autonomy should be understood as offering the means by which we can achieve freedom from domination by both our own inclinations and those of others, but that the achievement of autonomy should be understood as something that is only made possible, not made necessary, by the possession of free will. Contrary to Kant, I suggested that the extent to which we are free to achieve autonomy is a matter of degree, to be determined empirically, not an absolute that is given *a priori*. The particular techniques that Kant recommends in order to attain autocracy or self-mastery, which are described in Section III of this essay, would be entirely consistent with such an empirical, rather than transcendental, conception of freedom. Kant's early psychological argument for the value of autonomy, which is described in Section II, subsection A of this essay, would also be consistent with such a naturalistic approach to freedom of the will. It is clear that the Kant of the published writings in practical philosophy would not himself have been happy without both a transcendental guarantee of the existence of freedom of the will and an a priori argument for the unconditional obligation to be autonomous. But we might do better to settle for the empirical argument for the value of autonomy and the natural methods for the achievement of autocracy that Kant also provides.

Philosophy, University of Pennsylvania

HOW MUCH SHOULD WE VALUE AUTONOMY?*

By Marina Oshana

I. Introduction

Autonomy generally is a valued condition for persons in liberal cultures such as the United States. We uphold autonomous agents as the exemplar of persons who, by their judgment and action, authenticate the social and political principles and policies that advance their interests. I will begin by examining the concept of autonomy in Section II of this essay. In Section III, I will explore the idea that autonomy is valued because autonomous agents are persons whose judgment and actions serve to advance their interests in a democratic society. But the focus of this essay is on the phenomenon, which is not implausible in a culture such as that of the United States, of being "blinded" by the ideal of autonomy. What happens if we value autonomy too much?

I will examine three possible outcomes. One, our commitment might lead us to believe, falsely, that all persons deserve autonomy, such that incursions of autonomy are never justified. This situation can be avoided once we settle upon a class of persons who, by their conduct, deserve protection of their autonomy. This classification rests on a negative test for desert modeled on John Stuart Mill's *harm principle*. Section IV will be devoted to an exploration of this issue.

A second problematic outcome arises when the premium that we place upon autonomy is tested by the very independence that it secures for us. The events of September 11, 2001, have compelled us to question the extent to which we should (and do) continue to regard autonomy as a good. We must confront the possibility that extreme measures that abrogate full autonomy will need to be undertaken in exchange for heightened security. Relaxed civil liberties protections, intensified scrutiny, and modified legal standards illustrate this tension.[1] Because the scope of this

---

* I thank the editors of *Social Philosophy & Policy* for their thoughtful comments. I am also grateful to colleagues who critiqued an early version of this essay. In particular, I benefitted from the insights of Ellen Frankel Paul and James Stacey Taylor.

[1] The following account offers some insight:

> Consider the case of Rabih Haddad, a Lebanese national active in the Muslim-American community in Ann Arbor, Mich[igan]. Mr. Haddad, 41, is among 326 individuals jailed in the federal investigation being conducted in unprecedented secrecy since the Sept. 11 attacks. . . . Arrested at his Ann Arbor home on Dec. 14 on a minor immigration violation, Mr. Haddad has been shunted through a series of closed-door court hearings and detention facilities in Detroit, Monroe County, and Chicago. His crime? No official will say, although it apparently has something to do with the Global

essay does not permit an exploration of this issue, I mention it primarily for consideration, briefly touching on the subject in Section V.

An injudicious attachment to the ideal of autonomy might result in a third state of affairs that is more pernicious and less easily resolved than the previous two. The worry is that, if we value autonomy too much, we might advocate the use of paternalistic measures to compel persons whom we identify as nonautonomous, or insufficiently autonomous, to become (more) self-directed. Is it coherent to attempt to force autonomy in a person by means that deny autonomy? I will turn to this discussion in Sections VI and VII.

II. The Concept of Autonomy

I understand personal autonomy as the condition of being self-directed, of having authority over one's choices and actions whenever these are significant to the direction of one's life. Personal autonomy as I construe it is a "global" phenomenon, a property of a person's life that expresses and unifies the will and choices of the person.[2] By contrast, the "local" or occurrent sense of autonomy is a property of a person's acts or desires considered individually, and pertains to the manner in which a person acts in particular situations.

In the global sense, a self-directed individual is one who sets goals for her life, goals that she has selected from a range of options and that she can hope to achieve as the result of her own action. Such goals are formulated according to values, desires, and convictions that have developed in an uncoerced fashion. They are goals that the individual would affirm as important to her were she to reflect upon their origin and content. One who does not care about her goals, or lacks goals altogether, might be moved about by others to the extent that self-direction becomes illusory. In addition, and most important, persons who are autonomous are parties to ongoing social relations that enable them to direct their lives

---

Relief Foundation of Chicago, which he co-founded. Muslims say the organization is a charity but federal officials suspect it was funneling money to the al-Qaeda terrorist organization. All of the immigration court proceedings involving Mr. Haddad have been secret. . . . He is being held indefinitely and, in effect, incommunicado. . . . Mr. Haddad may be guilty, or he may be innocent, although that's not the issue here. It's the manner in which he is judged. If his detention and trial—assuming there is one— were to be handled in public, there could be little room for accusations of unfairness. As it is, secrecy invites skepticism that is corrosive to the trust that underlies our system of democratic government.

Editorial, "Justice in Open Court," *The Toledo Blade*, March 12, 2002, A6.

[2] A "global" or dispositional phenomenon of autonomy is developed by Robert Young in his *Personal Autonomy: Beyond Negative and Positive Liberty* (New York: St. Martin's Press, 1986). Also see Paul Benson, "Autonomy and Oppressive Socialization," *Social Theory and Practice* 17 (1991): 385–408; and Paul Benson, "Free Agency and Self-Worth," *Journal of Philosophy* 91, no. 12 (1994): 650–68.

with a minimum of interference.[3] An autonomous person is able to meet her goals without depending upon the judgments of others as to the goals' validity and importance. One is autonomous when one is "an independent source of activity in the world."[4]

This definition suggests that an autonomous person is in control of her choices, her actions, and her will. Some philosophers suggest that a weak form of control suffices for autonomy—or, more properly, for responsibility—charging that a person can remain in "guidance control" of his choices, actions, and will even when subject to conditions that could undermine self-governance.[5] For example, a person who, for reasons of drug addiction, coercion, subordinate rank, or weakness of will, could not do otherwise than perform a particular act (ingest a drug, relinquish money to a mugger, execute a military order, or lapse from a diet) might nevertheless be deemed in control of his actions, and responsible for them, if he would have performed the act anyway, independently and of his own free will. Thus, guidance control is possible even in the face of factors that are sufficient to determine one's actions.[6]

While guidance control might suffice for responsibility, I advocate a more stringent interpretation of being in control for autonomy. When we say that a person is self-governing because she is in control of her actions and choices, we are saying more than that the person's actions coincide with preferences or values that are her own. We are also saying that the person has the power to determine how she will live. Being autonomous is not simply a matter of having values and preferences that mirror those a person holds under conditions in which control is absent. Rather, being autonomous is a matter of directing one's life according to such values and preferences.

Autonomy or self-directedness, so described, calls for positive freedom. This is not just independence from the directives of others, not just unobstructed authority over the domain of one's life, and not simply rugged individualism of the sort that negative freedom is said to supply. It is positive liberty of the sort associated with the desire and ability for self-governance, or the psychological resources for self-governance.

Control of the sort that autonomy requires assumes of an agent certain psychological characteristics and a history of experiences conducive to

---

[3] See Marina Oshana, "Personal Autonomy and Society," *The Journal of Social Philosophy* 29, no. 1 (1998): 81–102. This conception of autonomy incorporates Thomas Hurka's view of autonomy as the condition of intentional causal agency that involves deliberate choice among a variety of actions. See Thomas Hurka, "Why Value Autonomy?" *Social Theory and Practice* 13, no. 3 (1987): 361–82.

[4] Robert Kane, *The Significance of Free Will* (New York: Oxford University Press, 1998), 206.

[5] For an extensive discussion of guidance control, see John Martin Fischer and Mark Ravizza, *Responsibility and Control: A Theory of Moral Responsibility* (Cambridge: Cambridge University Press, 1998).

[6] Note that the species of control that I describe could be specified in compatibilist or incompatibilist terms. I make no claim about the metaphysics of control in this essay.

self-directed agency. These suggest a capacity for autonomy, consisting of the minimum of qualities that a person must possess in order to lead a self-directed life. This capacity is not a bare, potential condition of the kind that we expect might be realized at some future moment, for where capacity is understood in this looser sense—as potentiality—an infant, a comatose being, and an intelligent computer would all be capable of self-government. A threshold must be satisfied: one must, say, have reasonably astute cognitive skills and a developed set of values in order to be actually autonomous. As the possession of these qualities is a matter of degree, so the capacity for autonomy is a matter of degree and can be cultivated more or less successfully in persons.

So, let us assume the following. An autonomous individual has knowledge of her circumstances and of the effective forces that are operative in these circumstances.[7] Control of the relevant sort requires that an autonomous person have the capacity to make decisions about matters that are pertinent to the nature and the direction of her life, and that she be disposed to do so. Such decisions, for example, concern a person's choice of lifestyle, partners, and career. Impediments to a person's control may consist of inner, psychological obstacles such as neurotic compulsion, excessively low self-esteem, weakness of will, or addiction. But impediments to autonomy are frequently of an external, or social, nature.[8] Manipulation and intimidation carried out by others on the individual, unreasonable conformist attitudes and role expectations, sexism, racism, or poverty might all count as external or social impediments of the relevant sort. An autonomous person not only has the capacity for independent decision but also exercises it; the individual must not succumb to the

---

[7] To be in control in this sense is to be "sensitive to environmental circumstances so as to allow oneself as much elbow room as possible." See Daniel Dennett, *Elbow Room: The Varieties of Free Will Worth Wanting* (Cambridge, MA: MIT Press, 1984). This requirement suggests that autonomous agents must be self-aware and able to avoid situations that undermine the pursuit of their life-plans. It also implies that they be rational in the sense described by Robert Young. Young says:

> [B]eing rational can be seen as significant [to autonomy] in the following two positive ways. First, it brings coherence into the relationship between a person's general purposes and his or her particular actions. Some degree of understanding of this relationship will be needed to ensure that actions performed on particular occasions do not seriously thwart or impede more dispositional concerns. Second, and more importantly, perhaps, rationality equips a person to assess critically the advice tendered by others, an increasingly important safeguard given the extent to which we are reliant on the testimony of others about matters of great moment like health, welfare, education, economic and political affairs and so on.

Young, *Personal Autonomy*, 13.

[8] Following Joel Feinberg, constraints upon autonomy may be categorized as encompassing internal positive and negative impediments, such as neuroses or lack of skill, respectively, and external positive and negative impediments, such as physical barriers or coercive threats and inadequate economic resources, respectively. See Joel Feinberg, *Social Philosophy* (Englewood Cliffs, NJ: Prentice-Hall, 1973), 13.

well-intentioned or malevolent attempts of others to control her decisions, nor must she be disposed to impose impediments upon herself.[9]

Clearly, a number of individuals lack this capacity as I have described it. For example, a small child, an individual afflicted with Alzheimer's disease, and an insane person lack the rudimentary ability to be self-governing. Absent from all three is the characteristic of being a good "local sociologist," of apprehending the complexities of one's external environment, of consistently distinguishing malevolence from benevolence, and of comprehending the normative expectations of other persons and adapting one's behavior accordingly. Absent from all three is the power of self-appraisal and the ability to plan, to fix on preferences, and to function in a farseeing, deliberative, and self-protective manner. All three are creatures for whom certain forms of supervision and protection are appropriate. (Ideally, of course, children will acquire the necessary characteristics for self-determination as they mature.)

Now, if we value autonomy too highly, we might attempt to free a child from the supervision of her parents before she is qualified to care for herself. (As a product of the alternative education trend and a former emancipated minor of the 1970s, I can attest to the questionable benefit of premature liberation.) Valuing autonomy too much, we might act in haste, expecting those who cannot assume direction for themselves to do so.[10] Indiscriminately embracing the ideal of autonomy has social costs as well, because not infrequently, the community, or the state, will have to assume support for those persons who are ill-equipped to care for themselves. Too often, the result is that the full autonomy of these persons will be abridged.

These cases must be distinguished from circumstances that are faced by persons who possess the general capacity-conditions for self-determination, but who are prevented for various reasons from living autonomous lives. An imprisoned individual, for example, lacks liberty to interact with others in a manner that gives her control over the direction of her life. She also lacks a range of options, which we expect of one who can direct her own life. Negative freedom—an absence of interference or constraint—is, therefore, a necessary condition of autonomy. Positive freedom—liberty of the sort associated with the desire and ability for self-governance, or the psychological resources for self-governance—is needed for autonomy as well. But negative and positive freedom do not suffice for autonomy. A paraplegic who requires, but does not receive, adequate physical therapy, or perhaps lacks a vehicle to provide him with a minimum of mo-

---

[9] To quote Young: "[T]o be autonomous is not merely to have a capacity, nor the opportunity to exercise the capacity. Autonomy is an *exercise-concept*, to use Charles Taylor's phrase." Young, *Personal Autonomy*, 49.

[10] James Stacey Taylor has pointed out, in correspondence, that this may just indicate a mistake on the part of the parent in how to respond to the value of autonomy, or a misunderstanding of how to foster properly the development of autonomy. Taylor is correct, but in some cases—my own, for example—this misunderstanding was accompanied by a disproportionate emphasis on the worth of autonomy.

bility, has both negative and positive freedom, but because he must depend on others he may fail to live in a self-governing fashion. Similarly, a person suffers no lack of freedom simply because abject poverty forces him to depend on the willingness of his government and the good graces of others for the availability of social services that are essential to his support and survival. Nevertheless, he can be described as self-governing only in an attenuated sense. Autonomy, then, calls for the presence of certain social, political, and economic arrangements. An autonomous person's choices must not merely be unobstructed (by others or by internal obstacles) but, where realistic, these choices must be socially, politically, and economically within his or her reach.

Some persons may deliberately forge lives in which autonomy is absent, though they possess the capacity and the freedom to do otherwise. Consider the situation of a woman living under a Taliban regime such as that which controlled Afghanistan until 2001. Suppose that this woman has embraced the role of subservience and the abdication of independence that it demands, out of reverence, a sense of purpose, and an earnest belief in the sanctity of this role as espoused in certain passages of the Qu'ran. Having previously enjoyed a successful career as a physician, this woman has since chosen, under conditions free of whatever factors might disable self-awareness, and with a considered appreciation of the implications of her decision, a life of utter dependence. She can no longer practice medicine (indeed, she is no longer permitted access to information about the science of medicine). She is not permitted to support herself financially. She has no voice in the manner and duration of any schooling that her children, particularly her daughters, may receive. She must remain costumed in cumbersome garb—a burqa—when in public. She is forbidden to enter common places of worship. She knows that any transgression, any show of independence counts as heretical defiance and invites punishment both swift and harsh. But a life of subservience is consistent with the Taliban woman's spiritual and social values, provides her with a sense of worth, and satisfies her notion of well-being.

I think that it is evident that the Taliban woman is not autonomous. In a "local" or occurrent sense of the term, she has chosen autonomously. Nevertheless, she fails to be autonomous in a "global" sense for the obvious reason that the life that she chooses, and toward which she experiences no alienation, is a life in which she is systematically subject to the ultimate will of others. Although the Taliban woman is "master of her will"—her original decision was made autonomously, she willingly renounces her rights, and she continues to express satisfaction with the life that she has selected for herself—she now has no practical authority over her situation.[11] Although she lives in a manner consonant with her pref-

---

[11] The case of the individual who willfully relinquishes his rights of self-government (and does so in an authentic manner, under suitable psychological and historical conditions),

erences, and succeeds in achieving what she believes is in her best interests, the choices that she makes are guided almost entirely by the judgments and recommendations of others. Although the Taliban woman does what she wants, what she wants frustrates the exercise of autonomy.[12]

Since autonomy calls for more than upholding a person's values, it is the conditions under which a person lives that must provide the framework against which personal autonomy is continually assessed. A lack of autonomy on the part of the Taliban woman is not merely due to the fact that she comes to depend on others. Nor can this lack of autonomy be minimized by the fact that she might retain the respect of others. Rather, her lack of autonomy is determined by what this dependency entails for her in her daily life, and the respect of others does not compensate for this loss.

It is a stretch to call a person "autonomous" whose genuine valuing of subservience or unquestioned adherence to religious tradition leads her to live a life of dependency. It diminishes the concept of autonomy to call such a human being autonomous in these conditions, for human beings are distinguished from other creatures precisely because of their deliberative and creative capacities. We may call such a person autonomous if we mistake well-being for autonomy, but the road to autonomy is not always the road to achieving one's aims. What a person might have reason to do in order to secure autonomy can diverge from what she has reason to do in order to secure what she values, or what comports with her conception of well-being. For example, deeply religious persons might believe that their interests are best served by following, without question, the edicts of their leaders. Such persons will not value or seek autonomy.[13]

---

preferring to live under the dictates of a religious order, offers an interesting case of one who might preserve some important measure of autonomy. It also illustrates the extent to which a person's autonomy is a function of his relations with others. Contrast the situation of the Taliban woman with that of a monk. In the case of the monk, some autonomy is preserved in that, every day, it is up to the individual to decide whether to remain in the order and to continue living in a manner that denies him a fuller range of freedom. The monk retains autonomy over a series of ongoing decisions to be subservient. Although an institution has power over him sufficient to compel him to behave in a certain way, the monk can recall this power within whatever frame of time is designated by the terms that he has accepted, in much the same way that individuals have the freedom to renege on their marriage vows or the legal authority to dissolve the terms of certain contracts. (Breaking the vow or dissolving the contract may, of course, carry a penalty that is sufficiently burdensome to make autonomy an impossibility. And of course, the nature of the contract, in terms of what is required of the individual, will be important for assessments of autonomy.)

[12] This means that "identification" and satisfaction are not sufficient for autonomy, even in the absence of certain negative constraints, as analyses sympathetic to the work of Harry Frankfurt maintain. As Young states, "[W]e may identify with a certain occurrent motivation in such a way as to undermine comprehensive or dispositional autonomy." Young, *Personal Autonomy*, 43.

[13] The distinction between the two different ideals of self-realization and autonomy is important. Joseph Raz raises the distinction, stating that although autonomy is a factor that contributes to self-realization, "[t]he autonomous person is the one who makes his own life, and he may choose the path of self-realization or reject it. Nor is autonomy a precondition of self-realization, for one may stumble into a life of self-realization or be manipulated into

Alternatively, we may want to call the Taliban woman autonomous because we think of autonomy as a condition relativized to the satisfaction of a person's desires, or decided entirely by the stance that a person adopts toward her choices, desires, affective states, and personal relations. But this mistake results from confusing autonomy with one of its potential advantages, namely, that it can lead to personal contentment. If I am correct, then it is false that chosen social roles of any variety must be permissible if a person is to be self-directed.

For why *should* autonomy be a condition compatible with any conception of the good, with any social role, or with every life-plan? I suspect that those of us in liberal societies are drawn to the idea that autonomy can "in principle be satisfied by an indefinite number of ways of life,"[14] and are wary of the idea that only certain social arrangements befit self-directed agents. Not everyone will include an autonomous life among the goals that he or she regards as integral to well-being, and to suggest that there is *an* ideal end or way of life is more likely than not to impose *our* ideal upon others. This smacks of hegemony.

Autonomy as I have described it can comport with a variety of social arrangements. But, as Robert Kane notes, what has been called "value pluralism," the idea that the legitimate "ends of men are many, and not all of them are compatible with others"[15] need not entail value relativism. Value pluralism of the kind that is required for free will and for autonomy "does not imply that any end or way of life is just as good as any other— for all persons, or for a particular person at a particular time."[16] It is not insensitive to state that the types of lives that a properly autonomous person can live are limited. Such lives need not accord with an archetype of autonomy that reflects the alleged perspective of Western society, where autonomy is valorized ("fetishized" might be more accurate if one accepts the broader allegation) as a condition of atomistic, self-created individuals, insulated from the influence and guidance of others.

To deny the autonomy of the Taliban woman is not to show disrespect or to demonstrate insensitivity to her values, choices, and commitments. One might well admire the woman for the depth of her commitment and the richness and fulfillment that this brings to her life, while rightly recognizing that such a life lacks autonomy. Similarly, one might esteem— even desire to emulate—an individual who forsakes all of her aspirations to lead a life of service. Nonetheless, it is not uncontroversial that we should value such a life and the social roles that it mandates. This is not because *our* culture does not happen to value this way of life, but because

it or reach it in some other way which is inconsistent with autonomy." Joseph Raz, *The Morality of Freedom* (Oxford: Clarendon Press, 1986), 376–77.
    [14] Isaiah Berlin, "Two Concepts of Liberty," in Isaiah Berlin, *Four Essays on Liberty* (Oxford: Oxford University Press, 1969), 169.
    [15] Kane, *The Significance of Free Will*, 203.
    [16] Ibid., 200.

it is a way of life that is inconsonant with autonomy, and autonomy itself is of considerable objective importance for all persons, whether or not it is of subjective importance to a particular individual.

III. Autonomy and Liberal Society

Some philosophers worry that autonomy is a condition that, at worst, necessitates the detachment of an agent from others and, at best, encourages this. Understanding autonomy in this manner, these philosophers question whether it is a desirable trait of persons. For example, these philosophers worry that insofar as the autonomous agent may be unresponsive to shared values and objective standards of good judgment, autonomy is a condition likely to disrupt various cooperative enterprises and relations premised on values such as caring and commitment. The worry is not that autonomy may nonetheless be valued immoderately. Rather, the concern is whether autonomy ought to be valued at all. I take issue elsewhere with these objections to an ideal of autonomy, and I will pursue the subject here only in an attenuated fashion.[17]

That autonomy as I have described it is valued as a means to realizing the ideal of democratic societies cannot be disputed. A democracy is, roughly, a sociopolitical alliance of agents who, through representation or direct participation, engage in the task of political governance. The judicial, the political, and the legislative systems of any liberal democracy rely on the participation of self-reliant, self-directed persons. It is through the activity of such persons that liberal political principles and policies are generated and garner legitimacy. Hence, a person who fails to be self-governing, whose reasons for choice and action are appropriated by others, lacks an essential component of democratic citizenship, namely, the authority to speak for oneself and to be an active participant in an important range of one's experiences.

In some circumstances this person may display a veneer of democratic involvement. She may, for example, vote, seek public office, or have legal action taken against her. Because she does not manage her own life-choices, however, the responsibility for representative governance that is assigned to her by the democratic ideal remains illusory. While such a person has liberty, she lacks autonomy. But the liberty of persons that is so essential to democratic society is of little practical value if the more primary value of autonomy is absent. Lawrence Haworth comments that in a situation of this sort, "although one confronts numerous and fecund options, one totally lacks [the] capacity to exercise them autonomously. One has choices to make, but consistently makes them heteronomously."[18]

---

[17] I address this concern in Marina Oshana, "The Autonomy Bogeyman," *Journal of Value Inquiry* 35, no. 2 (2001): 209-26.

[18] Lawrence Haworth, *Autonomy: An Essay in Philosophical Psychology and Ethics* (New Haven, CT: Yale University Press, 1986), 143.

More generally, agent autonomy is essential if any society, democratic or otherwise, is to survive. Consider a society in which a despotic regime is sovereign. Safeguarding the status quo appears to call for an absence of autonomy on the part of the citizenry. Autonomy is not broadly valued; the populace consists of persons who, worthy or not, capable or otherwise, are accorded a status similar to that of children. Those few who are autonomous undertake a parental role, supervising the activities and lives of others, by measures typically harsh. A political regime of this character can be sustained only with difficulty, even assuming that the populace is able to exercise self-restraint and to configure their lives to the arrangements determined by the authoritarian regime. Because the majority of persons would not be autonomous and so would be unaccustomed to decision-making, risk-taking, and innovation, there simply will be a minimum of persons who are qualified to assume the administrative burden of such a society.

Sustaining a despotic regime is a challenge for a more fundamental reason. As persons, we care about our ability to leave a trace, or a lasting impression, upon the world, a legacy made unique by our involvement. And we want this legacy to reflect a life of self-governance. We do not, as a rule, wish simply to reside in the world or to be moved through it. We are not simply objects made happy through the activities of others. Rather, we want to engage in activities that reflect self-competence and to pursue projects that bear our imprint rather than the imprint of other persons. This claim is contentious, but I think that evidence bears its truth. Whether our choices and actions be for good or for evil, we care that these choices and actions are ours, and that in forming them and in executing them we do not simply borrow from others but realize our autonomy.

One may experience contentment as a member of a despotic society. Indeed, absent autonomy, the intensity of pleasure and preference satisfaction may increase—think of a member of Walden Two, the fictional utopian society described by B. F. Skinner, or of a person attached to Robert Nozick's "experience machine." [19] But these people know a different and, I would contend, inferior variety of satisfaction than the contentment that is known by one who is a subject and not just an object, an agent and not a patient. Haworth has a point when he states: "Pleasure and preference satisfaction lose value in proportion as the pleased or satisfied individual lacks autonomy." [20]

IV. AUTONOMY AND DESERT

Whether one who is capable of autonomy, or self-determination, is *worthy* of an autonomous life remains an open question. Autonomy is the

[19] See B. F. Skinner, *Walden Two* (New York: Macmillan Press, 1962); and Robert Nozick, *Anarchy, State, and Utopia* (New York: Basic Books, 1974), 42–45.
[20] Haworth, *Autonomy*, 183.

default position; we assume that its *possession* is independent of the question of desert. But the idea that self-determination is a condition to be *promoted* only for deserving persons is quite plausible when self-determination is thought of as a characteristic that persons develop and retain in virtue of their relations to others. Although autonomy as I have been discussing it is a "global" state of persons, the issue of desert arises primarily when autonomy is regarded "locally," as a condition predicated of persons vis-à-vis a certain activity, situation, or class of rights enjoyed in a social context.[21]

The class of undeserving persons may be divided between those who are undeserving on moral grounds and those who are so for pragmatic reasons. Not every undeserving person is morally destitute. Consider the case of Nancy, a narcoleptic. Assume that Nancy is fully capable of assessing her motives for action and bearing responsibility for her actions. Assume, too, that although driving is not usually a necessary condition for autonomy, Nancy is employed as a travelling saleswoman. Driving is something that she must do if she is to keep her job, and jobs are hard to come by.

Nancy's occupation gives her reason to drive, although at grave risk to herself and others. By continuing to drive, Nancy exploits the qualities that befit her for self-determination in such a manner as to pose a danger to herself and to others. Denying Nancy the freedom to drive would diminish her autonomy, but in exercising self-determination, in acting autonomously, persons must be sensitive to the interests of others. Nancy's economic interests are important, and her subsistence needs must be met, but only in a way that poses no unjustified threat to others. (I say "unjustified" because there are, of course, numerous occupations that pose justified threats to others. Military activity, law enforcement, and the practice of medicine are examples.) As a rational agent and a member of society, Nancy has an obligation not to imperil others needlessly. Because she chooses to ignore this responsibility, she does not deserve autonomy with respect to her freedom to drive, and measures that restrict her autonomy are called for.

In a case such as Nancy's, the agent is regarded as an autonomous being, as a being in control of herself. She is also a responsible agent, able to appreciate the normative import of her conduct and accountable for her actions. Yet we find it neither necessary nor desirable to respect Nancy's autonomy in a way that we might think befits an ideal. The criterion

---

[21] In conversation and correspondence, James Stacey Taylor has pressed the following important point, which I can only mention in abbreviated fashion. This is that the idea that autonomy is conditional upon desert allows incursions upon autonomy whenever it is decided that a person has fallen short of some independently specified ideal of character or behavior. If, instead, autonomy is the default condition, and it is assumed that persons have a right (of sorts) to autonomy, then the burden of proof for justifiable incursions upon autonomy rests on the encroacher.

of desert acts as a constraint upon what we will do and should do in order to promote a person's autonomy. Valuing autonomy too highly may tempt us to overlook the desirability of this constraint.

Consider the following case.[22] Shelley is a schizophrenic. She is also a talented artist whose work is celebrated by the art establishment and commands a substantial price on the market. Unfortunately, Shelley is at her creative best when working under the momentum of her illness. Although her schizophrenia subjects her to torment, delusion, and unsettling antisocial behavior, it also supplies the thematic framework of her work, and enhances the vision and the breadth of her work. Taking her medication gives her life a prosaic quality: she feels lifeless and uninspired. Citing the values of artistic license and individual flourishing (not to mention the lucrative benefits that her artwork secures), Shelley chooses to discontinue use of her medication. Once off her medication, Shelley lacks autonomy; it is the schizophrenia, and not she, that motivates her behavior. But she regards her self-imposed, voluntary abridgment of personal autonomy as a manifestation of her individuality or self-expression. Are incursions to Shelley's autonomy justified? That is, is it permissible to force persons such as Shelley to take their medication when doing so means an irreplaceable loss of individual fulfillment?

What I will call the *negative test for autonomy* raises the issue of when a person's autonomy may justifiably be violated or rescinded. This test focuses on the criteria for desert. Under what conditions does the capable person no longer deserve protection of her autonomy? One way of formulating the test can be found in John Stuart Mill's effort to fuse an alliance between the spheres of liberty and authority. Mill argues that, since people are members of society (and of narrower, more formal associations), tensions will inevitably arise between the provinces of individual freedom and social authority.

Following Mill, I hold that under normal circumstances, individuality, as a manifestation of autonomy that we value, must be protected from the "tyranny" of social custom and the collective authority of society. This tyranny seeks

> to impose, by means other than civil penalties, its own ideas and practices as rules of conduct on those who dissent from them; to fetter the development and, if possible, prevent the formation of any individuality not in harmony with its aims. . . .[23]

---

[22] The example of the mentally ill artist was raised by Ellen Frankel Paul and others in discussion.

[23] John Stuart Mill, *On Liberty*, ed. Currin V. Shields (1859; reprint, New York: Macmillan, 1956), 7.

Because some threats to individuality are unavoidable, the variety of control and the extent of the power that can rightfully be exercised by society over an individual must be ascertained.

Mill does this by appealing to a general-interest principle known as the liberty principle. Negatively formulated as the *harm principle*, it states that

> the sole end for which mankind are warranted, individually and collectively, in interfering with the liberty of action of any of their number is self-protection. That the only purpose for which power can be rightfully exercised over any member of a civilized community, against his will, is to prevent harm to others. *His own good, either physical or moral, is not a sufficient warrant*.[24]

We rely on something very much like Mill's harm principle in determining when autonomy ought to be protected and preserved, and when it ought not to receive such protection. Like individuality, autonomy is a highly valued state for capable and deserving persons and requires for its preservation freedom from undue interference, or negative freedom.[25]

Additionally, the harm principle establishes useful parameters for individual autonomy by showing that autonomy can be cultivated "within the limits imposed by the rights and interests of others."[26] It does this by employing a distinction between self-regarding and other-regarding conduct. Self-regarding actions, thoughts, and opinions are, on Mill's account, those in which other members of society have no interest, because the expression of these affects only the individual himself directly and in the first instance. Mill maintains that *any* interference with those actions of an individual that are purely self-regarding constitutes an illegitimate violation of that person's self-determination. Thus,

> [m]en should be free to act upon their opinions . . . to carry these out in their lives without hindrance, either physical or moral, from their

---

[24] Ibid., 13, my emphasis.

[25] Berlin challenges Mill's claim that negative freedom—freedom from undue interference—is a necessary condition for human flourishing. Berlin argues that the link between the notions of negative liberty and the ideal of character that Mill envisions "is, at best, empirical," since ". . . integrity, love of truth, and fiery individualism" can be highly valued, and indeed can flourish, "in severely disciplined communities" as readily as they can in more tolerant communities. (Berlin, "Two Concepts of Liberty," 128.) I am not certain that this is true. Consider that Mill defends the value of not only truth and integrity, but also social progress. In order for the latter to ensue, the community must be responsive to the creatively nonconformist individual, and so it must loosen its reign upon the individual. Moreover, Mill claims only that *undue* interference must be absent; it is questionable whether he would call every instance of influence and discipline (such as that which certain religious communities embrace) "undue."

[26] Mill, *On Liberty*, 76.

fellow men, so long as it is at their own risk and peril. This last proviso is of course indispensable.[27]

When a person behaves in ways that we find injurious to the self-determination of others, either by "doing evil" or by failing to prevent evil, or when a person violates certain accepted codes for social behavior, or abdicates "a distinct and assignable obligation to any other person or persons," even when this action consists of injury that the person does to himself, "the case is taken out of the self-regarding class and becomes amenable to moral disapprobation in the proper sense of the term."[28] No longer in the realm of liberty, such conduct becomes subject to morality and law, where punitive measures that include a diminution of personal autonomy may be taken as justified and legitimate. We may interfere with the affairs of another person, even those that are of profound importance and interest to that person's life, when these pose a threat to others.

V. WHEN VALUING AUTONOMY IS AN ISSUE

What are the legitimate restrictions that can be placed upon autonomy when circumstances are *not* normal? Are the harm principle and the corollary distinction between self-regarding and other-regarding conduct subtle enough to provide parameters for autonomy at such times?

In less than normal circumstances, threats to the autonomy of deserving individuals can be great. Protections from the tyranny of majority sentiment, from encroachment upon civil liberties and constitutionally mandated rights, and from the infliction of loss, falsehood, duplicity, and the like take on a heightened urgency. In the aftermath of the December 7, 1941 attack on Pearl Harbor, Japanese-American citizens who had harmed no one were dispossessed of their autonomy and their property, and were treated in this way with the overwhelming approval of the United States populace. In the aftermath of the unprecedented terrorist events of September 11, 2001, circumstances have been anything but normal. A rekindled patriotism has tempered the willingness of many American citizens

[27] Ibid., 67. Mill correctly notes a "distinction between the loss of consideration which a person may rightly incur by defect of prudence or personal dignity, and the reprobation which is due to him for an offense against the rights of others." (Ibid., 96.) The difference here is one of a loss of respect or esteem from others in the first instance, and a loss of autonomy, or individuality, in the second. When a person's self-regarding actions are foolish, others may regard him with distaste, pity, or even contempt, but this lack of respect must never translate into a punitive act against the agent's individuality. In response to "that portion of [a person's] character and conduct which concern his own good . . . which do not affect the interests of others in their relations with him," we are entitled to visit upon the agent certain inconveniences or penalties. Such penalties may be quite severe—they may include forms of ostracism and discriminatory treatment. But these must be only the natural and inseparable result of the actor's conduct. (Ibid., 95.) And they must go no further than is permitted by the expression of our own individuality.
[28] Ibid., 99.

to criticize openly, or even question, the political and military policies of the United States. Restrictions that fetter individual autonomy have become commonplace and enjoy increasing public approval.[29] There is heightened support for surveillance cameras on select street corners of select urban neighborhoods. Passenger profiling and personal searches at public transport facilities have increased. Investigations of personal computer use and electronic communication have intensified. Persons have been detained, incommunicado, for unspecified crimes. Although restrictions on autonomy are not always or principally privacy concerns, privacy protections are generally essential for autonomy. The aforementioned security measures, both overt and covert, yield, *at a minimum*, a decline in the level of civil liberty that most of us cherish and regard as crucial to unimpaired self-governance. (Detainment by federal authorities for weeks or months unambiguously assails the detainee's exercise of self-government.)

If anything positive has come out of the horrific events of September 11, 2001, it is that the United States is a more unified, kinder, and gentler nation. Or so the story goes. But it is also a more vigilant and suspicious nation. So perhaps the following scenario is not too great a departure into fiction:

> The citizens of Bordertown are agitated by the events of September 11, 2001. Since that date, they have garnered increasing support for intensifying anti-immigration policies in the nation. Anti-immigration sentiment in the community runs high, and with some good reason. Bordertown is located in uncomfortable proximity to Migrantville, which is suspected as a breeding ground for terrorists. Although the law enforcement officials of Bordertown and of Migrantville have yet to confront indiscriminate violence against innocent members of the "migrant foreign element," the officials impose a curfew, rescind concealed weapons laws, and, in collusion with the media and local ecumenical councils, embark on a disinformation campaign that is intended to foster social unity.

[29] The Associated Press reported (June 12, 2002) that "four in five Americans would give up some freedoms to gain security": One-third of Americans surveyed favor making it easier for authorities to access private e-mail and phone conversations; more than 70 percent favor requiring U.S. citizens to carry identification cards with fingerprints. The *USA Patriot Act*, 107 P.L. 56, which was passed by the United States Congress in 2001, provides the Central Intelligence Agency with access to U.S. Justice Department records, including secret testimony developed in grand jury investigations. U.S. Attorney General John Ashcroft has issued executive directives allowing the Federal Bureau of Investigation (FBI) to eavesdrop on conversations between lawyers and their imprisoned clients in certain cases, and has given the FBI greater freedom to use wiretaps and to investigate people, even if they are not suspected of committing any crime. Certainly these amount to incursions upon privacy. How they affect the ability of persons to live self-governed lives remains to be seen: Self-governance and an open society go hand in hand.

These measures plainly erode the autonomy of the citizens. Are such measures justified as being in the best interest of the populace? Even if the end supports the means in this case, it is still an open question whether the cost in diminished autonomy is excessive.

When are such encroachments on autonomy warranted? Post-September 11, 2001, do we confront a situation akin to that described by Thomas E. Hill, Jr.? Hill remarks:

> If . . . the only way to persuade someone to make a decision that will prevent a riot or a series of murders were to make an otherwise impermissible threat or a nonrational appeal to his weaknesses, then surely most would grant that such interference would be justified. Though important, autonomy need not be considered an absolute right.[30]

Such scenarios remind us that although autonomy is a condition that we value in persons, it is not the sole or overarching good. Security may surpass autonomy in value and may justify constraints on the freedom necessary for autonomy. Attributes of character such as compassion, generosity, service to others, or a willingness to compromise may also exceed autonomy in importance.[31] Isaiah Berlin assumes that there are values higher than autonomy that bear protection, and the protection of which calls for restrictions on individual freedom. He states:

> I do not wish to say that individual freedom is, even in the most liberal societies, the sole, or even the dominant, criterion of social action. We compel children to be educated, and we forbid public executions. These are certainly curbs to freedom. We justify them on the ground that ignorance, or a barbarian upbringing, or cruel pleasures and excitements are worse for us than the amount of restraint needed to repress them.[32]

VI. Paternalism for the Sake of Autonomy

By expanding the criteria for desert, we might rightly narrow the class of persons against whom infringements to autonomy are in general unjustified. Candidates must respect the harm principle, and they must

---

[30] Thomas E. Hill, Jr., "Self-Respect Reconsidered," in Thomas E. Hill, Jr., *Autonomy and Self-Respect*, (Cambridge: Cambridge University Press, 1991), 259.

[31] I am, then, in agreement with Feinberg when he notes that "autonomy is not the whole of virtue, and may be made to look bad if it keeps bad company. (Imagine an inflexibly conscientious Robbespierre)." Joel Feinberg, *Harm to Self*, vol. 3 of *The Moral Limits of Criminal Law* (New York: Oxford University Press, 1986), 40.

[32] Berlin, "Two Concepts of Liberty," 169.

meet other conditions as well. Strengthening the criteria enables us to test our belief that autonomy is an optimal condition for persons. If autonomy is a condition that we think persons ought to enjoy, then to what extent should pains be taken to protect and promote that state? Is it permissible — and for the best — to take paternalistic steps to restore autonomy in deserving persons? When does interference with affairs that are of profound importance and interest to another person constitute a harm, a violation of the person's autonomy? As the stories of the Taliban woman and the schizophrenic artist suggest, certain attributes that might promote or strengthen a person's autonomy might be quite undesirable from the perspective of the good of the individual.[33]

While the harm principle permits the state to protect individuals against the choices and activities of others, and to restrict certain actions on the grounds of preventing harm to others, paternalistic actions cannot be justified by appealing to other-regarding harm. Let us understand paternalistic action as interference with a person's autonomy that seeks justification "by reasons referring exclusively to the welfare, good, happiness, needs, interests or values of the person. . . ."[34] We offend a person's autonomy by paternalistic means when we endeavor to impose on the person a conception of what is a worthy and proper life. We do this either by preventing the person from doing whatever she has decided to do, or by interfering with the way in which she reaches her decision.

---

[33] Consider the case of Mark, a megalomaniac. Mark can recover from his megalomania if provided with proper treatment. But in virtue of his neurosis, Mark is motivated to care for his family and to fulfill the role of a valued community leader. Because Mark is dominated by a neurotic disorder, he is not autonomous with regard to his behavior. Yet Mark is a more attentive parent and spouse, and a more estimable neighbor when motivated non-autonomously, by his neurosis, than he would be were he to undergo treatment for his megalomania and thus experience a full state of autonomy. Even if Mark would be better off were he to be freed of his neurosis, those who are close to him, whose interests he, presumably, holds dear, would likely suffer as a result.

[34] Gerald Dworkin, "Paternalism," *The Monist* 56 (1972): 65. I will confine my remarks to what Dworkin calls "pure" paternalism, and what Feinberg labels "direct" or "one-party" paternalism, where "the class of persons whose freedom is restricted . . . is identical with the class of persons whose benefit is intended to be promoted" by such restrictions (Dworkin, "Paternalism," 68). Feinberg contrasts paternalistic activity with the phenomenon of legal paternalism. Legal paternalism is expressed by the principle that "the need to prevent self-inflicted harm [is] a legitimizing reason for coercive legislation. . . ." (Feinberg, *Harm to Self*, 8). Legal paternalism concerns the manner in which criminal legislation can be granted moral legitimacy, and its tools are penal *regulations* that function as "coercive interferences with liberty" rather than paternalistic *actions* that need not involve or endorse coercive legislation. Hence, the target of paternalistic rules is always liberty of action, and paternalistic rules always involve the use of coercion or force. Legal paternalism, unlike the harm principle, is not mediated by the maxim that "a person is not wronged by that to which he consents. . . . B's consent to A's action, even though that action is harmful or dangerous to B's interests, exempts A from criminal liability under the harm principle, but does not exempt him under indirect legal paternalism." (Feinberg, *Harm to Self*, 11.)

Four things are required in order for an act to be paternalistic:

1. Since paternalism *just is* that which offends autonomy, those who are subject to paternalistic action must be capable of autonomy (though not necessarily deserving of autonomy). Therefore, children cannot be subjects of paternalistic action so construed.
2. The act uses compulsion (although not necessarily coercion) to promote the well-being of a subject, or to achieve some benefit that may or may not be recognized as a benefit by the one for whom it is intended.[35]
3. In cases where we wish to protect a person from a harm, incurring the harm requires the active cooperation of the victim.
4. To the extent that the agent is aware of the paternalistic measure, the agent does not (or would not) want to be treated in this way.[36]

Paternalism usurps autonomy because it substitutes one person's judgment for another's. Suppose that a friend in the United States military is tormented about his homosexuality, torn between his need to be forthright about his sexual orientation and his allegiance to the military policy of "don't ask, don't tell" on openness about homosexuality. If I reveal the homosexuality of my friend to his supervising officer because I believe that doing so will alleviate the unhappiness that my friend is experiencing, and in the long run will best promote his psychological esteem, I invade my friend's privacy, and I invade his autonomy. And my intervention most certainly invites substantial changes in my friend's life that he might fail to welcome. My motives need not be malicious. But because I have acted to promote what I perceive to be this person's well-being, where doing so is not welcome, my action is paternalistic.

Disquieting scenarios involving paternalism occur when persons who possess the capacity for self-determination *and* who are at least minimally deserving of self-determination (since they do not violate the harm principle) find their self-determination jeopardized by being subjected to even the most benevolent of paternalistic gestures. Interferences of this sort are worrying, if only because they threaten to make systematic violations of liberties more acceptable. Mill, Hill, and Berlin, among others, voice such worries.

---

[35] To "compel" action is to necessitate an action by force of some sort: it may include gentle persuasion or temptation. To "coerce" is to compel behavior by use of pressure, threats, or intimidation.

[36] Note that this list does not specify anything about the *manner* in which a person is prevented from exercising her autonomy. Whether manipulation, brute force, or rational persuasion is used is insufficient to determine cases of paternalism. Paternalism just consists in the practice of imposing a putative good on a person when that person does not welcome the imposition. See Dworkin, "Paternalism," 68.

In speaking of the value of individuality and the nature of self-regarding conduct, for example, Mill tells us that the person most interested in the well-being of an individual is the individual himself, and if the individual is a reasonable, mature adult, he should be granted "perfect freedom, legal and social, to do the action and stand the consequences."[37] No other person should tell him "not to do with his life for his own benefit what he chooses to do with it."[38]

Even when persons engage in behavior "which experience has shown not to be useful to any person's individuality," or act in ways that are "injurious to happiness and . . . a hindrance to improvement,"[39] intervention, says Mill, is permitted only to prevent a graver harm to the larger social body. In order to justify compelling a person to do what another believes is best, Mill adds, "the conduct from which it is desired to deter him *must be calculated to produce evil in someone else*. . . . Over his own body and mind, the individual is sovereign."[40]

Hill's concern is with the "many ways in which narrow utilitarian thinking can foster unwarranted interference in others' lives."[41] Although Hill restricts his discussion to the phenomenon of lying, his remarks have implications for the more general phenomenon of paternalistic interference. He offers several conceptions of autonomy, and he argues that each of these incorporates moral principles that oppose the phenomenon of benevolent lying as one that demonstrates a lack of respect for the autonomy of persons.

Hill claims that it is irrelevant whether the paternalistic intervention is intended to protect a person from discomfort or to augment that person's independence. When one knowledgeable, sane person is subject either to deliberate deception or to a voluntary withholding of information by another, "one's opportunity to live in rational control of one's life" is curtailed.[42] Paternalistic intervention displays a disrespect for persons by treating them as incapable of choosing their own courses of life.

Hill argues that, if we agree that individuals have a right to autonomy, then interferences to this right via paternalistic gestures such as benevolent lying will be justified only if the action that would occur in the absence of the paternalistic gesture is so disastrous as to override the individual's claim to autonomy as a right. What would count as suffi-

[37] Mill, *On Liberty*, 92.

[38] Ibid., 93.

[39] Ibid., 98.

[40] Ibid., 13, my emphasis. Note that what Mill appeals to here in defending the right of noninterference is the utility principle. His injunctions against paternalism as well as the harm principle emanate from the principle of utility. Berlin points out that other principles, such as the categorical imperative, prescriptions of natural law, or the inviolability of a social contract, might equally be employed. See Berlin, "Two Concepts of Liberty," 127.

[41] Thomas E. Hill, Jr., "Autonomy and Benevolent Lies," *The Journal of Value Inquiry* 18 (1984): 251.

[42] Ibid., 265. The offensive character of a paternalistic lie is commensurate with the extent to which the activity affected by the lie is significant for the individual's life-plan.

ciently disastrous remains an open question. Would the self-regarding aim of the individual to destroy his own autonomy qualify?

Berlin expresses similar concerns, though he restricts his comments to cautioning us against paternalistic acts that arise out of a particular interpretation of positive freedom. Specifically, Berlin asserts that the positive idea of freedom, understood as self-mastery, invites unwarranted interference when it is interpreted as the domination of the agent by his "real" or "ideal" self, as opposed to his baser, impulsive, and passionate nature.[43] Although positive freedom understood as "freedom by self-control" lends itself most readily to this partitioning of the self, Berlin notes that an account of negative freedom can lead to a similar result. Berlin states: "[T]he self that should not be interfered with is [not] the individual with his actual wishes and needs . . . but the 'real' man within, identified with the pursuit of some ideal purpose not dreamed of by his empirical self."[44] This account of the person accords reason the role of the dispassionate "true" self, and relegates the more empirical aspect of the agent to the lower, animal self. These persona are taken to be discordant: A struggle ensues between "the transcendent, dominant controller, and the empirical bundle of desires and passions to be disciplined and brought to heel."[45]

This idea of self-mastery assumes that it is only the self *qua* rational will whose wishes must be heeded, even when the individual demands otherwise. The outcome, Berlin argues, is that this true self takes on a fetishized character. It somehow becomes identified with whatever larger social or institutional collective body is given reign over the expressed wishes of the individual. Berlin remarks that just as

> [t]he reason within me . . . must eliminate and suppress my "lower" instincts, my passions and desires, which render me a slave; similarly . . . the higher elements in society—the better educated, the more rational, those who "possess the highest insight of their time and people"—may exercise compulsion to rationalize the irrational section of society. For . . . by obeying the rational man we obey ourselves: not indeed as we are, sunk in our ignorance and our passions . . . but as we could be if we were rational.[46]

The phenomenon that Berlin describes gives rise to what I will call *rational consent* varieties of paternalism. If the rational consent model is correct, then paternalistic action will be justified as long as it is taken in the name of the agent's true self. The action will not be viewed as one that

---

[43] Berlin, "Two Concepts of Liberty," 132, 134.
[44] Ibid., 134.
[45] Ibid.
[46] Ibid., 150.

the individual would want *were he otherwise*, but will be said to express what the individual does in fact really (though not expressly) want. Under such circumstances, argue advocates of the rational-consent justificatory scheme, no interference to the individual's freedom in fact occurs. Since the action is carried out by the individual's real self against his "less real" self, the individual is, in fact, the actor. As long as a person is not interfered with by factors alien to the person's rational (even if unrecognized) self, the person is autonomous.

However, this belief—that actions made by proxy for the rational true self are efforts that the individual *in fact* wills autonomously, even when these actions evoke the most intense rejection and resistance from the individual—is counterintuitive. It also carries tremendous potential for exploitation. Berlin, for example, worries that the two-self ideal breeds moral and political despotism. The assumption that the agent who does not act from his rational self fails to act freely entails that no brand of paternalistic action against such a person (no matter how sane that person appears and regardless of how offensive the paternalistic action) can be deemed a violation of the person's autonomy. Once the rational consent position is adopted,

> I am in a position to ignore the actual wishes of men or societies, to bully, oppress, torture them in the name, and on behalf, of their 'real' selves, in the secure knowledge that whatever is the true goal of man ... [it] must be identical with ... the free choice of his 'true', albeit often submerged and inarticulate, self.[47]

Requiring that the autonomous individual be ideally rational, disposed to sublimate her empirical nature for her dispassionate side, and making this the locus of individualism and personal freedom countenances a state of affairs potentially hostile to the negative species of freedom espoused in Mill's liberalism. It also severely limits the class of people whom we call autonomous. The idea that there is a particularly correct way of life, and a correct set of creeds that sustain the rationalist vision, invites intolerance and the suppression of opinions. No longer is autonomy an ideal associated with individual responsibility and self-mastery but, ironically, autonomy becomes a species of self-perfection. The case of the Taliban woman commands our attention in this regard. Ought paternalistic measures be taken in the name of her true self to remove her from the grip of the Taliban?

VII. Autonomy and the Value of Paternalism

As the preceding discussion indicates, it is especially difficult to weigh the value and desirability of autonomy against that of paternalism in

---

[47] Ibid., 133.

situations where a person's self-directed actions threaten the person's autonomy, and where paternalism might avert this threat.

Furthermore, there are varieties of paternalism. Gerald Dworkin distinguishes between "soft" (or "weak") and "hard" paternalistic acts. A necessary condition of soft paternalism is that the person for whom we act paternalistically is incompetent in some sense.[48] Interference with a person's autonomy is permitted when there is thought to be an occurrent or a dispositional defect in the decision-making capacities of the person who is interfered with, and when it is believed that consent would be forthcoming were the person's decision-making capacities revived.

The real challenge is posed by cases that we might want to characterize as appropriate targets for paternalistic intervention, but in which we lack a credible reason for deeming the agents incompetent and their actions involuntary. In such cases, Dworkin notes, "hard paternalism may be the only position which can justify restrictions on such actions."[49] "Hard" paternalism is the view that an acceptable reason for paternalistic legislation is the necessity of protecting competent adults, against their wills, from the harmful consequences of even their fully voluntary undertakings. Dworkin attempts to avoid the hard paternalistic position in such cases by arguing for a "hypothetical consent scheme for justifying paternalism" via the "soft" view. Justifications of paternalism based on hypothetical consent turn on the assumption that, to some degree, competent adult individuals are vulnerable to the same cognitive, emotional, and epistemic failings as are their less competent counterparts. It is also assumed that rational persons wish to protect themselves from cognitive deficiencies and incompetence. Dworkin's idea is that soft paternalism is justified when an agent's action is voluntarily undertaken, but it poses a real risk, of which the agent is not aware or does not sufficiently appreciate. Paternalistic protections or limitations on certain conduct are appropriate if they are ones that rational individuals antecedently would willingly and collectively establish, and would consent to as "social insurance policies."[50]

---

[48] Gerald Dworkin, "Paternalism: Some Second Thoughts," in Rolf Sartorius, ed., *Paternalism* (Minneapolis: University of Minnesota Press, 1983), 107. Feinberg also distinguishes between "soft" and "hard" paternalism but, instead of making soft paternalism a feature of the actor's competence, views it as determined by the involuntary nature of the harm suffered by the actor. The idea is that we can permissibly protect a person from self-regarding harm only when the harm is substantially nonvoluntary (or when intervention is required in order to determine whether it is voluntary or not). Soft paternalism is intended to affect only "wrongfully" suffered harm, i.e., harm that the subject does not consent to. Given that the person fails to consent to the harm, Feinberg rightly questions how action or legislation taken against the harm can truly be called paternalistic.

[49] Ibid., 109.

[50] Dworkin, "Paternalism," 78. The parameters of justifiable interferences will be determined in either of two ways. We might focus on the rationality and competence of the individuals involved or we might examine the decisions that the individual makes. On the former approach we ask whether the individual suffers from some degree of cognitive

For example, Dworkin notes that if we can show that a person who values slavery for its instrumental powers—believing, perhaps, that slavery will maximize some other, more highly desired good—suffers from a misapprehension, or a mistaken calculation about how best to obtain the primary good that he seeks, then we will be justified in imposing certain mandates regarding this person's behavior. Doing so "minimizes the risk of harm . . . at the cost of a trivial interference with . . . freedom."[51]

But when the targets of intervention are adults, the hypothetical consent model that is invoked to justify soft paternalistic restrictions lends itself to the worries that Berlin explores regarding rational consent models. Surely, every interference with freedom is not trivial, especially from the perspective of the one who is interfered with. Forcing the Taliban woman to abandon her way of life counts to her as a substantial harm, the cost of which is her purported flourishing. Yet Berlin concedes that there are times when it is defensible to compel a person to do one's will, or the will of a larger group, under the guise of promoting what the person would, in a more informed, mature, and reasonable state prefer. (Recall that civil liberties were retracted for the alleged benefit of the citizens of Bordertown and Migrantville.) Which interferences with individual freedom are defensible will reflect our understanding of what constitutes a well-developed life. Although action is taken for the sake of the agent, is said to be in the agent's interests, and is against the express wishes of the agent, in this case the difference—which Berlin believes to be a crucial one—is that interference is made in the name of an action that the individual would want *were he otherwise*. Paternalism is warranted in light of presumed future consent, as opposed to the presence of a "true, rational self." Again, the assumption is that the person will come to recognize and welcome these interferences as being in his or her best interest.

I do not think that Berlin's willingness to embrace a "best interests" defense of paternalism is any less subject to abuse than is the "true self" model for justification. Justifications for weak paternalism based on assumptions of rational consent or of future consent are problematic even though, as Dworkin notes, paternalistic interference is a less bitter pill where it (allegedly) "preserves and enhances for the individual his ability to rationally consider and carry out his own decisions."[52] Nonetheless, I

---

incompetence that causes her to weight abnormally some of her values, or to "discount unreasonably the probability or seriousness of future injury" ("Paternalism: Some Second Thoughts," 108). On the latter approach we wonder whether the person selects courses of action that are "far reaching, dangerous, and irreversible" ("Paternalism," 80), or are made under conditions of duress, or involve dangers not sufficiently understood or appreciated (ibid., 82).

[51] Dworkin, "Paternalism: Some Second Thoughts," 110. Dworkin believes that once the consent of the subject is acquired, "in interfering with such people we are in effect doing what they would do if they were fully rational. Hence we are not really opposing their will, hence we are not really interfering with their freedom" ("Paternalism," 77). But it is obvious that if consent is granted, then the action is no longer paternalistic.

[52] Dworkin, "Paternalism," 83.

believe that there are cases in which *strong* paternalistic measures ought to be employed as a means of discouraging certain autonomous behavior, of compelling certain autonomous behavior, and of enhancing autonomy where the capacity is present, but unfulfilled. I believe that this holds even when the target of the paternalistic gesture has not violated the harm principle, and so has not acted in ways that clearly permit infringements of autonomy.[53] Strong paternalistic intervention is sometimes needed to preserve the autonomy that is threatened by a competent and deserving person's self-regarding conduct. Robert Young argues for this point:

> Suppose S knows that heroin addiction causes severe physical harm and likely death before 30 years of age, but still chooses to take the drug because he wants the pleasure of the moment more than anything else. Assume, furthermore, that we independently have good grounds for believing S is emotionally stable and of sound reason. A policy of weak [soft] paternalism cannot in such a case justify intervention to prevent S's taking heroin. A strong paternalist . . . would argue for intervention where the consequences of S's action would be to undermine other more dispositional commitments.[54]

Since employing paternalistic measures to compel autonomy seems contradictory, it is the phenomenon on which I will focus. I believe that an argument in favor of strong paternalistic measures, even those taken against self-regarding harms, can be given when such measures are employed to minimize the sort of self-regarding harms that jeopardize autonomy, or individuality. This kind of argument challenges Mill's claim that the individual is always the best judge of his own interests, and that the evils produced by interferences with liberty are worse than any benefit obtained. Although I agree with Mill that there is a general principle that the individual is the best judge of his own interests, my view is that there are important exceptions to the principle that justify paternalistic interference, exceptions that surpass those that Mill himself acknowledged.

Mill argues that because paternalism affects conduct that is entirely self-regarding, it cannot be justified by citing the need to protect the interests of others. And because the individual is, arguably, the best judge of his own welfare, it is unlikely that compulsion would advance the interests of the individual, and it is quite likely that compulsion would

[53] The case of Mark, the megalomaniac, above at note 33, is an illustration of discouraging certain autonomous behavior. In challenging the assumption that autonomy is, for Mill, to be desired on instrumental grounds alone, James Bogen and Daniel M. Farrell note: "Autonomy may be desired for its own sake, even if it ceases to produce the mental state for which it was originally desired." See James Bogen and Daniel M. Farrell, "Freedom and Happiness in Mill's Defence of Liberty," *Philosophical Quarterly* 28, no. 113 (1978): 334.

[54] Young, *Personal Autonomy*, 68. The idea is that while S exhibits autonomy of desire, paternalistic measures might be employed to preserve S's autonomy of future action.

produce greater evil than it would prevent. Mill's reasoning is founded on the utilitarian cost-benefit calculus, but the claim that he wishes to defend is not supported by the cost-benefit analysis.

First, there is little proof that adult individuals always know their own interests. It is in a person's interest to be autonomous, but a person can be mistaken about whether or not he is autonomous, and about what his autonomy consists in. If autonomy is something we want to promote, then the failure of people to decide accurately about their autonomy might offer one reason in favor of paternalistic interferences, even when a person has decided in what he believes is his best interest. (Recall Hill's claim that the right to autonomy must be preserved, even when it is the self-regarding aim of the individual to destroy this right in himself.)

Second, as Mill himself should acknowledge, paternalistic action sometimes constitutes a lesser evil, or a greater good, than would obtain should the agent's action that it restrains go unchecked. Allowing a person to autonomously pursue a life in which more dispositional or global interests are circumscribed does not always make the person better off, even if the person is happy with the result. Mill writes:

> [An] . . . exception to the doctrine that individuals are the best judges of their own interest, is when an individual attempts to decide irrevocably now what will be best for his interest at some future and distant time. The presumption in favor of individual judgment is only legitimate, where the judgment is grounded on actual, and especially on present personal experience; not where it is formed antecedently to experience, and not suffered to be reversed even after experience has condemned it.[55]

For example, the value that Mill accords autonomy can be used to justify an argument against self-imposed slavery. Mill counts freely chosen slavery among those actions over which the individual is not sovereign, and says:

> The ground for thus limiting [the slave's] power of voluntarily disposing of his own lot in life is apparent, and is very clearly seen in this extreme case. The reason for not interfering, unless for the sake of others, with a person's voluntary acts is consideration for his liberty. . . . But by selling himself for a slave, he abdicates his liberty; he forgoes any future use of it beyond that single act. He therefore defeats, in his own case, the very purpose which is the justification of

---

[55] John Stuart Mill, *Principles of Political Economy*, 2 vols. (1848; reprint, New York: P. F. Collier & Sons, 1900), 459.

124 MARINA OSHANA

allowing him to dispose of himself. He is no longer free; but is
thenceforth in a position which has no longer the presumption in its
favour that would be afforded by his voluntarily remaining in it. *The
principle of freedom cannot require that he should be free not to be free.* It
is not freedom to be allowed to alienate his freedom.[56]

Mill's use of the term "freedom" equivocates between "liberty of action" and "individuality" or "autonomy." Thus, a better statement might
be that people should not be at liberty to relinquish their autonomy. But
his point is clear. Individuality or autonomy is too important a characteristic for persons to be without. Since it is that element of persons upon
which all other forms of freedom are grounded—including the freedom
to act—autonomy cannot be something that we are at liberty to disman-
tle. Consensual slavery, regardless of the gains that it might provide and
aside from any benefit to the enslaved, transforms the human subject into
a possession or object of another and accordingly defiles the enslaved
individual's autonomy. Once autonomy has been cast off, the person is in
no position to expect others to treat him with the respect for his individuality that typically disallows paternalism.

The following passage from Chapter 3 of *On Liberty* lends credence to
Mill's support of paternalism in such cases. Mill writes:

He who lets the world, or his own portion of it, choose his plan of life
for him has no need of any other faculty than the ape-like one of
imitation. . . . It is possible he may be guided in some good path, and
kept out of harm's way. . . . But what will be his comparative worth
as a human being? It really is of importance, not only what men do,
but also what manner of men they are that do it.[57]

The idea here is that autonomy acquires its value from other goods that
it makes viable, and from what it enables persons to do with their lives.
Strong paternalism is warranted solely to preserve more extensive autonomy or self-direction, greater freedom, and moral agency. We care about
being moral agents, even if, on occasion, we autonomously act in ways
that are not expressive of that concern. Thus, cases of voluntary slavery,
and perhaps cases in which a person willingly embraces a life of subservience, as does the Taliban woman, offer an exception to prohibitions on
paternalistic conduct. Such voluntary contractual obligations are prohibited because maintaining the freedom to make future choices is key. If we
accept this account, as I am inclined to do, then restrictions on autono-

[56] Mill, *On Liberty*, 125, my emphasis.
[57] Ibid., 71–72.

mously executed acts that eradicate one's dispositional or global autonomy can be upheld under a policy of judicious strong paternalism.[58]

Actions taken against conduct such as consensual slavery might even be explained by nonpaternalistic reasons, as when the explanation appeals to the interests of others. A nonpaternalistic argument in support of justified encroachments upon a person's individuality can be derived from Mill's contention that when a person "disables himself, by conduct purely self-regarding, from the performance of some definite duty"[59] to the public, intervening steps may be taken. When the sovereign individual lays claim to conduct that, though directly and primarily affecting himself also indirectly or derivatively affects the larger sphere within which he interacts, the utility principle is implemented.

Does the person who happily relinquishes his capacity for self-determination, as does the compliant slave and as does the Taliban woman, negatively affect the larger environment within which the person acts? No definite duty to the public has been abridged, but it is arguable in these two examples that a social offense has been committed in collusion with the society in which the action is performed. If the offense is of a magnitude that imperils the social basis for productive interchange within the social, political, and economic realms, then the utility principle could be invoked to support injunctions against the action. Classifying self-imposed slavery as a social offense of this proportion involves analyzing the implications of self-imposed slavery for the social structure in which it occurs. The same is true of a society in which 50 percent of the adult population is relegated, willingly or not, to the status of the Taliban woman. The same is also true of a society that, citing the value of artistic license and individuality, refuses to compel socially unstable, schizophrenic artists to take their medication.

Of course, a utilitarian calculus could conclude that autonomy is of less value to a society than is the sovereignty of the individual who chooses nonautonomy; society might greatly benefit from voluntary slavery, Taliban women, and schizophrenic artists. But if an absence of autonomy does significantly damage the very fabric of a person's cultural and political environment, then the calculus will decide that the benefits to all from the interchange among free persons outweigh those that accrue from interchange among free persons and those who lack autonomy. The decision to utilize paternalistic measures must, I think, depend on the extent to which a society counts autonomy as important for the integrity

---

[58] Young would include arguably less egregious behaviors among the acts for which strong paternalistic interference is justified. He mentions "restrictions placed on professional boxing between grossly ill-matched boxers, ... [and] voluntary participation in unnecessary, risky experiments," behaviors that are unquestionably imprudent but not clearly risks to, or sacrifices of, future autonomy. Young's claim lends itself to Berlin's worry discussed above in the text that one person's autonomy could become the subject of another's autocratic control. See Young, *Personal Autonomy*, 68.

[59] Mill, *On Liberty*, 70–71.

of its structure. In a society that bestows less social worth on autonomy, actions that diminish a person's autonomy, such as self-regarding slavery, might be targets for reproof or regret, but would not be regarded as social evils. Still, they might constitute a social evil if the longevity of the society could not be secured without autonomous persons.

VIII. Conclusion

The arguments that I have considered surrounding paternalism and interferences with autonomous behavior generally lend themselves to the following conclusions. First, autonomy *qua* individuality or individual freedom is not sacrosanct. There are times when we shall be permitted to override a person's right to noninterference, as when there are other, more exacting prerogatives that we want to protect.

I am not in a position to declare resolutely when the value of autonomy should be overridden, despite the cost to the individual. As Young notes, "[A]n individual's other values may come to assume at some time more importance for him than his autonomy, so the commitment we have to the value of autonomy is at best a defeasible commitment." [60]

There are many penumbral cases in which an individual's voluntary abdications of autonomy may fail to provide us with good or sufficient reason to intervene on a person's behalf. I am thinking of the lives embraced by persons in certain insular religious communities—the Amish, for example. Our respect for the good of value pluralism cautions restraint in such cases.

If we distinguish between autonomy and freedom, or liberty, then it may be that autonomy is one of those values for which freedom can be sacrificed. But autonomy, unlike freedom, is compatible with (and occasionally calls for) restrictions upon the parameters of individual behavior, or upon the sources of authority that govern an agent. The fact that it might be morally and legally incumbent upon us to caution others against their own behavior, to warn them of the punitive consequences that might follow their behavior, and to actually take steps to curtail their autonomy, does not mean that autonomy is not a valued state. This ideal remains intact, although uninstantiated in certain cases.

Even when a person's autonomy bears upon only those affairs in her life that are self-regarding, and is of fundamental importance to the pursuit and outcome of these affairs, autonomy is not inviolable. There are good arguments against respecting the autonomy of persons whose behavior undermines their self-governance, as in cases of consensual slavery. When these cases present themselves, interference may be justified and legitimate.

Philosophy, Bowling Green State University

[60] Young, *Personal Autonomy*, 73.

AUTONOMY, DURESS, AND COERCION*

By James Stacey Taylor

I. Introduction

For the past three decades philosophical discussions of both personal autonomy and what it is for a person to "identify" with her desires have been dominated by the "hierarchical" analyses of these concepts developed by Gerald Dworkin and Harry Frankfurt.[1] The longevity of these analyses is owed, in part, to the intuitive appeal of their shared claim that the concepts of autonomy and identification are to be analyzed in terms of hierarchies of desires, such that it is a necessary condition for a person to be autonomous with respect to (to identify with) a desire that moves her to act, that she desires that this desire so move her. (Conversely, on these analyses, a person will not be autonomous with respect to a desire that she is moved by, she will not identify with it, if she does not want to be so moved.) Despite the intuitive appeal of these analyses, however, Irving Thalberg has argued that they should be rejected.[2] This is because, he argues, a person who is forced to perform an action by being subjected to duress of a certain degree of harshness will desire to be moved by her desire to submit. Thus, he continues, the proponents of hierarchical analyses of autonomy and identification will be forced to hold that such a person acted willingly, and did not suffer from any impairment in her autonomy. This, Thalberg concludes, is so counterintuitive as to justify rejecting hierarchical analyses.

* I thank R. G. Frey, James W. Child, Fred D. Miller, Jr., Marina Oshana, Harry Frankfurt, Stefaan Cuypers, and Jim Gough for their helpful comments on a very early draft of this essay. Another draft of this essay was presented at the University of Texas at San Antonio Philosophy Symposium in 1999. I thank my commentator, John Hernandez, and my audience on that occasion (especially Michael Almeida) for their constructive criticisms. I especially thank Michael Bratman, Keith Lehrer, Bernard Berofsky, Jonathan Malino, and David Copp for their stimulating comments on this essay. Finally, I thank the editors of *Social Philosophy & Policy* for very helpful suggestions concerning the penultimate draft of this essay.
[1] Harry G. Frankfurt, "Freedom of the Will and the Concept of a Person," in Harry G. Frankfurt, ed., *The Importance of What We Care About* (Cambridge: Cambridge University Press, 1988), 11–25. Gerald Dworkin's early work on his hierarchical analysis of autonomy appears in two main sources: Gerald Dworkin, "Acting Freely," *Nous* 4, no. 4 (1970): 367–83; and Gerald Dworkin, "Autonomy and Behavior Control," in Thomas A. Mappes and Jane S. Zembaty, eds., *Biomedical Ethics* (New York: McGraw–Hill Book Company, 1981), 273–80.
[2] Irving Thalberg, "Hierarchical Analyses of Unfree Action," in John Christman, ed., *The Inner Citadel: Essays on Individual Autonomy* (Oxford: Oxford University Press, 1989), 123–36.

Thalberg's objections to the hierarchical analyses are striking, for they are the only objections that defenders of these analyses have not sought to counter.[3] Instead, it has come to be generally accepted by both defenders and critics of these analyses that Thalberg's objections show that these analyses must either be rejected outright or severely modified.[4] However, that Thalberg's objections are so widely accepted is unfortunate, for (as I will argue in this essay) they are based on a fundamental misunderstanding of Frankfurt's and Dworkin's hierarchical analyses—a misunderstanding that has been consistently overlooked.

Alas, any relief that my argument might provide to the defenders of these hierarchical analyses will be short-lived. Even when these analyses are properly understood, they *still* have counterintuitive implications when they are applied to a situation in which a person acts solely to avoid a threatened harm. However, the arguments in this essay do not lead only to negative conclusions, nor are they only of parochial concern to persons interested in hierarchical analyses of autonomy and identification. Rather, I will argue that, even though hierarchical analyses of autonomy and identification are seriously flawed, they can still provide the key to answering one of the perennial questions in the philosophy of action: Does a person who is forced to perform an action solely in order to avoid a threatened penalty thereby suffer from impaired autonomy?

---

[3] The three standard objections to hierarchical analyses of autonomy that defenders of hierarchical analyses have sought to counter are the regress *cum* incompleteness objection, the problem of authority, and the objection from manipulation. A concise statement of the regress *cum* incompleteness objection can be found in John Christman, "Introduction," in Christman, ed., *The Inner Citadel*, 8–12. The first outline of the problem of authority is found in Gary Watson, "Free Agency," *Journal of Philosophy* 72, no. 8 (1975): 205–20. The problem of manipulation is outlined in Michael Slote, "Understanding Free Will," in John Martin Fischer, ed., *Moral Responsibility* (Ithaca, NY: Cornell University Press, 1986), 124–39. A response to the regress *cum* incompleteness objection can be found in Keith Lehrer, "Freedom, Preference, and Autonomy," *Journal of Ethics* 1, no. 1 (1997): 3–25. A response to both the problem of authority and the regress *cum* incompleteness problem is offered in Stefaan E. Cuypers, "Autonomy beyond Voluntarism: In Defense of Hierarchy," *Canadian Journal of Philosophy* 30, no. 2 (2000): 225–56. Finally, difficulties that undermine the objection from manipulation are pressed in Richard Double, "Puppeteers, Hypnotists, and Neurosurgeons," *Philosophical Studies* 56 (1989): 163–73.

[4] Thalberg, for example, holds that these analyses should be rejected outright; see his "Hierarchical Analyses," 135. By contrast, while both Christman and Slote take Thalberg's objections to the hierarchical analyses of autonomy at their face value, these authors hold that, rather than showing that these analyses should be rejected completely, Thalberg's objections only demonstrate that they require some serious modifications. See Christman, "Introduction," 8–9; and Slote, "Understanding Free Will," 127. Similarly, in his most recent account of autonomy, Dworkin acknowledges that his analysis of autonomy requires modification (or, at least, clarification) in order to meet Thalberg's objections. See Gerald Dworkin, *The Theory and Practice of Autonomy* (Cambridge: Cambridge University Press, 1988), 18–20.

II. Hierarchical Analyses of Autonomy and Thalberg's Objections

A. Frankfurt's and Dworkin's hierarchical analyses of autonomy

As I noted above, the core feature shared by Frankfurt's and Dworkin's analyses of autonomy and identification is that these concepts are to be analyzed in terms of hierarchies of desire. (For the sake of clarity, from now on I will take the phrase "is autonomous with respect to her desire x" to be synonymous with the phrase "identifies with her desire that x,"[5] and the phrase "acts freely" to be synonymous with the phrase "is autonomous with respect to her actions.")[6] More specifically, on Frankfurt's original analysis of identification, a person identifies with a first-order desire that x that actually moves him to act if he *volitionally endorses* his desire that x. That is to say, a person identifies with (i.e., is autono-

---

[5] Although it is becoming standard to take Frankfurt's analysis of what it is for a person to identify with her desires to be an analysis of what it is for her to be autonomous with respect to them, to do so still requires some justification, for Frankfurt never explicitly states that his hierarchical analysis of identification is to be understood as an analysis of autonomy. Support for this understanding of his work, however, can be drawn from his "Autonomy, Necessity, and Love," in Harry G. Frankfurt, ed., *Necessity, Volition, and Love* (Cambridge: Cambridge University Press, 1999), 130-38. Here, Frankfurt argues, "The distinction between heteronomy and autonomy coincides . . . with the distinction between being passive and being active" (ibid., 133). In addition to this, in an earlier essay Frankfurt had argued that a person could be said to identify with his desires only if he is "active" with respect to them. (Harry G. Frankfurt, "Identification and Externality," in Frankfurt, ed., *The Importance of What We Care About*, 58-68.) Putting these two claims together, then, it can be seen that it would not be mistaken to hold that, in Frankfurt's view, for a person to "identify with" her desires is *also* for her to be "autonomous with respect to" them. Yet this claim must come with a caveat, since, in his most recent work on identification, Frankfurt argues that both persons and nonpersons can identify with their desires, but the latter will identify with their desires without having volitionally endorsed them after reflecting upon their desirability. (Harry G. Frankfurt, "The Faintest Passion," in Frankfurt, ed., *Necessity, Volition, and Love*, 105-6.) Since this is the case, and since Frankfurt argues that personal autonomy is grounded in the volitional structure of a person's will (Frankfurt, "Autonomy, Necessity, and Love," 132), it would be more accurate to claim that a person is autonomous with respect to those desires that she *reflectively* identifies with (i.e., those that she identifies with after volitionally endorsing them). This point is discussed more fully in James Stacey Taylor, "Book Review of *Necessity, Volition, and Love* by Harry G. Frankfurt," *Philosophical Quarterly* 51, no. 202 (2001): 114-16. Finally, if one remains unconvinced by this line of reasoning and believes that reflectively to identify with one's desires is not identical with being autonomous with respect to them, it should be noted that the arguments in this essay do not depend on one's acceptance of this understanding of the relationship between identification and autonomy. I thank John Martin Fischer for pressing me on this point.

[6] Just as Frankfurt does not use the term "autonomy" in his seminal essay "Freedom of the Will and the Concept of a Person," so, too, does Dworkin eschew this term in his essay "Acting Freely." However, in his later essay "Autonomy and Behavior Control," Dworkin explicitly notes that the authenticity component of the account of autonomy that he is developing herein was "more fully worked out" in "Acting Freely," where it played the same role in his account of acting freely. (Dworkin, "Autonomy and Behavior Control," 280 n. 5.) Given this, it would not be misguided to understand Dworkin's views in "Acting Freely" as being concerned with personal autonomy. However, once again, if one is unconvinced by such an argument, one should note that nothing in this essay rests on these terminological considerations.

mous with respect to) his effective first-order desire that x if he both desires to have the desire that x (i.e., he has a *second-order desire* that he have his desire that x) *and* he also wants his desire that x to move him to act (i.e., he does not merely endorse his desire that x with a second-order *desire*, but with a second-order *volition*).[7]

Similarly, on Dworkin's original analysis of autonomy, an "autonomous person is one who does *his own* thing." For Dworkin, it is "the attitude that . . . [the] . . . person takes towards the influences motivating him . . . [that] determines whether or not they are to be considered 'his'."[8] That is to say, on Dworkin's view, for a person to be autonomous with respect to the influences that motivate him to act, it is necessary that he endorse his being moved to act by them. In addition to the requirement that a person's motivations be *authentic* in this way, in his original analysis of autonomy Dworkin also required that a person enjoy both procedural independence and substantive independence with respect to his motivations. Here, a person possesses procedural independence with respect to his motivations if his desire to be moved to act by them has not been produced "by manipulation, deception, the withholding of relevant information, and so on."[9] A person possesses substantive independence with respect to his motivations if he does not "renounce his independence of thought or action" prior to developing them.[10]

On both Frankfurt's and Dworkin's hierarchical analyses, then, a person's autonomy will be impaired if he is moved to act by a desire that he has a second-order desire not to be moved by. In most cases, this is intuitively plausible. For example, if a person is subject to a neurotic compulsion constantly to wash his hands that he desires to be free from, his autonomy will be impaired if he is moved to act by a first-order desire to wash his hands that this neurosis causes him to have, and that he does not wish to be moved by.[11]

B. Thalberg's objections to the hierarchical analyses of autonomy

Thalberg's first objection to these hierarchical analyses is that they have counterintuitive results when they are applied to situations in which a person is forced to perform a certain action by being subjected to duress. To show this, Thalberg focuses on the way in which Frankfurt and Dworkin apply their hierarchical analyses to explain how it is that, when a person is subjected to duress and performs an action that complies with his threatener's desires, it can be said that he acted unwillingly (and thus

---

[7] Frankfurt, "Freedom of the Will," 14–22.
[8] Dworkin, "Autonomy and Behavior Control," 276.
[9] Ibid.
[10] Ibid.
[11] Although neither Frankfurt nor Dworkin uses this example, it serves well to demonstrate the intuitive plausibility of their hierarchical analyses.

suffers from impaired autonomy) even though he is performing the action that (given the circumstances that he is in) he most wants to perform.

Dworkin bases his discussion of this problem on an example in which a traveler surrenders his billfold to a highwayman in order to avoid being killed. Dworkin claims that, in this case, "What [the victim] doesn't want to do when faced with the highwayman is to hand money over in these circumstances, for these reasons." More generally, Dworkin asserts that persons "resent acting for certain reasons; they would not choose to be motivated in certain ways. They mind acting simply in order . . . to avoid unpleasant consequences." Dworkin adds that some "part of the human personality . . . takes up an 'attitude' toward the reasons, desires and motives" that determine one's conduct. He further notes that, as a result, "we consider ourselves compelled because we find it painful to act for these reasons."[12]

Thalberg infers from this that, in Dworkin's view, the highwayman's victim suffers from impaired autonomy when he hands over his billfold, because he has adopted a negative attitude toward that desire; he does not desire to be moved by this desire because he does not desire to hand over his billfold solely in order to avoid the unpleasant consequences of resistance. As Thalberg understands it, then, in Dworkin's view a person will suffer from impaired autonomy when he is moved to act by a desire that he does not want to be moved by, where one instance of this would be a case in which the individual concerned does not want to be moved by a desire because he resents acting for the reasons that led him to form the desire. (For example, he performs an action under duress solely in order to avoid the penalty with which he is threatened.) On this understanding of Dworkin's view, a person's autonomy will be impaired with respect to an action he performs, if he is moved to perform that action by a first-order desire whose motivational efficacy he repudiates at the second-order level of his desires.

According to Thalberg, Frankfurt offers a similarly hierarchical analysis of how it is that a person might suffer from impaired autonomy with respect to those actions that he performs as a result of being subject to coercion or duress. Discussing both threats and coercive offers in "Coercion and Moral Responsibility," Frankfurt describes an offer as coercive "when the person is moved into compliance by a desire . . . which he would overcome if he could . . . a desire by which he does not want to be driven." Frankfurt notes that the individual's autonomy may be violated by a threat in the same way: "In submitting to a threat, a person invariably does something that he does not really want to do."[13] As Thalberg

[12] Dworkin, "Acting Freely," 377–78. This quotation of Dworkin's view is from Thalberg, "Hierarchical Analyses," 125.

[13] Harry G. Frankfurt, "Coercion and Moral Responsibility," in Harry G. Frankfurt, ed., *The Importance of What We Care About*, 41–42. This quotation of Frankfurt's view is from Thalberg, "Hierarchical Analyses," 126.

understands this, Frankfurt's view is very similar to Dworkin's. A person will suffer from a lack of autonomy with respect to an action if he is moved to perform that action by a first-order desire that he volitionally repudiates; that is, he is moved to act by a first-order desire that he does not want to be moved by.

Thalberg's first objection to this hierarchical approach to analyzing the concept of autonomy is both elegant and simple. Thalberg argues that, on these hierarchical analyses, a person will only suffer from impaired autonomy with respect to those actions that he is coerced into performing, or that he performs under duress solely in order to avoid the penalty he is threatened with (his "compliant actions"), if he repudiates his first-order desire that actually moved him to act. Thalberg observes, however, that most persons who are subjected to coercion or duress "would, at the time and later, give second-order endorsement to their cautious [and compliant] motives. They are unlikely to yearn, from their elevated tribune, for more defiant ground-floor urges."[14] If this is so, Thalberg notes, then the hierarchical analysts are committed to claiming that most persons who are subject to coercion or duress do *not* thereby suffer from impaired autonomy, for they are not motivated to perform their compliant actions by first-order desires that they repudiate at the second-order level. As Thalberg points out, this conclusion is counterintuitive. However, Thalberg continues, if the hierarchical analysts of autonomy wish to avoid this counterintuitive result, they must claim that, when most persons are subjected to coercion or duress, they *do* wish to repudiate their prudent first-order desires to comply with the demands of their threateners. And this seems to be empirically false. Thus, Thalberg concludes, either the hierarchical analysts of autonomy are committed to the counterintuitive claim that most persons who are subject to coercion or duress are fully autonomous with respect to their compliant actions, or else the hierarchical analysts must attempt to salvage the plausibility of their position by falsely claiming that most persons thus constrained repudiate their effective first-order desires.[15]

In addition to this objection to the hierarchical analyses of autonomy, Thalberg also offers a second: "Dworkin and Frankfurt are mistaken, or

---

[14] Thalberg, "Hierarchical Analyses," 126.

[15] Thalberg's objection seems to work, not only against Frankfurt's original hierarchical analysis of what it is for a person to be autonomous with respect to these desires, but also against his most recent hierarchical analysis as it is outlined in Harry G. Frankfurt, "The Faintest Passion," 102-6. Here, Frankfurt argues that a person (reflectively) identifies with her first-order desires (i.e., is autonomous with respect to them) if she is satisfied with her volitional endorsement of them, where this satisfaction "is a matter of simply *having no interest* in making changes." ("The Faintest Passion," 104-5. Emphasis in original.) Since it appears that the typical compliant victim of duress would be satisfied, in this sense, with her volitional endorsement of her first-order desire to comply with her threatener's demands, Frankfurt once again appears committed either to the counterintuitive claim that the typical victim of duress is fully autonomous with respect to her compliant actions, or else to the false claim that such a victim will repudiate her effective first-order desires.

anyway guilty of exaggeration, when they suppose that what a constrained person 'doesn't want' is for some desire or other to move him." [16] Thalberg argues that the primary object of aversion of the victim of coercion or duress is more likely to be the consequences of his compliant actions (for example, that he has lost his billfold to a highwayman) than the fact that he was moved to perform his compliant actions by a certain first-order desire, or that he performed it for certain reasons. Since this is the more likely case, Thalberg argues, Dworkin and Frankfurt misdescribe the situation of the typical victim of coercion or duress to the extent that they hold that he is principally averse to his effective first-order desires, or that he acted for certain reasons, rather than to the actual losses that he has suffered. Thalberg therefore holds that, to be descriptively accurate, any account of why it is that a victim of coercion or duress suffers from an impairment in his autonomy should focus on his aversion to the situation that he finds himself in, and not on any aversion that he might be claimed to have toward those desires that moved him to comply or toward his reasons for such compliance.

III. RESPONSES TO THALBERG

Thalberg's objections to Frankfurt's and Dworkin's hierarchical analyses of autonomy are both persuasive and widely accepted. It is thus all the more unfortunate that these objections rest on a fundamental misunderstanding of their views.

Thalberg's first objection to the hierarchical approach to analyzing autonomy is based on the view that proponents of this approach are committed to two related claims. The first of these claims is that a person only suffers from impaired autonomy with respect to one of his actions if he is moved to perform that action by a first-order desire that he repudiates at his second-order level of motivation. The second of these claims is the converse of the first: if a person fully endorses the first-order desire that moves him to perform an action, then he will be fully autonomous with respect to that action. When taken together, these claims comprise what might be termed the *Assumption of the Transitivity of Autonomy*: that autonomy as a property of persons is transitive across their desires and actions.[17] On this assumption, if a person is autonomous with respect to

---

[16] Thalberg, "Hierarchical Analyses," 127.
[17] Although the Assumption of the Transitivity of Autonomy is never explicitly articulated, it underlies much of the discussion of Frankfurt's and Dworkin's work on coercion and duress. Christman, for example, implicitly accepts the assumption in his "Introduction" to *The Inner Citadel*, as do Slote in "Understanding Free Will"; David Zimmerman in "Making Do: Troubling Stoic Tendencies in an Otherwise Compelling Theory of Autonomy," *Canadian Journal of Philosophy* 30, no. 1 (2000): 25–54; and Susan Dimock in "Personal Autonomy, Freedom of Action, and Coercion," in Samantha Brennan, Tracy Isaacs, and Michael Milde, eds., *A Question of Values: New Canadian Perspectives in Ethics and Political Philosophy* (Atlanta, GA: Rodophi, 1997), 65–86. Moreover, some writers mistakenly understand Frank-

a desire D to degree n, then he will also be autonomous to degree n with respect to an action A that he is motivated to perform by desire D.

If the proponents of hierarchical analyses of autonomy are committed to this assumption, then Thalberg's first objection to them will hold, and these analyses must either be modified to accommodate it or else be rejected entirely. However, careful examination of these analyses will show that their proponents are *not* committed to this assumption. Indeed, Frankfurt even goes to some pains explicitly to reject it.

A. Autonomy and coercion

Before outlining how Frankfurt rejects the Assumption of the Transitivity of Autonomy, one should first outline his account of how a person who is *coerced* into performing an action suffers from impaired autonomy. This is because Frankfurt's discussion of coercion is often cited to support the view that he (and hierarchical analysts of autonomy in general) is only able to account for a person suffering from impaired autonomy by appealing to discord between different levels of desire in her motivational hierarchy. Since this view appears often (and since the defense of the hierarchical analyses of autonomy against Thalberg's objection will rest on the claim that this view of the hierarchical analyses is false), it would be useful to outline Frankfurt's account of the relationship that holds between coercion and autonomy-impairment in order to contrast it with his more nuanced (and overlooked) discussion of how persons who perform compliant actions under *duress* suffer from impaired autonomy.

For Frankfurt, when a person is coerced into performing an action by being threatened with a penalty if he does not comply, he is moved to act "by a desire which is not only irresistible but which he would overcome if he could."[18] In Frankfurt's view, such a person suffers from impaired autonomy because he is moved to act by a first-order desire that he does not volitionally endorse.

Frankfurt is often criticized for accounting for the autonomy-undermining nature of coercion in this way, for (as is frequently pointed out by his critics) persons who are coerced are not typically moved to comply with their threatener's wishes by "irresistible" desires that they would overcome if they could.[19] Instead, the typical victim of coercion is moved to comply by a desire that he could easily resist if he so desired, but which he acts upon because he fully endorses both his possession of

---

furt's and Dworkin's accounts of what it is for a person to be autonomous with respect to her desires to be accounts of what it is for her to be autonomous with respect to her actions. For example, see Ian Jennings, "Autonomy and Hierarchical Compatibilism," *South African Journal of Philosophy* 16, no. 2 (1997): 44–50.

[18] Frankfurt, "Coercion and Moral Responsibility," 42.

[19] See, for example, Thalberg, "Hierarchical Analyses," 126; and Zimmerman, "Making Do," 34–38. For an account of coercion that draws from Frankfurt's, see Denis G. Arnold, "Coercion and Moral Responsibility," *American Philosophical Quarterly* 38, no. 1 (2001): 53–67.

this desire and its moving him to act. Weighing the courses of action open to him, the typical victim of coercion decides to pursue the better part of valor and acts accordingly. This critical focus on Frankfurt's account of the autonomy-undermining nature of coercion is unfortunate, for two reasons. First, in focusing on Frankfurt's explicit discussion of coercion, there is a tendency for his commentators to overlook the fact that he does discuss the more "typical" case of coercion, although he refers to persons who are thus forced to act as victims of "duress," rather than as victims of "coercion." Consequently, Frankfurt is not guilty of taking the untypical for the typical, as David Zimmerman charges—although he is guilty of the lesser charge of using untypical terminology at the expense of the typical.[20] Second (and relatedly), by overlooking Frankfurt's discussion of how a person who acts under duress thereby suffers from impaired autonomy, Frankfurt's commentators are led to misconstrue his subtle and nuanced analysis of autonomous agency. This is because if one focuses on Frankfurt's discussion of coercion and is familiar with his hierarchical analysis of identification, it is easy to conclude that Frankfurt *accepts* the Assumption of the Transitivity of Autonomy. If one focuses solely on the combination of these two aspects of his overall view, it is likewise easy to conclude that Frankfurt holds that a person who is subject to a threat will only suffer from an impairment of his autonomy if he is thereby led to act by an irresistible desire that he wished to resist. However, since Frankfurt actually *rejects* this assumption in his discussion of the autonomy-impairing nature of duress (as I will argue in the following section), any account of his analysis of autonomous agency that focuses solely on his work on coercion and identification will fail to accurately represent his view.

B. Rejecting the Assumption of the Transitivity of Autonomy

Frankfurt's clearest rejection of the Assumption of the Transitivity of Autonomy occurs in his "Coercion and Moral Responsibility"—ironically, the very essay that Thalberg focuses on in developing his criticisms of the hierarchical approach.[21] In discussing a variant of Dworkin's highwayman example, in which a man is forced at gunpoint to hand over his billfold, Frankfurt notes that the person who is forced by the highway-

---

[20] Zimmerman, "Making Do," 38.

[21] Although the discussion in this section will focus on the work of Harry Frankfurt, since it contains the most explicit rejection of the Assumption of the Transitivity of Autonomy, the same arguments can also be used to defend Dworkin's hierarchical analysis of autonomy against Thalberg's objection. It should be noted, however, that at one point Dworkin does appear to endorse this assumption, when he writes that the victim of coercion (in the non-Frankfurt sense of duress) is motivated similarly to a kleptomaniac who is moved to act by resistible desires that she does not endorse. (Dworkin, "Acting Freely," 378.) However, this implied endorsement of the Assumption of the Transitivity of Autonomy is not central to Dworkin's view and could be repudiated without loss.

man into handing over his money "would not have defied the threat even
if he had been capable of doing so." Instead, "since he really does prefer
to give up his money than to die, he would doubtless have fought against
any impulse toward defiance which might have arisen in him."[22] Here,
then, Frankfurt allows that the motivational structure of the highwayman's victim might have been such that not only did he have a first-order
desire to hand over his billfold, but he also possessed a second-order
volition that this first-order desire lead him to act. However, despite this
harmony in the victim's hierarchy of desires, Frankfurt still holds that,
because this person acted to avoid a threatened harm, his autonomy *was*
impaired. It is clear that Frankfurt does *not* accept the Assumption of the
Transitivity of Autonomy, for if he did accept this assumption, he would
be committed to claiming that the autonomy of the highwayman's victim
was *not impaired at all*. Since this victim volitionally endorsed his effective
first-order desire, he was, according to Frankfurt's hierarchical analysis of
autonomy, fully autonomous with respect to it. Thus, if Frankfurt did
accept the Assumption of the Transitivity of Autonomy, he would also be
committed to claiming that the highwayman's victim was therefore also
fully autonomous with respect to his actions—and this is something that
Frankfurt explicitly denies.

The fact that Frankfurt allows that a person might volitionally endorse
his effective first-order desire to x when he does x under duress, and yet
still suffer from an impairment of his autonomy when he does x, shows
that Frankfurt does not accept the Assumption of the Transitivity of
Autonomy. However, the same observation does *not* show that Thalberg's
first objection to the hierarchical approach to analyzing autonomy (as
exemplified by Frankfurt's work) is mistaken. Even though Frankfurt
might *desire* to reject the Assumption of the Transitivity of Autonomy
(and claim to do so), the real question is whether or not he (and hierarchical analysts of autonomy in general) *can* so reject it, given his (and
their) previous theoretical commitments.

Fortunately for Frankfurt, he can reject the Assumption of the Transitivity of Autonomy despite his previous theoretical commitments. (This is
also true for hierarchical analysts of autonomy in general.) Thalberg was
correct to note that, when hierarchical analysts of autonomy attempt to
explain why it is that a person who is coerced to act or who acts under
duress suffers from impaired autonomy, they focus on the claim that such
a person "acts on a motive by which he would prefer not to be moved."[23]
However, Thalberg fails to recognize that this central claim is ambiguous.
On one reading, it could be understood as the claim that the compliant
victim of duress has an *absolute* preference not to be moved by the first-
order desire that actually moves him to act (i.e., he repudiates this desire).

---

[22] Frankfurt, "Coercion and Moral Responsibility," 43.
[23] Ibid., 44. See also Dworkin, "Acting Freely," 377.

Alternatively, it could be understood as the claim that the victim of duress has a *relative* preference that he not be moved by the desire that actually moves him to act (i.e., he would *prefer* to be moved by some *other* desire, but this preference does not entail that he repudiates the desire that actually moves him to act).

Recognizing this ambiguity is crucial if one is to understand correctly the hierarchical analysts' account of why a person who performs a compliant action under duress suffers from impaired autonomy. As is clear from his objection, Thalberg understands this central claim to attribute an absolute preference to the victim of duress not to be moved by his actual desire to comply; that is, the victim of duress will volitionally *repudiate* his first-order desire to comply. However, as I argued above, this cannot be the correct understanding of what the hierarchical analysts mean by their ambiguous central claim (i.e., that a person who is coerced to act or who acts under duress "acts on a motive by which he would prefer not to be moved"). Frankfurt allows that a person who performs an action under duress does thereby suffer from impaired autonomy *even if* he *endorses* his first-order desire to submit. Thus, the central claim of the hierarchical analysts should instead be understood as noting the fact that a person who acts under duress has a *relative* preference to not be moved by his actual desire to comply. In other words, he does not want to be moved by his desire to submit because (as Thalberg acknowledges) he would prefer to be in a different situation where he would be able to volitionally endorse a first-order desire *different* from that which he *actually* endorses without fear of incurring some harm. (And where, according to both Frankfurt and Dworkin, the typical victim of duress will also prefer to be in a different situation because he resents being in a situation where he has to act "simply in order to avoid unpleasant consequences with no attendant promotion of ... [his] ... own interests and welfare.")[24] A person who performs a compliant action under duress, and who thereby "acts on a motive by which he would prefer not to be moved," might volitionally *endorse* his first-order desire to comply, while still preferring that he not be in a situation where such endorsement is prudent. He thus prefers *not* to be moved by this first-order desire to comply, even though he volitionally endorses it, because he prefers to be in a situation such that he could act on a desire that would not move him to perform this compliant action. When their central claim is understood in this way, it is clear that the hierarchical analysts of autonomy are not subject to Thalberg's first objection, for they can accept that a person subject to duress might endorse his effective first-order desire to comply with his threatener's demands, and yet they still recognize that his autonomy was impaired. The hierarchical analysts of autonomy can thus retain their hierarchical

---

[24] Dworkin, "Acting Freely," 377. Frankfurt explicitly endorses Dworkin's view here in Frankfurt, "Coercion and Moral Responsibility," 44.

analyses of what it is for a person to be autonomous with respect to his desires, while rejecting the Assumption of the Transitivity of Autonomy.

From this discussion it can be seen that, on a generalized version of the hierarchical analysts' view, a person will suffer from impaired autonomy with respect to an action A if (i) he is motivated to perform action A by a first-order desire that he is not autonomous with respect to (i.e., one that he does not volitionally endorse); or (ii) he is motivated to perform action A by a desire that he is autonomous with respect to, but this desire is one that he would prefer not to be moved to act by, because he would prefer to be in a situation other than the one that he is actually in, where this preference for a different situation stems from his belief that, in the situation that he is in, he cannot act to improve his condition, but only to prevent it from becoming worse.

C. Autonomy and actions performed in situations of Type A

Although it is uncontroversial to state that condition (i) can be shared by all hierarchical analyses of autonomy, one might object that condition (ii) cannot similarly be shared by all such analyses, for it cannot be attributed to Frankfurt as part of his considered position. This is because, one might argue, condition (ii) appears to refer to actions that would be performed in a set of situations that comprise a subset of a larger set of situations that Frankfurt later describes (in "Three Concepts of Free Action") as "situations of Type A." [25] A situation of Type A is one in which a person's feeling "that he acted unwillingly derives from the fact that the external circumstances under which he acted were, as he perceived them, discordant with his desires," such that he was "actively discontented" with, or "resistant" to, the state of affairs in which he was forced to act. However, even though a person might be discontented with, or resistant to, the state of affairs in which he acts, Frankfurt holds that a person who acts in a situation of Type A nonetheless remains "autonomous within the limits of an unsatisfactory set of alternatives," and that the actions that he performs in this situation are still ones that he performs freely (i.e., autonomously). Even more worrisome for those who wish to regard Frankfurt as accepting condition (ii), Frankfurt goes on to claim explicitly that since a person can act autonomously in a situation of Type A, "it follows that actions may be performed freely [i.e., a person might be autonomous with respect to them] even when they are performed under duress." [26]

---

[25] Harry G. Frankfurt, "Three Concepts of Free Action," in Frankfurt, ed., *The Importance of What We Care About*, 47. The set of situations that are referred to in condition (ii) will comprise a subset of situations of Type A, rather then being coextensive with the set of situations of Type A, because not all situations of Type A will be ones in which a person resents having to act in order simply to maintain his condition rather than to improve it.

[26] Ibid., 49, 55.

Frankfurt's later position (as expressed in "Three Concepts of Free Action") certainly appears to be directly opposed to that which is attributed to him when condition (ii) is ascribed to him by virtue of his being a hierarchical analyst of autonomy. Nevertheless, two possible approaches can be taken to dispel Frankfurt's apparent opposition to condition (ii). The first approach is simply to note that Frankfurt makes it clear that he is not wedded to the claim that a person may act freely even if he acts under duress, for Frankfurt accepts that "it would be reasonable to require that no action be construed as having been performed freely if it was performed under duress, or under duress of a certain degree of harshness." [27] (A requirement that for the sake of clarity can be termed *Requirement 1*.) Consequently, attributing condition (ii) to Frankfurt need not be contrary to his expressed view.

However, to respond in this way to the objection that condition (ii) appears to be directly at odds with Frankfurt's views, as explicitly stated in "Three Concepts of Free Action," has a whiff about it of cheating. Rather than simply adopting this response, then, it would be far more satisfactory to show that the most coherent reading of Frankfurt's view lends support to the claim that he *should* accept Requirement 1, and thus condition (ii). To offer this more satisfactory response, one should first note that Frankfurt's reluctance explicitly to endorse Requirement 1 stems from the fact that he holds two further beliefs concerning the relationship between a person's acting freely (i.e., autonomously) and the question of whether he is morally responsible for his action. First, in addition to acknowledging that Requirement 1 is reasonable, Frankfurt also acknowledges that another requirement (*Requirement 2*) is also reasonable: "that a person can bear no moral responsibility except for what he has done freely." [28] Second, in addition to accepting the reasonableness of both Requirements 1 and 2, Frankfurt believes that a person who performs an action under duress is morally responsible for his performance of that action, even though, owing to the circumstances in which he performed it, he might not be praised or blamed for it.

Frankfurt thus finds himself in a quandary. If he accepts Requirement 1, a person who performs an action A under duress (or under duress of a certain degree of harshness) does not act freely; and so, if Frankfurt also accepts Requirement 2, this person is *not* morally responsible for his performance of action A. And Frankfurt does not accept that this is so. However, if Frankfurt wishes to maintain that this person *is* morally responsible for his performance of action A, by Requirement 2 he has to accept that he does A freely. But Frankfurt recognizes that he cannot accept this if he cleaves to Requirement 1.

[27] Ibid., 56.
[28] Ibid.

To show that it is not exegetically inaccurate to hold that Frankfurt accepts condition (ii), one must show that, given his expressed views, Frankfurt should hold Requirement 1. To achieve this, one must outline a way in which Requirements 1 and 2 can be reconciled such that Frankfurt can hold that although a person does not act freely (i.e., autonomously) when he acts under duress of a certain degree of harshness, he is *still* morally responsible for his actions.

Fortunately, such reconciliation can be achieved once it is recognized that Frankfurt does not accept the Assumption of the Transitivity of Autonomy; hence Frankfurt can distinguish between the degree to which a person is autonomous with respect to his desires and the degree to which he is autonomous with respect to his consequent actions. On Frankfurt's hierarchical analysis of what it is for a person to be autonomous with respect to his desires, a person who acts under duress (even under duress of a certain degree of harshness) will be autonomous with respect to the first-order desire that moved him to comply with the threat that confronted him. However, it is clear from his statements in "Coercion and Moral Responsibility," concerning the man who was forced at gunpoint to hand over his money to a highwayman, that Frankfurt does not accept that such a person is thereby fully autonomous with respect to his compliant action. Frankfurt might claim that attributions of moral responsibility should rest on whether the person being so assessed was autonomous with respect to the *desire* that moved him to perform the act that is in question. Thus, rather than adopting a stance of indifference as to which of the reasonable requirements he should accept and which he should reject, Frankfurt could modify Requirement 2 to read: a person must freely desire to perform an action (i.e., must be autonomous with respect to that first-order desire that led him to perform it) for him to be morally responsible for it. In this way, Frankfurt could retain both Requirement 1 and Requirement 2, and also his view that a person who performs an action under duress is morally responsible for it.

Having reconciled Requirements 1 and 2 in this way, one would not be mistaken to attribute condition (ii) to Frankfurt, even though his acceptance of both the (unmodified) Requirement 2, that a person is only morally responsible for what he does freely, and the view that a person may be morally responsible for the actions that he performs under duress, seems to imply that he cannot accept it. Not only is Frankfurt able to avoid Thalberg's first objection, since he is not committed to accepting the Assumption of the Transitivity of Autonomy (despite what is standardly believed), but he is also able to escape from the quandary in which he finds himself at the end of "Three Concepts of Free Action."

D. The response to Thalberg's second objection

In addition to avoiding Thalberg's first objection, the generalized hierarchical approach to analyzing autonomy is also able to avoid Thalberg's second objection, that a person under duress is not principally averse to being moved to act by a certain desire, but to the situation in which he finds himself. On this understanding of the hierarchical approach, its proponents can *agree* with Thalberg that, in cases of duress, the principal object of the victim's aversion is *not* the first-order desire that moves him to act, but, as expressed in condition (ii), the situation in which he finds himself. Of course, this response to Thalberg does not extend to cases in which a person is subject to coercion, for the hierarchical analysts would still claim that the autonomy of a victim of coercion is impaired, since he is moved to act by a desire that he does not volitionally endorse (by condition [i]). Despite appearances, however, such cases of coercion (rather than duress) are not susceptible to Thalberg's second objection. The reason they are not susceptible is simple: They are *defined* in such a way that they only include those cases where the victim's aversion is to his effective first-order desire, and not to his act or to the situation that he is in.

IV. Further Objections to Frankfurt's and Dworkin's Analyses

The generally accepted view that Thalberg's objections to Frankfurt's and Dworkin's hierarchical analyses of personal autonomy are either fatal to such analyses or demonstrate that they require serious modifications is, as I have thus far argued, mistaken. Moreover, once Frankfurt's and Dworkin's views have been properly understood (i.e., it is recognized that they are not committed to the Assumption of the Transitivity of Autonomy), it will be realized that they do not actually offer *hierarchical* analyses of why it is that a victim of duress who performs a compliant action thereby suffers from impaired autonomy. Instead, these apparently hierarchical analyses of what it is for a person to be autonomous with respect to her actions should be recognized as (to use a better term) *Situation-Averse* analyses, since they are based on the claim that the victim's autonomy is impaired owing to the situation that she is in, and not because she suffers from any disharmony in her motivational hierarchy.

A. Impairments of autonomy can differ in degree

Even though Frankfurt's and Dworkin's approaches to analyzing personal autonomy manage to avoid Thalberg's objections, they still suffer from significant theoretical difficulties. The first of these arises from the fact that a person can be more or less autonomous with respect to her actions, where (roughly) the degree to which she is autonomous with respect to them correlates to the degree to which it is she, and not someone else, who controls her performance of them.[29] It thereby follows that a person will suffer impaired autonomy with respect to her actions in proportion to the degree that she cedes control over them to someone else. This being so, a person who is threatened with a severe penalty unless she performs "an action within the week whose performance she disvalues" will suffer *less* impairment of her autonomy with respect to her consequent compliant action than will another victim of duress (such as the victim of Dworkin's highwayman) whose compliant action is specified in greater detail by his threatener. This is because the former victim of duress is able to exercise a greater degree of control over both *what* action she is to perform to avoid incurring the threatened penalty and *when* she is to perform it, than is the latter victim, who lacks control over both the nature ("Hand over your billfold!") and the timing ("Now!") of his compliant action. However, the Situation-Averse analyses outlined above aim only to explain how a person might suffer from impaired autonomy, *simpliciter*, when she performs compliant actions as a result of being subjected to duress. Such analyses cannot readily account for the fact that victims of duress might suffer from differing degrees of autonomy-impairment with respect to their compliant actions. Consequently, these analyses fail to offer a complete account of the relationship that holds between a person's being subject to duress and the consequent impairment of her autonomy when she performs the compliant actions that are required of her.

It might be tempting to respond to this first theoretical difficulty by modifying the Situation-Averse analyses, such that the autonomy of a victim of duress will be impaired in proportion to the degree that she resents acting solely to prevent her situation from worsening, rather than acting to improve it. This temptation should be resisted, however, for it commits the proponents of Situation-Averse analyses to claiming that, if the person in the above example whose compliant action was left unspecified by her threatener resents being subject to duress to a higher degree than does the victim of Dworkin's highwayman, then it will be she, and not the highway-robbery victim, who will suffer from the greater impairment in autonomy. Yet to claim this is to claim that the person who retains a greater degree of control over her actions suffers from a greater impairment of her autonomy with respect to those actions than the person who retains less control over his actions—and this is obviously mistaken.

B. The Anti-Stoic Objection

The difficulty that is posed by this suggested modification to the Situation-Averse analyses leads to the second major objection that such

[29] For an informative discussion of this point, see James W. Child, "Specific Commands, General Rules, and Degrees of Autonomy," *Canadian Journal of Law and Jurisprudence* 8, no. 2 (1995): 245–58.

analyses face: they have troubling Stoic implications. On these Situation-Averse analyses, a victim of duress will suffer from impaired autonomy with respect to her compliant actions if and only if she resents that she is performing these actions only to prevent her situation from getting worse, rather than to improve it. Thus, like the Stoic view of freedom, in which a person can become free by altering her expectations in the face of externally imposed constraints, so that these constraints are no longer felt as such, according to these Situation-Averse analyses, a victim of duress will not suffer from impaired autonomy if she *fails* to resent that she is moved to act only to prevent her situation from getting worse, rather than to improve it.

This view is mistaken, though. To see just how mistaken it is, consider the cases of Vinnie and Vera, who have both been held up at gunpoint in New York City and forced to hand over their billfolds. When confronted by the gunman, both Vinnie and Vera quickly decide that it would be prudent to comply with his demands, and they rapidly, volitionally endorse their first-order desires to comply with his threat. Vera, however, is outraged by what she takes to be a personal affront to the sanctity of her person—"Such a thing would never have happened to her in her hometown in Minnesota!"—and so deeply resents having to hand over her billfold in order to prevent her situation from (rapidly and bloodily) getting worse. As one would expect, then, the Situation-Averse analyses hold that Vera's autonomy is impaired with respect to her compliant action. By contrast, Vinnie, a native of the Bronx, simply regards the whole episode as part of the cost of living in New York City. (Indeed, rather than resenting his having to act for the reason that he did, Vinnie admires the gunman's *chutzpah* in holding him up in Macy's on a Saturday morning.) In this case, the Situation-Averse analyses hold that Vinnie does *not* suffer from any impairment of his autonomy. This cannot be correct, however, for to avoid being shot, Vinnie cedes to the gunman the *same* degree of control over his actions as did Vera. Since both Vinnie and Vera lack the same degree of self-direction with regard to their compliant actions, their autonomy with respect to their respective compliant actions must (*ceteris paribus*) be impaired to the same degree.

This objection to the Situation-Averse analyses can be termed the *Anti-Stoic Objection*, since it is based on denying the Stoic view of freedom as it is outlined above. This Anti-Stoic Objection can be generalized. Consider, for example, the slave who believes that it is his God-given lot in life to work solely to avoid being beaten, the political prisoner who fails to resent his incarceration because he believes that he will not have the courage openly to avow his political views outside the Gulag, and the downtrodden wife who has resigned herself to expect nothing better in life than constantly being told what to do by her husband. All three of these people suffer from impaired autonomy, even though each fails to resent being moved just to prevent his or her situation from becoming worse.[30] This because it is not the slave, the political prisoner, or the wife, but someone else, who controls which actions they perform and when. From considerations such as this, it appears that the Situation-Averse analyses have confused the degree to which a person suffers from impairment in her autonomy with the degree to which she suffers from a diminution in her well-being. The contented slave, the political prisoner, and the downtrodden wife might all be unaffected by the autonomy-undermining situations in which they find themselves—and this is why they fail to resent them. However, the fact that these persons fail to resent being moved to act for the reasons that they are moved to act does not show that their autonomy with respect to their actions is thereby unimpaired. Instead, it merely shows that these situations do not adversely affect the well-being of these individuals as much as one would expect. The Stoic retreat into the "inner citadel" of one's reason, soul, or noumenal self might protect one's well-being, but it still leaves one's autonomy undefended.[31]

V. THE ANALYSES OF CHRISTMAN AND SLOTE

Although Frankfurt's and Dworkin's Situation-Averse analyses of why a person who acts under duress thereby suffers from impaired autonomy are unsatisfactory, both John Christman and Michael Slote have held that the general approach that Dworkin and Frankfurt take to this problem is sufficiently promising to warrant further exploration.

A. Christman's analysis

In response to Thalberg's objections, Christman argues that a proponent of the hierarchical approach to analyzing personal autonomy need not evaluate the compliant action of a victim of duress as being one that he was fully autonomous with respect to, as Thalberg claimed.[32] Unfor-

---

[30] The example of a (real-life) Stoic slave is discussed in Sigurdur Krisstonson, "The Limits of Neutrality: Toward a Weakly Substantive Account of Autonomy," *Canadian Journal of Philosophy* 30, no. 2 (2000): 257–86. The example of the political prisoners who fail to resent their incarceration is discussed in Flint Schier, "The Kantian Gulag: Autonomy and the Liberal Conception of Freedom," in Dudley Knowles and John Skorupski, eds., *Virtue and Taste: Essays on Politics, Ethics, and Aesthetics* (Oxford: Blackwell, 1993), 1–17.

[31] Concerns about such a retreat were famously raised by Isaiah Berlin in *Four Essays on Liberty* (Oxford: Oxford University Press, 1969), 135–36. The worry that such Stoicism conflates the preservation of well-being with the preservation of one's ability to act freely (i.e., autonomously) has been expressed by Wright Neely in "Freedom and Desire," *Philosophical Review* 83, no. 1 (1974): 38. A similar objection has also been offered by David Zimmerman, "Making Do," 25–30.

[32] Christman, "Introduction," 8–9. Christman's failure to recognize Thalberg's misunderstanding of Frankfurt's and Dworkin's analyses indicates that he similarly failed to understand them properly, for, had he done so, he would have recognized that they were not susceptible to Thalberg's objections. Christman's modification of these analyses is thus

tunately, however, Christman did not reach this (correct) conclusion after recognizing that Thalberg had misunderstood the hierarchical analyses, for Christman accepted the conventional view that Thalberg's first objection to these analyses showed that they were in need of modification. Christman's response to Thalberg is based on an example of a bank teller who hands over his bank's money to a robber, solely in order to avoid being shot. Christman argues that the hierarchical analyses of autonomy could be salvaged if one accepts that, in such a case, "there are actually two operative desires that the agent has, both with the same object: giving over the money. The first is the desire to not be heroic in threatening situations. . . . [T]he other relevant desire is to give over the money *in this particular case.*"[33] Christman argues that these two desires "are importantly different because they have different origins: they were adopted for differing reasons and under different circumstances."[34] The bank teller's *first* desire, Christman argues, is one that he is autonomous with respect to, for he approves of the way in which he came to possess it.[35] According to Christman, however, the bank teller's *second* desire is not one that he is autonomous with respect to, for he does not approve of the way in which he came to possess this desire. He would not have formed this desire had he not been placed under duress. From this example, Christman concludes that "if one's account of autonomy requires that all the relevant desires causing an action be autonomously formed, then . . . [the bank teller] . . . is not autonomous" when he compliantly hands over the money to the robber.[36]

Although Christman's historical analysis of autonomy leads him to conclude correctly that persons who perform compliant actions under duress thereby suffer from impaired autonomy, his analysis suffers from several flaws that prevent it from being a fully satisfactory account of why this is so. The first two objections to Christman's historical analysis of why the compliant victim of duress suffers from impaired autonomy question the psychological plausibility of the motivational structure that Christman attributes to him. First, and most obviously, it is questionable whether the bank teller who complies with the robber's threat really possesses *two* operative first-order desires that share the object of handing over the money, as Christman claims. Instead, it is more likely that the

---

redundant, insofar as it is considered a defense of them against Thalberg's objections. This is not also to say, however, that Christman's modification lacks considerable merit in its own right as an attempt to explain how it is that the typical compliant victim of duress suffers from impaired autonomy, owing to his subjection.

[33] Ibid., 8. Emphasis in original.

[34] Ibid.

[35] For Christman's innovative historical account of what it is for a person to be autonomous with respect to his desires, see John Christman, "Autonomy: A Defense of the Split-Level Self," *Southern Journal of Philosophy* 21, no. 3 (1987): 281–93; and John Christman, "Autonomy and Personal History," *Canadian Journal of Philosophy* 21, no. 1 (1991): 1–24.

[36] Christman, "Introduction," 9.

teller has only *one* operative first-order desire to hand over the money, and it is this desire that moves him to act. Indeed, it seems that the only reason one might have to posit the existence of a *second* first-order desire is if one is a hierarchical analyst of autonomy who wishes to explain how a compliant victim of duress suffers from impaired autonomy, and who accepts Thalberg's (mistaken) view that the only way that one can explain this (while at the same time retaining the hierarchical approach to autonomy) is to posit that such a victim suffers from motivational discord across his different levels of desire. This point leads to the second objection to Christman's account. As Thalberg noted, the most likely object of the teller's aversion is *not* his operative first-order desire (or that operative first-order desire whose conditions of formation he does not approve of) but to the *situation* that he is in.[37] And if this is so, then any account of why a person who performs a compliant action under duress thereby suffers from impaired autonomy that is based on this person's aversion to one or another of his desires will rest on an inaccurate description of such a victim's actual motivational state.

In addition to these two objections, which apply specifically to Christman's historical analysis, Christman's approach is also subject to the objections that beset Frankfurt's and Dworkin's (properly understood) Situation-Averse analyses. Like these analyses, Christman's lacks the theoretical resources to explain why it is that a person who is afforded considerable latitude with respect to both *what* compliant action she will perform and *when* she will perform it, suffers from *less* impairment of her autonomy than a person whose compliant action is specified in detail by her threatener. Furthermore, Christman's analysis also has the same troubling Stoic implications that beset the earlier Situation-Averse analyses of Frankfurt and Dworkin. This is because, on Christman's analysis, a person's autonomy with respect to her compliant action will be unimpaired if two conditions are met: (1) she does *not* object to one of her operative first-order desires being formed by her being placed under duress, and (2) she also has no objection as to how she came to have her other, previously formed, operative first-order desire with the same object. If this is the case, then persons who are Stoically resigned to their lot (such as the slave, the wife, and the political prisoner in the examples that I mentioned above) will be held to suffer from no impairment in their autonomy, even if they are constantly forced to perform actions under duress. And, as was noted above, this is highly counterintuitive.

B. *Slote's analysis*

Christman's historical analysis, then, is no more persuasive than the Situation-Averse analyses that he intends it to replace—indeed, given its

---

[37] Thalberg, "Hierarchical Analyses," 127.

susceptibility to the additional objections that I outlined in the preceding section, it appears to fare worse. Alas, Slote's development of Frankfurt's and Dworkin's analyses fares little better. Analyzing why it is that a person who acts in compliance to a threat thereby suffers from an impairment of his autonomy, Slote begins by focusing on the claim that such a person will *resent* being placed under duress. Slote argues that the resentment that a person is likely to feel when he is placed under duress signifies a desire or a wish to defy the person who is placing him under duress, or to retaliate against that person. This being so, Slote continues, the victim of duress "will have various momentary/fragmentary fantasies of heroic defiance, or foiling, or retaliation, with appropriate accompanying thoughts."[38] Consequently, Slote argues, the victim will be *ambivalent* about his own compliance, and to the extent that he resents having to act in this way and wishes that he had chosen to defy his threatener, he will reproach himself for choosing to save his own skin. In complying with the threat, then, "such a person acts from a desire by which he wishes not to be moved to act, even given the alternatives that he confronts. There is in him a conflict between a first-order desire to comply (and play it safe) and an ultimately frustrated second-order volition that that desire not be effective and that . . . he should overcome that safe-playing desire through appropriate heroics or defiance."[39] Slote concludes that there is no need to reformulate Frankfurt's views to respond to the possibility that Frankfurt is committed to the mistaken claim that victims of duress will be fully autonomous with respect to their compliant actions, since, owing to the motivational ambivalence that they experience, such persons will *not* count as being autonomous with respect to their effective first-order desires to comply.

The first objection to Slote's analysis comes from David Zimmerman, who has noted that it rests on the claim that, if a person resents being moved to perform a compliant action, then he will automatically form a second-order volition that he not be moved by his first-order desire to comply. However, Zimmerman argues, it is not at all clear that this will happen, because the mere fact that a person resents a certain state of affairs need not lead to him judging that he should resist it.[40] Thus, even though the typical compliant victim of duress might resent being forced to comply with the demands of his threatener, he is not necessarily subject to any motivational ambivalence, for his resentment need not automatically lead him to form a second-order volition repudiating his effective first-order desire to comply. If Slote's analysis is correct, then there might be some compliant (and resentful) victims of duress whose autonomy remains unimpaired, despite their subjection.

[38] Slote, "Understanding Free Will," 127.
[39] Ibid.
[40] Zimmerman, "Making Do," 47.

Yet, even if one accepts, for the sake of argument, that Slote is correct to claim that a person's feelings of resentment will lead to his volitional repudiation of his effective first-order desire to comply, Slote's focus on a person's motivational ambivalence as the source of impaired autonomy has the counterintuitive implication that even a person who exercises significant control over his life does not act autonomously, *unless* he does not suffer from any serious doubts about the advisability of his actions. To see this, consider an example that was developed by Paul Benson, which I am using here to different purpose: Charlotte, a "white, middle-class American woman," comes to adulthood in the 1880s, and "finds the rigid, conventional roles that women of her class are expected to take up—wife, mother and housekeeper—to be nearly intolerable."[41] Charlotte thoroughly detests the conventional role that she is expected to play, and leaves her husband and children in order to pursue an artistic career—an occupation that, owing to her socialization, she agrees is "an unsuitable job for a woman" (if I may borrow that description here, as has another philosopher, from novelist P. D. James).[42] However, Charlotte does not leave her family as a result of having undergone a feminist version of St. Paul's conversion on the road to Damascus. Instead, owing to her internalization of her era's norms of femininity, Charlotte's decision to abandon her family and pursue a career is agonizingly difficult for her, and even after she has made this decision, she continues to experience "various momentary/fragmentary fantasies" of returning to her family and living as a dutiful (if frustrated) Victorian wife and mother. Moreover, these "momentary/fragmentary fantasies" of return that Charlotte experiences are not merely idle daydreams, for they lead her to feel so guilty about leaving her family that she forms a second-order volition that repudiates her effective first-order desire to pursue her career. Nevertheless, despite the guilt that she experiences, Charlotte still, all things considered, believes that she should continue to pursue her artistic yearnings, and so her desire to do so still moves her to act.

Charlotte thus experiences the same sort of motivational ambivalence that Slote's compliant victim of duress experiences, for they both experience a motivational conflict at the level of their second-order volitions. However, rather than claiming that, as a result of this motivational am-

---

[41] Paul Benson, "Feeling Crazy: Self-Worth and the Social Character of Responsibility," in Catriona Mackenzie and Natalie Stoljar, eds., *Relational Autonomy: Feminist Perspectives on Autonomy, Agency, and the Social Self* (Oxford: Oxford University Press, 2000), 74. It should be noted that Benson developed the example of Charlotte in order to illustrate his views concerning the relationship between a person's self-worth and her moral responsibility for her actions, rather than to illuminate the conditions that are required for a person to be autonomous with respect to her actions. The following discussion in the text of this example might thus not be pertinent to Benson's own use of it.

[42] A similar example is given by Marina Oshana, who also recognizes the appropriateness of the title of P. D. James's novel, *An Unsuitable Job for a Woman*, in Oshana's discussion of her own example. Marina Oshana, "The Autonomy Bogeyman," *Journal of Value Inquiry* 35 (2001): 220.

bivalence, Charlotte is *not* autonomous with respect to her acts of leaving her family and pursuing her career, it is far more plausible to claim that she is *highly* autonomous with respect to these acts, for they demonstrate that she is directing the course of her own life despite considerable social pressure not to do so. But if this is so, it cannot be the case that a person's experience of motivational ambivalence at the level of her second-order volitions is sufficient for her to be held to suffer from impaired autonomy.

Of course, one might rightly object that this criticism of Slote's analysis trades heavily on the intuition that Charlotte *is* acting autonomously when she leaves her husband to pursue a life of art—and that simply *claiming* that this is so is not the same as *showing* that it is so. In order to make the above objection to Slote's analysis compelling, then, one must fill out the details of Charlotte's motivational structure. For this objection to hold, it must be plausible to attribute to Charlotte a motivational structure that is structurally identical to that which Slote holds is possessed by a compliant victim of duress. Moreover, it must be the case that, when the details of Charlotte's motivational structure are filled out, it is clear that there is a theoretical basis (rather than a merely intuitive one) for considering her to be autonomous with respect to her pursuit of her artistic career.

As I argued above, it is plausible to hold that, like Slote's compliant victim of duress, Charlotte suffers from conflicting second-order volitions. Now, as Thalberg noted, most compliant victims of duress, all things considered, *endorse* their effective first-order desires to comply. To develop Thalberg's insight further, one can attribute to such persons the possession of a *third*-order volition endorsing their pro-compliance, second-order volitions (i.e., all things considered, they prefer to be moved to comply rather than to resist). Since this is so, for Charlotte's motivational structure to be structurally identical to that of the compliant victim of duress, it must be plausible to ascribe to Charlotte a third-order volition endorsing her effective first-order desire to pursue her career. And this is indeed the case, for it is plausible that she might, all things considered, endorse her desire to pursue an artistic career and leave her family. Thus, since one can plausibly ascribe structurally identical motivational patterns to both Charlotte and the compliant victim of duress, and since the details of these motivational patterns (having been filled out) provide a theoretical basis for holding Charlotte to be autonomous with respect to her pursuit of her career, Slote is faced with a dilemma. He can either continue to claim that second-order volitional ambivalence suffices for a person to suffer from impaired autonomy, or he can accept that a person's being subject to such volitional ambivalence is not sufficient for her to suffer from impaired autonomy. If Slote chooses the first horn of this dilemma, he will be committed to the claim that Charlotte's autonomy is impaired when she defies social custom and pursues her own goals. This claim is highly counterintuitive. However, if he chooses the second horn of this dilemma, then his account of why it is that a compliant victim of duress suffers from impaired autonomy is incomplete.[43]

VI. WHY THE COMPLIANT VICTIM OF DURESS SUFFERS FROM IMPAIRED AUTONOMY

From this discussion it is clear that there is something very baffling about the status of actions that a person performs solely in order to avoid incurring a threatened penalty. A person who is subjected to duress *chooses* to perform her compliant actions after deciding that her performance of them offers the least unattractive option from a set of unpalatable alternatives with which she is faced. Since she thus desires to perform these actions, and this desire moves her to perform them, it seems, prima facie, plausible to claim that she is fully self-directed, fully autonomous, with respect to their performance. However, to claim that a person who is *forced* to perform a series of compliant actions by being subjected to duress is a paradigm of someone who is engaged in autonomous self-direction seems clearly mistaken. The most obvious way of resolving this difficulty is, of course, to deny one or the other of the intuitions that these claims express. However, it would be far more satisfying to provide an account of personal autonomy that is able to respond to both of these tugs of intuition, when it is applied to a situation in which a person acts solely in order to comply with a threat.

A. An informative false start

Given that one can reject the Assumption of the Transitivity of Autonomy, the clearest way to provide an account of personal autonomy that is able to respond to both of these tugs of intuition is to follow the lead of Frankfurt and Dworkin, and to develop an account in which it is a necessary but not a sufficient condition for a person to be autonomous with respect to her actions, that she be autonomous with respect to her effective first-order desires. One could thus argue that, although the compliant victim of duress might be autonomous with respect to the effective first-order desire that moves her to perform her compliant action, she is still *not* autonomous with respect to the act itself. Since this is so, it is tempting to argue that a person who performs a compliant action under duress is moved to act by the effective first-order desire that w: "to do whatever my threatener tells me I must do to avoid incurring the penalty I am threatened with." Given her situation, this person might be autonomous with respect to this desire. (She might volitionally endorse it and be satisfied with it; it might be authentically hers, and she might be both substan-

---

[43] Worse yet, Zimmerman argues that Slote's position is incoherent. Zimmerman, "Making Do," 48–50.

tively and procedurally independent with respect to it; she might decide to treat it as reason-giving; and so forth.)[44] However, to satisfy her desire that w, she will cede control over her actions to her threatener, and thus suffer from impaired autonomy with respect to these actions.

This *Simple Analysis*, as it may be called, certainly satisfies both of the intuitions that are expressed in the aforementioned claims. The intuition that the compliant victim of duress retains full autonomy even under duress because she *chose* to act as she did, is satisfied, since she *is* autonomous with respect to her effective first-order desire to comply. Similarly, the intuition that she suffers from impaired autonomy as a result of being *forced* to act as she did is also satisfied, since to satisfy her desire that w, she ceded control over her actions to her threatener. Nevertheless, the temptation to account in this way for the impaired autonomy of a compliant victim of duress should be resisted, for several reasons.

First, it is not clear that the actual first-order desire that moves a compliant victim of duress to perform her compliant action is as general and open-ended as the above desire that w. For example, when a highwayman's victim hands over his billfold in order to avoid being shot, it is plausible to assume that at least part of the object of his effective first-order desire concerns the specific action that he is being forced to perform. But this is overlooked by the Simple Analysis, which holds that the object of this victim's effective first-order desire is that of the desire that w.

From this first objection to the Simple Analysis, one can also develop a second: the *Objection from Illegitimate Redescription*. The Simple Analysis appears to rest on the presupposition that it is legitimate to redescribe the intentional object of a person's effective first-order desire. (For example, the intentional object of the effective first-order desire of the victim of the highwayman should not be described as "handing over my billfold to avoid being shot," but as "performing an action that will preserve my well-being.") It is doubtful that such redescription is legitimate.[45] However, even if such redescription were legitimate, it would be self-defeating to aim to satisfy *both* of the intuitions expressed earlier by developing an analysis, which rests on this basis, of why it is that the compliant victim of duress suffers from impaired autonomy. This is because, if it is legitimate to redescribe the objects of a person's effective first-order desires in this way, then there seems to be no principled objection to allowing her *actions* to be similarly redescribed as well. If this were the case, then the compliant actions of any such victim of duress might be described as

---

[44] These accounts of what it is for a person to be autonomous with respect to her effective first-order desires are, respectively, those of Frankfurt in "Freedom of the Will" and "The Faintest Passion," Dworkin in "Autonomy and Behavior Control," and Michael E. Bratman in "Identification, Decision, and Treating as a Reason," *Philosophical Topics* 24, no. 2 (1996): 1–18.

[45] Dworkin expresses doubts about such redescription in "Acting Freely," 372–75.

those "that secure her well-being." With this redescription of the compliant victim's actions in hand, it is a simple matter, on this analysis, to move
to the claim that the victim is autonomous with respect to *both* her effective first-order desires and her consequent actions. This is because, under
this revised description of her actions, no mention is made of the victim's
ceding any control over them to another. Instead, she merely desires to act
so as to secure her well-being and she does so. But to make this claim is
inconsistent with the Simple Analysis, for in making it one denies that the
compliant victim's autonomy is impaired. The Simple Analysis, then,
faces two immediate and related difficulties. First, to defend it one will
have to establish the legitimacy of redescribing the victim's effective first-
order desires. Second, even if the legitimacy of such redescription *can* be
established, it seems that there will be no principled objection to holding
that the compliant victim of duress is autonomous with respect to both
her effective first-order desires and her actions.

In order for one to defend the Simple Analysis further, one might do so
by noting that these two objections to it are based on the understanding
that the Simple Analysis is committed to the claim that the typical compliant victim of duress is moved to act by the first-order desire that
w —and this is not so. Instead, it is consistent with the Simple Analysis to
hold that the compliant victim of duress forms her desire that w *prior* to
her forming her effective (and more specific) first-order desire that p
("to hand over her billfold"), such that she forms her desire that p to
satisfy her desire that w. Unfortunately, this revised version of the Simple
Analysis will not suffice either, for if this revised description of the motivational structure of the compliant victim of duress were accurate, she
would cede control not only of her actions to her threatener, but also of
her effective first-order desires. This is because it appears that, after the
compliant victim of duress has formed the desire that w, it will be up to
her threatener what actions she will perform, and thus it will *also* be up
to him what specific first-order desires she will need to form, in order to
be appropriately moved to act to satisfy her prior desire that w. And if this
is the case, then the compliant victim of duress will *not* retain her autonomy with respect to her effective first-order desires that p. But if this is so,
then the Simple Analysis will no longer satisfy both of the intuitions
expressed above, for if one accepts this revised version of the Simple
Analysis, one will regard the victim of duress as failing to exercise any
autonomy at all, after she has acted to satisfy her desire that w.

As an attempt to account for both of the intuitions expressed above, the
Simple Analysis is thus caught in a dilemma. In its original form, this
analysis must establish that it is theoretically legitimate to redescribe the
effective first-order desires of the victims of duress who comply with the
demands of their threateners. However, if the legitimacy of such redescription is established, it will lead to the development of an alternative analysis of how to characterize the autonomy of a compliant victim of duress—

one that does not satisfy the second intuition (i.e., that the victim of duress suffers from impaired autonomy through being forced to act as she did). Yet, if the Simple Analysis is revised to avoid this problem in the way outlined here, it will no longer satisfy the first of the two intuitions (i.e., that the compliant victim of duress retains full autonomy even under duress because she *chose* to act as she did).

B. Learning from the Simple Analysis

Despite these difficulties faced by the Simple Analysis, there is still something intuitively compelling about its core idea that the effective first-order desire that moves the compliant victim of duress to act is one whose satisfaction involves her ceding control over her actions to another. This core idea, then, might be retained as the basis for an alternative analysis that will satisfy both of the intuitions expressed in the preceding subsection. Furthermore, one can also draw from the previously discussed objections to the Simple Analysis an idea of what counterintuitive traps should be avoided by a satisfactory account of why a compliant victim of duress suffers from impaired autonomy.

The first set of objections to the Simple Analysis showed that one should not assume that one can intentionally describe the object of a compliant victim's effective first-order desire without making reference to the particular act that it moves her to perform. In addition to this, the second set of objections to the Simple Analysis showed that, to satisfy both of the intuitions discussed above, one cannot posit that the compliant victim of duress abdicated complete control over her compliant actions to her threatener. This second point is reinforced by the fact that persons who are subject to duress do not simply perform *any* act that their threatener requires of them in order to avoid incurring the threatened penalty. Instead, persons subject to duress will assess whether or not they are willing to perform the particular act required of them in order to avoid the threatened penalty, where the severity of the penalty might be sufficient to move them to perform some actions, but not others. From these two objections to the Simple Analysis, it can be seen that a satisfactory analysis of how it is that a compliant victim of duress suffers from impaired autonomy will have to recognize *both* (1) that the object of the victim's effective first-order desire should include a reference to the specific act that she is required to perform, *and* (2) that the victim will herself decide whether or not to perform the particular act that her threatener requires of her.

It is easy to construe this second condition as requiring that a satisfactory analysis must be one that regards the compliant victim of duress as a person who assesses whether or not she will choose to perform the act her threatener requires of her. However, this is precisely how *not* to understand this second condition, for to view the victim's deliberative process in this way is to misunderstand her situation. This is because when a person under duress deliberates about whether or not to perform the action that her threatener requires of her, she is not deliberating as to whether or not she should *perform* this action, but whether or not she should *resist* being forced to do it. This distinction between the possible deliberative aims that might be ascribed to a person who is subject to duress is not without a difference, for it points to the different default positions that are held by a person who is not subject to duress and by one who is. For the former, the default conclusion of her deliberative process is (typically) that she *will not* perform the action she is considering (i.e., she will not perform it unless she believes that she has a reason to do so). For the latter, the default position is (typically) that she *will* perform the action that she is considering (i.e., she will perform it unless she believes that she has a reason to resist doing so). Thus, if a person who is subjected to duress decides that she should perform the act that is required of her by her threatener, in order to avoid the penalty that he is threatening her with, then she will not be moved to act by the desire to perform this action *simpliciter*. Instead, she will be moved to act by the desire "not to resist another's attempt to exercise control over me such that I perform act *x* at his behest."

Once it is recognized that it is *this* desire that moves the compliant victim of duress to act, a satisfactory account of how it is that such a victim suffers from impaired autonomy can be developed, along lines similar to that of the Simple Analysis. On this new account (the *Revised Simple Analysis*) the compliant victim of duress *is* autonomous with respect to her effective first-order desire to fail to resist her threatener and thus to perform the act that he requires of her. (This satisfies the first intuition expressed at the beginning of this section.) However, since the satisfaction of this desire involves her relinquishing control to her threatener, the victim of duress suffers from impaired autonomy with respect to her compliant action. (This satisfies the second intuition.) Moreover, in addition to satisfying both of these intuitions, the Revised Simple Analysis also satisfies the two requirements that were outlined earlier in this section: (1) the effective first-order desire that the compliant victim of duress is posited to have includes, as part of its intentional object, a reference to the specific act that she is required to perform; and (2) it is the case that the victim herself decides whether or not to resist performing the act that her threatener requires of her.

VII. CONCLUSION

It is now time to take stock. I have argued that Frankfurt's and Dworkin's highly influential analyses of identification and personal autonomy have been misunderstood, for it has been assumed by their critics and supporters alike that they are committed to the Assumption of the Transitivity of Autonomy when, in fact, they are not. It has also been argued in this essay that, once it has been recognized that neither Frankfurt nor Dworkin are committed to this assumption, Thalberg's objections to their hierarchical approach to analyzing autonomy are unfounded. However, that this is so can provide only cold comfort to the proponents of such hierarchical analyses of autonomy, for even when these analyses are properly understood, they still suffer from significant theoretical difficulties.

Nevertheless, this discussion of Frankfurt's and Dworkin's analyses did not arrive only at this rather dispiriting conclusion. Rather, in making clear both what the Assumption of the Transitivity of Autonomy is and the fact that it can be rejected, this discussion paved the way for development of the Revised Simple Analysis of why it is that a compliant victim of duress suffers from impaired autonomy. The Revised Simple Analysis satisfies both of the (apparently conflicting) intuitions that surround the question of whether or not a person who compliantly acts under duress thereby suffers from impaired autonomy.

I noted at the start of this essay that the issues that I planned to discuss are not only of parochial interest to those who are concerned with Thalberg's criticisms of the hierarchical approach to analyzing personal autonomy, but are also of interest to others who are engaged by the perennial question of whether a person who compliantly performs an action under duress thereby suffers from impaired autonomy. However, the issues in this essay are of even broader interest than this, for once the possibility of rejecting the Assumption of the Transitivity of Autonomy has been explicitly recognized, one can also see that it is possible that a theoretically complete analysis of personal autonomy might require that different conditions hold for a person to be autonomous with respect to her desires and with respect to her actions. This recognition is important, for such distinctions may well have significant implications for those areas of moral philosophy in which the nature and value of personal autonomy play a central role.

Philosophy, Louisiana State University

AUTONOMY AND HIERARCHY*

By Michael E. Bratman

I. The Autonomy-Hierarchy Thesis

In autonomous action the agent herself directs and governs the action. But what is it for the agent herself to direct and to govern? One theme in a series of articles by Harry G. Frankfurt is that we can make progress in answering this question by appeal to *higher-order conative attitudes.*[1] Frankfurt's original version of this idea is that in acting of one's own free will, one is not acting simply because one desires so to act. Rather, it is also true that this desire motivates one's action because one desires that this desire motivate one's action. This latter desire about the motivational role of one's desire is a second-order desire. It is, in particular, what Frankfurt calls a second-order "volition." And, according to Frankfurt's original proposal, acting of one's own free will involves in this way such second-order, and sometimes yet higher order, volitions.[2]

Frankfurt's hierarchical proposal has met with a number of challenges and has been subject to clarification and emendation.[3] I myself have elsewhere tried to map out some details of this debate.[4] My concern here, however, is with the very idea that there is a close connection between autonomous agency and motivational hierarchy.

* Thanks to William Brewer, Alisa Carse, John Fischer, Nadeem Hussain, Margaret Little, Alfred Mele, Elijah Millgram, Henry Richardson, Neil Roughley, Ralph Wedgewood, and audiences at the Georgetown University Philosophy Department and the Social Philosophy and Policy Center, Bowling Green State University. Special thanks to Gideon Yaffe for a series of very helpful discussions. Work on this essay was supported by a fellowship from the John Simon Guggenheim Memorial Foundation.

[1] See Harry G. Frankfurt, *The Importance of What We Care About* (Cambridge: Cambridge University Press, 1988). See also Gerald Dworkin, "Acting Freely," *Nous* 4 (1970): 367–83; Wright Neely, "Freedom and Desire," *Philosophical Review* 83 (1974): 32–54; and Keith Lehrer, "Freedom, Preference, and Autonomy," *The Journal of Ethics* 1, no. 1 (1997): 3–25.

[2] Frankfurt, "Freedom of the Will and the Concept of a Person," in Frankfurt, *The Importance of What We Care About*, 11–25.

[3] For an important, early response to Frankfurt's original essay, see Gary Watson, "Free Agency," *Journal of Philosophy* 72 (1975): 205–20. Watson offers an alternative approach, one that replaces appeal to motivational hierarchy with an appeal to a distinction between motivational and evaluative orderings. Watson also points to at least two potential concerns for the hierarchical approach: (1) a concern about the grounds for seeing higher-order desires as having a stronger claim to speak for the agent than do lower-order desires, without embarking on an unacceptable regress; and (2) a concern about the idea that, in deliberation, we reflect on our desires rather than directly on our options. I discuss this second concern below, in the main text of this essay.

[4] Michael E. Bratman, "Identification, Decision, and Treating as a Reason," in Bratman, *Faces of Intention* (New York: Cambridge University Press, 1999), 185–206.

Of course, much depends on what kind of close connection one has in mind. Some might argue that all cases of human autonomous agency essentially involve motivational hierarchy. But I will focus on a somewhat weaker claim. As I see it, talk of autonomous agency and of autonomous action is talk of a highly abstract property of agents and actions, one that involves agential direction and governance of action. We can ask, what kinds of psychological functioning in human agents are such that they can constitute or realize this abstract property?[5] And we can consider the view that at least one central kind of psychological functioning that can constitute or realize human autonomous agency involves motivational hierarchy. That is, it involves the functioning of higher-order conative attitudes that concern the presence and/or functioning of conative attitudes. Perhaps there are other forms of functioning that could also claim to realize a kind of human autonomy. If there are, then we will want to understand their relation to the hierarchical model. But, at the least, a central kind of functioning that can realize human autonomy involves conative hierarchy. Or so it may be claimed. Let us call this the *autonomy-hierarchy (AH) thesis*. And let us ask why we should accept this thesis.[6]

Gary Watson points to reasons to be skeptical about accepting the AH thesis.[7] Watson notes that agents "do not (or need not usually) ask themselves which of their desires they want to be effective in action; they ask themselves which course of action is most worth pursuing. The initial practical question is about courses of action and not about themselves."[8] It seems to me that Watson is right in arguing that the "initial practical question" that is explicitly and consciously raised in one's practical reasoning is ordinarily about "courses of action" and not about ourselves. But it is one thing to acknowledge this point about the "initial practical question" and another thing to reject the idea that, in at least one central kind of case, autonomy involves motivational hierarchy.

---

[5] Here I am, broadly speaking, following both Frankfurt and J. David Velleman. See, in particular, J. David Velleman, "What Happens When Someone Acts?" in Velleman, *The Possibility of Practical Reason* (Oxford: Oxford University Press, 2000), 123-43. In speaking of functioning that realizes such an abstract property, however, I am making room for the possibility of multiple realizations. I am unsure whether Frankfurt or Velleman would also want to do so. (My appeal in the text to a "central kind of functioning" signals that my concern is with the limited claim that one theoretically important realization involves motivational hierarchy.) Let me also note here that, as I understand the notion of functioning, not all causal impacts will be included in an attitude's functioning.

[6] In Michael E. Bratman, "Reflection, Planning, and Temporally Extended Agency," *Philosophical Review* 109, no. 1 (2000): 35-61, I explore the role, in strong forms of human agency, of higher-order policies concerning the functioning of first-order desires in one's motivationally effective practical reasoning. A number of individuals have asked whether such policies about practical reasoning need to be higher order. (Samuel Scheffler once raised this question in a particularly helpful way in correspondence.) The present essay responds to these concerns.

[7] Watson, "Free Agency," 205-20.

[8] Ibid., 219.

Indeed, I believe that higher-order conative attitudes play a significant role in central cases of autonomous agency, and so we should accept the AH thesis. In support of this view I offer here two lines of argument. One line of argument (the one that will be my main focus here) derives from the role of valuing in central cases of autonomy, and from pressures on such valuing to involve hierarchy. This argument draws on the idea that an autonomous agent not only governs her actions, but also governs the practical reasoning from which those actions issue. A second line of argument for the AH thesis derives from the idea that an autonomous agent's governance of her own practical reasoning involves her understanding of this reasoning as so governed. In each case, there are reasons to think that a central model of psychological functioning that can at least partly constitute or realize human autonomous agency will make essential appeal to motivational hierarchy. The first step in advancing these arguments is to reflect on the phenomenon of valuing.

II. Valuing and Two Problems for Human Agents

It is sometimes useful in the philosophy of action to see certain features of human agency as (at least, implicit) responses to pervasive and systematic problems that human agents face. I think that this strategy is especially useful when we consider what it is to value something. In particular, I think that we can see valuing as a response to two different, though related, problems that reflective human agents face. I shall describe what these problems are, how valuing constitutes a response to them, and what light this sheds on the higher-order structure of valuing. I shall then explain why it is plausible to see such valuing as central to autonomy.

Many problems that we face as human beings are faced by a wide range of nonhuman agents as well; but some problems that we face are limited to agents who are, like us, reflective in certain ways. Here, I highlight two problems of the latter sort. The first concerns reflective self-management. We are creatures who are affected and moved by complex forms of motivation, and we sometimes find ourselves needing to reflect on, and respond to, these forms of motivation.[9] Suppose that I find myself angry, resentful, and desiring retribution. I am, however, reflective: I ask myself whether, as we say, I "really want" to pursue retribution or, rather, to turn the other cheek. I thereby face a problem of reflective self-management.

The second problem begins to arise once we make judgments of value, judgments that we see as intersubjectively accountable in characteristic

[9] This is a central Frankfurtian theme. The idea of casting this problem together with the problem, noted below in the text, of underdetermination by value judgment parallels aspects of Marth C. Nussbaum's discussion in her *The Fragility of Goodness: Luck and Ethics in Greek Tragedy and Philosophy* (Cambridge: Cambridge University Press, 1986), chap. 4.

ways.[10] On reflection, we can reasonably come to judge that there are many things that have value. We can also reasonably come to believe that a coherent human life frequently involves decisions and/or the assignment of weights, priorities, or other forms of significance that go beyond and are underdetermined by these prior, intersubjectively accountable judgments of value.[11] A dramatic case can be found in a version of Sartre's famous example.[12] A young man sees the value of fighting with the Free French, and he also sees the value of staying with his mother. With respect to these judgments, he may expect an appropriate form of intersubjective convergence. The young man also, however, believes that a coherent, temporally extended life requires some sort of specific, wholehearted commitment to one of these valuable activities over the other, a commitment with respect to which he may well not expect relevant intersubjective convergence. Granted, he may suppose that after he has arrived at a commitment to, say, the Free French, the value of loyalty to his commitment becomes salient; and about *this* value he may expect relevant intersubjective convergence. But this does not undermine the observation that there was underdetermination of the contours of the young man's life by his value judgments prior to arriving at his commitment.

I will call these two problems, respectively, problems of *self-management* and problems of *underdetermination (of the contours of one's life) by value judgment*. These are not only problems that philosophers have in theorizing about human agency. They are pervasive, practical problems faced by ordinary human agents.

This is not to say that these problems are normally ones with which we are explicitly and consciously concerned in our everyday practical thinking. Rather, much of our ordinary, day-to-day practical thinking takes for

---

[10] In "A Desire of One's Own" (*Journal of Philosophy*, forthcoming), I note several different ways of interpreting this constraint of intersubjectivity. We might, for example, see a judgment of value as made from a Humean "common point of view," or as a judgment that those who are appropriately rational and informed would converge in a relevant way, or as involving the expression of a demand on others to converge in relevant ways. And other interpretations are possible. For our present purposes we do not need to settle on a specific interpretation, though for ease of exposition I will sometimes write in ways that fit most naturally with the second of these interpretations. For a version of this second interpretation see Michael Smith, *The Moral Problem* (Oxford: Basil Blackwell, 1994), 151–77.

[11] A number of philosophers have emphasized ways in which such judgments of value can underdetermine the specific contours of an individual life. For present purposes I will take it for granted, without further argument, that there frequently is some such underdetermination. See, e.g., Isaiah Berlin, *Four Essays on Liberty* (Oxford: Oxford University Press, 1969); Robert Nozick, *Philosophical Explanations* (Cambridge, MA: Harvard University Press, 1981), esp. 446–50; and Joseph Raz, *The Morality of Freedom* (Oxford: Oxford University Press, 1986), chap. 14. Consider also T. M. Scanlon's remark that "one cannot respond to every value or pursue every end that is worthwhile, and a central part of life for a rational creature lies in selecting those things that it will pursue." T. M. Scanlon, *What We Owe to Each Other* (Cambridge, MA: Harvard University Press, 1998), 119.

[12] Jean-Paul Sartre, "Existentialism Is a Humanism," in W. Kaufmann, ed., *Existentialism from Dostoevsky to Sartre* (1956; reprint, rev. and expanded, New York: Meridian/Penguin, 1975), 354–56.

granted background structures that help to constitute our solutions to these problems. Watson may well be right in noting that we ordinarily do not reflect explicitly and directly on our motivation. Instead, the direct target of our explicit practical reasoning frequently concerns what to do. Nevertheless, our management of our motivation is one of the problems that needs to be addressed by the structures that help to shape our practical reasoning. More generally, our coordinated responses to problems of self-management and of underdetermination by value judgment are, so to speak, part of the deep structure of our ordinary practical thinking. Or so I propose.

When we see our practical thinking in this way, we can ask the question: What features of such thinking enter into our solutions to the problems of self-management and underdetermination by value judgment? My conjecture is that human agents tend to incorporate into their practical thinking a unified—as it were, simultaneous—solution to this pair of problems. This unified solution is valuing.

III. Valuing and Policies about Practical Reasoning

I propose that human agents tend to incorporate into their practical thinking valuing understood in a certain way. What I have in mind is this: Policies are intentions that are general in relevant ways.[13] We have policies of action. We also have policies, or policy-like attitudes,[14] that concern the significance that is to be given to certain considerations in our motivationally effective practical reasoning concerning our own conduct.[15] I might, for example, have a policy that gives no weight at all to revenge, another policy that gives great weight to family, and yet another policy that gives little or no weight to my own contribution to political goals. On the one hand, such policies partly constitute my stance with respect to relevant motivation, such as a desire for revenge, that might come up for reflective assessment. On the other hand, some policies of this sort constitute my response to the problem of fashioning a life with a coherent shape in the face of underdetermination by value judgment. Such policies, or policy-like attitudes, about practical reasoning are a kind of valuing, one that constitutes a unified response to problems of self-management and of underdetermination by value judgment.

---

[13] My discussion throughout this essay assumes the approach to intention that I have called "the planning theory" and that I present in Michael E. Bratman, *Intention, Plans, and Practical Reason* (Cambridge, MA: Harvard University Press, 1987; reissued by CSLI Publications, 1999). I discuss policies, esp., at 87–91. I also discuss policies in Michael E. Bratman, "Intention and Personal Policies," *Philosophical Perspectives* 3 (1989): 443–69.

[14] Concerning this qualification see my discussion of what I call "quasi-policies" in Michael E. Bratman, "Reflection, Planning, and Temporally Extended Agency," 57–60. In most of my discussion here I will not keep repeating this qualification (though I will return to it briefly below in note 51).

[15] Cp. Nozick, *Philosophical Explanations*, 446–49.

I have touched on some of these themes elsewhere. In "Valuing and the Will," I pursue a project of Gricean "creature construction."[16] This project introduces forms of valuing as steps in the "construction" of a series of fictional creatures, in pursuit of a (partial) model of actual human agents. We begin with a creature who has certain broadly conative attitudes—desires in a broad sense—and certain belief-like cognitive attitudes. Early in the project of creature construction, we envision a creature whose desires have been suitably exposed to its relevant beliefs and in that sense are "considered." We then turn to a creature who engages in a primitive form of deliberation, in which its considered desires determine the weight that is given to various factors, where the weight that is given matches the degree to which these considered desires tend to move the creature to action. The considered desires of such a creature can be thought of as a primitive kind of valuing.

A more complex creature, however, might be more reflective about her desires, including her considered desires, and might ask herself how she "really wants" such desires, and what they are for, to enter into her deliberation and motivation. An intelligible output of such reflection would be a higher-order policy, or policy-like attitude, about that creature's treatment of her desires as providing, for her motivationally effective deliberation, *justifying* considerations for action.[17] In "Valuing and the Will," I call such policies *self-governing* policies, and I argue that they constitute an important kind of valuing.[18]

It is helpful, here, to distinguish two different ways in which a first-order desire may enter into practical reasoning.[19] Suppose, for example, that my desire for revenge motivates action by way of associated practical reasoning. In one case the content of my (defeasible) reasoning might be expressed as follows:

---

[16] The basic idea of creature construction comes from Paul Grice. Grice aimed to "construct (in imagination, of course) according to certain principles of construction, a type of creature, or rather a sequence of types of creature, to serve as a model (or models) for actual creatures." See Paul Grice, "Method in Philosophical Psychology (From the Banal to the Bizarre)," Presidential Address, *Proceedings and Addresses of the American Philosophical Association* 68 (1974–75): 37. My discussion is in Michael E. Bratman, "Valuing and the Will," *Philosophical Perspectives* 14 (2000): 249–65.

[17] For some intermediate steps in this construction see "Valuing and the Will," 252–57.

[18] In the central case that I consider in "Valuing and the Will," the self-governing policy concerns first-order motivation that is already present. I also note, however, that there can be cases in which the policy involves, rather, a commitment to acquiring certain desires; and such a policy might concern one's treatment of certain desires, were one to acquire them.

For a related but different conception of a connection between valuing and policies, see David Copp, *Morality, Normativity, and Society* (New York: Oxford University Press, 1995), 177–78.

[19] For a closely related distinction see Philip Pettit and Michael Smith, "Backgrounding Desire," *Philosophical Review* 99 (1990): 565–92. In what follows, my first case corresponds to cases in which, in their terminology, the desire is in the "foreground." My second case is similar to one kind of case in which, in their terminology, the desire is in the "background."

MODEL 1
(a) I desire revenge.
Action *A* would promote revenge.
So I have a justifying reason for *A*-ing.
So I will *A*.

Here (a) is, as is said, the major premise.[20] In a second case, in contrast, my reasoning has as its major premise an appropriate expression of my desire, or of a thought involved in my having that desire. So, for example, we might in the second case see the major premise as:

(b) Revenge is a justifying consideration.

where (b) is an expression of my desire, or of a thought involved in my having that desire.[21] The content of my (defeasible) reasoning would then be along the lines of:

MODEL 2
(b) Revenge is a justifying consideration.
Action *A* would promote revenge.
So I have a justifying reason for *A*-ing.
So I will *A*.

(Here [b] is understood in the indicated way.)[22]

Now, a self-governing policy that eschews my treating my desire for revenge as reason-providing in my motivationally effective practical reasoning will eschew practical reasoning of both sorts. Indeed, it might do this even in some cases in which my desire really does involve a thought or judgment along the lines of (b). A self-governing policy that supports

[20] We might also see (a) as alluding to further conditions that the desire fulfills, for example, that it is a considered desire.

[21] Appeal to an evaluative expression of the desire is characteristic of Donald Davidson's views about practical reasoning. See, e.g., Donald Davidson, "Intending," reprinted in Donald Davidson, *Essays on Actions and Events* (Oxford: Oxford University Press, 1980), 85–86. John Cooper emphasizes how, on Aristotle's theory of virtues of character, even appetites and forms of anger and grief involve judgments about the good or what ought to be done, although these judgments are not themselves based on reasoning that aims at determining what is good or what ought to be done. Cooper also emphasizes the permanence of these nonrational desires even in a human being of Aristotelian virtue of character. See John M. Cooper, "Some Remarks on Aristotle's Moral Psychology," reprinted in Cooper, *Reason and Emotion: Essays on Ancient Moral Psychology and Ethical Theory* (Princeton, NJ: Princeton University Press, 1999), 237–52.

[22] We might try to see (b), when it is an expression of (a thought involved in) my desire, as sometimes involving an implicit indexical element:

Revenge is a justifying consideration (from *my* point of view).

We would then need to address the broadly Frankfurtian issue of which point of view is *mine*. This is the issue of agential authority that I turn to briefly below in Section V. A consequence of the approach to agential authority sketched in Section V (see also note 39) is that there are desires that are not appropriately expressed in this way.

my treating my desire as reason-providing in my motivationally effective practical reasoning will support practical reasoning of one or both of these sorts. Note that even in the case in which such a policy concerns only practical reasoning along the lines of Model 2, the policy still concerns the cited functioning of the relevant desire in that reasoning. The policy is a higher-order policy about that functioning of the desire, even though the relevant premise in the policy-supported reasoning—premise (b)—does not itself refer to that desire, but is, rather, an expression of that desire or of an involved thought.[23]

Now, as they emerge from the story of creature construction as so far developed, higher-order, self-governing policies are primarily a response to concerns with reflective management of one's motivational system. In contrast, in "A Desire of One's Own," I highlight not only these issues of self-management, but also the problem that is posed for our agency by our judgments about multiple, conflicting values that, at least so far as we can see, underdetermine what particular, coherent shape our lives are to take.[24] I suggest that our response to this problem will consist, in one important type of case, in policies, or policy-like attitudes, that say what justifying significance to give to various considerations in our motivationally effective deliberations and practical reasoning about our own action.[25] So, to use an example from "A Desire of One's Own," consider a person—let us call her Jones—who sees the value in sexual activity and who also sees the value of a certain kind of life of abstinence. Jones might

[23] Let me note two complexities. The first concerns Model 2. In some cases the desire for X will, even prior to an endorsing policy, already involve a thought of X as a justifying consideration, or will at least be plausibly expressible along the lines of (b). But there are, I think, also cases which do not fit well into such a picture: for some cases of pre-reflective anger, for example, this will seem to be an overly intellectualistic picture. Nevertheless, if in a case of this latter sort one does arrive at a self-governing policy in support of treating the anger as reason-providing, then this policy may infuse or shape the anger so that it becomes (or involves a thought that is) expressible in this way. So the reasoning supported by the policy can be Model 2 reasoning.

A second complexity concerns motivation in the absence of either kind of practical reasoning. An agent who rejects her desire for revenge has a self-governing policy of not allowing that desire to lead to action by way of Model 1 or Model 2 practical reasoning. I think we can also suppose that the agent's policy rejects an effective motivational role for that desire, even if that role does not involve such practical reasoning—perhaps the desire of a Frankfurtian "unwilling addict" could in some cases motivate action in this latter way. However, it is policies specifically about the roles of desires in motivationally effective practical reasoning that are central to autonomous action; or so I will be claiming below in the text. These policies will be my main concern here.

[24] Bratman, "A Desire of One's Own." For such talk about the "shape" of our lives see Charles Taylor, "Leading a Life," in Ruth Chang, ed., *Incommensurability, Incomparability, and Practical Reason* (Cambridge, MA: Harvard University Press, 1997), 183.

[25] I discuss this idea further in Michael E. Bratman, "Shared Valuing and Frameworks for Practical Reasoning," in R. Jay Wallace, Philip Pettit, Samuel Scheffler, and Michael Smith, eds., *Reason and Value: Themes from the Moral Philosophy of Joseph Raz* (Oxford University Press, forthcoming). Note that the idea is *not* that such policies directly change what is valuable—though there is room for an indirect impact by way of the value of living in accord with such policies, once they are adopted.

then arrive, on reflection, at a policy of giving no positive weight to her sexual activity. She sees that there are alternative, nonabstaining ways of living that have value, but in creating for herself a life of abstinence she puts the value of her sexual activity aside, so to speak. Although she does not expect relevant intersubjective convergence on living such a life, she arrives at a policy, or policy-like attitude, concerning her own motivationally effective practical reasoning. And given the role of such a policy (or policy-like attitude) in her practical reasoning and action, it seems reasonable to see it as constituting a kind of valuing.

IV. Two Problems, One Solution?

A salient response to the problem of self-management and to the problem of underdetermination by value judgment involves policies concerning one's own motivationally effective practical reasoning. Such policies say what significance to give to certain considerations in this reasoning. Such policies constitute an important kind of valuing. Valuing in this sense is related to, but is to be distinguished from, judging what is good.[26] Indeed, this distinction lies at the heart of the usefulness of such valuing as a response to the problem of underdetermination by value judgment.

One might, however, question whether this is really a single solution to our pair of problems. After all, although our respective responses to these problems involve policies about practical reasoning, there seems to be a difference in the kind of policy that is cited. The policies that are cited as a response to problems of self-management are primarily higher-order responses to separable forms of motivation: desires for revenge or for sexual activity, for example. The policies about practical reasoning that are a response to concerns about underdetermination by value judgment do not need to be about separable forms of motivation, though they may be. Perhaps in response to his dilemma, the young man in Sartre's example settles on a policy of giving weight to helping the Free French, but not to helping his mother. So described, this policy does not seem to be about the functioning of separable forms of motivation. It seems rather directly to support (defeasible) reasoning along the lines of:

Model 3
(c) Helping the Free French is a justifying consideration.
A would help the Free French.
So I have justifying reason to do *A*.
So I will *A*.

---

[26] For this distinction see David Lewis, "Dispositional Theories of Value," in Lewis, *Papers in Ethics and Social Philosophy* (New York: Cambridge University Press, 2000), 68–94; Gary Watson, "Free Action and Free Will," *Mind* 96 (1987): 150; and Gilbert Harman, "Desired Desires," in Harman, *Explaining Value and Other Essays in Moral Philosophy* (Oxford: Oxford University Press, 2000), 117–36, esp. 129–30.

At the same time, this policy seems to reject analogous reasoning concerning the young man helping his mother. Here, premise (c)—in contrast with premise (b) in Model 2—need not be an expression of (a thought involved in) a separable desire. So, we might wonder how policies of practical reasoning that are involved in our solution to problems of self-management are related to policies that constitute our solution to problems of underdetermination by value judgment. Do we really have a single solution to our pair of problems?

I think that the basic point to make here is that we need to respond to both problems, and there will be, at the least, a requirement that an agent's responses to these problems mesh with each other. There will be pressure on our young man, for example, not to have policies that give predominant weight to helping the Free French, but that nevertheless encourage the effective influence on his relevant Model 1 or Model 2 practical reasoning of his powerful desire to stay with his mother. In pursuit of a model of autonomy we want a model of a more or less unified agent, one whose agency involves both reflective management of his motivation and a response to underdetermination by value judgment. As reflective human agents, we have both a problem of self-management and a problem of responding to underdetermination by value judgment with a form of, so to speak, limited self-creation.[27] I have been assuming that the latter problem is pervasive. The pervasiveness of the former problem is ensured by the pervasiveness of forms of motivation—including appetites, and forms of anger and grief—that can pose problems of self-management.[28] We seek coordinated solutions to both problems: as we might say, the self that emerges from self-management should be coordinated with the self that emerges from limited self-creation.

We can develop the point further by returning to creature construction. My discussion in "Valuing and the Will" ends with a creature who has self-governing policies concerning which desired ends to treat as justifying considerations in (as I have here described it) her motivationally effective Model 1 or Model 2 deliberation. Such policies play central roles in the organization of the agent's own thought and action over time. They also play central roles in various forms of social organization, coordination, and cooperation. After all, much of our ability to work with and to coordinate with others depends on our grasp of the justifying significance that they give to various considerations in their practical thinking.

This role in social coordination points to the enormous significance of these forms of coordination in the creature's life, a point that Allan Gibbard

[27] For such talk of self-creation see Raz, *The Morality of Freedom*, 385–90; and Joseph Raz, "The Truth in Particularism," in Raz, *Engaging Reason: On the Theory of Value and Action* (Oxford: Oxford University Press, 1999), 242–45.
[28] See Cooper, "Some Remarks on Aristotle's Moral Psychology," esp. 247–50, where Cooper highlights the contrast with the Stoics.

has emphasized with great insight.[29] As Gibbard might say, pressures for social coordination will lead to pressure on our creature to try to articulate, explain, and, to some extent, defend and justify her self-governing policies to others in her social world. This suggests that we can expect to emerge—in a later stage of creature construction—some sort of intersubjectively accountable views about values and/or reasons.[30] But at that point we can also expect that these further views will have a feature highlighted by our second problem: given the need for intersubjective accountability, these views will tend to leave unsettled many questions about the particular contours of an individual agent's life. These views will tend, by themselves, to underdetermine, to underspecify, how one is to live.[31] At least, this is reasonable to expect, given the assumption that such underdetermination is common. So a creature's self-governing policies, formed initially in response to problems of self-management, may be in a position to do "double duty" in this later stage of creature construction. They also may be in a position to help constitute her response to underdetermination by her intersubjectively accountable value judgments.[32] In this way the creature's responses to our pair of problems can be expected to mesh.

We can also consider matters from the other direction, by beginning with policies of practical reasoning that are a direct response to underdetermination by value judgment. Let us here return to Jones. Jones has arrived at a policy of abstinence, a policy that precludes giving positive deliberative weight in her life to her sexual activity. This is her own, distinctive response to underdetermination of the contours of her life by her prior judgments about the good in a human life of sexual activity, on the one hand, and of abstinence as a part of a certain kind of religious observance, on the other hand. Now, this policy seems to be directly about how to weigh certain considerations in her Model 3 practical reasoning, and not about the functioning of separable first-order motivation. But it is likely that in order for this policy to be effective, it will need to involve or be associated with a policy, or policy-like attitude, of putting to

---

[29] Allan Gibbard, *Wise Choices, Apt Feelings* (Cambridge, MA: Harvard University Press, 1990). While I think that Gibbard's focus on issues about social coordination is of great importance, I see my discussion here as neutral concerning the debate between Gibbard's expressivist understanding of value judgment and certain more cognitivist approaches. This is part of an overall strategy—a kind of method of avoidance, to use John Rawls's terminology—of trying to articulate important structures of human agency in ways that are available to a range of different views in metaethics.

[30] I think that we can also expect forms of shared *valuing* (in contrast with shared judgments of value) to emerge. See Bratman, "Shared Valuing and Frameworks for Practical Reasoning."

[31] I think that this is implicit, for example, in Gibbard's effort to distinguish between an "existential commitment" and accepting "a norm as a requirement of rationality." See Gibbard, *Wise Choices, Apt Feelings*, 166–70.

[32] Which is not to say that these self-governing policies may not themselves be responsive to the creature's judgments of value.

one side in her motivationally effective practical reasoning considerations provided by her felt sexual desires. It will need to involve or be associated with a policy of not treating those desires as providing justifying considerations for her Model 1 or Model 2 practical deliberation.

Or consider the young man who settles on a life of fighting with the Free French. This will "mesh" (in the way that I mentioned above) only if he has a way of managing the impact on his deliberation and motivation both of his inclinations not to fight—that is, his affections and concerns for his mother, his fears of battle—and of his affections and concerns for the Free French. A policy of giving weight in his motivationally effective Model 3 practical reasoning to his work with the Free French, but not to his mother's needs for his attention, will likely be effective only if it involves or is associated with such forms of self-management. So there will be pressure on the young man for associated higher-order policies of self-management, policies that concern relevant practical reasoning along the lines of Models 1 and/or 2.

If we begin with problems of self-management, then we arrive first at self-governing policies that are, in part, about the management of the functioning of one's first-order motivations. We arrive later at the idea that such policies can also constitute (part of) a response to underdetermination by intersubjectively accountable value judgments. If, instead, we begin with the latter problem about underdetermination, then we arrive first at policies about the significance of certain considerations in one's motivationally effective practical reasoning, and second at associated higher-order policies about the management of the impact of relevant forms of motivation on one's effective motivation and practical reasoning. I surmise that the differences are not differences in the basic model of human agency, but in our route to that model. At the heart of the model in each case are policies about what is to be given significance in one's motivationally effective practical reasoning. And, given the kind of creatures that human agents are, these policies will normally involve or be associated with policies that concern the management of relevant forms of motivation in practical reasoning and action.[33]

This is not yet to identify these two kinds of policies concerning practical reasoning. The AH thesis does not depend on such identification. The thesis needs only to insist that hierarchical policies are an element in a central case of human autonomy. Nevertheless, I think that there is normally reason for a kind of identification. What we have seen is that in reflective agents like us there is substantial pressure toward a unified

---

[33] A fuller discussion also would consider both "quasi-policies" (see note 14 above) and "singular commitments." See Michael E. Bratman, "Hierarchy, Circularity, and Double Reduction," in Sarah Buss and Lee Overton, eds., *Contours of Agency: Essays on Themes from Harry Frankfurt* (Cambridge, MA: MIT Press, 2002), 65–85. These complexities can be put to one side here, however, since our primary concern is with a kind of hierarchy involved in all of these phenomena.

cluster of forms of functioning—a cluster that involves coordinated, cross-temporal, policy-like control of practical reasoning along the lines of Models 1, 2, and 3. This suggests that we see the underlying source of this cluster as a single, complex policy or policy-like attitude. In a central case such a policy will be something like this:

> It will be a policy of giving justifying significance to consideration X in motivationally effective Model 3 reasoning, in part by way of appropriate control of associated motivationally effective practical reasoning along the lines of Models 1 and/or 2.

In a central case, this will be the form that a self-governing policy will take. Although the genesis of such a policy might only sometimes include explicitly higher order reflection on first-order motivation, its function and content will be, in part, higher order in the indicated ways.[34] Such (to some extent) higher-order policies are an important form of valuing.

V. Valuing and Autonomy

And they are a form of valuing whose control of action can partly realize or constitute a human agent's direction and governance of action, and thus, the agent's autonomy. Or so I maintain. It is time to say why.

In autonomous action, as I have said, an agent directs and governs her action. Note that there are two different ideas here: agential *direction* and agential *governance*. As I see it, in agential direction there is sufficient unity and organization of the motives of action for their functioning to constitute direction by the agent.[35] Agential governance is a particular form of such agential direction: agential governance is agential direction that appropriately involves the agent's treatment of certain considerations as justifying reasons for action. Autonomous action involves a form of agential direction that also constitutes agential governance. And I want to describe what these phenomena of agential direction and agential governance consist in without appealing to a homunculus account, that is, to a "little person in the head who does the work."

Without appealing to a homunculus account, my strategy is to see agential direction and governance as being realized by appropriate forms of psychological functioning.[36] There is agential direction of action when action is under the control of attitudes whose role in the agent's psychology gives them authority to speak for the agent, to establish the agent's

---

[34] I consider in the text below, in Section VI, the objection that there may be a gap here between function and content.

[35] See Frankfurt's work on wholeheartedness in, for example, Harry G. Frankfurt, "The Faintest Passion," reprinted in Frankfurt, *Necessity, Volition, and Love* (Cambridge: Cambridge University Press, 1999), 95–107.

[36] See note 5 above.

point of view—gives them, in other words, agential authority. This agential direction of action is, furthermore, a form of agential governance of action only when these attitudes control action by way of the agent's treatment of relevant considerations as justifying reasons for action, that is, as having subjective normative authority for her.[37]

When we approach autonomous action in this way, valuing of the sort that we have been discussing seems to be a natural candidate for an attitude whose control of action can, in part, realize the agent's direction and governance of action. On the one hand, self-governing policies play central roles in supporting and constituting important forms of cross-temporal organization and coordination in an agent's life. As long as an agent's self-governing policies are not involved in conflict that undermines these cross-temporal organizing roles, we have reason to see such policies as having agential authority.[38] Hence, we likewise have reason to see their control of action as realizing agential direction of action. On the other hand, such policies function, in particular, by way of helping to shape the agent's operative, background framework of justifying reasons.[39] To borrow terminology from J. David Velleman, the policies' control of action is part of a story not only of motivation, but also of rational guidance.[40] This is why agential direction of action that is realized by the controlling role of such policies constitutes, at least in part, agential *governance* of action. Taken together with the arguments that I have just offered, that such self-governing policies involve (or bring with them) motivational hierarchy, this leads us to the view that motivational hierarchy is at the heart of at least one important realization of human autonomy. This leads us, that is, to the AH thesis.

This argument for the AH thesis has two main steps. The first step is to articulate what we might call design specifications for an autonomous agent.[41] I have, so far, cited two design specifications: sufficient organization of motivation to constitute agential direction, and motivation that involves rational guidance in a way that further qualifies this agential direction as agential governance. The second step in defending the AH

---

[37] Concerning these two kinds of authority, see Michael E. Bratman, "Two Problems About Human Agency," *Proceedings of the Aristotelian Society* 101 (2001): 309–26.

[38] I expand on these matters, and their relation to ideas about personal identity, in Bratman, "Reflection, Planning, and Temporally Extended Agency." In pages 48–51 of that essay I describe the cited nonconflict condition as a version of what Frankfurt calls "satisfaction." In my discussion of higher-order policies (below in the text) I will take it for granted that some such satisfaction condition is realized. A full account of satisfaction would also need to consider the significance of conflict with singular commitments concerning what to treat as justifying (see note 33 above).

[39] We might say that such self-governing policies help constitute the agent's justificatory point of view. So if such a self-governing policy were to reject a desire for X, and that desire were nevertheless to involve the thought that X is a justifying consideration from that agent's point of view, that thought would be false.

[40] Velleman, "The Guise of the Good," in *The Possibility of Practical Reason*, 99–122.

[41] Cp. Velleman, "Introduction," in *The Possibility of Practical Reason*, 11.

thesis is to argue that a model in which higher-order self-governing policies function in the indicated ways would satisfy these design specifications.[42]

Must the kind of rational guidance that is needed for autonomy also involve sufficient responsiveness to what is judged to be good and/or is good?[43] My response here is to leave this question open, since either answer is compatible with the present argument for the AH thesis.

A final point on valuing and autonomy is that there might be actions that are not the direct issue of the kinds of policy-directed practical reasoning that I have cited, but that are sufficiently related to such reasoning to be candidates for autonomous action in an extended sense. Once we have in hand our basic model of autonomous agency, we can allow for such extensions in our account of autonomous action.

VI. Two Objections and the Autonomy-Transparency Thesis

I now consider a pair of closely related objections to this way of defending the AH thesis. Each objection acknowledges the role of reasoning-guiding policies in an important realization of human autonomy. Each objection nevertheless goes on to challenge the idea that such policies need be hierarchical.

The first objection concerns self-management. Suppose you find yourself desiring revenge. You stop to reflect, and you arrive at a commitment not to give weight in your practical reasoning to revenge. This commitment, or policy, is certainly a response to an antecedent desire for revenge, but why must its *content* make explicit reference to the functioning of that desire? Why can't its content simply reject forms of Model 3 reasoning that give positive weight to revenge? Granted, for such a commitment to be effective it must somehow involve management of the impact on one's practical reasoning and action of one's désire for revenge. But this does not show that the content of the guiding policy must refer somehow to the functioning of one's desire and cannot simply be the rejection of Model 3 reasoning that gives positive weight to revenge. So it is not clear that what is needed are higher-order policies of the sort highlighted by the AH thesis.

---

[42] On this account autonomous action is compatible with the persistence of first-order motivation that diverges from what is supported by one's self-governing policies. Within the proposed model, what autonomy requires is that one's self-governing policies actually do guide one's relevant reasoning and action. Further, there can be cases—e.g., our case of principled sexual abstinence—in which one's self-governing policy rejects a desire for X even though one acknowledges the value of X.

[43] See Susan Wolf, *Freedom Within Reason* (Oxford: Oxford University Press, 1990); but see also Gary Watson, "Two Faces of Responsibility," *Philosophical Topics* 24 (1996): 240. Relatedly, we might also consider a constraint that, at the least, the relevant self-governing policies not favor one's own loss of autonomy or complete domination by others. Here, again, we need not settle the issue in order to argue for the AH thesis.

The second objection concerns limited self-creation (responding to underdetermination by value judgment). Recall Jones's policy of sexual abstinence, which I discussed in Section IV. I have said that, to be effective, this policy will likely need to involve a policy of eschewing the demands of felt sexual desires on her motivationally effective deliberations. The second objection to the AH thesis grants that for Jones's policy of sexual abstinence to be effective, there will normally need to be management of the impact on her deliberation and action of felt sexual desires. However, this objection claims that it does not follow that the *content* of her policy of abstinence will need to refer explicitly to this management of contrary desires. Her policy can simply eschew appeal in her Model 3 deliberation to her sexual activity as a justifying consideration. So it does not follow that her policy is higher order in its content.

Both objections to the way that the AH thesis has been defended thus far grant that the psychological functioning that issues from the reasoning-guiding policies whose control can partly realize human autonomy will normally include some form of management of the impact of relevant first-order motivation on practical reasoning and action. But both objections insist that it does not follow that the reasoning-guiding policies must themselves be higher order in their content.

Now, we might simply respond that there are cases and cases. As long as there are common cases in which autonomy is realized by the functioning of reasoning-guiding policies that are higher order, the AH thesis stands. But I think that we can make a stronger claim than that here.

Our concern is, after all, with *autonomous* agency. For such agency, some sort of modest condition of *transparency* seems apt in characterizing the relation between, on the one hand, known significant functioning that is supported by a reasoning-guiding policy and, on the other hand, the content of that policy. We can put the idea this way:

> If one knows that the effective functioning of the practical reasoning that is supported by one's reasoning-guiding policy at the same time significantly involves management of the roles of relevant motivation, and if one's ensuing action is self-governed, then the content of one's reasoning-guiding policy will refer to, and support, this management of motivation.

The idea here is that, in the absence of such transparency, the functioning of the reasoning-guiding policy would not be sufficient to ensure an agent's governance of his or her ensuing action. Let us call this the *autonomy-transparency (AT) thesis*. The AT thesis helps to block the current pair of objections. These objections depend on driving a wedge between the psychological functioning that issues from the reasoning-guiding policy and the content of that policy. The AT thesis blocks this wedge for cases of autonomy in which the agent has the requisite self-knowledge.

And since the requisite self-knowledge need only be a fairly general knowledge of the need for management of motivation—a kind of self-knowledge that is compatible with only partial knowledge of the specific complexities of one's actual motivation—it seems plausible to suppose that an autonomous agent will be knowledgeable in this way.

VII. Transparency and Self-Governed Practical Reasoning

I believe that, if accepted, the autonomy-transparency (AT) thesis effectively blocks the cited two objections to the autonomy-hierarchy (AH) thesis, but why should we accept the AT thesis? My answer appeals to pressures on an autonomous agent to govern not only her action but also the practical reasoning from which her action issues.[44]

Let us begin by noting that the fact that there is practical reasoning leading to action, and that this reasoning has normative or evaluative content, does not yet ensure that the agent governs the reasoning. There can be cases of motivationally effective practical reasoning about which we will want to say—borrowing a phrase from Gibbard—that the agent is not governing the reasoning but is instead in the "grip" of concerns that drive the reasoning.[45] This might happen, for example, in a case involving a strong desire for revenge and associated thoughts about what degree or type of revenge is deserved. One's motivationally effective practical reasoning might be in the grip of this desire and these normative thoughts.

So the model of (a central case of) autonomous agency that we have been developing—a model that appeals to the role of self-governing policies in guiding reasoning and action—needs to include psychological functioning that ensures that the agent is not in the grip of relevant concerns but is, rather, governing her own, relevant practical reasoning. Suppose, then, that relevant practical reasoning, and its control of action, involves in an important way psychological functioning of type F. And suppose that the agent does govern that reasoning and knows that it involves this F-type functioning. We can expect that the agent's governance of her reasoning will extend to that known functioning. And the natural way, within the model, to ensure agential governance of that F-type functioning is to build support for such functioning into the content of a self-governing policy that guides her reasoning. And this is a condition that will be violated when the agent's reasoning is, instead, in the grip of a certain consideration.

---

[44] As I understand her views, this is a theme in Christine M. Korsgaard's *The Sources of Normativity* (Cambridge: Cambridge University Press, 1996), chap. 3. It appears here in my discussion as, in effect, a third design specification on autonomous agents.

[45] Gibbard, *Wise Choices, Apt Feelings*, 60. I discuss the significance of such cases also in Bratman, "Hierarchy, Circularity, and Double Reduction" and in Bratman, "Two Problems About Human Agency."

Return now to the AT thesis. This thesis, which I described at the end of the preceding section, concerns cases of self-governed actions that are the issue of practical reasoning that is guided by a relevant self-governing policy, P. According to the AT thesis, if the agent in such a case knows that the effective functioning of that practical reasoning significantly involves management of her relevant motivation, then the content of P will refer to and support this management of motivation. We have now observed that if, in such a case, the action is self-governed, then so is the practical reasoning from which it issues. And we have also observed that if an agent is to govern her practical reasoning in such a case, then she must govern known, important F-type functioning involved in that reasoning and its control of action. We have, further, provided a model of psychological functioning that would realize such agential governance of that reasoning. And within this model, the agential governance of this F-type functioning will involve guidance by a policy whose content supports this F-type functioning. The AT thesis is, then, a special case of this general feature of this model of self-governed practical reasoning—a special case in which F is the management of the cited functioning of relevant motivation. This means that at least a central case of autonomous agency will involve the kind of transparency that is needed to complete our first argument for the AH thesis.

Related concerns about transparency also suggest a second line of support for the AH thesis; or so I now proceed to argue.

VIII. THE SECOND LINE OF ARGUMENT: POLICIES ABOUT SELF-GOVERNED PRACTICAL REASONING

According to the model that we have been developing, an autonomous agent's reasoning-guiding policies guide practical reasoning that is, in part because of this guidance, governed by the agent. That this reasoning is agentially governed is, I take it, something that the autonomous agent will normally know and endorse. But then a natural extension of our reflections on transparency suggests that the agent's guiding policy will be a policy that favors practical reasoning that is governed by herself. Within the model, however, in order to be governed by the agent the reasoning needs to be guided by a relevant self-governing policy. So it will be plausible to expect that the reasoning-guiding policy is, in part, about its own role in guiding the reasoning. This is to build into the content of the policy that guides the practical reasoning the condition that this same practical reasoning be appropriately guided by that very policy. And this is to draw on work by Gilbert Harman and others on forms of *reflexivity in intentions*.[46]

---

[46] Gilbert Harman, "Practical Reasoning," in Harman, *Change in View* (Cambridge, MA: MIT Press, 1986), chap. 8; and Harman, "Desired Desires." See also Alan Donagan, *Choice:*

Harman, in particular, has argued that a "positive" intention in favor of an action will be "an intention that something will happen in a way that is controlled or guided by" that very intention. In this sense, a positive intention "is reflexive or self-referential—it refers to itself."[47] Harman cautions that this does not require that the agent have "an explicit mental representation of her intention."[48] What is required, however, is that what the intention favors is that there be a certain process that is suitably dependent on, and responsive to, that intention itself.

Consider, then, a case in which one knowingly governs practical reasoning in which one gives positive weight to revenge. The idea now is that one's policy of giving weight in one's reasoning to revenge will be a policy that one's reasoning give such weight to revenge, in part, *because of* this very policy. It will be a policy of giving such weight as a matter of this very policy.

This suggests that, at least in certain central cases of autonomous action, the self-governing policies that guide the underlying practical reasoning will be reflexive;[49] that is, they will be in part about their own guidance of the practical reasoning.[50] Such a reflexive self-governing policy will be a higher-order conative attitude. It will be a policy about the functioning in reasoning of a certain policy, namely, itself. So we arrive again, as promised, at a form of motivational hierarchy.

Note, however, that this form of motivational hierarchy is different from that at stake in our first line of argument. According to our first line of argument, valuing involves policies that are, in part, about the role of desires, and/or of what they are for, in providing justifying premises in motivationally effective Model 1 or Model 2 practical reasoning. According to the second line of argument that I have just sketched, the practical reasoning of an autonomous agent, at least in a central case, involves policies that are, in part, supportive of their very own functioning in guiding practical reasoning. The functioning of these self-governing pol-

---

The Essential Element in Human Action (London: Routledge & Kegan Paul, 1987), 88; John Searle, *Intentionality* (New York: Cambridge University Press, 1983); and J. David Velleman, *Practical Reflection* (Princeton, NJ: Princeton University Press, 1989). For an important critique of these ideas, see Alfred Mele, *Springs of Action: Understanding Intentional Behavior* (New York: Oxford University Press, 1992), chap. 11; Harman's response is in Harman, "Desired Desires."

[47] Harman, "Desired Desires," 121. Let me note that I am not here endorsing Harman's general view that all positive intentions are reflexive. I am only using his idea of reflexive intentions to make progress with the special case of self-governed practical reasoning.

[48] Ibid., 124. Harman notes here a parallel with John Perry's observation that (as Harman writes) "a child can have the thought that 'it is raining' without having any concepts of places or times and without any inner mental representations of particular places and times, even though the content of the child's thought concerns rain at a particular place and a particular time."

[49] Related ideas about reflexivity can be found in Keith Lehrer, *Self-Trust: A Study of Reason, Knowledge, and Autonomy* (New York: Oxford University Press, 1997), 100–102.

[50] I offer a related argument for seeing such policies as reflexive in Bratman, "Two Problems About Human Agency," 323.

icies, which is reflexively supported in this way, is their very own guidance of practical reasoning along the lines of any of Models 1 through 3.

IX. CONCLUSION

Recall Watson's observation that in normal cases of practical reasoning "the initial practical question" is "about courses of action and not about ourselves." My defense of the autonomy-hierarchy (AH) thesis is consistent with this view. My claim is not about the initial practical question, but about the background structures that are brought to bear in trying to answer this question. I have argued that, in central cases of autonomous action, these background structures involve higher-order self-governing policies. While we frequently take for granted such structures in our practical reasoning, we have seen reason to think that they are present in at least certain central cases of autonomy.

Granted, I have left open the possibility that other kinds of background structures might also satisfy our design specifications for autonomy. Faced with such an alternative proposal, we would want to see whether our design specifications are indeed satisfied, and, if so, whether there are, at bottom, significant similarities with our model of self-governing policies.[51] But such prospects can be left open here.

Now, recall that Frankfurt's original appeal to motivational hierarchy—to what he called higher-order "volitions"—was an appeal to higher-order conative support for the functioning of a first-order desire as an effective motive of action.[52] I have been led here to higher-order policies not only in support of forms of functioning (along the lines of Models 1 or 2) of first-order motivation in one's practical reasoning and action, but also in reflexive support of their own framework-providing role. Both of these forms of policy-supported functioning in practical reasoning go beyond the bare motivational role of first-order desires, which is the concern of (at least, the original version of) Frankfurtian higher-order volitions. Nevertheless, the approach to autonomy that has emerged here shares with Frankfurt's approach the basic idea that some hierarchical structures provide an important element of at least one central case of autonomous human agency.

The AH thesis is a thesis about important kinds of contemporaneous psychological functioning that can partly realize human autonomous agency. Certain issues about the history of elements in this functioning remain open. In particular, it may be that, in the end, a full story about human autonomy will also need to appeal to some sort of historical condition that blocks certain extreme cases of manipulation, brainwash-

---

[51] And, if so, whether the idea of a quasi-policy can usefully capture these similarities.
[52] Frankfurt, "Freedom of the Will and the Concept of a Person," 16. But see the modification of this idea in Harry G. Frankfurt, "Identification and Wholeheartedness," in Frankfurt, *The Importance of What We Care About*, 159-76.

ing, and the like.[53] This is not an issue to be settled here.[54] But before we can settle this issue, we need the best account available of the structural conditions involved on the occasion of autonomous action. My concern here has been to argue that our account of such structural conditions should endorse a version of the autonomy-hierarchy (AH) thesis.

Philosophy, Stanford University

---

[53] See John Martin Fischer and Mark Ravizza, *Responsibility and Control: A Theory of Moral Responsibility* (New York: Cambridge University Press, 1998); and Keith Lehrer, "Reason and Autonomy" (in this volume). See also Bratman, "Fischer and Ravizza on Moral Responsibility and History," *Philosophy and Phenomenological Research* 61, no. 2 (2000): 453–58. Note, though, that the present issue is autonomy, not the related but different idea of moral responsibility. (See Gary Watson's distinction between "attributability" and "accountability" in Watson, "Two Faces of Responsibility.")

[54] Of course, if the specification of the content of the relevant attitudes is ineluctably historical (for reasons developed by, among others, Tyler Burge and Hilary Putnam), then we would need to appeal to such content-fixing historical considerations. But that is a different matter.

REASON AND AUTONOMY

By Keith Lehrer

I. Introduction

Reason has co-opted our conception of autonomy. My purpose is to set autonomy free. Here is the problem: some philosophers, Kant most notably, have said that governing your life by reason or by being responsive to reason is the source of autonomy.[1] But there is a paradox concealed in these plausible claims. On the one hand, a person can be enslaved to reason and lack autonomy because of this kind of bondage. On the other hand, if reason has no influence, then it appears that one would be the slave of one's passions, and, however eloquently Hume might have written about reason being the slave of the passions,[2] there is something odd about the idea that a person who is enslaved by his passions is autonomous. The paradox, which I shall call *the paradox of reason*, is that if we are governed by reason in what we choose, then we are in bondage to reason in what we choose, and we are not autonomous. Yet, if we are not governed by reason, then we do not govern ourselves in what we choose, and again we are not autonomous.

I do not think that this paradox is a mere sophism of philosophy. At the level of phenomenology, we might feel that if we are governed by reason, then we are constrained by it, and if we are not governed by reason, then we are not in control. For to be governed by reason is to be moved by rational considerations in how we choose to act and live, but being moved by rational considerations, by the rational choice of means to ends, for example, is a form of causation. Once the concept of autonomy is properly understood, though, we can resolve the paradox. The resolution requires that we understand that whether we are governed by reason must be an autonomous choice even when we are governed by reason in this choice. This raises the question, however, of which comes first, the choice to be governed by reason, or the governance of reason in the choice. Thus, the paradox deepens. For if, on the one hand, the choice to be governed by reason precedes any governance of choice by reason, then this initial choice is not governed by reason, and we are not autonomous. On the other hand, if the choice to be governed by reason is governed by reason, then we are constrained by reason and not autonomous in the

---

[1] Immanuel Kant, *Foundations of the Metaphysics of Morals*, trans. Lewis White Beck (Indianapolis, IN: Bobbs-Merrill, 1959).

[2] David Hume, *A Treatise of Human Nature* (London: John Noon, 1739), bk. II, sec. III.

choice. Which comes first, we might ask, the autonomous choice to be governed by reason or the governance of reason in autonomous choice? Whatever the answer, it appears that the conclusion is that we are not autonomous in that choice.

To resolve the problem, we shall need a clear conception of autonomy and an analysis of autonomy that is adequate to extricate ourselves from the paradox. Freedom and autonomy are closely connected, and it is, in terms of ordinary usage, difficult to distinguish between them. However, freedom seems more closely connected with not being constrained by external and internal conditions, while autonomy seems to require some positive condition of being empowered. I shall not make too much of the distinction, however, because once one becomes philosophically reflective about freedom, one begins to demand an account of positive empowerment in a satisfactory account of freedom. Thus, freedom and autonomy get joined. It is, however, important to keep in mind that there are many forms of freedom (freedom to do what one chooses, for example) that are greatly valued even if they do not ensure autonomy. But what is autonomy?

II. INTERNAL AUTONOMY: BEYOND DESIRE

I shall offer an account of autonomy as an internal condition. The account could easily be expanded to include external conditions of freedom, but that is not my concern here. I am interested in the internal conditions that must be satisfied for the will to be autonomous, for us to be autonomous in choice, putting aside any external conditions. So let us look at the internal conditions. Desire or some stronger conative state is a natural starting point. Are we autonomous when we do what we desire? Some philosophers, such as Harry G. Frankfurt, for example, argue that we have free will when we do what we desire, with the proviso that we have a higher-order desire, that is, a second-order desire with which we are satisfied, that endorses our first-order desire.[3] It must be conceded to such a position that a person will claim that he is acting of his own free will when he does what he desires and, moreover, when he desires to have the desire in question. However, if the matter is left without further comment or qualification, doubts easily arise. Suppose that a person's desire, and even the desire for the desire, are not subject to the supervision of reason. Whatever the person desires, looking inward he desires to desire, and, looking outward, he does. We might imagine that the person just automatically desires to desire what he desires without reflection or the intervention of rational processes. Given conflict between desires, this may appear unrealistic, but it is not difficult to imagine a person so constructed that his desires, though they conflict, are automatically ordered. Perhaps his desires are ordered by

---

[3] Harry G. Frankfurt, "Freedom of the Will and the Concept of a Person," *Journal of Philosophy* 68 (1971): 5–20.

some internal mechanism, perhaps by the intervention of another, with ties between equally appealing desires arbitrarily resolved, so that the highest-ranked desire brings with it a desire for that desire. The person does what he desires and desires to desire. The person will feel as though he is acting of his free will.

Would we agree that such a person is acting autonomously? When we reflect that harmony between first- and second-order desires arises automatically by an internal mechanism of which the agent may be innocent, it appears that the answer is negative. Simply put, it might not be up to an agent that she does what she desires, and it might not be up to the agent that she desires what she does or, furthermore, that she has the second-order desire that automatically accords with her first-order desire. The desires favor the act at all levels, but it is not up to the agent that she desires what she does at the first or second level. Moreover, desire does not seem sufficient to express autonomy, whether a desire is a first- or second-order desire, because desires may arise in us quite automatically and in a way that is indifferent to our approval or rational evaluation. The same could be true of even higher order desires. The appropriate state to express autonomy should be one that we choose, that is up to us, rather than a state such as being desirous, which in many instances, perhaps the most typical, arises in us without our approval or consent. This is what motivates the idea that autonomous choice should be the expression of rational processes, or at least subject to the supervision of rational processes. In short, the objection is that autonomous choice should be directed by or, at least, approved and evaluated by an agent who is engaged in rational processes. But there is nothing in desire, whether at the first or second level, to ensure any connection with evaluation or rational processes whatever.

It should be further noted that in the most natural use of the expression "desire," a person sometimes autonomously chooses to do something that the person has no desire to do. As I contemplate filling out my tax form, I am as certain as I am about any aspect of my psychology that I have no desire to fill out my tax form. I do not think that I am at all unusual in this respect. Someone might object that I might have a desire to avoid the consequences of not completing the form, and about this they would be right. But, in addition, I am convinced of the importance of taxation. I am convinced of the utility of it. I vote against candidates who would lower or eliminate taxes. I am convinced, as a result of reflecting on the appropriate role of government, of the importance of taxation in a democratic society. I also see the importance, of course, of balancing public expenditure and private wealth, but I approve of taxation, though I do not desire to be taxed or to fill out my tax form to pay my taxes. My approval, indeed, my moral approval of taxation, does not produce a desire for it. In terms of desire, I am like everyone else who desires not to pay taxes and not to fill out tax forms.

Now, I may be mistaken in my views about taxation. I consider myself fallible in this matter as in other matters, and so I see that those who are opposed to taxation on libertarian grounds have an argument. Rational reflection leads me to the opposite conclusion, however. When I pay my taxes and fill out the tax form to pay my taxes, I am following the directive of my rational consideration. But I still have no desire whatever to subject myself to the very unpleasant task of filling out the form or, for that matter, writing a check and parting with my money. It is just that I am convinced that this is what I ought to do. I simply do not have a desire to do what I am convinced I ought to do. I choose to do what I think I ought to do because of reasons that I have for thinking that I ought to do it, without desire nudging me to do what I think that I ought to do. *Pace* Hume, reason need not serve the passions. It has other business. I do not have to wait for a desire to arise in me to drive my sense of obligation to action. I am autonomous in the matter; it is up to me whether I go where reason and obligation direct. I do not, having reflected on what I ought to do and having reached a conclusion, sit by helplessly waiting for some desire to lead me to act. It is up to me, whether I like or dread this fact, and I am the author of my choice.

III. PREFERENCE AND METAMENTAL ASCENT

Still, one might ask, "Isn't there some disposition, perhaps not desire, that leads me to choose what I am convinced I ought to do?" Am I not disposed to do what I am convinced by reason that I ought to do? The answer is affirmative. I prefer to do what I am convinced I ought to do, even though I do not desire to do what I am convinced I ought to do. People often prefer to do what they desire, but not always, as the example of filling out tax forms illustrates. But even in the tax case there is a difference between preference and desire. I may prefer to satisfy a desire or prefer not to satisfy the desire, or I may prefer to ignore a desire and do what I consider to be rational or obligatory without thereby satisfying the desire. So it is crucial for us to distinguish between preference and desire. My theory of the matter, which I have articulated in some detail elsewhere, is that a philosophically satisfactory theory of the mind will distinguish between a first-order state of desire and a higher-order state of preference, which differs from desire, including even higher order desires.[4] The choice of the words "desire" and "preference" seems appropriate to my theoretical usage, but neither ordinary nor philosophical usage is consistent on this linguistic point. So my usage requires some elucidation and illustration.

---

[4] Keith Lehrer, *Self-Trust: A Study of Reason, Knowledge, and Autonomy* (Oxford: Clarendon Press, 1997), 11–12.

Let us begin with garden-variety desires, the kind that often arise in us in confusion. I desire to paint Finger Rock Canyon. I also desire to meet Jennifer for coffee to discuss virtue. Moreover, the weather is perfect for a swim at the Recreation Center, and so I have a desire for a swim. There is a conflict among my desires because I cannot arrange to satisfy all of these desires. I must decide which of the desires I prefer to satisfy. I move, almost imperceptibly, from desire to the metamental level of the evaluation of desire. The metamental level of evaluation is a higher-order level of evaluation of a first-order mental state. Evaluation of desires may lead me to deliberate, though it need not. I may have a fixed intention resulting from prior reflection to give priority to one sort of desire, the desire to paint, for example, having reflected that unless I paint when the spirit moves me, when the desire and impulse are present, I shall lack inspiration. I think of *preference* as a disposition to choose given the opportunity, which incorporates higher-order evaluation. The distinction between first-order desire and preference to satisfy a desire becomes apparent as soon as conflict arises among our desires. When conflict arises, we confront the need to decide which desire we prefer to satisfy.

It should be noted that this metamental ascent to evaluation and preference is a feature of our mental and metamental capacities. I am not arguing that it is impossible to resolve conflict without metamental ascent. I am claiming, on the basis of observation, that we do it this way. We are able to place our desires before the bar of judgment and evaluate their merits. Moreover, such a perspective often enables us to see how to resolve conflict and maximize the satisfaction of desires. The evaluation of desires must enter into this process if we are moral and rational. Some desires are immoral and others irrational, so reflection on how to satisfy our desires typically presupposes evaluation of desires and the formation of preferences concerning which ones to satisfy. Even so, it is possible to imagine a creature who is incapable of metamental ascent with exactly the same dispositions to choose as we possess. There is an obvious argument to this conclusion.

Imagine a most rational person, Kant perhaps, who seeks to form all preferences by rational deliberation and who chooses throughout his life in accord with those rational preferences. Now imagine a second being, Pseudokant, who completely lacks any capacity for higher-order evaluation but has exactly the same dispositions to choose as Kant does. Pseudokant lacks preference as I construe the notion because he lacks the capacity for higher-order evaluation, but he may have the same dispositions to choose as Kant does when confronted with desires and conflicting desires, though Pseudokant's dispositions are all embedded in his first-order mind. So what is the advantage of metamental ascent and higher-order evaluation? The process is heuristic and provides for our plasticity, our ability to change, to change our principles, and even to change how we change. We might have been made as first-order creatures with unreflective principles and dispositions for conflict resolution. But then we would lack the plasticity to change our principles for choice because we could not override them. Given our metamental capacity, we can both evaluate how to choose and how to change how we choose. Of course, we can imagine, once again, Pseudokant always choosing in the same way that Kant or any other rational person does. There is no difficulty, in principle, in imagining the existence of such a being as Pseudokant, however difficult it might be to imagine how he came to be. The claim that we choose by evaluating our desires is supported by observation and explained by the heuristic of metamental plasticity, that is, plasticity resulting from our higher-order mental life. Moreover, our autonomy depends on this metamental capacity and the plasticity of our mental life. Autonomy without plasticity is a contradiction.

Of course, preference, even when autonomous, may be principled. One use of principle, and an important one, is to have a rule of thumb for the satisfaction of unproblematic desires in order to provide for an economy of effort. We do not need to reflect on the question of whether to satisfy each desire that arises because some desires are innocuous. Such desires may be satisfied without deliberation in ordinary circumstances, for example, drinking a glass of water from the tap when one is thirsty and has a desire to drink. The satisfaction of such a desire without thinking about whether to satisfy it or not in ordinary circumstances is neither irrational nor immoral. Suppose then that one satisfies such a desire without reflection. Does it follow that one is, therefore, operating exactly like Pseudokant responding entirely at the first level? Some unreflective behavior is no doubt automatic, but we should not assume that the preference to satisfy desires without reflecting upon them is entirely controlled at the first level. The higher-order certification of some desires in ordinary circumstances remains, when we are autonomous, under the power and influence of the metamind. The rule or principle to satisfy such desires without deliberation is a rule of thumb that is defeasible and may be overridden. The role of the rule is rather like an intention to satisfy such desires, as Michael E. Bratman analyzes intention.[5] An intention, as he analyzes it, may direct choice without reflection but is open to reconsideration and, indeed, alteration. We see this when circumstances change. If there is concern about whether the water might be degraded or poisoned, we become more reflective about whether to drink. To convince oneself of this, consider the way in which we unreflectively satisfy the desire to open mail that is addressed to us, until circumstances change and raise our suspicions about whether our mail might be contaminated and whether there could be danger in following the usual rule of thumb. We then see that the rule or principle that embodied our preference is not an auto-

[5] Michael E. Bratman, *Intention, Plans, and Practical Reason* (Cambridge, MA: Harvard University Press, 1987).

matic first-order operation, but is an intention to follow a rule under metamental supervision and is subject to reconsideration and revision.

IV. Autonomous Preference

Now let us turn from our account of preference to the promised account of autonomous preference. Frankfurt has insisted, and correctly so, on the importance of higher-order desires.[6] He suggests that freedom requires that first-order desires must accord with second-order desires for us to act freely. There has been much controversy about whether a person whose first- and second-order desires are in accord therefore acts freely in the satisfaction of the first-order desire. The question is whether such accord among our desires is sufficient for freedom. One might think it necessary to add some counterfactual condition to the effect that if one had a first-order desire to act otherwise, one would have acted otherwise, and whether if one had a second-order desire to have a different first-order desire, one would have had a different first-order desire. However, it seems essential to note that such additional requirements would be unrealistic. First-order desires do not ordinarily disappear when we evaluate them negatively, as immoral, irrational, or just undeserving of satisfaction. If second-order desires were like first-order desires, that is, genuine desires arising in us as desires do, then they would not necessarily disappear as a result of negative evaluation either. The distinction between second-order desires and preferences is that the latter, unlike the former, are states of evaluation, positive evaluation, that ascend beyond the first level to the evaluation of it. Thus, we require the metamental ascent to preference in order to make sense of autonomy.

Moreover, just as accord among our desires is not sufficient for autonomous preference, it is not necessary either. Conflict among desires is compatible with autonomous preference. Indeed, we are acutely aware of our autonomy when we have a conflict between our desires. For then we are forced to reflect upon our desires and form a preference, hopefully an autonomous preference, for the satisfaction of some but not all of our desires, or, perhaps, for none of them. Moreover, the conflict among desires may be a conflict among desires at different levels. I might have a desire to eat some rich food laden with butter. I might have a second-order desire not to have such a desire because of a concern for the effect of butter on my arteries and a desire to have healthy arteries. I might even have a third-order desire to be a more fatalistic character who was not so concerned about his health. And so forth. I might be rife with conflicting desires that articulate themselves at different levels without my freedom or autonomy being infringed upon in a significant way. Indeed, I may take some pleasure in looking upon all these unruly desires and putting

---

[6] Frankfurt, "Freedom of the Will and the Concept of a Person," 5-20.

them in some order to form a preference about whether to satisfy the desire to eat the buttery food on this occasion. It is, I might reflect, up to me and in my power to determine which of these desires I shall prefer to satisfy. I might find this reflection to be a source of satisfaction, seeing myself as empowered to choose, or a source of anxiety, seeing myself as responsible for the choice. Which desires, if any, I evaluate positively and prefer to satisfy is up to me, however, when I am autonomous in my preference.

Having noted that autonomy pertains to preference rather than desire, the question immediately arises as to what is required for a preference to be autonomous. Should we say that it is the nature of preference to provide autonomy? Are higher-order evaluation and the formation of preference necessarily autonomous? The usual objection is that preference, even if metamental, does not provide us with a secure prophylactic against manipulation. Although we are concerned with the autonomy of an internal state, that is, preference, rather than the success of action in the external world, we recognize that compulsion, whether it originates internally or externally, threatens autonomy. Indeed, the objection might proceed, metamental ascent merely provides us with greater cognitive advantages. As a result of metamental ascent, we might know what we desire and what the merits and demerits of satisfying a desire are, but such information, though it might ensure us against some forms of ignorance about our desires, does not ensure us against other forms of manipulation. For our metamental evaluations and resulting preferences might themselves be under the control of another agent. How we evaluate and what we prefer might be in his power, not ours. In this case, our preferences, no matter how rational and moral they might appear to us, could be a reflection of the power that another has over us rather than an exercise of our autonomy. The ascent to preference is necessary for autonomy, but it is not sufficient to ensure it.

What must we add to preferences to ensure that they are autonomous? Will higher-order preferences or counterfactual conditions concerning preferences provide the needed prophylactic? Suppose, for example, that moving from the inflexibility of desire to the plasticity of preference, we consider whether a higher-order preference for a lower level of preference suffices for autonomy of the lower-level preference. It is clear from our considerations of higher-order desires why this higher-order preference for a lower preference does not suffice for the autonomy of the latter. The entire preference structure, from the lowest to the highest level preference, might be in the control of another agent and be manipulated by this other agent.

Consider, then, the addition of counterfactual conditions, ones to the effect that if I had preferred to have other preferences than I do, then I would have had other preferences. Thus, for example, suppose that if I had preferred at the second level not to have my preference to paint

Finger Rock Canyon, then I would not have had my first-order preference to paint it, even, though, in fact, I have a first-order preference to paint it. Does this ensure, as G. E. Moore once suggested concerning choice, that I am free or autonomous?[7] Unfortunately, it does not, and the objection is familiar from the discussion concerning Moore and his followers. The second-order preference might not be in my control but again may be manipulated by another agent. Thus, even if my first-order preference would have been different if my second-order preference had been different, this does not ensure that I am autonomous in the first-order preference, because I might not be autonomous in the second-order preference. The latter might not be under my control.

In an earlier attempt to meet this objection, I suggested iterating the counterfactual condition and requiring that if I had preferred at any level to have a different preference at the next lower level, then I would have had a different preference at the next lower level.[8] My purpose was to ensure that I had an answer to the question of whether my preference at any level is in my power. My answer to the question of whether the preference at some specified level is in my power would be that if I had preferred to prefer otherwise at the specified level, then I would have preferred otherwise at that level. Is this counterfactual condition sufficient for the preference being in my power? Again, there is a difficulty concerning control raised by Peter Van Inwagen[9] and Krister Segerberg.[10] It is that the sequence of higher-order preferences and the counterfactual conditions concerning preferences might be in the control of another agent. Imagine that what I do prefer and what I would prefer if I had preferred to prefer otherwise are completely controlled by another. To get specific about the control, suppose that a small computer chip was secretly installed in my brain. Call it, as I have, a "braino," which enables an external operator to determine what preferences I have. In fact, all of my preferences are controlled by the operator. It might then be true that if I had preferred to have other preferences, I would have had other preferences, but this is because the operator with the braino would have determined that I had other preferences. It is not my autonomy but his control of the braino that determines what preference I do have and, moreover, would have at each level.

To capture the notion of autonomy, something more is required than just preference, something more than just preferences over preferences, and something more than counterfactual influence of preferences over

---

[7] G. E. Moore, *Ethics* (Oxford: Oxford University Press, 1912), chap. 6.

[8] Keith Lehrer, "Preferences, Conditionals, and Freedom," in Keith Lehrer, *Metamind* (Oxford: Clarendon Press, 1990), chap. 3, reprinted from Peter Van Inwagen, ed., *Time and Cause: Essays Presented to Richard Taylor* (Dordrecht, The Netherlands: Reidel, 1980).

[9] Peter Van Inwagen, *An Essay on Free Will* (Oxford: Clarendon Press, 1983), chap. 4.

[10] Krister Segerberg, "Could Have but Did Not," *Pacific Philosophical Quarterly* 64 (1983): 230–41.

preferences. But what? Someone might be inclined to give up the quest for explanation at this point and just answer, "autonomy." A philosopher will not give up the quest for explanation, however, until there is proof that none can be given. For it is the goal of philosophy, and of this philosopher, to explain as much as possible and to leave as little unexplained as we must. One further attempt at explanation is to appeal to a notion of agency or agent causality. Thomas Reid (1710–96) suggests that liberty requires that I determine my volitions, which include my preferences, and that this suffices.[11] Reid uses the notion of "liberty" as I do "autonomy," so Reid would claim that to be autonomous in my preferences, I must be the cause of them. Others, most notably Richard Taylor[12] and Roderick M. Chisholm,[13] have reintroduced this doctrine into discussion in the latter part of the twentieth century. Some have found the notion of agent causality to be unintelligible, but Reid argues that this is the primary notion of causality, though unanalyzable. Other notions of causality, Reid alleges, are but metaphorical extensions of it. So to ensure the presence of autonomy and to avoid the problem of manipulation, Reid might just have added that the autonomous agent must be the cause of his or her preferences. Should we settle for this solution?

Seeking to explain as much as we can and to leave as little unexplained as we must, we need to ask whether we can analyze this notion of agent causality. I suggest that we need not take the notion as primitive, but that we can explain it. So let us take a few further steps toward explanation. First of all, let us make explicit the notion of a preference structure concerning some action A. By this I shall mean a first-order preference concerning action A and other, higher-order preferences pertaining to action A. One simple example of a preference structure would be a preference to paint Finger Rock Canyon, a second-order preference to have this first-order preference, and a third-order preference to have the second-order preference, and so on up the orders of preference as far as they extend. This is an integrated structure of level-specific preference without conflict. As we noted above, however, autonomous preference may be based on a preference structure that contains conflict. Moreover, the higher-order preferences need not be stratified by levels, that is, they need not be level-specific. For example, a preference concerning all of my preferences pertaining to action A would not be level-specific.

Moreover, autonomous preference need not depend on an infinite hierarchy of preference, though an infinite hierarchy of preferences is possible. We can suppose that a person has an infinite hierarchy, especially an integrated one, since preferences are functional states, not occurrent states.

---

[11] Thomas Reid, *Essays on the Active Powers of Man*, 8th ed., William Hamilton, ed. (Edinburgh: James Thin, 1895), Essay 4.

[12] Richard Taylor, *Action and Purpose* (Englewood Cliffs, NJ: Prentice-Hall, 1966).

[13] Roderick M. Chisholm, "Freedom and Action," in Keith Lehrer, ed., *Freedom and Determinism* (New York: Random House, 1966), 11–44.

A functional state is, like a dispositional state, one that is a standing state having a certain role and functioning in a determinate manner in thought, reasoning, and choice. Moreover, since preferences are functional states, there is no need to suppose that they can be understood in a momentary intuition. The understanding of them may itself be computational or functional. In the simple example considered above, there is no difficulty with computing higher-order preferences from lower-level ones or, for that matter, lower-level preferences from higher-order ones. The computational rule says this: to go up a preference level, just add a preference to the last preference considered, and to go down a preference level, just delete the last preference from the last preference considered. However, an infinite hierarchy of preferences is neither sufficient for autonomy, as we noted above, nor necessary, for reasons that we shall now consider.

An autonomous preference may be level-ambiguous and incorporate conflict. Suppose, for example, that I consider all preferences that I have concerning an action A and find that, whatever conflicts or other peculiarities I discern, I am satisfied with the preference structure just as it is. I evaluate it positively. Thus, I prefer to have this preference structure, including all of my preferences pertaining to action A—to writing this essay, for example. I might prefer to have this preference. Indeed, I do. This is not without conflict, but all things considered, I prefer to have all the preferences that I do concerning writing this essay. Notice, however, that this very preference to have the preferences that I do concerning writing this essay is, itself, a preference concerning writing this essay. So this preference, being a preference for having the preference structure containing all my preferences concerning writing the essay, is contained in the preference structure because it is also a preference concerning writing this essay. This preference for the preference structure is not level-specific. This preference for the preference structure is a preference for the preferences within the preference structure. Since the preferences within the preference structure are preferences of differing levels, the preference for those preferences is not level-specific.

Let us call this preference for the preference structure, or more personally, my preference for my preference structure to do A, my *power preference* concerning A. I shall argue that such a preference empowers me and is the basis of my autonomy. A philosopher who is determined to stratify preferences by levels might suppose that it would be possible to assign the power preference a higher level than any of the preferences in the preference structure. It is a preference "over" the preferences in the preference structure. This attempt to assign a level to the power preference, in addition to being a deviant notion of "level," would be a mistake, however. The reason noted above is that the power preference is itself a preference in the preference structure pertaining to A. The power preference is a preference concerning preferences pertaining to action A. Thus, my preference for the preference structure loops back onto itself in the preference structure. It is a preference for all of the preferences in the preference structure, including itself. This is the secret source of the power of the preference.

The loop of the power preference back onto itself in the preference structure is a special feature of the autonomy of preference. Consider my preference for A. Now suppose that a question arises as to the autonomy of the preference. I might try to assure myself or another agent that the preference is autonomous by appealing to a preference for that preference. But this will leave the question of the autonomy of that next level preference unanswered. One might, of course, argue that the first preference to do A is autonomous because of the second preference for the first, even if the second preference is not autonomous, but this would leave us with the need to explain how a second preference that is not autonomous could be sufficient to ensure the autonomy of the first preference. One might just insist that it is sufficient without explanation, but that would leave us with an unexplained "surd," and one seeking, as I do, to explain as much as possible, will not be satisfied with a "surd."

To avoid the "surd," one might embrace a regress and add a third preference for the second, a fourth for the third, to answer the question of whether the first preference is autonomous. So one might embrace a regress of explanations to avoid the "surd." The infinite regress, though it is not vicious because preferences are functional states, is not satisfying either. For it leaves open the question of whether the infinite sequence is autonomous. By contrast, the power preference answers all questions about preferences concerning preferences pertaining to A in a single preference, the preference for the preference structure. Since this preference loops back onto itself as a preference in the preference structure, it contains within itself a preference for itself and avoids the "surd" and the regress. The question whether it is preferred is answered by the preference itself without need to appeal to another preference, and the explanation for why it is autonomous is that it is preferred in a way that is sufficient to ensure that it and all the other preferences in the preference structure are preferences that the agent prefers to have. A power preference ties the preferences in the preference structure up, down, and together in a loop of preference that empowers us.

Is the power preference sufficient to ensure autonomy? It frees preference of external semantic constraints because of the self-referential feature of it. In this way it is like the claim, "All true sentences are true," which says of other true sentences that they are true and, at the same time, if it is true, says of itself that it is true. In a similar way the power preferences—my preference to have the preference structure that I do have pertaining to action A—is a preference for all the other preferences that I have pertaining to the action and, at the same time, it is a preference for having the power preference itself. The semantic ungroundedness discussed by Saul Kripke[14] might be considered a semantic defect, but, as Vann McGee[15] has shown, the ungroundedness of a sentence does not mean that it lacks a truth value. Rather, the ungroundedness means that the truth value is a matter of choice. Consider again the sentence, "All true sentences are true." This sentence, if true, says of itself, as well as other sentences, something that might be expressed by the sentence, "This sentence is true." The truth of this latter sentence, if it is true, is not grounded in any antecedently specified truth conditions. Let us say, therefore, that this latter sentence is "ungrounded." We can choose to assign it a truth value: for example, we can choose to assign it the value "true," but this choice will not be grounded in any antecedently specified truth conditions. So the ungroundedness of the power preference does not mean that there is no truth value to the claim that such a power preference exists, but only that the truth value depends on choice. The ungroundedness provides a kind of semantic independence, therefore, which is a virtue of the power preference as a condition of autonomy. We want the autonomy of our preference to depend on our preference itself, and preference is the dispositional surrogate of choice.

The internal structure and, indeed, the semantic structure of the power preference reveals its merit for the role of explicating autonomy. However, this does not mean that the power preference is a sufficient condition for autonomous preference. There are two reasons for this. The first concerns the possibility of external manipulation. The second concerns the possibility of internal compulsion. Consideration of both will take us back to the paradox of reason with which we began. Consider the possibility of external manipulation. A power preference, though semantically ungrounded, may result from choice, and choice may be externally controlled. Another person might direct my thoughts and preferences. We can imagine a braino installed in my brain, as we did above, which is controlled by another person who operates the braino to cause me to form my preferences, including a preference for having the preference structure that I have. The braino might be used to cause my power preference. Without electronic control of my brain, another person might make use of psychological compulsion. If another person knows that a certain line of reasoning, perhaps one that appeals to religious authority, will make me choose to prefer a course of action and to prefer to have a preference structure pertaining to this course of action, then I am subject to manipulation by the other person in my choice of a power preference by a line of reasoning that appeals to religious authority.

It is clear that such causation of the power preference deprives me of autonomy, however satisfied I might be with the power preference. My

[14] Saul Kripke, "Outline of a Theory of Truth," *Journal of Philosophy* 72, no. 19, Seventy-Second Annual Meeting, American Philosophical Association, Eastern Division (Nov. 6, 1975): 690–716.
[15] Vann McGee, *Truth, Vagueness, and Paradox* (Indianapolis, IN: Hackett Publishing, 1991).

preference for the preference structure that I have, including this preference itself, might be controlled by another person. Should we conclude from this that a power preference must be uncaused, as libertarians might propose, to ensure that the preference is autonomous? This proposal might appear promising as a solution to the problem, until we remember that we need some positive account of how a person can be the cause of his or her preferences. The mere fact that a preference of mine is uncaused, even a power preference, does not ensure that the preference is up to me or that I am the cause of it. In short, the denial of causal etiology of a power preference leaves us without a positive account of a relationship of an agent to a preference to ensure that it is autonomous. Are we caught in a dilemma then? Must we say that if my preference, even a power preference, is caused, then it is not free because it is caused, and if it is uncaused, then here, too, it is not free because I am not the cause of my preference? Is there any explanation of how I can be the cause of a preference, including my power preference, which precludes control of my preferences by another or by some compulsion?

V. THE PRIMACY CONDITION

The answer to this question and the solution to the dilemma is contained in the formulation of the problem. What we must require is that the power preference be a preference that a person has because he or she prefers to have that preference. Moreover, we need to require that the person has the power preference that he or she has because he or she prefers to have it in a rather special way. Most simply put, the preference for having the power preference must be the primary explanation for why he or she has the power preference. Thus, to obtain an account of autonomy that satisfies the appropriate external as well as internal conditions on autonomy, we must require that a preference for the power preference on the part of the agent, which is internal to the power preference, as we have noted, is the primary explanation of the existence of the power preference. There may be many components to a complete explanation of a preference, but for the preference to be autonomous, the preference for the power preference must be the primary explanation of the preference itself. This condition will be called *the primacy condition*.

Let us recall that a power preference is a preference for having the preferences that one has pertaining to some specific action A. Thus, on an account of autonomy in terms of the power preference and satisfaction of the primacy condition, a person might be autonomous with respect to some actions but not others. A bolder theory of autonomy might hold that we are autonomous with respect to all of our preferences concerning all of our preferred actions. The result of such a theory would resemble in this respect a Sartrian theory of freedom affirming that all of our choices are both free and uncaused.[16] However, the psychology of preference appears to allow for failure of autonomy of preference resulting from the power of desire if, for example, the strength of a desire overpowers the activity of metamental evaluation in the formation of preference. Many libertarians, Reid for one,[17] have conceded that, though the will is sometimes free, it is at other times overwhelmed by desire or passion. This appears to me to be the truth of the matter. What is of paramount importance, however, is the looping structure of the power preference satisfying the primacy condition. A power preference is a preference for the preferences that one has concerning doing A, writing this paper, for example. The power preference itself concerns A, writing this paper, and is, therefore, a preference for itself as well as for other preferences in the preference structure. When one has this power preference because one prefers to have it, and in a way that satisfies the primacy condition, the preference is autonomous.

VI. AGENT CAUSALITY EXPLAINED

Let us note the advantages of this account and then return to the paradox of reason. First of all, a power preference that satisfies the primacy condition offers us an explanation of agent causality. Such a preference is one that I have because I am the cause of the preference. If I have a preference because I prefer to have it, then I and not someone else am the cause of the preference. Consider again the case of the braino. In that case, the operator of the braino, not I, is the cause of my preferences, even my power preferences. In such a case, I do not have a preference because I prefer to have it. I have it because the braino operator prefers that I have it. I have the preferences that I do because he operates the machine rather than because I prefer to have them. When he causes me to have a preference for a course of action and to prefer to have the preference structure that I have pertaining to the action, the latter is a power preference. There is a failure of autonomy here because the primacy condition is not satisfied. The primary explanation of why I have the power preference is that he causes it, not that I do. Alternatively, if the primacy condition is satisfied, and I have the power preference because I prefer to have it, then the preference cannot be controlled by the operator of the braino. (If it were, then I would not have the preference because I preferred to have it.) When the primacy condition is satisfied, I am the cause of the power preference in that I have that preference because I prefer to have it.

This account of agent causality avoids the regress and "surd." There is no regress because the power preference loops back onto itself and is a

[16] Jean-Paul Sartre, *Being and Nothingness*, trans. Hazel E. Barnes (New York: Philosophical Library, 1956).
[17] Reid, *Essays on the Active Powers of Man*, Essay 4.

preference for itself as well as for other preferences pertaining to the action *A*. There is no "surd," because there is no appeal to a self causing a preference in some unexplained or mysterious way. On the contrary, the explanation for the preference is a preference, and causation of preferences by preferences is not mysterious. The looping character of the preference might seem to introduce something odd if not mysterious. Isn't the idea of a preference existing because it is a preference for itself a mysterious one? The answer, which will be elaborated upon further when we consider the solution to the paradox of reason, is that components in a structure can be mutually supporting in ordinary causal terms. Consider a structure built of three flat boards leaning against the sides of a small triangle-shaped board placed at the top. If you remove the triangle, the structure will collapse. Each of the components contributes causally to the support of the structure, and the triangle at the top plays the role of supporting the three boards leaning against its sides. The triangle contributes causally to holding itself in place in the structure as it contributes causally to holding the boards in place. It is a kind of keystone in the structure. This kind of mutual causal support is commonplace and not mysterious. My claim is that the structure of preferences causally resembles this physical structure. The power preference playing the role of the triangle may be causally supported by the other preferences in the structure at the same time that it causally supports the structure and, indirectly, the position of itself within the structure.

VII. Causality and the Power Preference

The metaphor of a structure containing three boards and a triangle calls to our attention the need for considering the position of the power preference in satisfying the primacy condition in the "structure" of causes. First of all, consider the causal influence of the preferences of another agent. We appear to obtain a paradoxical result if we concede, as we must, that we sometimes have the preferences that we do because of the preferences of others. For surely we can autonomously prefer to satisfy the preferences of another. But how can I have the preferences that I do pertaining to an action because I prefer to have them if I have the preferences that I do because of the preferences that you have? This paradox concerning the preferences of others leads naturally to the internal paradox of reason. For how can I have the preferences that I do pertaining to an action because I prefer to have them if I have the preferences that I do because of the *reasons* that I have for these preferences?

Let us consider the paradox concerning the preferences of others. The solution to it rests on drawing a distinction between different ways in which I can be influenced by the preferences of another person. At one extreme, there is the control of my preferences in some concealed way by another so that I do not even perceive that I am controlled at all. A bit less extreme is the case in which I prefer what I do because of my knowledge of the preferences of another person whom I have a compulsive desire or impulse to satisfy. Extreme cases of obsession with another person, whether as the result of my love or the other's charismatic power, may have the result that I cannot help preferring what I perceive the other to prefer. It is not just that I desire to do what the other prefers. It is rather that the other has an influence over me of such a systematic sort that it extends beyond my first-order desire to higher-level evaluation and preference. Obsessive love or charismatic power may have this feature. In these states, my mind and metamind are taken over by the other, so that whatever the other values, I value, and whatever the other prefers, I prefer. There is no autonomy here, for I prefer what I do not because I prefer to have that preference, but because of the influence of the other.

Can I autonomously prefer what the other prefers? I can. If I prefer to satisfy the preferences of the other because I prefer to have such preferences, then I am autonomous. On the contrary, if I prefer to satisfy the preferences of the other but I do not have that preference because I prefer to have it, I may be enslaved to the other. In short, whether I am autonomous depends on whether the preference that I have for satisfying the preferences of the other results from a power preference which satisfies the primacy condition. If I have the power preference because I prefer to have it, then I am autonomous. If not, I may be in bondage to the powers of the other. It does not matter for my autonomy whether I prefer to satisfy the preferences of the other or not. What matters is why I have that preference. To be autonomous, I must have the preference because I prefer to have it.

VIII. The Paradox of Reason Solved

These reflections on the paradox concerning the preferences of others lead to the solution of the paradox of reason. How can I have the preferences that I do because I prefer to have them if I have these preferences because of the reasons that I have for having them? The answer is more complicated than the explanation of how we can autonomously prefer to satisfy the preferences of another person, but the fundamental idea is the same. I can be enslaved by reasons just as I can be enslaved by the preferences of another, but preferring something because of the reasons that I have for preferring it, like preferring something because of the preferences of another, need not be bondage. If the response to reasons like the response to the preferences of another has a primary explanation in my power preferences, then the response may be autonomous in spite of the causal influences. Another person could have such amorous or charismatic power over me as to supply me with reasons that become my reasons for forming a preference because of his or her power over me. If I cannot resist the other person, then my preference, though it is one for which I have reasons, is not autonomous. It does not matter whether the reasons are good reasons or bad ones. If I respond to them because of the power of the other, if the power of the other is the primary explanation of why I form my preference in accord with these reasons, then my preference is not autonomous.

I may, however, form a preference in accord with reasons in a way that is compatible with autonomy. The way should now be clear. If I form a preference in accord with reasons because I prefer to form my preference in accord with these reasons and this preference accords with a power preference for the preference satisfying the primacy condition, then I am autonomous in preferring what I do for the reasons that I have. I can autonomously prefer to form preferences in accord with reasons, and when I do form preferences in accord with such reasons, I autonomously prefer what I do for these reasons. The basic solution to the paradox of reason is that I autonomously prefer to form preferences in accord with reasons.

It might seem that this solution to the paradox of reason only calls up another paradox, however. For now it seems that I can only form autonomous preferences in accord with reasons if I first have an autonomous preference for proceeding in this way. This naturally raises the question of whether these autonomous preferences for forming preferences in accord with reasons may themselves be formed in accord with reasons. It appears, therefore, that we might be forced to concede that some autonomous preferences cannot be formed in accord with reasons, namely, the autonomous preference to form preferences in accord with reasons. As Sartre suggests concerning some choices, it appears that some autonomous preferences must be without justification and without excuse.[18] We might put the issue as a dilemma: Either some autonomous preferences must be formed without reasons, namely, autonomous preferences for forming preferences in accord with reasons, or some preferences must be formed in accord with reasons without an autonomous preference for forming them in that way. On either alternative, not all autonomous preferences can be formed in accord with reasons.

The dilemma is a false one, however. A preference can be formed in accord with reasons at the same time that a preference is formed to be guided by reasons in forming preferences. Consider a difficult choice. Someone is trying to decide whether to change her career in a major way. As she remarks on the difficulty of the choice, we advise her that, since she is a philosopher, all she needs to do is tally up her reasons and decide. She may justly reply that we do not understand the seriousness of the matter, for she has to decide which reasons are to guide her decision. Put another way, though it may be important for her to reflect on the reasons

[18] I was not able to link this interpretation to a specific passage, for his prose has a charmingly diffuse character, but I am indebted to Jean-Paul Sartre, *Being and Nothingness*.

that she has, she must evaluate them and decide which ones she prefers to guide her decision. In fact, the choice of what career she will prefer and the choice of what reasons will determine her preference may well occur together. When she has a preference for forming her career preference in accord with some reasons and not others, she may, at the same time, form her preference in accord with those reasons. In fact, the decision to prefer one career over another and the decision to form her preferences in accord with some reasons over others may coincide functionally as well as temporally. Her preference to pursue a career that she finds personally rewarding may be functionally equivalent to preferring to form her preference concerning her career for the reason that she finds the career personally rewarding. Which comes first, the career preference, or the preference to be guided by the reasons that support this career preference? This question is answered by denying that one has to come before the other. The career preference and the preference to be guided by reasons that support this career preference may occur at the same time.

A critic may persist and claim that even if they occur at the same time, one must be the cause or explanation of the other and, therefore, have causal or explanatory precedence or dominance over the other. The reply is that the career preference and the preference to form such preferences by reasons may be mutually supportive in the way that two cards leaning against each other are mutually supportive or, to take my favorite metaphor, in the way that stones in an arch support the keystone as it supports them, so that the structure remains standing because of a loop of mutual support. Suppose, too, that the critic of my theory is moved to protest that even if the career preference and the preference to be guided by reasons that support the career preference are simultaneous and mutually supportive, there is a problem about the autonomy of the preference to be guided by reasons that support the career preference. What would make this preference autonomous? The answer, of course, is that the preference must be a preference that the person has because she prefers the preference structure concerning that preference; that is, there is a power preference satisfying the primacy condition for that preference. It is, therefore, autonomous.

Can the formation of preference for some special reason, because it satisfies the categorical imperative, for example, suffice for autonomy without the satisfaction of the primacy condition? To test this idea, consider a philosopher, similar to Kant, who forms a preference to tell the truth and not to lie, for the reason that it satisfies the categorical imperative. Is this sufficient for the person to be autonomous in choosing to tell the truth? Suppose that a person, Catecomp, forms his preferences for the reason that they satisfy the categorical imperative, but Catecomp is a victim of a braino implanted in his brain, which allows the operator, Controller, to determine what reasons will move Catecomp to form his preferences. Controller chooses to make Catecomp be guided by the categorical imperative in his formation of preferences. Catecomp is not autonomous, no matter how perfectly he is guided by the categorical imperative, because he is controlled by another person in how he forms his preferences. The problem for Catecomp is not that he fails to form his preferences on the basis of the categorical imperative, but that his formation of preferences on the basis of the categorical imperative, even if he prefers to form preferences in this way, is the result of the intervention of Controller. Catecomp does not form preferences because he prefers to form preferences on the basis of the categorical imperative, but because Controller makes him form his preferences in this way. Notice that even if Controller creates a preference in Catecomp for forming preferences in a way that satisfies the categorical imperative, Catecomp will not have this preference because he prefers to have it. In short, he will lack a power preference satisfying the primacy condition for a preference for forming his preferences in the way that he does. Autonomy supplements rationality rather than being a consequence of it.

IX. Reason and Autonomy: The Ultrapreference

A host of talented contemporary authors, John Martin Fischer[19] and J. David Velleman,[20] for example, have tried to reduce freedom or autonomy to the influence and governance of reasons in preference and choice. But any such account will fall short unless it somehow guarantees that a person is autonomous in the way in which the person is influenced by or governed by reasons. The influence and governance by reasons, no matter how admirably rational, can be controlled by another person. The result is that the controlled individual lacks freedom and autonomy. We must add autonomy to any account of being influenced or governed by reasons, rather than expect that autonomy should be a consequence of such influence or governance. The preference to be guided or governed by a system of reasons, SR, in forming a preference, P, must be autonomous in order for the preference P, guided by reasons, to be autonomous. Does this preference to be so guided or governed lead us to a regress of preferences?

It does not. Call the preference to be guided or governed by a system of reasons an *ultrapreference*. Now suppose that there is a power preference satisfying the primacy condition for the ultrapreference. This power preference may have the features of any other preference. It may be a preference in a preference structure, and the person may prefer to have this structure because the person prefers to have it. In short, there may be a power preference for the preference structure containing the ultrapref-

---

[19] John Martin Fischer, *The Metaphysics of Free Will: An Essay on Control*, Aristotelian Society Series, vol. 14 (Cambridge, MA: Blackwell, 1994).
[20] J. David Velleman, "What Happens When Someone Acts?" *Mind* 101, no. 403 (1992): 461–81.

erence. The looping character of the power preference again avoids the regress and the "surd." Must the ultrapreference be a preference that a person forms, as Sartre suggests, without justification and without excuse? Not at all. The ultrapreference may be a preference that the person forms guided or governed by the system of reasons, SR. The ultrapreference is governed by the system of reasons, SR, at the same time that the ultrapreference is a preference to be governed by SR, and so there is a loop of preference back on to itself. This loop of preference, which may include the power preference in the governance by the system of reasons, SR, is the loop of autonomy that ties autonomy and rationality together.

X. A Summary on Preferences, Reason, and Autonomy

Let us retrace our path and end with a consideration of the perennial problem of freedom and determinism, reinterpreted as the problem of autonomy and determinism. We began by asking how we might solve the paradox of reason, that is, if we are governed by reasons in our preferences, then we are in bondage to reason and not autonomous; whereas if we are not governed by reason, then we are not autonomous. We noted that the solution is that we may have an autonomous preference to be guided by reasons in forming our preferences. Moreover, this autonomous preference itself may be guided by the reasons that we prefer to be guided by. This becomes possible once one notes that autonomous preference results from a power preference for one's preference structure. This power preference is itself a preference in the preference structure and, therefore, loops back onto itself. The result is that the autonomous preference is a volition of which I am the cause, in the sense that I have the preference because I prefer to have it. No regress results from this account of autonomy. Finally, we are not left with some "surd" of an unexplained or unjustified preference. The preference is explained by the fact that I have it because I prefer to have it and for the reasons that I prefer to have govern my preferences.

XI. Conclusion: Arational Autonomy, Causation, and Determinism

We are left with two perennial problems that we are now in a position to answer. The first concerns whether we must be governed by reasons in order to be autonomous. The view of autonomy advanced in this essay is compatible with arationalism. Suppose that a person prefers at time t not to be guided by reasons in the future. He may even have reasons for this at time t. Moreover, his preference for not being guided by reasons in the future may be autonomous. Consider any time later than t. At such a time, the person may autonomously prefer what he does without being guided by reasons at that time. He might not even be guided by the reasons that he had at t for preferring not to be guided by reasons in the future. The future that was referred to at t is now present, and he might not be guided by any reasons, including the earlier ones, in his present preferences. His present preferences may, nonetheless, be preferences in a preference structure that he has because he prefers to have it. He has become arationally autonomous. Rationality is compatible with autonomy, but autonomy supplements rationality.

The second problem is whether the account of autonomy that I have proposed is compatible with causal determinism. The answer will, of course, depend on how one defines determinism. The simplest answer is that autonomous preference is compatible with the preference being causally explained. Moreover, the conditions of causal explanation may extend in a sequence as far back in time as one cares to imagine. All that is required for autonomy is that the primary explanation for the power preference be that the person has the preference because he or she prefers to have it. There might be some secondary explanation, and further explanation beyond that, and so forth back into the indefinite past. One might object that remote explanations, no matter how secondary, are causal conditions over which the person had no control. The answer is that there are always causal conditions of our preferences over which we had no control, for example, our being born. If it is asked whether we could have preferred otherwise, we may answer briefly that we could have, provided that we were autonomous in our power preference and would have been autonomous in our power preference had we preferred otherwise. Once again, this is compatible with a causal explanation of preference that extends in a secondary way as far back into the past as one cares to imagine. The burden of compatibilism is to explain the difference between causation that makes us free in our preferences and causation that puts us in bondage so that, understanding this difference, we do not fear the forces of nature but, instead, find our autonomy within the natural universe. We have found it. When we prefer to have the preference structure that we do pertaining to our preferences because we prefer to have them, we find a place for our autonomy in the natural order of things free of bondage. Autonomous preference and the actions that result from it provide us with the dignity of being causal agents in the causal order. Autonomy provides us a place of liberty in the natural world of cause and effect.

Philosophy, University of Arizona

IDENTIFICATION, THE SELF, AND AUTONOMY

By Bernard Berofsky

I. Introduction

Autonomy, we suppose, is self-regulation or self-direction. There is a distinct idea that is easily confused with self-direction, namely, self-expression, self-fulfillment, or self-realization. (I do not mean to suggest that the latter three terms are all synonymous. But in this essay, whatever differences there are among them play no role, so I will use them interchangeably.) Although it will turn out paradoxically that autonomy is *neither* self-regulation *nor* self-realization, it is reasonable to suppose that the former is a superior candidate. My teacher of Indian religion, Dr. Subodh Roy, blind from birth, chose not to undergo an operation that would have made him sighted because he believed, perhaps rightly, that the ability to see would interfere with his religious quest. He thereby chose not to realize one of his fundamental human capacities, one whose cultivation has produced some of the finest fruits of civilization. Joseph Raz describes a case in which a man places his life in jeopardy by undertaking a trip to deliver medical aid to a group of people in a distant place. Since he will be unable to secure food for several days, he, in effect, subordinates one of his own basic needs or interests to a goal that he deems more important.[1] There is no reason to believe that, in refusing to express or realize a dimension of self, either Dr. Roy or Raz's philanthropist have failed to act autonomously.

Of course, there is also no reason to believe that these two men's actions do not "express the self" even if they suppress other facets of the self. What then renders self-regulation, suitably qualified, superior as the analysis of autonomy to self-realization?

II. Autonomy and Choice

To begin to address this question, consider the following example. Malcolm has recently become a father. He never chose to sire a child and never dreamed of assuming the responsibilities of fatherhood. To his initial surprise, he discovers himself taking on the role of a father with all of its trappings and entanglements. He finds that a powerful bond be-

---

[1] Joseph Raz, *The Morality of Freedom* (Oxford: Clarendon Press, 1986), 296.

tween him and his son is developing. Malcolm also finds that much of his time and energy are directed toward nurturing their relationship. His free time, his finances, and the range of his options are becoming drastically diminished. He is unable to resist certain sorts of entreaties and to do or even to contemplate actions that would place his child in harm's way. Of course, Malcolm cannot imagine doing or even choosing to do serious harm to his son; the prospect is sufficiently repellent as to paralyze his will. Indeed, were he given the opportunity to acquire power to harm his son, he would unhesitatingly refuse. Yet, in spite of the extensive diminution of his time, finances, and options, Malcolm also finds that he is thoroughly pleased about the sort of person whom he has become and the life that he is leading. Indeed, the very encumbrances that Malcolm experiences are essential to the expansiveness that his self undergoes through the relationship. He thoroughly endorses the limits on his will: a loving father is precisely one who cannot choose to harm his son.

Eventually, Malcolm is unable even to imagine living any other life. He comes now to be defined by the connections that have arisen by chance, not by choice. He is subject to what Harry G. Frankfurt calls "volitional necessity."[2]

Malcolm is not only thoroughly content with his life and its limitations, he is also pleased that he has reached this point in ways other than through acts of choice. Malcolm has fallen in love and to fall is precisely not to choose. In "falling" in love, one finds oneself bound to a person (or perhaps an ideology, a movement, or a job), and one is happy to be swept along by the rhythm and demands of the relationship. One prefers not to choose to engage in many of the activities, nor to undergo the emotions and patterns of thinking, that are intrinsic to an *act* of love. For if Malcolm had been presented with an opportunity to choose, he would have had the power to exercise a degree of control that would have undermined the nature and special quality of his involvement with his son.

Many of the most important activities in life are the very ones in which we happily lose a great deal of control to the other. When mathematician Andrew Wiles discovered a glitch in his proof of Fermat's Last Theorem, he did not want to will his way out of his deep frustrations. He could not decide to fix the proof. He was bound by the nature of the structures that he was studying and would have it no other way. He was glad that he was not the voluntarist God of Descartes, who has full control over mathematical relationships. Wiles had to and wanted to *discover* what was wrong with his proof.

Given that Malcolm identifies himself so completely with his life as a father, we may justly regard him as self-realized—his actions reflect the fundamental project that defines him. But he took no active regulatory

---

[2] Harry G. Frankfurt, "On the Necessity of Ideals," in Frankfurt, *Necessity, Volition, and Love* (Cambridge: Cambridge University Press, 1999), 108–16.

role in the process of becoming a father. So why might one be inclined to describe Malcolm as an autonomous agent? Yes, Malcolm is a thoroughly fulfilled individual, preferring not to be different in any fundamental way, especially in those spheres in which his life is now largely governed by outside forces. But this is a description that could be provided for paradigmatic instances of *heteronomy*, for example, Sister Rossetta of the Heaven's Gate cult, who is a completely brainwashed individual under the domination of Do, the cult leader. She, too, identifies herself with her life and regards her actions as an expression of her underlying nature.

Malcolm *might* have reached this point autonomously. But to control the direction of his life, he would have had to *engage* in *independent, reflective decision-making*. For consider scenarios without reflective decision. Had Malcolm, having chosen to eschew fatherhood, been the victim of a deception that brought him grudgingly into this state, the fact that he eventually embraced his condition would appear to be a basis for regarding him as perhaps fortunate, but hardly autonomous. Or, had Malcolm actually reflected on the merits of fatherhood once it was upon him, the process might have taken place under the powerful influence of Malcolm's feelings for his son and their relationship, an influence that might have been sufficiently strong to overwhelm his capacity for independent judgment. So even if the heteronomous attachment of Sister Rossetta to Do is different from the attachment of Malcolm to his son, the latter relationship may incorporate a genuine loss of autonomy. An autonomous Malcolm, in contrast, would have been able to reflect on the wisdom of nourishing powerful impulses and emotions and respond accordingly. He would not have had to be constrained to endorse the ideal of fatherhood and might well have embraced it freely. Under *these* conditions, the reduction of control implicit in parenthood would no longer be a ground for reduced autonomy. But without having chosen the ideal of parental love at some key stages along the way, Malcolm will simply be contented and fulfilled, perhaps self-realized, but not autonomous. Thus, reflection on Malcolm's status reveals the superiority of an account in terms of self-regulation rather than self-realization.

But is it not unrealistic to suppose that we choose our ideals? Do they not draw us in by their compelling attractiveness? Yes. But the point is that beings who are under the sway of ideals in this way *may* fail to meet the conditions of autonomous decision-making—conditions that we assume can be spelled out, although we have yet to do so—and appeals to self-realization are not going to change this fact.

Two distinct conditions bearing on Malcolm's autonomy have been identified. In order to be autonomous Malcolm must (1) determine his relationship to his child, and (2) determine it on the basis of reflection that is sufficiently independent to be counted autonomous. If Malcolm fails to choose at all (that is, if he fails the first condition), then he is content or fulfilled rather than autonomous. If he chooses under the undue influence of external forces (if he fails the second condition), then he is too dependent on others, and possibly lacking in sufficient self-control, to be counted autonomous.

Without choice, even in an ideal environment, all we would have are creatures revealing their natures. These might be fully contented animals, or human members of a tribe for whom individual expression has not yet arisen as an issue. Autonomy, as the Western ideal that it is, demands tension between an individual and the group, tension that is resolved in decision-making. One does not control one's affairs in the relevant sense by living a life that is totally fulfilling and conflict-free.

Nonhuman systems, for example, robots, are "autonomous" when they incorporate self-correcting mechanisms such as an internal thermostat, which could be compared to the mechanism within us that regulates internal bodily temperature. The robots' mechanisms operate automatically, that is, an environmental stimulus initiates action by the mechanism in such a way as to produce the "desired" outcome. We do not conceive our *selves* as operating in this automatic way and, therefore, we import into our conception of autonomy the demand that control be exercised at the conscious level. Self-regulation in the case of personal autonomy presupposes a conception of the self that links it to our status as conscious beings. I am not autonomous if I am acting on "autopilot," no matter how independent of the environment the relevant mechanism is and no matter how desirable or sophisticated the outcome happens to be—hence the demand that control in the human sphere be exercised through (conscious) decision-making.

Of course, we can imagine a creature, Jill, who is so fortunate that, at any stage of her life, she discovers, even after ideal reflection, that the values that she would like to guide the formation of specific motives happen, in all cases, to be the ones that do guide her. Jill need make no adjustments in her will. Hence, if she also discovers that she can never decide otherwise, this would not faze her. She may endorse, but she does not determine, her life. Is she autonomous?

We can raise the hypothetical question: Would Jill have had the power to bring her decisions into line with her deliberations were there a discrepancy? If we think of Jill as autonomous, then I believe that we are presupposing an affirmative answer to this question. Jill approves of her life, that is, her values and desires, as well as the specific decisions that she makes on the basis of them after a thorough, rational, and independent evaluation. She cannot be faulted for failing to exercise powers to change when there are no good reasons to exercise such powers. Although no actual practical decisions are called for, the judgment of autonomy introduces at least counterfactual choice for Jill. If Jill's decisions were ultimately those of a distinct coercive power, her acquiescence would not confer autonomy on her.[3] Thus, to return to Malcolm, in saying that he must choose parental love in order to be autonomous, we do not mean that the state of love must be *created* by his choice. His endorsement suffices so long as it is rendered autonomously and is accompanied by the capacity and disposition to make adjustments in accordance with the results of reflection.

A harder line on the importance of choice—an insistence on actual determination by one's decision—would fail because this demand would lead to incoherence. It is a truism that we do not create ourselves ab initio. Once we reach the stage at which our first gropings for independence and self-mastery take place, a good deal of our nature is already in place. The wildest-eyed believer in free will asks only for free selection from options that, in reality, have already been drastically reduced by the forces of heredity and environment. Similarly, an account of autonomy for human beings, creatures who begin life as completely heteronomous, must permit a transition to autonomy that is achieved through critical appraisal of inculcated values and desires. An adult who is willing and able to make adjustments in accordance with an independent critical appraisal is not deficient in autonomy just because he approves of some elements that are already in place.[4]

Another consideration undermines the radical demand that all elements that enter into decision-making be the result of an act of choice by a mature agent. Decision-making cannot be undertaken unless the context permits certain elements to be fixed—not themselves the objects of deliberation—in order that practical reasoning about other elements may proceed. If everything is "up for grabs," then any particular choice is bound to be arbitrary and nonrational. One cannot hope to canvas all possible objections to, or be in certain possession of all relevant knowledge concerning, a course of action; the process of reason-giving must end, necessarily leaving us with a surd, at least in this context. We risk immobilization if we seek perfect rationality or perfect control.

Yet, we can say more to the lovers of "ideal autonomy." For example, even if some elements must be assumed so that practical reasoning may sensibly commence, one need not suppose that assumed matters may not themselves be the subject of evaluation in another context.[5] Moreover, the fact that much important decision-making depends on perspectives that have been provided to an agent in a process of molding that takes place

[3] We do not even have to suppose that a content Jill has the ability to change the direction of her life during her content phase. All we need to suppose for counterfactual choice is that she *would be able and disposed to change* if, through (autonomous) reflection, she came to disapprove of her life. Since the ability (and/or disposition) to change may arise only when Jill detects problems, we need not, therefore, even take a stand on the relation of autonomy to alternate possibilities.

[4] I am grateful to James Stacey Taylor for helpful suggestions on this point.

[5] See Bernard Berofsky, *Liberation from Self: A Theory of Personal Autonomy* (Cambridge: Cambridge University Press, 1995), 124–25.

prior to the age of reason need not undermine the mature agent's autonomy as much as is ordinarily assumed. Although I cannot present arguments here, I believe that the arbitrariness of some perspectives may be removed through objective grounding (for example, inculcated beliefs may become known to be true), and the arbitrariness of those that cannot be so removed may be shown not to be intrinsically inferior to other possibilities.

Given that Malcolm exercises reflective and independent endorsement and has not reached the state of fatherhood through manipulation or coercion, we can then concede that his current inability to change does not undo his autonomy. For counterfactual control is the power to change *if* one detects a reason to do so. Discontent may be a necessary condition of the power to change, in which case Malcolm is currently powerless. He cannot alter his condition, but he could alter it if he wished to. There is, then, a real distinction between Malcolm and an agent whose autonomy is genuinely impaired, that is, one who cannot now or under hypothetical conditions, restore his life to a satisfactory state.

Even if we understand self-regulation as the proposed analysans of autonomy along the more moderate lines that I have just laid out, decision-making is a core notion in the account. Since decisions can be made under duress, or on the basis of values inculcated from without, or by one who is emotionally disturbed, it would be natural now to undertake the project of more carefully delineating the conditions of autonomous decision-making, for example, critical competence, independence, relevant knowledge, emotional stability, and the like. The picture of self-regulation that we would then be projecting is that of the regulation *of* decisions *by* various states and conditions that meet the requirements of autonomy. But then it would appear that the self, as this system of states and conditions, would be essentially passive. Although, like any set of states or conditions, the self can have causal efficacy, decisions would be the *result of* rather than *constitutive of* self-activity. In recognizing the importance of the difference between a decision that emanates from the self and one that really arises from external sources through manipulation, coercion, selective socialization, and the like, we are led to construe the self as a system that is distinct from the decisions that it occasionally explains.

This position appears to abandon the very starting point of the discussion. For I claimed above that autonomy or self-direction for human persons presupposes a self that is essentially a conscious decision-maker. I rejected the idea that mere explanation of action in terms of features of the self suffices as an account of autonomy; this idea would assimilate our autonomy to that of a self-adjusting mechanism. In an effort to reaffirm the original position, to insist on the fundamentally active nature of the self, some philosophers posit a special sort of self-constituting decision that disregards or bypasses the psychic system. In this paper, I wish to evaluate this point of view, which I shall call *Self-Constituting Decision Theory* or *SCDT*.

III. Decision-Making and Self-Control

Before we turn directly to SCDT, we may still wonder why decision-making is so important to self-control. What does decision-making provide that makes us identify our *selves* with it? First of all, if the element of consciousness is crucial, then we should consider whether it is possible for decisions to take place without our realizing it. We do indeed say things like, "I see by the coordinated series of actions that you have taken that you have decided to bring me to ruin." May not the individual to whom this is addressed honestly claim that he is unaware that this is so? Yet may it not also be the case that the person has indeed been motivated by a desire to ruin the speaker? Of course, we do allow motivation by unconscious desire, but we have a problem with unconscious decision. Here, though, the allegation is that there has been a coordinated series of actions that reveals not only intelligence and purposiveness, but also something like a commitment to an outcome. Yet without conscious concurrence from the one who acts, we are loath to regard the agent as fully engaged or responsible.

Consciousness may be deemed important in connection with the ancient tradition in philosophy of identifying agency with rational agency. Thus, direction by an agent can only be understood in terms of guidance by reason. Raz says, "Our life is our own when it is under our control and that means when our various emotions, hopes, desires, intentions, and action are guided by reason."[6] The argument for the essential role of consciousness in agency would then rest on the thought that desires that operate unconsciously do so, not as reasons, but rather, as Donald Davidson says, as mental causes.[7]

Many philosophers have challenged the identification of autonomy with rational action on the grounds that true autonomy would permit the very rejection of rationality itself.[8] But even if this challenge is mistaken or incoherent, a direct rebuttal of the argument for the essential role of consciousness in agency is possible. The assumption that unconscious desires can operate only as causes, never as reasons, may be challenged. In many deliberations, there are considerations that ought to bear on a decision, which an ideally rational agent would take into account. Nomy Arpaly has argued that sometimes such considerations do play a role in

---

[6] Joseph Raz, *Engaging Reason: On the Theory of Value and Action* (Oxford: Oxford University Press, 1999), 1.

[7] See Donald Davidson, "Two Paradoxes of Irrationality," in Richard A. Wollheim and James Hopkins, eds., *Philosophical Essays on Freud* (Cambridge: Cambridge University Press, 1982), 289–305.

[8] See, for example, Robert Nozick, *Philosophical Explanations* (Cambridge, MA: Harvard University Press, 1981), 354; and Lawrence Crocker, *Positive Liberty: An Essay in Normative Political Philosophy* (The Hague: Martinus Nijhoff, 1980), 36–43.

decision-making even if they do not enter into reflection.[9] Oftimes, circumstances prevent an agent from knowing at the time or even later what all of her reasons for action are. Sometimes these circumstances are benign. For example, we have to decide quickly and so we rely on our "instincts," that is, we do the sort of thing that we have done before without thinking.[10] In the past we formed a conscious intention on the basis of a consideration. We now confront a very similar situation and are unaware at this time that we are again invoking the same sort of reason to guide us. It just never enters our reflections, although later we may recognize the force of this reason. Sometimes, however, we actively resist the emergence in consciousness of earlier-established reasons, and they function undetected with a directness and a power that isolate them from the normal effects of a rational monologue or dialogue. Then, our reasons are not behaving as reasons, and we relegate them to the status of causes. Failing to respond as rational agents would respond to novel factors bearing on the reasonableness of acting on such reasons, we find that we are responding instead to a brute causal mechanism.

Since we can act from reasons in a rational manner even when they do not enter the conscious arena, why is self-determination for a rational self a matter of *conscious* decision-making? Rational decision-making on the unconscious level may at times occur, but it cannot become the norm. Many important decisions demand a delicate weighting of many factors and a large amount of information from disparate sources. We may have to take into account multiple moral demands and commitments, as well as a variety of nonmoral preferences with varying strengths and degrees of personal significance. Consciousness is then essential for the occasional complex deliberations that lead to the hard and important decisions that we face, especially those that take place when our lives are not going well on "autopilot." If serious reconsideration is called for, we cannot control our lives satisfactorily without conscious deliberation.

IV. IDENTIFICATION AS SELF-CONSTITUTING: SCDT

Since autonomous agents must take an active role in the direction of their lives, much attention has been paid in recent decades to the precise character that this direction should take. Since our own desires can enslave us just as much as an outside force can, the decisions that we regard as crucial are often ones regarding the desirability or acceptability of leading a life dominated by the desires that, in fact, happen to be guiding our actions.

---

[9] Nomy Arpaly, "On Acting Rationally against One's Best Judgment," *Ethics* 110, no. 3 (2000): 488–513.
[10] Ibid., 506–7.

It is by now generally recognized that the simple fact that one might want to be moved by a certain desire is insufficient to ensure autonomy. As early discussions of Frankfurt's writings revealed, any worries about the insufficiency of an account of autonomy as the ability to do what one wants to do would extend to an account of autonomy as the ability to act upon those wants that one wants to act upon. Subsequent discussions, by Frankfurt and others, have introduced a variety of other sorts of considerations that are deemed relevant to the issue. Frankfurt himself has introduced the concepts of endorsement and identification as key, and he has striven to interpret these notions in such a way as to preserve the core meaning of autonomy as *self*-rule. Thus, the agent's reflective endorsement of, or identification with, certain of his (effective) desires and passions as the ones that he cares most about is constitutive of the very essence of the agent and thereby establishes his autonomy.[11] (To be sure, in facing certain conflicts, we can identify with desires in a weaker sense. When we need to establish priorities, we may accord certain desires a low level of priority without expelling them from the self.)

If identification, as autonomy-conferring, cannot be a merely passive state such as a (second-order) desire, then we had better not interpret it as a belief—equally passive—that a desire, process, or goal is valuable in one way or another. But the goal of reflection is often the formulation of such a belief. In moments of reflection Malcolm might want to know whether fatherhood is a good thing or, perhaps, whether it is a good thing for him at this stage in his life.

Gary Watson, in a well-known critique of Frankfurt's earlier works, has advanced the view that autonomy is indeed constituted by the coherence of one's motivational system with one's evaluational system, thereby claiming that the autonomy-conferring state might well be just a belief.[12] I am autonomous (or free) if my actions are guided by desires that I happen to believe are ones that it is good (worthy, desirable) to act upon.

But Frankfurt's earlier works insisted upon a more active, higher-order role for an agent. One must *do* something before a desire becomes one's own in the relevant sense. An endorsement is not just a belief; it is an act of appropriation, typically rendered on those desires that one thereby certifies as important, as expressive of what one cares about.

Whatever it is that one is doing to those desires that get endorsed, it is clear that this doctrine of Frankfurt's is very different from Watson's. For one thing, I can believe that some state of affairs is valuable without actively valuing it, that is, without being disposed to take steps to care for or nurture it. Watson came to acknowledge this later, observing that we may not identify with our own evaluations, and I have developed this

---

[11] Frankfurt, "On the Necessity of Ideals," 110–14.
[12] Gary Watson, "Free Agency," *Journal of Philosophy* 72, no. 8 (1975): 205–20.

theme elsewhere.[13] We can love the life that we are leading even if we must acknowledge that it lacks any "real" merit and that we would not recommend it to others. So there can be a breach between a person's evaluation on the one hand and his caring or identification on the other.

Watson regarded people like this as perverse. But I believe that this phenomenon is more common than that characterization would suggest. We agree that it is all too common for one's evaluations to clash with powerful desires. But when this happens, some thinkers hesitate to allow that a person might actually value or care about the object of these powerful desires. Some powerful desires are, to be sure, totally repudiated by a person victimized by them. But the view that one cannot value the object of those desires that one decides are unworthy of endorsement rests upon an unreasonable standard for the conversion of a desire into a (personal) value, and I shall argue this point below. I know that a gambling life has little to recommend it, but I cannot help loving it, and I would choose it all over again.

Independently of this complexity, heteronomy is not constituted just by the discord between one's motivational and evaluational systems. Suppose that I acknowledge that I ought to care for my ailing mother, but I really do not much care for her or for the project of caring for her. Harmony can be restored by providing extrinsic incentives for taking care of my mother, by having discovered, say, that she is thinking of rewriting her will. Here, I now want to care for my mother and believe that a good son is obliged to do so, but it is not this belief that is moving me to act in the right way. If evaluations are important to autonomy, then they must cohere with a mode of motivation that is determined by these evaluations. It will not do just to be moved to act in accordance with the demand that is expressed in the evaluation. I can even care for my mother and believe that I should care for my mother because children ought to assume these responsibilities, yet not be motivated in the right way. I might, for example, harbor powerful incestuous desires that are doing the causal work. The grounds on which one normally judges that one should take care of one's mother do not include the desire to nurture a romantic relationship with her. If evaluations are important to autonomy, then they should mesh with or even determine the reasons that one is motivated.

Suppose, then, that I am moved to assume the burden of caring for my mother for the right reasons (children have an obligation to their parents) without really caring for her. Consequently, I regard my responsibility as a burden, as a chore that I must perform. It would be a mistake to conclude that the assumption of responsibility is not one of my values, for I am committed to acting on it because I believe that I should be so committed. But if my allegiance to morality is accompanied by a sense of

[13] Gary Watson, "Free Action and Free Will," *Mind* 96, no. 382 (1987): 145–72. See Berofsky, *Liberation from Self*, chap. 5.

alienation rather than a sense of fulfillment, then I may fail to identify with this powerful moral streak in my personality. Although I regard myself as a good person, I view my conscience as a fetter.[14] In this case, insofar as my moral belief induces moral motivation leading to morally praiseworthy behavior, we have even more than just harmony between evaluational and motivational systems. My motivations have been brought into line because of my evaluations. Although it strikes me that in this case I am neither free nor autonomous, I emerge as autonomous on a harmony-style account.

Advocates of a harmony-style account cannot evade this result by appealing to the presence of desires that conflict with the effective ones, for conflict is ubiquitous in those who are judged to be free or autonomous. (After an unwilling smoker finally conquers his addiction, he may harbor urges to smoke that he unambivalently keeps under control.) Thus, we see the merit of an alternative account of autonomy such as Frankfurt's. The smoker identifies with his desire to quit, but I do not identify with my relationship with my mother nor the moral principle that moves me to act. The smoker cares about or values quitting, but I do not care about or value (in the right way) my mother or morality. We need to go beyond evaluations.

If identification or endorsement is not a cognitive state, then what is it? As I stated above, Frankfurt thinks of it as appropriation, as an instance of metaphysical hubris. "The person, in making a decision by which he identifies with a desire, *constitutes himself*."[15] This is mine; that is not; I have spoken. At other times, the language of authority rather than appropriation is used. Through this act, I am authorizing, that is, establishing authorhood or ownership. But what exactly does this mean?

Frankfurt emphasizes the volitional or conative dimension of this act to distinguish it both from the cognitive dimension that we have been discussing, as well as from the affective dimension. Endorsement is not the having of any special sort of feeling, even though it may typically be accompanied by certain feelings. Caring, for Frankfurt, is also a conative state. "That a person cares about or that he loves something has less to do with how things make him feel, or with his opinions about them, than with the more or less stable motivational structures that shape his preferences and that guide and limit his conduct."[16] A variant of this idea is Michael Bratman's version, according to which identification with a desire or the act that establishes "ownership" of the desire is a policy in

<hr/>

[14] One of the problems with Susan Wolf's theory of freedom (*Freedom within Reason* [New York: Oxford University Press, 1990]) is that I count as a free agent on her view because I am acting for the right reasons. See Berofsky, *Liberation from Self*, 72–75.

[15] Harry G. Frankfurt, "The Importance of What We Care About," in Frankfurt, *The Importance of What We Care About: Philosophical Essays* (Cambridge: Cambridge University Press, 1988), 170.

[16] Frankfurt, "Autonomy, Necessity, and Love," in Frankfurt, *Necessity, Volition, and Love*, 129.

favor of treating that desire as reason-providing in motivationally effective practical reasoning.[17] It is a forward-looking commitment to treat certain facts about oneself as justifying reasons for action.

If, as I have argued, identification is not simply wanting, and not simply approving, and not simply believing, and not simply feeling a certain way, yet it is a mental act directed to the will, then it would indeed have to be a decision, or a commitment, or the adoption of a plan or policy. Although, until now, we have associated such acts with caring or love, the fact of caring must be distinguished from the act of identification itself. Just as there can be a breach between evaluation and either caring or identification, so can there be cases of identification without caring *so long as identification is defined in terms of mental action alone.* The case of the reluctant son indicates that one can be committed to act in certain ways and to regard one's (weak) desires to do certain acts, such as helping one's mom, as good reasons to do so, without caring for the object of one's attention. The problem goes deep. One may not in general care about being moral in spite of a commitment to a moral path, as the above example demonstrated. And the commitment itself may involve constraints on future choices and decisions without implicating the phenomenon of caring: for example, one is convinced through moral reflection that desires to be good ought to be cultivated.

Although a conceptual distinction can be made, it may be argued that identification without caring is psychologically impossible. As human beings, we do not form commitments, adopt policies, or make identifications unless we care about the goal that is necessarily driving us. Frankfurt characterizes love (a species of caring) as conceptually linked to the desires that explain the mental actions. "What a person loves helps to determine the choices that he makes and the actions that he is eager or unwilling to perform." [18]

The claim of psychological impossibility can be challenged. There are people who become resigned to a way of life that they believe they are trapped in, and they are weary of continued struggle. Although they care for little, they do not want to rock the boat, and so they commit themselves to staying the course. Yes, a person of this sort cares a little about stability, or loyalty, or getting through the day without disaster, but he is basically acting out of world-weariness. It is a mistake to suppose that a person to whom life has been sufficiently cruel so as to render him incapable of love or passion is thereby unable to order his will.[19] Even if his

---

[17] Michael E. Bratman, "Identification, Decision, and Treating as a Reason," in Bratman, *Faces of Intention: Selected Essays on Intention and Agency* (Cambridge: Cambridge University Press, 1999), 197–98.

[18] Frankfurt, "Autonomy, Necessity, and Love," 129. Does the reference to eagerness import affect into the account of love?

[19] If identification can be severed from care, it can a fortiori be severed from love. Love is a stronger emotion because one can care about something that one does not love. See Eleonore Stump, "Persons: Identification and Freedom," *Philosophical Topics* 24, no. 2 (1996): 183–214.

will is moved by a desire for stability, it is not at all moved *because* he cares about the object, the future of which he is committed to take into account in his deliberations. If identification can be severed from care and can be severed from judgment and affect, as it was above, then can identification alone ground autonomous agency?

In Bratman's version of this idea, an agent must be satisfied with his decision in the sense that it does not conflict with competing decisions and does not, therefore, create a divided will.[20] Bratman concludes that, should an addict be resigned to his condition, he may be free of a divided will, in which case he *has* identified with his addiction.

Bratman objects to Frankfurt's more recent interpretations of identification just because Frankfurt has abandoned the position that decisions are important. Frankfurt replaces the act of decision with the (passive) state of wholeheartedness, characterized negatively in terms of the absence of any discontent or inclination to change.[21] Bratman and Frankfurt both demand satisfaction, but Bratman insists on the interpretation of identification as a bona fide act.

In spite of the centrality of the concept of identification in recent philosophical accounts of autonomy, the term is pretty much a philosopher's term, and I, therefore, have no pretheoretic intuitions to guide me in resolving these disputes among proponents of SCDT. My subject is autonomy, however, and my pretheoretic intuitions regarding it incline me strongly to believe that Sister Rossetta lacks autonomy even if she "identifies" in either Bratman's or Frankfurt's sense of this term. I turn now to a defense of this position.

V. The Limits of Identification

Identification can be reflective, impulsive, or somewhere in between. No one would suppose that reflection undermines autonomy.[22] Indeed, Frankfurt insists that reflection prevents wantonhood[23] and that wholehearted identification arises only as a consequence of an appraisal of one's psychic condition.[24] So, let us suppose that identification (here, with O) is reflective. Even so, an agent can lack information of different sorts that would have led her not to identify with O had she possessed it. An agent may be misinformed about (1) whether O is really satisfying in the long run, (2) the motives leading her to identify with O, and (3) what it is she is really identifying with.

---

[20] Bratman, "Identification, Decision, and Treating as a Reason," 200–201.
[21] Harry G. Frankfurt, "The Faintest Passion," in Frankfurt, *Necessity, Volition, and Love,* 102–5.
[22] Although one can be too reflective at times, obviously reflection is often important and not in general antithetical to autonomy.
[23] Wantonhood is the state of not caring about which desire moves us to action.
[24] Frankfurt, "The Faintest Passion," 105.

The third possibility is controversial. But even Frankfurt concedes that people may be mistaken "about what is moving them in their choices and in their actions."[25] They may also be "mistaken *concerning what they love*."[26] And he makes similar remarks about care. If we cannot help identifying with what we love, then we must sometimes identify with something that we are not aware we are identifying with. A woman can rightly say, as the song says, that her lover is really in love, not with her, but with love (or loving).[27] A scholar can believe herself to be devoted to the pursuit of truth, unaware that she is devoted really to the pursuit of acclaim by her peers.

These cases highlight unclarities in the concept of the object of identification. In each such case, we can try to avoid having to think of the agent as ignorant of the object by relocating the ignorance at the level of reasons. Harry knowingly loves Sally, but does not realize that the reason is that Sally is merely an instance of a love relationship with Harry. Wilma loves her sociological research, but does not realize that the reason is that the research is a means to acclaim. In effect, the relocation strategy would expand the second type of ignorance (ignorance of motive) to protect against the third (ignorance of object). But the strategy fails because what a person loves determines the policies and commitments that one undertakes, including policies concerning the structure of one's motivations. Yet in each of these cases, different commitments are associated with what we have called different reasons. When the excitement of loving dissipates, Harry will seek love elsewhere, thereby revealing that Sally was not really the object of his love at all. And when Wilma fails to receive praise from her colleagues, she will abandon her scholarship, thereby revealing—at least to others, if not herself—that the scholarship itself is not what interested her in the first place. What we have called the reasons must enter into the characterization of the object of identification if we want to preserve the idea that the object determines one's policies vis-à-vis the direction of one's motivations and the specific future choices that one makes.

These results imply that the conscious product of reflection whose goal is the formation of a fundamental commitment is not a case of self-formation ex nihilo. The process is, at least in part, one of discovery, and it can go awry in ordinary creatures in several ways.

Suppose that we now simply append relevant knowledge in all its forms to wholehearted commitment or the like in order to define autonomous agency.[28] This step is not just a simple emendation of SCDT. For

[25] Frankfurt, "Autonomy, Necessity, and Love," 130.
[26] Ibid.
[27] Richard Rodgers (music) and Lorenz Hart (lyrics), "Falling in Love with Love," from the 1938 Rodgers and Hart musical, *The Boys from Syracuse*.
[28] Perhaps this is Frankfurt's intention when he talks of understanding and appreciating one's condition as requirements of wholeheartedness. See Frankfurt, "The Faintest Passion," 105.

we are significantly closer now to the more conventional approach to autonomy suggested in my discussion of the Malcolm example. We insisted there that mental action is indeed crucial to autonomy; Malcolm must decide to continue the path that he is on. But this decision is autonomous only if it meets various constraints such as knowledge, independence, mental health, and so forth.

Before we conclude that, by themselves, acts of identification just cannot live up to the demands that are placed upon them—that SCDT fails—we will ponder the possibility of a last-ditch effort to pull the mental act of identification up by its own bootstraps so that it can do all of the work of self-formation on its own.

Here is the argument. Knowledge be damned; if Selma identifies wholeheartedly with acclaim, structures her motivations accordingly, and, unlike Wilma, is not hampered in the pursuit of her goals, then she is an autonomous agent.

After all, why should knowledge matter in this context? If Fred spends his whole life driven by a desire to reach the top of the corporate ladder, manages to climb many rungs, and faces no serious obstacles on his ascent, but dies before realizing that success would have felt empty and would have led to a reappraisal, the outcome of which would have been Fred's repudiation of his core value, why should we deny that Fred led an autonomous life? Fred wholeheartedly identified with success in terms of climbing the corporate ladder and, as a consequence, led a life in accordance with this value. We all perform value experiments. The failure of this experiment is a testimony to the shallowness of Fred's choice, but not necessarily to his heteronomy.

Although we can disagree about the delineation of conditions that we wish to impose on identification, we cannot be sanguine about the wholesale abandonment of reasonable conditions of autonomous decision-making, including knowledge. Let us expand the picture of Selma, the woman who identifies wholeheartedly with acclaim, structures her motivations accordingly, and proceeds unimpeded to fulfill her goals. Like Wilma, Selma is unaware that she would repudiate acclaim were she to achieve it, for she would find it totally unfulfilling. She is even unaware that she has identified with and seeks acclaim. (This possibility has been conceded by the friends of identification.) She believes that she loves scholarship for its own sake. She lacks self-knowledge, for she would be deeply ashamed of herself were she to discover the truth, and her unconscious fear of feeling this way leads her to bury the knowledge of her motivations. Acclaim is very important to her because she is deeply jealous of her sister, upon whom Selma believes all parental love was heaped. (Actually, Selma's parents loved her equally, but, needing to wallow in self-pity, she does not want to recognize this fact.) This jealousy reveals itself in many ways—in feelings, verbal and nonverbal behavior, and dreams—but Selma continues to misinterpret these manifestations in order to preserve a self-image that she is more comfortable with. If Selma were to discover these facts about herself, she would change her life dramatically. Not only would she abandon the pursuit of her scholarly reputation, but also she would abandon the mistaken object of identification, scholarship. After all, she never really cared about it. And she would change careers altogether. But she never makes these discoveries.

Acts of identification, commitments, and policies do not arise in a vacuum. My intuitive response to Selma—that she completely lacks autonomy—reveals to me that the contours of the self cannot be confined to the immediate environment of acts of identification.[29]

If my conclusion requires more support, then we may compound the story along lines that have become familiar in the critical literature. Not only may the agent lack transparency in the above ways, but also failure to know "the what" and/or "the why" of identification may be explicable in terms of extrinsic origins that are obviously autonomy-nullifying. We may, for example, trot out the philosopher's "demon neurologist," that all-powerful, evil physician who manipulates a subject's brain without regard for the subject's mental life, causing her to have the mental states (for example, acts of identification) that the demon neurologist desires her to have. A similar scenario is that of Do, the cult leader who manipulates Sister Rossetta, causing her to identify with his goals. It would be ludicrous to suppose that this act of identification is an instance of self-creation, hence autonomy. Sister Rossetta identifies with the goals of Do as the result of an act in which she is basically enslaved by him.

It is difficult to imagine a more obvious truism than that we act for reasons and on the basis of beliefs, but the thought that we must link the self to conscious decision-making in order to form a conception of our own autonomy must be modified by this recognition, or we will be defining autonomy not for us, but for God. We must observe again that many of the desires and beliefs that we possess, feel thoroughly comfortable with, and act from, evolved from our childhood, a time during which we lacked control over our destiny. No plausible account of autonomy can relegate *all* of these desires and beliefs to limbo until an agent performs an act of identification, commitment, or endorsement. The project of distinguishing desires that are genuinely mine from the rest requires us to define the right sort of independence from external sources. Desires can arise through interpersonal relationships in an autonomy-preserving way (for example, benign advice) and in an autonomy-nullifying way (for example, brainwashing). There is a variety of intermediate forms— manipulation, temptation, and coercion, for example—each of which comes in degrees, and this variety makes it impossible to draw a sharp boundary

---

[29] I do not wish to deny the originative role of decision-making. We need not be pushed and pulled by our motives. Also, the fact that identification does not take place in a vacuum does not mean that the act itself cannot generate desires that have great motivating power and steer us along important lines.

between desires that arise from within and those that are imposed from without.

Also, it has become increasingly clear that much of our behavior, our motives, and our capacities is under the control of our self-conceptions. Much of our conceptualization and interpretation of the environment and our own actions takes place in accord with our need to maintain a self-conception or self-image, or with our need to enhance this self-image, or at least with a need to render our behavior intelligible and coherent, given this self-conception. Cognitive dissonance research and self-perception studies reveal that we distort the subjects of interpretation in order to fulfill these goals, whether or not the self-image or self-conception that we import to interpretation is accurate. In other words, we frequently distort our picture of ourselves and the world in order to maintain a distorted self-image!

In the face of all of these possibilities, proponents of SCDT are burying their heads in the sand when they propose an account of autonomy that would be limited to a pristine act of identification. It makes sense to distinguish desires that belong to the self from those that do not, *antecedent to* acts of identification, in which case we must incorporate into an account of autonomous identification or decision-making a requirement of motivational autonomy, namely, the demand that the motives that are driving me already be genuinely mine.

VI. ALIENATION

If identification lacks the metaphysical clout that some have ascribed to it, so does alienation. One cannot, in other words, expel a desire from the self just through a pristine act of repudiation, no matter how emphatic. Indeed, as we saw above, if repudiation is constituted by a value judgment, then we cannot even be sure that a sincere repudiation will entail that an object of a desire is of no value to us any longer.

Suppose, for example, that Harry A's whole life has been driven by an overwhelming desire to exterminate Armenians. Having met a nice Armenian, Harry A begins to reflect on his values and eventually repudiates his Armenian project, although he continues to find himself driven by it. He suffers, therefore, from the familiar conflict between motivation and evaluation. But conflicts of this kind are quite complex, as we have seen. For example, Harry A may not harbor just a negative moral evaluation of his conduct. He may also feel utterly alienated from what he now thinks of as a dangerous compulsion. (In calling the impulse a "compulsion," I do not mean to imply that the agent cannot refrain from acting on it, although, obviously, it is at least very difficult for him not to succumb to it. In this way, we preserve the possibility of choices to refrain and do not, therefore, automatically rule out the possibility of autonomy in this sphere.)

Although Harry A continues his nefarious activities in spite of sincere efforts at reform, he no longer identifies himself with them, and he no longer sees them as flowing from him. Moreover, suppose that this facet of Harry A's life does not permeate other facets all that much. He does not dwell on it, and his feelings, behavior, and motivational system operate independently of the compulsion to kill Armenians. Every so often these murderous impulses come upon him, and it is difficult for him to refrain from acting upon them. Once the episodes end, he picks up his life as if the compulsion had never existed. Even though the action emanating from the impulse is intentional, the intention is not a component of a pattern of intentional behavior. The action is not part of a project whose history is one component of the agent's sense of his continuing identity as a person. Rather, the impulse and resultant intention rupture his sense of an ongoing life that is, to some extent, under his control. If we wish to characterize this example as a case of expulsion from the self of particular desires, the ground for so doing is not just repudiation, but, rather, the fact that the impulses are cut off from the rest of Harry A's life and are perceived by him as lacking in personal value. These impulses no longer make sense in relation to his other interests and values, and he may be undertaking steps to eliminate these urges. I would concede that Harry A is heteronomous (in this sphere of his life) in a pretty straightforward way.

Other scenarios that incorporate projects that we continue in spite of repudiation are more difficult to characterize. For example, in the case of Harry B, the anti-Armenian compulsion plays a significant role in other aspects of his life. He dwells on it, he has nightmares, he spends much of his time in therapy, and his behavior toward others is adversely affected. Here, Harry B is not just repudiating the behavior; he would prefer to be rid of the ancillary business as well. He thinks of himself as victimized by his compulsion. If he were to be rid of it, there would be no adverse consequences to his psyche. The greater significance of the compulsion is only causal in character and is important to Harry B only in the way that a deadly disease is.

Harry C is in the same situation as Harry B, except that the compulsion does play a key role in Harry C's psychic organization. The behavior serves a basic protective role for Harry C, such that success at its abolition would release fears and unresolved conflicts that would be personally devastating. Harry C is not aware of any of this, but he would choose not to change if he became aware—the pain would be too great. Although he repudiates the compulsion because it lacks any intrinsic personal value, his conscious desire to be rid of it is based on ignorance. The compulsion serves an indispensable personal function for Harry C.

Harry D is like Harry C except that Harry D experiences enormous personal satisfaction when he acts on his impulses and he does not, therefore, wish to be different. He dwells on his behavior, but only because he likes to savor the experience. The very danger of the enterprise is invigorating. The image of himself as an exterminator is deeply embedded in his psyche, and he perceives his own motivations and the world in terms of this image. He finds it depressing that his conscience has issued a negative report. He realizes that there is little to be said in favor of his project beyond the personal fulfillment that he derives from it. He knows that he should stop and is, therefore, taking preliminary steps to do so. But, as in the example above of my failure to identify with my obligation to care for my mother, Harry D does not identify with his evaluations. Although Harry D is unaware of the importance of his compulsion to his very sanity, he "fortunately" is not sufficiently interested in ending his project, anyway. Harry D seems to me to be a clear case in which repudiation does not add up to expulsion.

VII. THE ROLE OF REFLECTION

The inclination to permit a move from repudiation to expulsion is the consequence of conferring undue metaphysical weight on reflection. I argued above for the necessity of conscious deliberation to autonomy. But deliberation as a prelude to decision-making can take place without a self-conscious appraisal of the forces at play in the deliberative process. As we are using the term here, *reflection* refers to the deeper, second-order process in which an agent steps back to undertake such an appraisal. One must concede the significance to autonomy of reflective identification *as a type*. Mature beings think before they act and must occasionally think deeply so as to raise the possibility of adjusting their wills as well as their behavior, depending on the results of their reflective activity. In characterizing individual selves, however, we must guard against the tendency to give excessive due to the specific products of reflection. These outcomes cannot take metaphysical priority over the sum of psychological facts that establish both the centrality of the genocidal impulse to Harry D's psychological economy and the personal, positive significance that it possesses. Yes, I experience occasional, weird promptings that play no significant role in my life, that I am taking steps to eliminate, and that I utterly repudiate. That these sorts of isolated impulses may be treated as "external" to myself does not entitle me to eject fundamental desires that are deeply satisfying, that play a central role in the explanation of my verbal and nonverbal behavior and experience, and the dislodging of which would be deeply disruptive.

If Harry A is heteronomous because he is moved by "external" forces, is Harry D autonomous because he is moved by "internal" forces? Although I pointed out above that conflict is a fact of life even for autonomous agents, Harry D's conflict and ambivalence may be quite deep. He at times exercises choice on behalf of his highly satisfying genocidal project and at other times, under the sway of his moral reflections, he seriously ponders steps that he might take to suppress and to eliminate his geno-cidal urges.[30]

In order to produce a plausible answer to the above and similar hard questions, we must revisit the conceptual starting point of this discussion. In seeking an account of autonomy, we look to the phenomenon of con-scious decision-making as crucial. We then confront the need to expand the sphere of relevance in order to incorporate the causal neighborhood in which we find the bases for decision-making. And now we are forced to acknowledge that this neighborhood also houses some pretty seedy char-acters: (1) beliefs, the falsity of which is self-induced through the need to protect the self and one's self-conception; and (2) stated reasons for action that disguise genuine ones. That these genuine reasons fail to make their way to consciousness is also explained in terms of needs that often remain unconscious, such as the need to produce consistency in, or to maintain or enhance, one's self-image. These elements are not external to us in the way in which Do's interests are external to those of Sister Rossetta. And, at least for Harry D, they are not external in the sense in which completely repudiated impulses and addictions may be so counted.

At a weekly meeting of Exterminators Anonymous, Harry D speaks truly when he says, "My name is Harry and I am an exterminator." This is true, not in a trivial sense, but rather, in the sense that his behavior, feelings, fantasies, speech, and deepest concerns are driven by the desire to eliminate Armenians. We should not forget that in spite of the negative judgment that he casts upon his feelings, he actually does find himself hating Armenians and relishing his actions against them. Nor should we forget that the abandonment of this project would produce in Harry D profound personal upheaval and great distress. Moreover, his feelings of shame make no sense if he is not really an exterminator. Although Harry repudiates himself, how can one deny that his project expresses one of his core values?

VIII. REFLECTION, IDENTIFICATION, AND AUTONOMY

In examining the role of reflection for the characters whom we have called Harry, we reach the paradoxical result that self-*direction* is compat-ible with heteronomy! To see this, let us introduce Harry E, who is similar to Harry D, except that Harry E is equipped with many qualities that are important to autonomy. Unlike Harry D, Harry E is not guilty of self-delusion. He knows exactly why he does what he does and why it is important to him; he has all relevant knowledge, including knowledge of the psychologically harmful results of extinguishing his deadly desires.

---

[30] Harry D is not a clear case of the sort of ambivalence that Frankfurt describes (see Frankfurt, "The Faintest Passion"), because Harry D does, in the end, side with his geno-cidal impulses in spite of serious reservations.

Although none of us creates our desires from scratch, we hope that some sort of line can be drawn between those that arise "naturally" and those that are the consequence of manipulation, coercion, mental illness, etc. Suppose, then, that Harry E's desire to kill Armenians does not arise in one of these "external" ways. The individual decisions that he has made along the way have been made autonomously: they have been informed, dispassionate, and driven by desires that were not the consequence of manipulation, coercion, etc. Perhaps Harry E had misgivings early on. But when he reaches the stage of mature reflection, he concludes that, taking all considerations into account, moral and nonmoral, he would prefer not to be making the decisions and commitments that he has been making on behalf of the project of extermination. In other words, he would choose to be a different sort of person if he could. His ambivalence is not so deep that he cannot ultimately side with his moral nature.

"Self-regulation" cannot be a synonym of "autonomy," etymology notwithstanding, if it requires that the system that is doing the regulation incorporate the deepest or most important components of the self. For Harry E's actions *are* under the control of forces that represent what is most important to him; he *is* choosing his life. Moreover, given that he is independent, informed, uncoerced, free of mental illness, etc., Harry E fulfills the requirements of autonomy as well as anyone else does. There is no serious case to be made that his life is directed from without. But his reflective condemnation of himself establishes his heteronomy *even if the reflection itself meets the requirements of autonomy*!

What has emerged is that considerations bearing on the autonomous character of a decision arise at two points. We first look at the etiology of decision. If deliberations do not bear on decision, if, for example, one is a slave, then approval or reflective endorsement by the slave of her state does not undo her debilitating condition. Reflection is a sham if one lacks the power to make one's own decisions. Second, we look at reflection, which introduces another set of autonomy requirements. For we must suppose that Harry E's reflective repudiation of his project is itself autonomous, that is, independent, uncoerced, etc. Although conflict is a fact of life even for autonomous individuals, such agents cannot abide a deep schism between their reflective and their active natures.

IX. CONCLUSION

We have tried, on the one hand, to avoid an irrational reverence toward the rational and, on the other, to pay the right sort of homage to our reflective natures. Even though reflection can be faulty in many ways, its ideal dictates must govern the will of an autonomous agent. A sincere, informed, stable, mentally healthy, independent, and rational evaluation must guide an autonomous agent such that its dictates fundamentally mesh with his *nonreflective nature*.[31] If one's intellect has not achieved a sufficient foothold in the self, what one professes to be important upon ideal reflection may not yet in fact be so. But one cannot be counted autonomous unless one is actually guided by values and principles endorsed by autonomous reflection. The demands of autonomy will go unrealized if professed ideals do not find sufficient mooring in the self. So Harry E's autonomous rejection of himself renders him heteronomous in spite of the fact that he is expressing himself and is regulating his actions by his choices.

The fact that Harry E sides with morality upon reflection is incidental. One can just as easily concoct a case of self-regulation without autonomy in which a moral agent repudiates her morality for the sake of self-interest, although she finds her morality to be a fetter that she is unable to cast off. Imagine a woman who has been given a moral education that meets the most rigorous standards of wise persons in her community. She grows up to be a model of propriety until, as a young adult, she finds herself developing powerful immoral proclivities. Although she never veers from the path of morality, she eventually comes to view her moral nature as an impediment to being the sort of person whom she would ideally prefer to be. I cannot argue here that she may ultimately form an *autonomous* (and rational) judgment that, all things considered, she would choose to scuttle the moral life in favor of an immoral form of self-expression. But if this is possible, then we have a case like Harry E, a person who is self-directed, yet heteronomous.

I will not proceed to produce even in outline a statement of *necessary and* sufficient conditions of autonomy, that is, to consider examples in which reflective endorsement is short of ideal and/or the conflict between it and self-governance is not as deep. Rather, my goals have been (1) to return the phenomena of identification and endorsement to the context in which they belong, namely, elements of a self whose broader contours must be introduced into an account of autonomy, thereby refuting SCDT; and (2) to concede the importance of reflection as key to our understanding of autonomy, without assigning to it the metaphysical significance implicit in the (mistaken) view that its ideal form must coincide with self-determination.

Philosophy, Columbia University

---

[31] Meshing, rather than governing, may suffice. When we reach the age of reflection, a great deal is already in place and much of it is untouchable. As I said above in the text, no one would be autonomous if we demanded that ideal reflection actually be the source of one's values, desires, and fundamental choices.

SOME TENSIONS BETWEEN AUTONOMY
AND SELF-GOVERNANCE

By Jonathan Jacobs

I. Introduction

The notions of autonomy and self-governance each capture something crucial about the moral dimensions of agents and actions. These notions are central to the ways in which we conceptualize ourselves and others. The concept of autonomy is especially crucial to understanding the distinct status of moral agents. For its part, self-governance has a significant relation to the evaluation of agents as individuals with *particular* characters, leading *particular* sorts of lives, and performing *particular* actions. Neither notion—autonomy nor self-governance—fully assimilates or dominates the other. Moreover, there are some important strains between them. There are certain forms of regard that the autonomy of an agent *demands* that are at odds with what an agent's exercise of self-governance *merits*. In this essay I plan to show this, and offer a diagnosis of why this is the case.

The discussion will proceed as follows. In Sections II and III of this essay, I shall suggest general ways in which considerations concerning autonomy and self-governance are distinct and also very important to moral theorizing. In Sections IV and V, I shall look at ways in which these considerations bear upon responsibility for character and action. In Section VI, I shall consider how the foregoing discussion raises important questions concerning the justification of punishment. Then, in Section VII and the brief concluding section, I shall look at why there are certain ways in which considerations of moral psychology having to do with self-governance put pressure on normative considerations having to do with autonomy. I shall also examine why this results in some important moral perplexities. Punishment is not the only context in which these perplexities occur, but it is an especially effective one for identifying and diagnosing them.

I shall refer to Kant rather extensively, especially in regard to autonomy. This is because of the way in which elements of Kantian moral philosophy have become fixtures of a great deal of moral thinking. In the discussion of self-governance, I shall likewise make several references to Aristotle, because of the importance of his arguments and insights. This is not a textual study, and there are, of course, many different notions of both autonomy and self-governance, but tethering the discussion to Kant and to Aristotle will lend it a valuable manageability and focus.

221

II. Autonomy and Moral Status

Autonomy is widely held to be the basis for the distinct status of rational agents. This status is not conferred, cannot be withdrawn, and locates each person in the moral world because each is a rational agent. A key element of the Kantian version of this concept is that respect for persons as participants in a moral order is neither discretionary nor dependent upon attaining a contingent status. It does not depend upon the sentiments of others, the achievement of some end, or the realization of one or another perfection. It is owed to each agent simply as a rational agent.

In Kant's view, as articulated in his *Foundations of the Metaphysics of Morals*, autonomy determines the distinct status of rational agents because "[a]utonomy of the will is that property of it by which it is a law to itself independently of any property of objects of volition."[1] Rational nature is the capacity to be normatively self-legislating, the capacity for participation in moral life. Self-legislation is crucial to moral status because through it, persons are ends in themselves: "Now morality is the condition under which alone a rational being can be an end in itself, because only through it is it possible to be a legislative member in the realm of ends. Thus morality and humanity, so far as it is capable of morality, alone have dignity."[2] Kant continues, "Autonomy is thus the basis of the dignity of both human nature and every rational nature."[3] The most familiar and synoptic rendering of this view is that persons are ends in themselves, which is a notion that has considerable currency even apart from explicit commitment to specific Kantian theses.

Kant asks, "What else, then, can the freedom of the will be but autonomy, i.e., the property of the will to be a law to itself?"[4] And he concludes, "Therefore a free will and a will under moral laws are identical."[5] The same capacity that formulates the moral law also provides conclusive reasons to fulfill moral requirements, and enables us to do so. Morality is essentially grounded in our rational nature, and rationality is sufficient to ascertain what is morally necessary. Thus, it is also part of Kant's view, as Stephen Darwall writes, that "the very considerations that make an action morally obligatory must also be conclusive reasons for acting—reasons on the basis of which we can *act*."[6] In acting morally, we are autonomous because we are obligated by reasons of which we are the authors, and only in acting morally are we fully free, rational beings.

---

[1] Immanuel Kant, *Foundations of the Metaphysics of Morals*, ed. and trans. Lewis White Beck (Indianapolis, IN: Bobbs-Merrill, 1959), 59.

[2] Ibid., 53.

[3] Ibid., 54.

[4] Ibid., 65.

[5] Ibid.

[6] Stephen Darwall, *The British Moralists and the Internal 'Ought', 1640–1740* (New York: Cambridge University Press, 1995), 322–23.

A key feature of this conception of morality and autonomy as mutually entailing is that the demands of the moral law are not beyond our capacity—the moral *ought* implies *can*. With regard to the moral law, says Kant, "We ought to conform to it; consequently we must *be able* to do so."[7] In an earlier passage, he states, "For when the moral law commands that we *ought* now to be better men, it follows inevitably that we must *be able* to be better men."[8] Even one's own history of immorality does not fully alienate the agent from the moral law or defeat his capacity to act rightly:

> However evil a man has been up to the very moment of an impend-
> ing free act (so that evil has actually become custom or second na-
> ture) it was not only his duty to have been better [in the past], it is
> now still his duty to better himself.[9]

Insofar as we are rational, we cannot alienate ourselves from the appeal and the authority of the moral law:

> When we present examples of honesty of purpose, of steadfastness in
> following good maxims, and of sympathy and general benevolence
> even with great sacrifice of advantages and comfort, there is no man,
> not even the most malicious villain (provided he is otherwise accus-
> tomed to using his reason), who does not wish that he also might
> have these qualities.[10]

No agent who is still in possession of his reason is morally irretrievable. Reason is the source of morality, and where it is not expunged it can re-engage the agent to moral considerations.

Moreover, for Kant autonomy is the basis for a "systematic union of rational beings through common objective laws."[11] Kant holds that autonomy not only locates agents in a common moral world, but also *connects* them together in it. He argues:

> The concept of each rational being as a being that must regard itself
> as giving universal law through all the maxims of its will, so that it
> may judge itself and its actions from this standpoint, leads to a very
> fruitful concept, namely, that of a *realm of ends*.[12]

---

[7] Immanuel Kant, *Religion Within the Limits of Reason Alone*, trans. Theodore M. Greene and Hoyt H. Hudson (New York: Harper & Row, 1960), 55.

[8] Ibid., 46.

[9] Ibid., 36.

[10] Kant, *Foundations of the Metaphysics of Morals*, 73.

[11] Ibid., 52.

[12] Ibid., 51.

We can recognize each person as an end in itself, and as such, as
sovereign and subject in a rational moral order. This is Kant's basic
idea of an "ethical commonwealth."[13] He explains: "A union of men
under merely moral laws, patterned on the above idea ['the sovereignty of the good principle'] may be called an *ethical*, and as far as
these laws are public, an *ethico-civil* (in contrast to a *juridico-civil*) society or an ethical commonwealth."[14]

Commenting on Kant's view of the realm of ends, David Wiggins
remarks:

> This is the solidarity of all beings that partake in the noumenal, the
> solidarity of all rational beings. Even for creatures such as us, crea-
> tures who are not completely rational, the kingdom of ends, the
> systematic union of rational beings under common self-legislated
> rational laws, is an unforgettable rational ideal. This is the kingdom
> to which—in so far as we are rational—we cannot help but aspire to
> belong.[15]

We are participants in a common moral world because of reason, and we
are able to construct shareable moral ideals because of reason. We can be
cut off from each other by vice, inattention, selfishness, and in countless
other ways. But it is rational autonomy that enables us both to be self-
legislating and to share an ideal of moral community.

Overall, this conception of autonomy makes for a twofold moral democracy. Each individual has equal status as a participant in the moral
order, and each is equally capable of sustaining that status, because *ought*
implies *can*. We do not all act in ways that are morally worthy, but each
of us is a locus of equal moral worth and the dignity that is founded on
autonomy.

While many elements of Kant's conception of rational personality and
its nonempirical nature are not widely embraced, key elements of his
conception of morality as grounded in rational autonomy figure centrally
in a great deal of recent moral theorizing. For example, the claim that the
capacity for rational agency determines a distinct and equal status for
individuals as participants in the moral world is a fixture of much moral
theorizing. For example, John Rawls repeatedly refers to persons as "free
and equal" and says the following about his view:

> The essential idea is that such procedures [by which first principles
> are selected] must be suitably founded on practical reason, or, more

---

[13] Kant, *Religion Within the Limits of Reason Alone*, 86.
[14] Ibid.
[15] David Wiggins, "Categorical Requirements," in Rosalind Hursthouse, Gavin Lawrence,
and Warren Quinn, eds., *Virtues and Reasons: Philippa Foot and Moral Theory: Essays in Honour
of Philippa Foot* (Oxford: Clarendon Press, 1998), 326.

exactly, on notions which characterize persons as reasonable and rational and which are incorporated into the way in which, as such persons, they represent to themselves their free and equal moral personality.[16]

This is Kantian in the sense that the principles that are properly constructed by rational agents must reflect the ways in which they are free and equal. Likewise reflecting the influence of Kant on recent moral theory, Alan Donagan writes:

> Since they are negatively free, the actions of a rational being have a causality higher than those of a brute animal; and it is because of that higher kind of causality that rational beings are ends in themselves — ends which are not producible but which exist independently of the actions done for their sake. It is as ends in themselves that rational beings find in their own natures a ground for the law they lay down for themselves.[17]

Frances Kamm, another philosopher who emphasizes rational agency, uses the idiom of "the high inviolability of persons."[18] She says, "If people are morally inviolable in a certain way, then, I believe, they have a *higher*—and not merely a different status."[19] This status is grounded in their being rational agents.

Focusing on a different aspect of autonomy, Christine Korsgaard argues, "If complete normative skepticism is to be avoided—if there is such a thing as a reason for action—then humanity, as the source of all reasons and values, must be valued for its own sake."[20] Normativity and moral obligation have their source in "[the] capacity for self-conscious reflection about our own actions. . . ."[21] This is the same as the basis for having reasons to act *at all*.

> If we do not treat our humanity as a normative identity, none of our other identities can be normative, and then we can have no reasons to act at all. Moral identity is therefore inescapable. Second, and for that reason, moral identity exerts a kind of governing role over the

[16] John Rawls, "Kantian Constructivism in Moral Theory," in Stephen Darwall, Allan Gibbard, and Peter Railton, eds., *Moral Discourse & Practice: Some Philosophical Approaches* (New York: Oxford University Press, 1997), 256.

[17] Alan Donagan, *The Theory of Morality* (Chicago, IL: University of Chicago Press, 1977), 233.

[18] Frances Kamm, "Nonconsequentialism," in Hugh LaFollette, ed., *The Blackwell Guide to Ethical Theory* (Oxford: Blackwell, 2000), 217.

[19] Ibid.

[20] Christine M. Korsgaard, with G. A. Cohen et al., *The Sources of Normativity* (Cambridge: Cambridge University Press, 1996), 122.

[21] Ibid., 19.

other kinds. Practical conceptions of your identity which are fundamentally inconsistent with the value of humanity must be given
up.[22]

In Korsgaard's view, our capacity for reflection on action-guiding considerations gives us a kind of authority over our actions, grounded in
autonomy. This is the basis of the moral identity of rational agents, and
each rational agent has moral standing on account of it.

Part of the appeal of the Kantian notion of rational agency as determining the distinct and equal status of agents in a moral democracy is
that this notion frees moral standing from determination by tradition,
ancestry, membership in an estate, wealth, affiliation, or even birth order
(all of which have much to do with luck or chance). The Kantian framework not only assigns a crucial role to reason—after all, so did Plato's and
Aristotle's ethics, and Aquinas's, too, for that matter—but also takes reason to be autonomous in fashioning morality. Kant's view differs from
these in the way in which the operation of reason in determining principles is autonomous in a particularly strong sense. Any determination of
rational principles by considerations that are grounded in anything external to reason itself would, for Kant, constitute heteronomy. As Rawls
has put it:

> Heteronomy obtains not only when first principles are fixed by the
> special psychological constitution of human nature, as in Hume, but
> also when they are fixed by an order of universals or concepts grasped
> by rational intuition, as in Plato's realm of forms or in Leibniz's
> hierarchy of perfections.[23]

Reason has normative authority in its own right, and its principles are
accessible to any agent who has not lost his reason. The general contours
of this approach to moral theorizing have been widely endorsed and
variously developed, even when other elements of Kant's view have been
abandoned. Whatever specific aspect of autonomy they might emphasize
or take to be basic, it is plain that many philosophers hold the view that
autonomy determines a distinct moral status for rational agents.

III. Self-Governance and the Voluntariness of Character

There is another fundamental dimension of moral evaluation and significance. It concerns features of agents that are not status-determining
but concern what they are *like* and what they *do*. These features are objects
of appraisal *within* the world of valuation of actions and agents. These

[22] Ibid., 129–30.
[23] John Rawls, "Kantian Constructivism in Moral Theory," 256.

features reflect modes of self-governance, the activity through which a rational agent fashions a mode of substantive, practical engagement with the world. We are self-governing in that we *lead* lives—we fashion ends, we act upon values, we pursue interests and concerns that we conceptualize, and with regard to which we exercise deliberative rationality. This is not a metaphysical claim presupposing a metaphysical notion of free will. It is a point about the distinctive character of human lives and modes of self-conception, and how we conceptualize each other. Human beings give their lives valuative shape and content through specific modes of self-governance.

To a large extent, self-governance is a matter of how agents exercise their capacities for voluntary activity. A person does not become a voluntary agent at some particular point. The agent exercises voluntariness all along, although the character of it changes as the agent matures and grows in rational capacity and experience. Responsibility is calibrated accordingly. The behavior of a young child in reaching for something is voluntary, even though there may be no conscious, deliberative rationality involved, and the behavior of a sixteen-year-old in deciding what clique to join is typically voluntary, even if peer pressure and other influences are at work. The responsibility that we find appropriate to attribute to a thirty-year-old is more extensive because of the way in which his action expresses mature character. Voluntariness has a wide range of expression, and it can be exercised more or less consciously or deliberately. In general, however, it is on account of voluntariness that we find it appropriate to attribute responsibility to agents for their characteristics and their actions.

A great deal of early habituation is a training in self-governance, a matter of encouraging attachment to certain kinds of objects, and shaping modes of attention, perception, and receptivity. Habituation is not a matter of imposing dispositions on someone. In abusive or coercive forms it may be that, but more often it is a process of educating a person's capacities for voluntariness and self-governance. This is why it is appropriate to attribute responsibility to mature agents. Their characters reflect commitments, concerns, policies of action, and modes of valuing that, in turn, reflect who they are as voluntary agents. Self-governance is the form that voluntariness takes in a rational being. Or put another way, rational agents are capable of voluntariness that is also self-governance. Aristotle, for example, notes: "For children and the other animals share in what is voluntary, but not in decision; and the actions we do on the spur of the moment are said to be voluntary, but not to express decision."[24] Animals never become self-governing in the ways that human beings can, and habituation of the young is so crucial because it is training (for better or worse) in self-governance.

---

[24] Aristotle, *Nicomachean Ethics*, trans. Terence Irwin (Indianapolis, IN: Hackett Publishing Co., 1985), III, 2, 1111b9–10.

Much of the habituation that we undergo is in the service of acquiring *rational* habits, habits of seeing things in certain ways, recognizing various considerations as reasons for action, and strategies of deliberation. Moreover, as we mature in our rationality we increasingly habituate *ourselves*. The process by which we come to have stable dispositions to respond, to choose, and to act is increasingly self-governed. Aristotle remarks: "We deliberate about what is up to us, i.e. about the actions we can do . . . [f]or causes seem to include nature, necessity and fortune, but besides them mind and everything [operating] through human agency." [25] The Aristotelian view, endorsed here, is that we are voluntary originators of action, both before our rational capacities are developed and once they are. In maturing, our self-motion is more and more deliberate, even if we reason poorly or inattentively.

An individual, in maturity, typically settles into more or less fixed dispositions. Indeed, a crucial dimension of what it is to *have* a character is that the agent has stable, action-guiding dispositions, and dispositions of affect, motivation, and receptivity. We do not regard a person's attributes as simply welcome or unwelcome, desirable or undesirable. We see them as features of a self-determining individual who does not just happen to be that way entirely on account of luck or necessity. While multiple influences are at work on each of us, what we make of these influences is partly determined by how we exercise self-governance. The character that we each acquire is, in substantial respects, voluntary.

Indeed, we tend to identify with many of our own persistent, characteristic dispositions. Sometimes we identify so strongly that even when we acknowledge their defects, the fact that they are our own, and are partially constitutive of us, poses an obstacle to changing them. Often, habit is pleasing just because it is "second nature." Although we are capable of adopting a critical stance toward some of our characteristics, we may withhold the effort to change them, not because we think change is impossible, but because there is comfort in the familiarity of "second nature."

In sum, to a substantial extent, we become who we are on account of the manner in which we exercise self-governance. Agents' states of character are more fully their responsibility as they are more fully able to decide to act on values and attitudes with which they identify, and which they recognize as reflecting their own commitments, concerns, and policies of action. As Bernard Williams puts it:

[I]f one acknowledges responsibility for anything, one must acknowledge responsibility for decisions and action which are expressions of

---

[25] Ibid., 1112a31–33.

character—to be an expression of character is perhaps the most sub-stantial way in which an action can be one's own.[26]

Self-governance does not require that an agent be immune to luck or necessity. Nor does it require that a large "menu" of options be presented to the agent. The person who is raised in certain traditions, to the exclusion of seeing and doing things in other ways, and to whom it does not occur to think and act differently, can still exhibit a substantial degree of voluntariness and self-governance in leading his life. A duke may be acting exactly as the duke would act; namely, as the duke has acted for generations. He has been raised and educated to act that way. But the duke is no less a voluntary agent. In many cases, compliance, willingness, and endorsement of ends and practices are sufficient for the voluntariness of acts and states. The duke may give little thought to whether there is any other way for him to act. In fact, the thought that there might be any other way may strike him as absurd. Perhaps his endorsements are not thoughtful or critical. But they are the endorsements of a voluntary, rational agent, not an automaton.

We generally do not know what difference will be made to our characters by specific acts, and the fact that a state is voluntary does not imply that the agent had complete control over its initiation and establishment. However, as Aristotle remarks, we do know that, in general, "each type of activity produces the corresponding character."[27] We do not know how many forays into battle without cowering make for a courageous soldier, nor do we know how many lies cause one to be a liar—but it is facing risks and dangers without flinching, running, or equivocating that makes for courage, and it is lying that makes liars, and so forth.

IV. CHARACTER AND PRACTICAL NECESSITY

A person may voluntarily acquire qualities of character that she did not intend to acquire, and which she is then unable to alter, and still be responsible for them and for the actions that flow from them. Although one may strive to establish a certain type of disposition, dispositions can be the result of voluntary activity even if what results is not something explicitly intended. In addition, character attributes determine, to a large extent, what is possible and what is necessary for an agent. In addition to the "have to" of law, of rule-following, of moral requirement, of social custom, and of biological imperative, is the "have to" of character and self-governance.

---

[26] Bernard Williams, "Practical Necessity," in Williams, *Moral Luck: Philosophical Papers, 1973–1980* (Cambridge: Cambridge University Press, 1981), 130.

[27] Aristotle, *Nicomachean Ethics*, III, 5, 1114a7.

Again, Aristotle is an especially valuable resource for developing this claim. He notes, for example, that the conditions for actions being virtuous acts are that the agent first "must know [that he is doing virtuous actions]; second, he must decide on them, and decide on them for themselves; and, third, he must also do them from a firm and unchanging state."[28] In Aristotle's view, and in the view that I am developing, the virtuous agent grasps and appreciates what is ethically salient, and also reasons well to what is required. He then proceeds to act in a way that is undistracted and free of motivational conflict. This is not thoughtless or mechanical, but is the result of employing an array of concepts and making certain discriminations, which inevitably leave many other, possibly action-relevant considerations out of the picture.

John McDowell uses the language of "silencing" to characterize the way in which a virtuous agent's manner of seeing things brings certain reason-making facts into view and excludes others. He says that for the virtuous agent:

> the dictates of virtue, if properly appreciated, are not weighed with other reasons at all, not even on a scale which always tips on their side. If a situation in which virtue imposes a requirement is genuinely conceived as such, according to this view, then considerations which, in the absence of the requirement, would have constituted reasons for acting otherwise are silenced altogether—not overridden—by the requirement.[29]

McDowell is talking about an ideal of virtue. It may be a rare individual whose character silences reasons for acting that conflict with what virtue requires. But the main point remains unaffected. It would be incorrect to say that the virtuous agent and the vicious agent apprehend the same action-guiding considerations but respond to them differently. Rather, these agents have different conceptions of what are the action-guiding considerations in the situation. As McDowell points out:

> It would be wrong to infer that the conceptions of situations which constitute the reasons are available to people who are not swayed by them, and weigh with those who are swayed only contingently upon their possession of an independent desire. . . . Their status as reasons is hypothetical only in this truistic sense: they sway only those who have them.[30]

[28] Ibid., II, 4, 1105a30–35.
[29] John McDowell, "Are Moral Requirements Hypothetical Imperatives?" *Proceedings of the Aristotelian Society* Supp. Vol. 52 (1978): 26.
[30] Ibid., 23.

The vicious agent may be rational—he has conceptions of good and bad, and he may show care and resolve in enacting them. Vice is not clear evidence of a failure of rationality on the part of the vicious agent. Also, vice can silence as well as virtue can. In the seriously and persistently vicious agent, what is in accord with vice does not simply override what virtue requires. What virtue requires is silenced, and the considerations that have significance for the virtuous agent do not count as action-guiding reasons for the vicious agent even if they are brought to his attention. That is the difference, for example, between a cruelly vicious person who inflicts suffering because he really believes that his victim deserves to suffer, and the agent who succumbs to a vengeful passion, but is able to recognize it as a moral lapse. The cruelly or persistently vicious agent is doing what he thinks he ought to do, and he would stand by his actions even upon consideration. He is responding to what he takes to be rational imperatives. He is someone for whom what is morally necessary is not practically necessary, on account of his character. This agent might not even recognize what is morally required.

Much of what an agent does is practically necessary in the sense that it reflects firmly established states of character or perhaps the aspiration to exhibit or acquire a certain state of character. Those states or the determination to establish them can constitute real limitations on what an agent takes to be possible and what enters into her deliberation and intention. The exclusion of other possibilities is often not a matter of inattention, lack of information, or thoughtlessness (though it may sometimes be one of these). It may, instead, be a matter of the agent exercising a habit of judgment and action that particularly reflects what she takes into account and cares about (for better or worse). The acts of an uncoerced, aware, rational adult are voluntary acts even if they are of the sort of which we say, "she could not help it" because of the sort of person that she is. "Being in character" is not an alternative to being voluntary; "being in character" is a fundamental mode of acting voluntarily.

An upshot of this view of self-governance and character is that moral considerations are not equally accessible to all rational agents. These considerations may be *available*, in the sense that they are not epistemically out of reach to such an extent that agents cannot be reasonably expected to know them, but they still may not be *accessible* to all agents. (I shall say more about this distinction in Section V.) There are agents who cannot bring moral considerations into view and properly appreciate them. Given the wrongness or perversity of their values and motives, they do not acknowledge or respond to ethically sound considerations. They act for reasons that they endorse, and they weigh considerations, deploy normative concepts, and so forth. But their modes of self-governance preclude them from correctly appreciating and responding to ethical considerations, or at least some important kinds of them. Normatively sound rationality is an achievement, and these agents progressively disable themselves for it, while remaining voluntary, responsible individuals.

Facts about self-governance, the role of voluntariness in the establishment of character, and the way in which states of character determine practical necessity and impossibility for individual agents push us toward the conclusion that, while moral requirements are categorically imperative, this does not imply that they are cognitively and motivationally accessible to all rational agents. There are agents who do not recognize their wrong actions as such. These agents do not appreciate their wrong actions as lapses from values and standards that they recognize; their actions are in accord with the values and standards that they endorse. Thus, there are some agents who cannot, in any practically effective way, appreciate the wrongness of their actions. In many cases, however, this does not defeat responsibility.

V. CHARACTER AND ACCOUNTABILITY

Gary Watson suggests a distinction between attributions of moral fault, on the one hand, and practices of moral accountability, on the other. This distinction will help us to explicate the tension between autonomy and self-governance. Judgments concerning attribution of moral faults are made from what he calls the "aretaic perspective,"[31] and we can think of this "as concerned with the question of what activities and ways of life are most choiceworthy."[32] In aretaic evaluation we are concerned with the degrees of excellence or the deficiencies of agents' characters and actions, that is, the ways in which they are admirable or not, or worthy of praise or not. We are not necessarily concerned with whether agents' actions are morally right or wrong. Judgments of *accountability*, however, concern "particular moral norms"[33] and the agent being "accountable to us or to others"[34] on the basis of "certain expectations or demands or requirements."[35]

Explaining what he means by accountability, Watson writes:

> To require or demand certain behavior of an agent is to lay it down that unless the agent so behaves she will be liable to certain adverse or unwelcome treatment. For convenience, I shall call the diverse forms of adverse treatment "sanctions." Holding accountable thus involves the idea of liability to sanctions. To be entitled to make demands, then, is to be entitled to impose conditions of liability.[36]

[31] Gary Watson, "Two Faces of Responsibility," *Philosophical Topics* 24, no. 2 (1996): 231.
[32] Ibid.
[33] Ibid.
[34] Ibid.
[35] Ibid., 235.
[36] Ibid., 236–37.

In this way, "holding [someone] responsible goes beyond aretaic apprais-al."[37] We sometimes find fault with agents without necessarily regarding those agents as being *at fault* for a specific wrong. They might be found selfish, shallow, cold, or perhaps even repugnant, but there may not be a specific wrong act for which they are liable. Similarly, we might admire and praise people for their composure, consideration, reliability, and the like, without also making specific judgments concerning their moral ac-countability. Watson says:

> Attributability has an importance to ethical life that is distinct from concerns about accountability. Responsibility is important to issues about what it is to lead a life, indeed about what it is to have a life in the biographical sense, and about the quality and character of that life. These issues reflect one face of responsibility (what I will call its aretaic face). Concerns about accountability reflect another.[38]

This distinction brings into relief the ways in which evaluations of agents answer to different kinds of considerations.

Aretaic appraisal concerns matters that reflect the agent's mode of self-governance. "Because aretaic appraisals implicate one's practical iden-tity," Watson writes, "they have ethical depth in an obvious sense." He further explains:

> This brings out the way in which aretaic appraisal involves an attri-bution of responsibility. To adopt an end, to commit oneself to a conception of value in this way, is a way of taking responsibility. To stand for something is to take a stand, to be ready to stand up for, to defend, to affirm, to answer for. Hence one notion of responsibility — *responsibility as attributability* — belongs to the very notion of practical identity.[39]

Accountability, in contrast to attributability, concerns what can be ex-pected or demanded of an agent. It concerns liability to sanctions, not just susceptibility to appraisal. Accordingly, Watson notes that an important difference between accountability and attributability is that the former "raises issues of fairness that do not arise for aretaic appraisal."[40]

One way to see that autonomy and self-governance can be in tension is to recognize that agents can be accountable even when, in certain re-spects, it was not practically possible for them to do what they ought to have done, because aretaic features alienate them from what accountabil-

[37] Ibid., 238.
[38] Ibid., 229.
[39] Ibid., 234.
[40] Ibid., 235.

ity demands. There are cases in which what is morally required is *available, but is not accessible*, because of agents' habits and characters. The relevant moral understanding is abroad, but some agents are deeply alienated from it by their characters. Are *these* agents properly liable to sanction? Many of them are.

The agents of chief concern here are full participants in the moral order because they *could have* acquired correct understanding and morally sound motives, but these are now seemingly out of reach because of the states of character that the agents have settled into. They are not irrational, though they are firmly attached to wrong values, which they believe are normatively sound. Such agents reject attempts to get them to revise their beliefs and commitments, though this does not indicate incompetence or disability that would disqualify the agents for accountability.

Susan Wolf argues that "an individual is responsible if and only if she is able to form her actions on the basis of her values *and* she is able to form her values on the basis of what is True and Good."[41] She writes:

> Whatever the explanation that prevents the agent from being able to do the right thing for the right reasons, our intuitions seem to support the claim that the agent does not deserve blame. If an agent is incapable of doing the right thing for the right reasons, then it is not her fault that she stumbles into doing something wrong.[42]

When the deformation of an agent's values can be traced to factors that the agent could not control, we diminish her accountability. These factors, in Wolf's view, might be such things as the wrongness of prevailing norms, such as in the slaveholding American South in the nineteenth century or in Germany in the 1930s. (These are examples that Wolf employs, and I shall critique them below.) Wolf says, "[I]nsofar as we do regard social processes and norms as potential obstacles to sound moral judgments, we lessen the blame we would otherwise direct toward individuals who, surrounded by these obstacles, fail to reach these judgments."[43] The aretaic failures of nonresistant citizens in the slaveholding South or in Nazi Germany underwrite attributions of fault, but these failures do not, at least to the same extent, underwrite blame. Given the powerful influences operating on these agents, suggests Wolf, they are less than fully accountable because we can see why it was reasonable for them to have developed the values and commitments that they had. Their actions were voluntary, and they were acting on values that they endorsed, but they were prevented from seeing things in any other way. Thus, they are not fully accountable for their wrong actions.

[41] Susan Wolf, *Freedom Within Reason* (New York: Oxford University Press, 1990), 75.
[42] Ibid., 81.
[43] Ibid., 122.

I have suggested a distinction between correct values being available and being accessible. The agents to whom Wolf refers are, I think, agents to whom correct values *were* available (even if, in some ways, not accessible), and that is a reason *not* to lessen blame. At least there is a question about whether to lessen it. These are agents who could have known better. First, they could have known better in the general sense that they were competent rational agents. We are considering agents who were not deranged, insane, or cognitively handicapped. Second, at crucial stages in their development, they did have the plasticity of character and capacity for learning that could have enabled them to acquire different valuative attachments, attitudes, and motivational policies. In the process of coming to have valuative commitments and firmly established states of character, these agents exercised voluntariness no less than agents who acquired virtues. For all of the influences at work on the agents whom Wolf cites in her examples, they were not victims of compulsion, coercion, or the destruction of their capacities for practical rationality—although they were encouraged in habits of mind that were wrong or perverse. (Of course, some agents are victims of destructive influences, and of course, such agents' responsibility is appropriately diminished. Being raised by abusive, violent people who keep you in confinement and deny you interaction with other people will destroy your capacity to acquire a character with normal emotionality and to exercise self-governance.) Third, a sounder moral understanding was not so remote from the agents in Wolf's examples that it is utterly unreasonable to expect any of them to have acquired it. There were, indeed, powerful forces militating against endorsement of values other than the prevailing ones. But, the prevailing ones were contested, and challenges to them were well known.

Let us (plausibly) suppose that Josef Goebbels, for example, reached a point where he could not consider a way of seeing things other than through Nazi ideology. Let us also (plausibly) suppose that there were powerful influences at work on him that were instrumental in motivating him to be a Nazi zealot. His surroundings shaped his character, and his character became fixed in a way that cut him off from "the True and the Good" (as Wolf puts it). Neither of these considerations automatically tips the balance against his accountability. The Nazi zealot and the defender of slavery live in social worlds that do not render them incapable of correct moral understanding, though they may be beyond the reach of right reason because of the habits of mind, motivation, and sensibility that have become second nature to them. This is to say, blameworthiness does not always require avoidability.

In the antebellum South, many people, even among those who tolerated, condoned, or supported slavery, understood that it was wrong, but for a number of reasons failed to take steps to oppose or abolish it. These were agents who could perceive that slavery was immoral, even if they did not oppose it. There were other Southerners for whom correct values were epistemically inaccessible. They were profoundly alienated from sound ethical understanding: they were resolute defenders of the institution of slavery and genuinely believed in its rightness. Once settled into their way of seeing things, perhaps they could not have known better, and they could not do what they ought to have done. What was right had become inaccessible to them because of their fixity of character and the way that it cut them off from correct moral understanding. They would not recognize accountability for perpetuating unjust practices, because they did not think that they were wrong. These persons too, I believe, are responsible agents, on account of the availability of correct ethical considerations and the fact that they voluntarily became the sorts of agents whom they were.[44]

That there are such agents is an important illustration of the tension between autonomy and self-governance. These agents merit respect as participants in the moral order. We owe it to them to address them as such, to regard them as moral agents, and to appeal to them as rational. Still, we might not have any reasonable expectation that they are capable of ethically appropriate responses because of the ways in which their characters shape what they take to be practically necessary.

VI. PERPLEXITIES CONCERNING PUNISHMENT

Even though some agents appear to have put sound ethical considerations out of their reach, there are both epistemic and moral reasons to be very cautious about concluding that such agents are incorrigible. We do not know with certainty, even in our own cases, if and when dispositions have become altogether fixed. Kant, for example, had few illusions about the human capacity for evil, but strongly cautioned against thinking that we are ever in a position to judge that an agent is so fixed in vice that we cannot interact with him as with a fully rational agent.[45] Respect for persons as rational authors of their actions requires a certain kind of humility. We are not to presume to know others so well that we can confidently regard them as irretrievably alienated from morality. Neither are we to regard an individual (except in cases where there clearly is coercion, compulsion, or some other unmistakably agency-defeating cause) as less than the author of his actions.

---

[44] See Philippa Foot's *Human Goodness* (Oxford: Clarendon Press, 2001), where she states a similar position. She says: "Ignorance itself may be voluntary, as when in present-day Britain, an arms dealer takes care not to enquire whether the weapons he is shipping to one country will not be shipped on to a repressive regime. Or if he 'enquires', his conclusion may be guided by self-interest rather than by the evidence at hand: he holds a convenient opinion that does not absolve him, because it is not held, as we say, in good faith" (70). In a footnote to this passage, she writes: "Many of the beliefs of slave owners, and of white people under South Africa's apartheid regime, must have been of this kind" (70).

[45] Kant makes this point in *Religion Within the Limits of Reason Alone*. See, for example, pp. 16 and 35.

In addition to exercising this sort of humility, we also *morally* owe it to others not to abandon them, not to "write them off," so to speak, as incorrigible. To regard agents as less than fully accountable might appear to be a way of showing sympathetic concern, but it is actually a denial of their autonomy and a way of regarding them as less than full agents. R. A. Duff makes the moral point about respect and corrigibility as follows:

> We owe it to every moral agent to treat him as one who can be brought to reform and redeem himself—to keep trying however vainly, to reach the good that is in him, and to appeal to his capacity for moral understanding and concern. To talk thus of "the good that is in him" is not to make some psychological claim to the effect that he "really" cares for the values which he flouts: it is rather to combine the conceptual claim that every moral agent has the capacity or potential for moral development and reform, with the moral claim that we should never give up hope of bringing him to actualize that potential.[46]

If we cease to regard an agent as capable of correct moral acknowledgments and rationally motivated, ethical reform, then we have diminished the agent and damaged the unity of the moral world by making adjustments in that agent's status.

On the one hand, no rational agent is to be despised or treated with less than the respect owed to a participant in the moral order. This is because virtue is not a necessary credential for moral standing, and the autonomy of rational agents fixes that status. On the other hand, there are agents who not only act wrongly on a regular basis, but also seem to have characteristics that make it practically impossible for them to attain sound normative understanding and act upon it.

The tension between autonomy and self-governance is felt particularly strongly in respect to the issue of punishment. In punishing an offender, we deliberately impose harm as a strategy of appealing to him as a rational agent. Apart from consequentialist aims that punishment might have, it is a mode of address that includes the offender in the moral order. Duff expresses this view as follows:

> Punishment, like moral blame, respects and addresses the criminal as a rational moral agent: it seeks his understanding and his assent; it aims to bring him to repent his crime, and to reform himself, by communicating to him the reasons which justify our condemnation of his conduct.[47]

---

[46] R. A. Duff, "Expression, Penance, and Reform," in Jeffrie G. Murphy, ed., *Punishment and Rehabilitation*, 3rd ed. (Belmont, CA: Wadsworth Publishing Company, 1995), 198.
[47] Ibid., 174.

Furthermore, "punishment is part of that continuing dialogue with the criminal through which the law aims to guide his conduct by appealing to relevant reasons."[48] It is not merely a striking back, an institutionalized form of expressing outrage, or a form of control aimed at those who make mischief. Punishment takes seriously the agent's participation in the moral community and the importance of restoring the agent's relations to the rest of the moral community. Morally justified punishment is a strategy through which sound ethical understanding is intended to be made accessible to an agent who needs to connect or reconnect with it, through acknowledgment of having done wrong.

The significance of this cannot be undermined by pointing out that it is well known that punishment often fails to motivate moral self-correction, and that, indeed, it often worsens those who are punished. There are agents who *could* respond in a constructive way, but do not. This is indeed lamentable, but it is a distinct issue. Our present concern is the appropriateness of punishing agents who are not *able* to recognize the justice of sanctioning them, because of their firm attachment to wrong values. It is not merely that they do not respond by acknowledging their wrongdoing; rather, there are reasons to think that they *cannot*.

This issue is also distinct from certain other kinds of situations involving fundamental moral disagreements. Agents who disagree (say, on capital punishment, abortion, or physician-assisted suicide) may still recognize one another as holding their views in good faith, as willing to listen to reason, and as common participants in a shared moral world, even though their disagreements might become rancorous. On specific issues they might find that they can make no progress, and the dialectic grinds to a halt. But it is a *dialectic* that grinds to a halt, and there is, to a large extent, a common framework within which it takes place and halts. The situation is quite different if one party believes that it is perfectly all right to treat certain people in exclusionary ways, and to deny them basic rights, or to take no account of their welfare, *because* people "like that" are inferior and despicable, and they deserve no better. In this case, there is hardly room for meaningful dialectic if the advocate of this view, upon reflection, really believes it and dismisses considerations that confute it. There can be cases of deep disagreement that do not challenge or threaten the overall fabric of the moral community, and in which it is possible for agents to sustain respect for each other. Those are not the kinds of cases at issue here. The present focus is the character of the agents, not the contested nature of the issues.

In one respect, the issue of character might not be thought to be so important. It could be argued that what is important is that offenders be punished, and that we should only punish agents who are rational and competent, and not influenced by disease, coercion, or compulsion. We

[48] Ibid.

can, the objection goes, make the relevant exculpatory and exempting discriminations, when appropriate, without complicating the issue with reference to the fact that there are rationally unreachable agents. Offenders need to be stopped and punished. Whether the criminal can ethically recompose himself is a separate matter, which does not determine the legitimacy of punishment. Perhaps the need to control those who engage in violent, wrongful acts is enough to justify punishing them. Watson, for example, notes that even if the agent suffered the misfortune of a very rotten background and various deprivations, this "does not shield victim-criminals from legal sanctions."[49] He adds, "We still protect ourselves against [criminals'] murderous assaults; we hunt them down, lock them up, shoot them. . . . Seeing the criminal as himself a victim will not prevent us from shutting the cage or pulling the trigger."[50] It is true that certain social concerns are met by punishing offenders, even when moral purposes are unfulfilled. Punishment is necessary to fulfill certain purposes of social regulation. However, it is important that Watson also notes that "these responses will then tend to seem regulative rather than retributive. In a disconcerting way, they lose their normal expressive function."[51] He finds this disconcerting because the expressive function ought to be tied to moral purpose, and not just to social control. The expressive function is the aspect of punishment through which it is a communicative engagement concerning values. I would add that, in a society in which the moral legitimacy of its institutions and practices is important as the basis of conformity to its norms, more than the regulative function of punishment is at issue.

Along these lines, Herbert Morris argues that among the conditions for morally justified punishment are that "the norms addressed to persons are generally just and that the society is to some substantial extent one in which those who are liable to punishment have roughly equal opportunities to conform to those just norms."[52] In addition, the theory "presupposes that there is a general commitment among persons to the values underlying them."[53] Suppose that a society has basically just norms and that its institutional practices are basically just. Still, it is almost certain that there will be members of the society who do not share a commitment to these norms, though they had the opportunity to acquire that commitment and to conform to them. The norms were available for adoption, although the combined effect of circumstances and voluntary activity made them inaccessible to some agents. Some of their actions are shame-

[49] Watson, "Two Faces of Responsibility," 240.
[50] Ibid.
[51] Ibid.
[52] Herbert Morris, "A Paternalistic Theory of Punishment," in Jeffrie G. Murphy, ed., *Punishment and Rehabilitation*, 165.
[53] Ibid.

less moral outrages, and the agents have no interest in revising their values and commitments. They may even scorn correct values.

These agents may still properly be subject to punishment because they possess the relevant sort of normative competence to be self-governing and responsible. *Normative competence* is not the same as virtue. To be normatively competent, an agent must use normative concepts in a coherent way and make various types of valuative distinctions and judgments. This is not a wanton or a psychopath who has no concern for what moves him to act. This is not someone who, out of desperation or rage, runs amuck. The agent in question may have articulate and elaborate rationales for his views and actions. He acts on the basis of valuations. However, he is so thoroughly alienated from the true and the good that society's norms are not *really* accessible to him, even though they were and are available.

VII. Forgiveness and Hatred

Considerations of moral psychology put pressure on the framework of morality as structured by autonomy in the way we have indicated. This pressure is especially evident in regard to punishment, but it also emerges in related questions concerning retributive hatred and forgiveness. By *retributive hatred* I do not mean malice, but an attitude by which we insist on the punitive suffering that an offender deserves and find it gratifying that the offender should suffer.[54] The morality of hatred in general involves many difficulties, but there is one that stands out in the present context: Can agents forfeit our respect for them as participants in the moral world and be properly regarded as loathsome, inferior creatures? Suppose that an agent is strongly attached to wrong values, regards those values as correct, and acts on them with a sense of justification. Given the agent's commitments and sincerity, we are moved to find him loathsome, as though he is "not one of us" and cannot be accommodated in the moral world along with other agents. Has he forfeited his distinct and equal status as a moral agent, and are we thus justified in our loathing?

According to Jean Hampton, while retributive punishment or hatred of a person's worst character traits may be morally well placed, we should not reach the point of regarding the wrongdoer "not merely as cloaked in evil, but as himself a bad thing."[55] In a passage a few pages earlier she writes:

> But I can remain emotionally opposed to someone's action, and still come to be supportive of, even reconciled to, *her*, if I am able to

---

[54] I borrow the term "retributive hatred" from Jeffrie G. Murphy, who introduces it in "Hatred: A Qualified Defense," in Jeffrie G. Murphy and Jean Hampton, *Forgiveness and Mercy* (New York: Cambridge University Press, 1988), 90.

[55] Jean Hampton, "The Retributive Idea," in Murphy and Hampton, *Forgiveness and Mercy*, 152.

dissociate her from the action and reapprove of her. This is precisely what I cannot do if I morally hate the wrongdoer.[56]

This is an attempt at retributivism without retributive hatred. It is also part of an argument for forgiveness following punishment. Hampton appeals to the considerations that I mentioned above, concerning our uncertainty about whether any agents are altogether incorrigible, as well as to the teachings of Christianity. She asks, "Aren't we obliged to have faith in a decent core within, even if it is a core which we are completely unable to see?"[57] Whatever evidence there is in the aretaic dimension, we may lack a sufficiency of evidence to determine that the person is "morally dead"[58] and thus reduced in moral standing. We cannot confidently claim that we are morally better. Perhaps we were lucky to have had better surroundings, better examples, and better opportunities. We can, and should, denounce the offender's acts and the character states that motivated them, but we should not hate the offender. We owe it to the offender's better self, and to our own better selves, to be both restrained in our hatred and generous in our willingness to reapprove of the agent. (This might be a way of recognizing serious aretaic defects without also allowing that recognition to disturb the respect owed to the individual as a rationally autonomous agent.)

Even if an individual has seemingly destroyed the basis for respecting him, it is not appropriate (Hampton suggests) for us to withdraw respect for this person as a moral agent. That respect is not contingent on virtue. Hampton notes that a presupposition of retributivism, as she understands it, is a "Kantian theory of human worth, which makes people intrinsically, objectively, and equally valuable."[59] We should always look to the agent's capacity to morally redeem himself, rather than withdraw respect because of his vices. This harks back to what we noted about autonomy at the outset of this essay. Autonomy determines the status of an individual as a moral agent, based on his rationality, which is the capacity to participate effectively in the moral order and to orient himself to what morality requires. Self-governance may disfigure this capacity through the way that self-governance is exercised, but it is the capacity for autonomy that determines the individual as a moral agent with special standing.

It is undeniable that retributive hatred can become unruly and minatory in ways that fail to respect the hated agent as a fellow rational being. Still, the willingness to forgive and to reapprove a moral offender can distract us from the genuine evil that he has done. It can be symptomatic

56 Ibid., 148.
57 Ibid., 151.
58 Ibid., 153.
59 Ibid., 124.

of an unwillingness to see evil for what it is. Sometimes, forgiveness is
motivated by the fact that the offender is no longer dangerous or fear-
some simply because he is in custody and at our mercy. Adam Smith
remarks that "[w]hen the guilty is about to suffer that just retaliation, . . .
when he ceases to be an object of fear, with the generous and humane he
begins to be an object of pity."[60] To counterbalance this urge to pardon
the criminal, Smith recommends that the generous and humane remind
themselves of

> the general interest of society. . . . They [ought to] reflect that mercy
> to the guilty is cruelty to the innocent, and oppose to the emotions of
> compassion which they feel for a particular person, a more enlarged
> compassion which they feel for mankind.[61]

It can be very difficult to reconcile ourselves to the fact that some agents
may be as deeply or enduringly vicious as they seem to be. Perhaps some
are hateful in ways that merit retributive hatred. There is a danger that
forgiveness will be corrupted (whether or not we admit it) into a kind of
narcissism, in which the concern is primarily for our own (perceived)
virtue, rather than for the evil with which we must deal.

Granted, Hampton was not suggesting that we forgo punishment. We
can punish *and* forgive. This would be a way of sustaining respect and
avoiding retributive hatred. However, the moral purpose of forgiveness is
fulfilled only when there is some realistic chance of uptake of the gift.
Some agents are unreachable, unrepentant, and utterly devoted to wrong
or perverse values. God can forgive them because God can infuse receptivity to grace. But *we* cannot do that. There certainly seem to be some
agents who are unreachable by us. The fact that we might find gratification (which is not the same as joy) in their punishment and suffering does
not disqualify retributive hatred as a proper expression of fidelity to
correct values and norms. Epistemic and moral humility are in order here,
but so, too, is resolve to see that correct values are upheld and that "the
victim's value receives its proper defense."[62]

In most cases of punishment, an offender is capable of acknowledging
his wrong and recognizing the justice of his punishment. The respect
owed to the offender is not in doubt, and retributive hatred is either out
of place, or it should be forgone without difficulty. But the agent in
question in less typical cases is not like that. He gives every sign that there
is no better self to reach through punishment or to respond to forgiveness.
It may be asking too much to expect virtuous agents *not* to feel retributive
hatred for such an unrepentant agent, or to forgive him, even after pun-

---

[60] Adam Smith, *The Theory of Moral Sentiments* (Indianapolis, IN: Liberty Fund, 1984), 88.
[61] Ibid., 88–89.
[62] Hampton, "The Retributive Idea," 131.

ishing him. There are times (many of them) when it is wrong not to forgive. But there are also agents whose vice is sufficiently profound and so centrally a part of their practical identities that forgiving them only makes sense on the basis of a misrepresentation of their characters and their capacities to connect (or reconnect) to correct values. There seem to be agents whose viciousness is of such a nature that it threatens our respect for them as rational beings. At least it calls that respect into doubt, even though it is a type of fundamental regard that is supposed to be protected from judgments or decisions to confer or withdraw it. If there are agents who merit retributive hatred, then there is a source of serious strain on the normative framework for autonomy, to which respect is crucial.

This is not a concession to our baser selves. It is an acknowledgment of important features (involving sentiment and judgment) of the commitment to justice and to correct values. As Jeffrie Murphy puts the point, "we may say that retributive hatred is a strategy designed to see (and to let the victim see) that people get their just deserts; as such it is neither irrational nor immoral." [63] The hatred can reflect the strength of our attachment to certain values, rather than mere or sheer malice. Retributive hatred is not always wrong simply because it is hatred—and forgiveness is not always right, simply because it is forgiveness. A virtuous agent respects other agents, can tell the difference between vengeance and retributive hatred, and works at keeping the former from infecting the latter. However, a virtuous agent finds no justice or satisfaction when a wrongdoer does *not* suffer at all: Kant remarks at the beginning of the *Foundations of the Metaphysics of Morals*, "It need hardly be mentioned that the sight of a being adorned with no feature of a pure and good will, yet enjoying uninterrupted prosperity, can never give pleasure to a rational impartial observer." [64] We need to consider seriously whether a vicious and seemingly incorrigible agent can be found so repugnant that we find it not just acceptable but gratifying that he suffers (just punishment).

VIII. Conclusion

Rational agency *demands* respect, we might say, while the virtuous exercise of self-governance *merits* it. Respect is owed to rational agents as having a distinct and equal status. The agent whose self-governance is profoundly and persistently vicious may merit our loathing to such a degree that we experience doubts about his standing as a participant in the moral order. This is not a license to degrade, humiliate, or abuse that person, but, at the same time, there may be serious obstacles to forgiveness and restoration of respect. A shameless, dreadfully bad person who

---

[63] Murphy, "Hatred: A Qualified Defense," 95.
[64] Kant, *Foundations of the Metaphysics of Morals*, 9.

has no inclination to morally retrieve himself may exhaust the bases for the full measure of respect that rational agency otherwise seems to demand.

Part of the explanation for this forfeiture of respect is that aretaic features are not merely accessories to an agent's rational nature. They are the expression and realization of it. The degree to which the normative framework that requires respect for persons actually structures the moral world depends upon the extent to which agents are virtuous. The normative framework is merely ideal or notional *unless* the ways in which people exercise self-governance actualize and sustain it. Vicious self-governance can threaten the respect that is owed to an agent on the grounds of autonomy. What autonomy demands and what self-governance merits may pull in opposite directions. Thus, there remain difficult questions about whether one's standing in the moral order can be relinquished on account of how one exercises self-governance. This is one way in which the concepts that we use to map the moral landscape may fail to bring complete clarity.

Philosophy and Religion, Colgate University

AUTONOMY FROM THE VIEWPOINT
OF TELEOLOGICAL BEHAVIORISM

By Howard Rachlin

I. Introduction

I will argue that the autonomy of a particular act of a particular person depends on the pattern of behavior in which it is embedded. I call this *conditional autonomy*. A person's act is conditionally autonomous or not, relative to other acts at other times. Consider an example of a person crossing the street. On the one hand, this act might not be done for its own sake, but may fit into some ongoing long-term behavioral pattern that is personally beneficial to the person crossing the street—such as regularly buying groceries in the supermarket (which happens to be across the street). On the other hand, crossing the street might be done simply for its own sake. If such an act were considered to be autonomous, regardless of its temporal context, its autonomy would be *unconditional*. However, I will argue that whereas conditional autonomy is a highly useful social concept, indeed a necessary concept, for any human society, unconditional autonomy is a useless concept that actually impedes our efforts to understand and explain human behavior.

Before making this argument I need to discuss the psychological viewpoint from which it comes, a viewpoint I call *teleological behaviorism*. In order to do this, I first need to distinguish between cognitive psychology and behavioral psychology (as I understand these terms), and then, to distinguish between Skinnerian behaviorism (the form of behaviorism that most people are familiar with) and teleological behaviorism.

II. Cognitive Psychology and Behavioral Psychology

Figure 1 shows, in a general way, how behavioral and cognitive theorists conceptualize choice behavior. The thick vertical line represents the boundary between the person and the world. To the right of the thick line is an example of a cognitive organization of behavior; to the left, a behavioral organization. The four heavy horizontal arrows represent the variables of both cognitive and behavioral psychologies—events in the world affecting the person and behavior of the person observable in the world. The upper arrow heading from the world into the person represents information—signals relevant to important events in the world. The upper arrow going to the left is verbal behavior—what the person

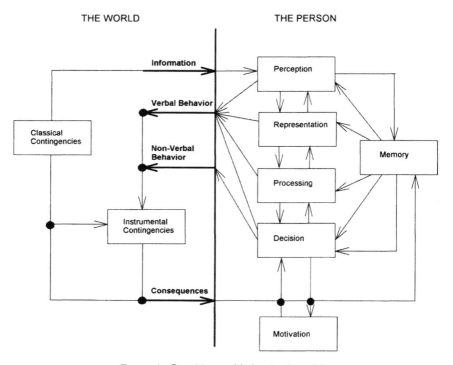

FIGURE 1. Cognitive and behavioral models

says and writes. The lower arrow going to the left is nonverbal behavior—
the actual choices that a person makes. The lower arrow going to the right
indicates consequences, or outcomes, of his or her choices.

The elements of cognitive theory (in very simplistic and abstract form,
not intended to reflect any particular theory) are the internal mechanisms
that mediate between the arrows going in and the arrows going out
between the person and the world. (See the boxes and thin arrows to the
right of the thick vertical line.) Information, in the form of instructions
and experimental displays, is first perceived, then represented and pro-
cessed, and finally a decision is made on the basis of it. All of these
processes are influenced by memory. In addition, processes may be altered by motives coming up from below. The workings of some or all of
these mechanisms are (in some cognitive theories) accessible to introspection and expressible by verbal behavior. When a decision is made, that
decision is expressed in verbal or nonverbal behavior or some combination of the two. Finally, the outcome of the decision (consequences) is
retained in memory and may affect future operation of any component of
the decision mechanism.

Figure 1 is a simplistic model and does not indicate any of the quite
complex and elaborate submechanisms (neural networks or parallel pro-

cessing) that may operate within or across the boxes in the figure. There is some dispute within cognitive psychology about which, if any, internal mechanisms contain submechanisms that work on logical principles, and where, if anywhere in the process, principles of optimality apply. Moreover, strictly speaking, a purely cognitive theory is silent about the physiological instantiation (the hardware) corresponding to the flow of information (the software) represented in Figure 1. The workings of the boxes labeled perception, representation, memory, and so forth, and their interaction as an information processing system, are what cognitive theories are all about.

What goes on to the right of the heavy vertical line of Figure 1 (that is, what goes on in the cognitive realm) is unquestionably interesting and important. No behaviorist can deny that. Nevertheless, the behaviorist is fundamentally interested, not in the principles underlying internal mechanisms, but in the principles underlying the behavior itself. The cognitivist and the behaviorist both want, ultimately, to *explain* current behavior—to answer the question, "Why is this person acting in this way?" Their explanations of current behavior, however, refer to different events. The cognitivist, in explaining current actions, refers to current events inside the organism; the behaviorist, in explaining current actions, refers to past actions and past environmental events, and to the relations over time between those events and actions. The behavioral equivalent to a cognitive mechanism is a contingency. But, unlike a cognitive mechanism, a contingency has no meaning at an instant of time. For example, a student's grade point average, or GPA, is presumably contingent on his or her study habits; but no particular GPA value can be traced to any particular act of studying. Study habits are definable only over extended time periods.

No behaviorist, not even a teleological behaviorist like me, denies that there are mechanisms inside the person mediating between the incoming and outgoing arrows of Figure 1. The organism is not empty. But, just as the cognitive psychologist may be interested fundamentally in the internal software and only secondarily, if at all, in the particular underlying hardware (the particular brain physiology), so the behaviorist is interested fundamentally in the relations in the world or environment between the four thick arrows of Figure 1, and only secondarily in the mechanisms (software or hardware) that mediate between the ingoing and outgoing arrows.

III. Skinnerian Behaviorism

Skinnerian analysis proceeds as follows. There is some behavior in which you are interested (say, addiction). First you look for a single stimulus in the environment that reliably causes that behavior. I think that most reasonable people will agree that there is no such single environmental cause of addiction; if there were, we could cure addiction simply by eliminating its stimulus. Failing to find a stimulus, Skinnerian analysis bids you to look for a *reinforcer*, to ask, "What are the consequences of any given bit of behavior?"

Suppose that I receive a written invitation to speak at a conference. I prepare the talk, go to the conference, and deliver the talk. (Presumably this is voluntary behavior.) You could ask *how* I do it, tracing a chain of internal events from the typed words entering my eyes, engaging my cognitive system, and finally causing me to stand up and speak. Or you could ask, "What are the reinforcers (and punishers)?" This would involve an examination of the consequences of my behavior as they affect me—and these might include the chance to enjoy the attention of my audience for a while, or perhaps the chance to influence them, or to improve my research, thanks to feedback from audience members. You would have to look for similar behavior by me in the past and similar consequences. These, Skinner says, are the true causes of my present behavior. I may have better access to my own behavior and its consequences than the audience could have (because I am always there when I am behaving), and this is an advantage for me. However, my audience has an objective view that I do not have, and that is an advantage for them. (The behavior therapist aims to work with this advantage.)

What is wrong with this method of analyzing behavior? The problem is that, just as it is not possible, in almost any interesting case, to find a single external stimulus as the cause of behavior, it is likewise not possible to find an external reinforcer in many interesting cases. For example, although a member of my audience might easily discover reinforcers for my talk, he will not be able to find a reinforcer for any particular sentence. Yet, according to Skinner, every individual act (each sentence, each word) must have its individual, immediate reinforcer—either a primary reinforcer (like a pellet of food offered to a rat) or a secondary reinforcer (like the mere sound of the food hopper moving in a Skinner box). It is often impossible, though, to trace every individual act of a laboratory rat (let alone a human being) to its particular reinforcement.

This problem is apparent in my primary research area: self-control. On the one hand, it is easy to explain *failures* of self-control in terms of immediate reinforcement. If I have a second or third cocktail at a party, the reinforcers of my behavior—the cocktails themselves—are easy to spot. But what if the waiter tries to hand me a cocktail, and I refuse? What reinforces that act? What reinforces *success* in self-control? I refuse the cocktail and exactly nothing happens.[1] The usual tactic of the behavior

---

[1] One could say that not vomiting and not getting into embarrassing social situations are discrete reinforcers of a particular drink refusal. But if the absence of these particular aversive events is to explain a particular refusal, then their absence must be distinguished from the absence of any of the infinite number of other conceivable aversive events (experiencing electric shock, being boiled in oil, etc.) that are not contingent on drinking but are

analyst at this point is to postulate some sort of inner self-reinforcement—
my satisfaction perhaps. When I refuse the third drink I might covertly
pat myself on the back for resisting temptation. (I will discuss self-
reinforcement in more detail later in this essay.) But to postulate such an
internal mechanism is to engage in cognitive analysis rather than behavioral analysis (as I have defined it). Cognitive psychologists are much
better at postulating internal mechanisms than behaviorists are—cognitive
psychologists are trained for it—and the behaviorist begins to look overly
simplistic. This is the problem with Skinnerian behaviorism, which is a
problem that has been pointed out many times.[2]

IV. Teleological Behaviorism

When confronted with a clearly voluntary act (like refusing a cocktail)
for which there is no apparent external reinforcement, teleological behaviorism looks, not into the organism, but into the past and future, for
patterns of behavior.[3] According to teleological behaviorism, the question
of why I am giving a talk cannot be broken up into the questions of why
I am speaking this sentence, why I am speaking the next sentence, and so
forth. Rather, teleological behaviorism examines why I am giving the talk
as a whole—the *extrinsic* social reinforcers as well as the *intrinsic* value of
the activity itself.[4] If I had to decide whether to utter each sentence
individually, I would be tongue-tied, since there is no reinforcement for
each sentence individually. Similarly, in the area of self-control, there is no
reinforcement for each act of refusing a cocktail (to cite my earlier example) or, for that matter, for refusing an individual cigarette, hit of heroin,
or so forth. It is sometimes said that the reinforcement for such acts is
delayed. But if I refuse a single cocktail tonight I will not wake up three
weeks from today, suddenly a healthier, happier person. A single act of
self-control is not reinforced—*now or ever*. Reinforcement is to be found,

---

also generally absent after drink refusal. The most straightforward way to make this distinction is to point to the negative correlation over time between drink refusal and vomiting
or getting into embarrassing social situations (i.e., the more drink refusal, the less vomiting
there is). But, in Skinner's model, negative correlations cannot work by themselves. They
must be reduced to specific reinforcers following specific responses. In order to effect this
reduction, Skinnerian behaviorism has to postulate unobserved internal stimuli, responses,
and reinforcers.

[2] William Baum, *Understanding Behaviorism: Science, Behavior, and Culture* (New York: Harper
Collins, 1994); John Staddon, *The New Behaviorism: Mind, Mechanism, and Society* (Philadelphia, PA: Psychology Press, 2001).

[3] Howard Rachlin, *Behavior and Mind: The Roots of Modern Psychology* (New York: Oxford
University Press, 1994); Howard Rachlin, "Teleological Behaviorism," *American Psychologist*
47 (1992): 1371–82.

[4] Intrinsic value is determined not by introspection or physiological or biological investigation, but by the position of the pattern on a value scale or in a utility function. Value and
utility are determined, in turn, by behavioral observation. Eating, for example, is a highly
valued act, not because it is pleasurable or stimulates a "pleasure center" in the brain, but
because eating is frequently chosen over other acts.

not in individual acts, but in the value (or utility) of a pattern of acts repeated over time. This value may be extrinsic to the pattern—such as social approval—or intrinsic in the pattern itself, such as the enhanced enjoyment of food when eating is well regulated.[5]

To put this argument more formally, suppose that there is a long activity lasting T time units and a short activity lasting t time units where $T = Nt$. A problem of self-control arises when two conditions are satisfied:

$$A: V_T > NV_t, \text{ and}$$

$$B: V_t > V_{T/N},$$

where V stands for value. In other words, a problem of self-control arises when the value of a longer activity is greater than that of an equal duration of repetitions of a shorter activity and the value of the shorter activity is greater than that of an equal fraction of the longer activity.[6]

For example, suppose that you were driving from New York to California. You like both classical and popular music, so you take along ten classical compact discs (CDs) and ten pop CDs to play on your car's CD player during the trip. Let us assume that the order of your preference (illustrated in Figure 2) is as follows:

(1) listening to a whole one-hour-long symphony;
(2) listening to a three-minute-long popular song;
(3) listening to three minutes of the symphony.

The problem is, of course, that in order to listen to the whole symphony (first on your list) you must listen to the first three minutes of the symphony (last on your list). Hence, the immediate choice is always between (3) and (2) (the popular song). If you always do what you immediately prefer, you are likely to reach California without ever having heard the symphony. Of course, you could listen to just one popular song and then the symphony, but after listening to the song, you would be in the same position that you were in originally. The value of the symphony (as the gestalt psychologists never tire of pointing out) lies not in the sum of the values of its parts—even in the sum of the delay-discounted values of its parts; it lies in the symphony as a whole. You can see this by imagining how you would feel if a CD were defective and the last three minutes of a symphony were missing. You would not consider that you had 57/60th

---

[5] In dealing with individual human behavior, the behaviorist calculates reinforcement value in terms of consummatory behavior rather than in terms of the goods themselves being bought. For an individual, value (or utility for that matter) is primarily in eating the apple and only secondarily in having the apple.

[6] By an *activity* I mean an instance of a class of activities defined functionally (an *operant* in Skinner's terms). Thus, eating a large steak for dinner and eating a pint of ice cream that night while watching TV would be two instances of the same class of activity—overeating.

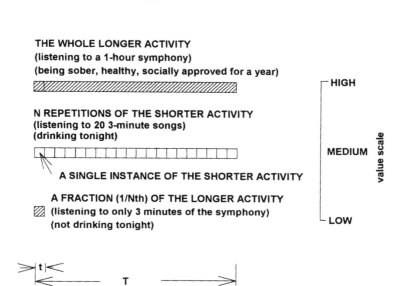

FIGURE 2. How inconsistency of valuation of long and short duration activities cause problems in self-control

worth of enjoyment from the CD. Most likely, the whole experience would be ruined, even though you had already listened to, and presumably enjoyed, fifty-seven minutes of the symphony.

The same considerations apply in most instances of human self-control — for example, the choice between studying and not studying, between reading a novel and watching a TV program, or between being sober and having too much to drink. The alcoholic does not choose to be an alcoholic. He prefers not to be one. His preference ordering is:

(1) not being an alcoholic;
(2) drinking tonight;
(3) not drinking tonight.

He just chooses to drink tonight, and tonight, and tonight—and ends up as an alcoholic without ever having chosen to be one.

The cognitive psychologist naturally sees self-control in terms of internal mechanisms; the teleological behaviorist sees self-control as more or

less valuable behavioral patterns, reinforced in different behavioral contexts *as whole patterns*. This difference between the behavioral and cognitive approaches is not just a semantic issue. It determines where you
should look—into the person or into the person's past (the person's reinforcement history, in Skinner's terms)—to discover the causes of her
behavior.

V. NEGATIVE AND POSITIVE ADDICTIONS

A negative addiction is the behavioral pattern that we are most accustomed to calling addictive—that of the alcoholic, or the heroin or cocaine
addict, or the cigarette smoker.[7] Negative addictions come about not
because they are chosen as such, but because of two prior properties.
First, there exists an inverse proportionality between the rate of the addictive activity and the value of each addictive act. If the rate of the
addictive activity is initially low, the value of each alcoholic drink, drug
dose, or cigarette is high. But as the rate increases, tolerance develops,
reducing the value of each alcoholic drink, drug dose, or cigarette. The
alcoholic, drinking at a high rate, needs a quart of gin to achieve the effect
that a single martini would have in a social drinker. Second, as high rates
of addictive activity reduce the value of each addictive act, they also
reduce the value of all alternatives to that act. That is, negative addictions
reduce the quality of life. As alcoholism develops, for example (and the
value of each individual drink drops), relationships with family, friends,
coworkers, and the drinker's general health also deteriorate. If, as alcoholism progresses, the rate of deterioration of the value of alternative
activities deteriorates as fast or faster than that of drinking itself, drinking
will remain the most highly valued of all available activities, or even gain
in relative value, as it loses in absolute value. As a character in Linda
Yablonski's novel *Junk* says, "However good or bad you feel, heroin
makes you feel better."[8] At low rates, choosing the addictive activity
increases an already high overall value; at high rates, choosing the addictive activity keeps an already low overall value from decreasing further.[9]

Positive addictions work in an opposite manner to negative ones. As
the rate of a positive addictive activity increases, the value of an individual episode increases as well; as the rate decreases, the value of an individual episode decreases as well. Such addictions require learning or
practice to attain high value: examples include listening to classical music,

[7] The distinction between negative and positive addictions comes from George J. Stigler
and Gary S. Becker, "De Gustibus Non Est Disputandum," *American Economic Review* 67
(1977): 76–90.
[8] Linda Yablonski, *The Story of Junk: A Novel* (New York: Ferrer, Straus, and Giroux, 1997),
as quoted in Sue Halpern, "The Awful Truth," *New York Review of Books*, September 25, 1997,
p. 13.
[9] Technically, as the rate increases the addictive activity changes from a positive reinforcer
to a negative reinforcer.

exercising, doing crossword puzzles, or collecting stamps. Most importantly, *social* activity is a *positive* addiction. As the rate of social activity increases, the value of each positively addictive act increases. If the value of any alternative to the act does not increase faster than that of the act, the act's increased value will cause further increases in its rate, which will, in turn, increase its value still further, and so on, resulting in the positive addictions we observe.

In the case of social activity, a child's appropriate social behavior must be externally reinforced in order to be maintained.[10] That is, a child must learn to behave appropriately in a given society. As we grow older, the more we engage in social activity, the more social support we get from other people in return. Experiments in my laboratory with undergraduate subjects have shown that socially cooperative behavior depends on the probability that it will be reciprocated by others.[11] Thus, social activity may be extrinsically reinforced.

Along with offering *extrinsic* reinforcement, social activity, when it forms a coherent pattern, is *intrinsically* of high value. As in the previous examples of positive addictions, like doing crossword puzzles, listening to classical music, engaging in sports, etc., social activity beyond a certain rate is performed for its own sake (i.e., frequently chosen over other activities). Yet, the less we engage in social activities, the more we retire into our own shells, the more difficult it becomes to start social activity again, and the less intrinsically valuable social activity becomes. The same holds for other positive addictions. For example, I have been skiing four times in my life, each separated far enough from the other times that I had to learn all over again how to ski. I never graduated from the beginner's slope. Needless to say, I do not enjoy skiing.

Although positive addictions develop in a manner opposite to negative ones, there is evidence that positive addictions are substitutable for negative addictions. I have proposed a theory of addiction, called *relative addiction theory*, which says that the most fundamental way (although not necessarily the only way or even the most effective way) to get rid of a negative addiction is to substitute a positive addiction for it.[12] Effecting such substitutions, however, is not a simple matter, since all during the recovery the particular negatively addictive act will be higher in value than the particular positively addictive act: the alcoholic will always prefer the local bar to dinner with his family. What is required, as in most acts of self-control, is for choices to be made between patterns of acts extending over time rather than between particular acts.

[10] Mary D. S. Ainsworth and John Bowlby, "An Ethological Approach to Personality Development," *American Psychologist* 46 (1991): 333–41.

[11] Forest Baker and Howard Rachlin, "Probability of Reciprocation in Prisoner's Dilemma Games," *Journal of Behavioral Decision Making* 14 (2001): 51–67.

[12] Howard Rachlin, "Four Teleological Theories of Addiction," *Psychonomic Bulletin and Review* 4 (1997): 462–73.

As in the example, in the previous section, of the CD with the missing
three minutes of music at the end, the value of the act at the beginning of
the sequence is *provisional*. The value of the first fifty-seven minutes of
listening to the hour-long symphony will depend on what happens during the last three minutes—even though those fifty-seven minutes are in
the past and presumably have already been experienced. The same would
be true for doing a crossword puzzle. My enjoyment of the puzzle depends strongly on whether I finish it. But my enjoyment or, very frequently, frustration, applies to the whole of the time I spend doing the
puzzle.[13] My choice to listen to the symphony or do the puzzle, therefore,
must be a choice to listen to the *whole* symphony or do the *whole* puzzle;
the value of these activities derives from the patterns of the activities, not
from the sums of the values of their parts.

VI. Unconditional Autonomy

Many of the philosophical difficulties with the concept of autonomy
come from insisting that we be able to classify a given act as unconditionally autonomous or unconditionally not autonomous before we know
what pattern the act is part of. The belief that we can classify particular
acts unconditionally comes from a cognitive view of behavior. In a cognitive model, everything you would want to know about a particular act
is given by the instantaneous state of the various internal mechanisms
that form the efficient cause of the act. If the state of those mechanisms
were known—either by inference from past and present behavior, or by
introspection by the behaving person—the value, the degree of autonomy, the purpose, the meaning, and the relevant context of the act would
also be known. But, from the viewpoint of teleological behaviorism, none
of these qualities can be known absolutely—all are provisional.[14]

Imagine that you see a snippet of film that shows a man swinging a
hammer. But what is he *actually* doing? Now consider the following alternative descriptions. He is:

(1) swinging a hammer
(2) hammering a nail
(3) joining one piece of wood to another
(4) building a floor
(5) building a house

[13] The test is whether, after discovering the missing three-minute final section of the CD,
I play the CD again. (I would not play it again; if you would, then what if six or nine or
twelve minutes were missing? At some point the whole CD must lose its value.)

[14] A probability is provisional in the same sense. A given probability can always change
depending on future events. But, like a probability, as more and more behavior is observed
the meaning of a particular act can be known better and better—by the observer as well as
(or better than) by the actor.

(6) providing shelter for his family
(7) supporting his family
(8) being a good husband and father
(9) being a good person

All of these may be valid descriptions of his behavior. Based on the snippet of film you saw, all you can say is that he is swinging the hammer. He might have been swinging it at someone's head. But if you said, "He's just swinging the hammer," someone else who saw more of the film might, with justice, say, "Yes, he's swinging the hammer, but what he's *really* doing is hammering a nail." A third person who has seen even more of the film might then correct the second in a similar way: "Yes, he's hammering a nail, but what he's *really* doing is building a floor." We can envision such a process until we get to a godlike observer who has sat through a film of virtually this man's entire life and can make the final judgment: "He's being a good person." To paraphrase Ovid (*Metamorphoses*, III): No one must be counted good until his last funeral rites are paid.

The important point is that all of the descriptions, listed from (1) through (9), are descriptions of the man's behavior. As you go down the list, more and more context is incorporated into the description, but that context is always behavioral. The final godlike observer need not look into the man's heart as long as he has looked at the complete film of the man's life. Then the observer can say, "He is a good man," without fear of contradiction—regardless of the state of the man's heart. The validity of any of the above descriptions may be settled by moving the camera back or by showing more film, earlier and later.

This teleological and behavioristic way of assessing an activity is different from the usual way of doing so. Usually, as you go down a list of possible descriptions or explanations, you are supposed to be going deeper and deeper into the man himself—deeper and deeper into his internal intentions, his internal consciousness, his nervous system, or his soul (where the soul is considered to be some nonmaterial, internal entity). In a sense, the usual conception has to be true: if the man is building a house, some internal mechanism must be causing his movements. Correspondingly, if a sound system is playing Beethoven's Fifth Symphony, there must be some mechanism that causes what we hear—AM, FM, LP, CD, or tape. But the mechanism is not the thing we are describing. For a sound system to be playing Beethoven's Fifth Symphony, Beethoven's Fifth Symphony must be coming out of the system, regardless of the mechanism. Similarly, for a man to support his family, he must support his family, regardless of the mechanism that prompts him to behave.

You might say that there is a difference between the man who intentionally swings a hammer and the man who accidently swings a hammer—even though the two men are behaving alike. You might also say that the difference resides inside them. But, again, while it is true that something inside of people must mediate behavioral differences, the difference between intention and accident *is* behavioral. The difference between a man purposely swinging a hammer and a man accidentally swinging a hammer can be resolved, not by looking inside him, but by looking at more of his behavior. A man accidentally swinging a hammer will not be hammering a nail or building a floor.

VII. CONDITIONAL AUTONOMY

A useful distinction between autonomous behavior and nonautonomous behavior can be based on the distinction between self-controlled and non-self-controlled (or impulsive) behavior. Such a distinction may help in attributing responsibility to people for their own actions. A person would then be deemed responsible for his actions to the degree that those actions were self-controlled. Attributing responsibility allows, in turn, the efficient construction of social contingencies of reward and punishment. But there would be no point in rewarding or punishing actions that cannot be controlled by reward and punishment. Therefore, to classify an act as autonomous, it must be controllable by its consequences.

Skinner called acts that are controllable by their consequences "operants." He distinguished operants from what he called "respondents," acts controlled by their antecedents. The antecedents to which Skinner referred were the classical environmental stimuli—the food powder injected into the mouth of a hungry dog causing salivation, the blow of a rubber hammer on the patellar tendon causing a knee jerk.[15]

Respondents were said to be *elicited*; operants were said to be *emitted*. A behavioral conception of unconditional autonomy, if such were possible, might rest on this distinction: emitted acts (acts controllable by their consequences) would be autonomous; elicited acts (acts controllable by their antecedents) would not be autonomous. The problem with this notion is that *any* act—even salivation, pupillary constriction, or heart rate— can be controlled, at least to some extent, by its consequences. Moreover, some acts, clearly controlled by their consequences (such as an alcoholic's drinking), would seem most usefully classified as nonautonomous.

The literature on addiction often refers to addiction as slavery. I believe that a useful definition of autonomy should take this commonsense notion into account. The addict is a slave, however, not because some inner

---

[15] Some critics of Skinner, including some philosophers, seem to believe that the postulation of such stimuli-response (S-R) connections was his entire goal. Their criticisms, if they are criticisms of the notion that psychology's goal is to track down every response to its immediately antecedent stimulus, should really be directed toward cognitive and physiological psychology. It is these psychologists who, if they cannot find an immediately antecedent stimulus for a response in the environment, undertake to search for one in the interior of the organism. And, if they cannot find one, they invent one and give it a name— such as willpower.

force is compelling each movement he makes. Reaching out for the glass, grasping it, lifting it to his mouth, are all physiologically voluntary acts, not reflexes. The addict is a slave because the reinforcement of his act is strong and immediate, however brief.

A person with a positive addiction, on the other hand, is not a slave. Once the long-term pattern of a positive addiction attains its high intrinsic value, each act that comprises that pattern is, I would say, an autonomous act. Each act has, by itself, no extrinsic reinforcement, immediate or delayed. Nor is it intrinsically reinforced; on the contrary, its immediate alternatives may be highly preferred to it. Its value is contingent on being embedded within a pattern of other acts. That is what makes it autonomous.

An unconditional autonomy, based merely on whether or not an act can be controlled by its consequences, would include virtually any individual act, including those acts society would want to classify as nonautonomous, and such an inclusive conception would therefore be useless. Realizing this, Skinner rejected the concept of autonomous actions entirely.

Is there a behavioral conception of autonomy that would make a useful social distinction between acts for which a person is responsible and acts for which a person is not responsible? To answer this question, we need to expand Skinner's operant/respondent classification from two to four kinds of acts: (1) *Respondents*, reflexes clearly attributable to an external stimulus; (2) *Emitted operants*, acts of high intrinsic value, like eating, that are done for their own sake; (3) *Reinforced operants*, acts, like paying for a loaf of bread, that are done not for their own sake, but for the sake of an extrinsic reinforcer; and (4) *Self-controlled acts*, acts, like pedaling on an exercise bicycle or refusing a drink, that are of low intrinsic value yet never extrinsically reinforced, which are nevertheless part of a pattern of acts of high intrinsic value (a healthy life or an active social life, for example). Acts in this last category are conditionally autonomous.

Aristotle drew a famous analogy between the pattern of an individual person's acts over time and the pattern of acts of a group of people. In *Posterior Analytics* (II, 19) he said that the pattern of acts (the universal) comes about through individual actions (the particulars) "like a rout in battle stopped by first one man making a stand and then another, until the original formation has been restored."[16] In a battle, one soldier alone knows that he cannot possibly survive the onslaught of a pursuing army. That soldier also knows that his action can potentially influence the actions of others and, therefore, establish a pattern of resistance. Similarly, in ordinary life, one night's abstinence from a bad habit would be futile against the pursuing army of temptations. It would be futile, that is, were it not for the connections in our behavior between one night and the

[16] Aristotle, *Posterior Analytics*, trans. E. M. Edghill, in Richard McKeon, ed., *The Basic Works of Aristotle* (New York: Random House, 1941).

next—were it not for our ability to organize our behavior into patterns extending over time (as a military formation extends over space). That is, some particular acts are not intrinsically valuable in themselves, but become valuable when massed into patterns (or habits).

I have argued that at least some of these patterns are valuable for society, as well as for the individual.[17] Bicycling to work rather than driving, for example, may be preferable in the long run for a person (in terms of health gained), as well as for society (in terms of pollution avoided), but it might not be preferred to driving in the short run (in terms of personal discomfort and energy expended). *Although particular acts of social cooperation may not be intrinsically valued by the particular person performing them, the pattern of acts, of which the individual acts are a part, may be intrinsically valuable to that person.* In other words, the problem of self-control and that of social control are intertwined. While patterns of behavior that are beneficial to society may also be intrinsically valuable for the individual person in the long run, the individual acts that comprise those patterns may not be intrinsically valuable and would not be chosen over their alternatives without extrinsic reinforcement (or punishment of their alternatives). From the viewpoint of teleological behaviorism, society's primary function, *vis-à-vis* its members, is to arrange contingencies of reinforcement and punishment so as to establish these beneficial patterns.

What then makes an act autonomous? A particular act is autonomous when it *would not* be chosen over its particular alternatives, but is part of an intrinsically valuable pattern of behavior that *would* be chosen over alternative patterns. The alcoholic, for example, might not refuse a particular drink but might at the same time prefer not to be an alcoholic. Thus, his refusal of the drink would be an autonomous act relative to his drinking the drink. How contingencies of reinforcement and punishment might best be arranged, so that people will pattern their behavior and not make decisions on a case-by-case basis, is an empirical question and the subject of my research on self-control.[18]

VIII. INTERNALIZATION

The teleological behavioral approach to autonomy is completely external. No particular internal processes are presupposed. The degree to which an act is autonomous does not depend on the actor's introspection or feeling of freedom, nor on the action or lack of action of any of the mechanisms in the boxes on the right side of Figure 1.[19]

---

[17] Howard Rachlin, "Altruism and Selfishness," *Behavioral and Brain Sciences* (forthcoming).

[18] Howard Rachlin, *The Science of Self-Control* (Cambridge, MA: Harvard University Press, 2000).

[19] It depends to some extent on the *perception* of freedom, but the perception is that of the observer (or that of the actor as an observer of the consequences of his own actions).

Consider the sequence of events as a complex pattern is learned—a girl learning to play the piano, for example. At first, each particular key press must be learned individually and reinforced by the teacher, but soon chords and chord sequences become learning units. Then, a whole musical piece may be reinforced—by the teacher's approval, by the girl's parents, by the applause of her audience. Finally, perhaps, piano playing becomes intrinsically reinforced; that is, the girl may reach a stage at which playing the piano becomes valuable to her in itself. She plays the piano even when all extrinsic reinforcers are removed. Reaching this point (and she certainly might not reach it—even, or perhaps especially, if she becomes a professional musician) does not mean that reinforcement has become internalized. It does not mean that her playing is reinforced by internal applause, internal pats on her internal back, internal satisfaction, or internal stimulation of some "pleasure center" in her brain. It means that, when offered repeated choices between playing a whole sonata (with no extrinsic reinforcement) and other valued activities requiring equal time (say, watching a TV program or reading a magazine article), she frequently chooses to play the sonata.

From the viewpoint of teleological behaviorism, moreover, the intrinsic value of her piano playing refers not to what she *would do* now, at this particular point in time, but to what she *does* in the long run, including what she does in the future. Thus, the value of any pattern of acts is always provisional. Like the value of the first fifty-seven minutes of the symphony on the CD in the example presented previously, the value of the girl's piano playing depends on future events, as well as past events. The moral implication of this conception is that future behavior may have the power to redeem past behavior—by altering its context. Whether a professional pianist's present concert (followed by applause and money) is intrinsically valued by her will depend on her future, as well as her past, behavior (whether she continues to play the piano in her retirement, for example).

Most psychologists, including many who call themselves behaviorists, would not accept this behavioral view of reinforcement. They believe that the processes of reinforcement and punishment may be internalized. Positive internal events such as satisfaction are supposed to reinforce internal responses; negative internal events such as guilt are supposed to punish internal responses. The whole left part of Figure 1 is transposed into an internal representation within the right part. This internal mechanism is then held to be responsible for autonomous behavior, understood in terms of some form of self-regulation, self-governance, or self-direction.

The concept of internal reinforcement and punishment has both logical and empirical problems. As early as 1896, John Dewey argued that con-

---

However, the observer's perception in this case is his *overt* behavior of classifying acts as more or less autonomous.

cepts such as *stimulus*, *response*, and the then-recently postulated *reinforcement* had meaning only in terms of input to and output from the organism as a whole.[20] Inside the organism there are physiological events such as nerve firings, which could respond to prior nerve firings and stimulate other nerve firings, but there is no clear point (unless there is an homunculus) at which stimuli on one side could be divided from responses on the other.[21]

More recently, philosopher Rowland Stout has developed this critique, arguing against what he calls "the internal shift," that is, the process of taking concepts defined originally in terms of behavior of whole organisms over time, reifying them, and projecting the reified object inside the organism.[22]

Despite their logical problems, the concepts of self-reinforcement and self-punishment have survived and even thrived in psychology. As one would suspect, they are very difficult to test. Since self-reinforcement and self-punishment are supposed to occur wholly within the person, they are impossible to observe. By definition, satisfaction is a pleasant emotion and guilt is a painful one. But there is no evidence that these emotions can reinforce or punish behavior—reinforce the refusal of a drink or punish the taking of it, for example. An alcoholic is more likely to take another drink to get rid of the guilt of having taken the previous one. Like slapping yourself on the hand or hitting your head with the heel of your hand, or even kicking yourself, guilt may serve to enhance the feedback—to remind you that you did, indeed, have the drink. But guilt does not punish the taking of the drink, as an electric shock punishes a rat's pressing a lever in a Skinner box. If an alcoholic could press a button, *before* he had the drink, so as to deliver an electric shock *after* he had the drink, that would be an effective form of self-control. This is similar to the way Antabuse (a drug that makes drinking painful) works. But, just as alcoholics generally refuse to take Antabuse, the alcoholic would probably not press the button. Once the drink is taken, pressing the button would be futile. It would be no more effective as punishment than slapping yourself on the hand.

Some people say that they reinforce their own writing behavior, for example, by keeping a bowl of peanuts on the table and eating one after each page. "Self-reinforcement" of this kind may actually help a person to write. If so, how does it work? The problem for the theorist is to explain why the peanut is ever withheld. A reinforcer must be more valuable than

---

[20] John Dewey, "The Reflex-Arc Concept in Psychology," *Psychological Review* 3 (1896): 357–70.

[21] It would be possible to draw a line around the brain and then to speak of stimuli to the brain and responses of it, but all theories of internal reinforcement proposed thus far have reinforcement taking place *within* the brain.

[22] Rowland Stout, *Things That Happen Because They Should* (Oxford: Oxford University Press, 1996).

the reinforced act. If peanuts can reinforce writing a page, eating a peanut would have to be more valuable than writing a page; otherwise, why not eat a peanut after each paragraph, after each sentence, after each word, or, since it is preferred to writing, why not eat a peanut before writing or instead of writing? Writing may well be extrinsically reinforced—by fame, money, tenure. But can it be reinforced by peanut eating? If the other rewards were taken away, and if writing an article were not intrinsically reinforcing, could such an activity be reinforced by eating peanuts?

In an attempt to study how self-reinforcement actually works, a group of dieters were invited to "reinforce" their own weight loss by taking money from a dish placed next to the scale at weekly weigh-ins. Sure enough, the dieters who did this lost more weight than another group with no dish of money next to the scale. However, a third group, whose members actually put money into the dish proportional to the amount of weight lost—and, thus, if self-punishment were possible, would have been "punishing" themselves for weight lost—actually lost the most weight.[23] The true reinforcers in this experiment were social approval and health gain, not the few dollars taken from a dish. Taking the money served as vivid feedback—it underscored the behavior. Taking the money was a way of saying, "Yes, I did lose the weight and will get the reward." Putting money into the dish evidently served as even more vivid feedback. Thus, with all of its logical difficulties, the concept of self-reinforcement apparently labors under empirical difficulties, too.

IX. Objections to a Behavioral View of Autonomy

There is something admittedly unsatisfying about this wholly behavioral view of autonomy—as there is about behavioral explanations in general. However, I would like to emphasize that the usual objection to behaviorism—that two people may do the same thing, but do it for different reasons—does not apply to teleological behaviorism. Even though two people may be doing the same thing at this very moment, if they are doing it for different reasons, they will be doing different things before and after this moment.

I was once asked by prominent neuropsychologist Jeffrey Gray, "What is the difference between two awake individuals, one of them stone deaf, who are both sitting immobile in a room in which a recording is playing a Mozart string quartet?"[24] The answer to that question is, "One of them is hearing the music and one is not." But what does it mean, to a behaviorist, to hear something? To be a normally hearing person means that the

---

[23] Leonides Castro and Howard Rachlin, "Self-Reward, Self-Monitoring, and Self-Punishment as Feedback in Weight Control," *Behavior Therapy* 11 (1980): 38–48.
[24] As quoted in John Staddon, *The New Behaviorism: Mind, Mechanism, and Society* (Philadelphia, PA: Psychology Press, 2001), 177.

present act is part of a series of actions significantly correlated with sounds; to be deaf means that no such correlation exists. The actions (or inaction) of the hearing and deaf individuals at the present moment are overlapping points in two entirely different correlations. Asking Gray's question is like asking, "What is the difference between Picasso and a kindergarten child who both at this moment put a drop of yellow in the upper left corner of a painting?" The difference, of course, lies in what they do before and after this moment.

But behavioral explanations are still unsatisfying. They seem circular — not just teleological but tautological. I claim, though, that behavioral explanations of behavior need not be circular, whereas physiological or cognitive or even spiritual explanations of behavior are often circular. Let me begin to defend this claim with a little bit of history — that of the concept of reinforcement.

The unadorned concept of reinforcement is, in itself, circular: If a reinforcer is made contingent on a particular act, it will increase the frequency of that act. Question: What is a reinforcer? Answer: Anything that increases the frequency of an act it is contingent upon. Attempts to break out of this circularity have defined reinforcement in nonbehavioral terms: a reinforcer is anything that feels satisfying, or anything that reduces a biological need, or anything that reduces a drive, or anything that stimulates a certain area of the brain. However satisfying these definitions may be, none of them has held up (although with the development of magnetic resonance imaging [MRI] machines, the last one is having a comeback). All of these definitions either have fatal exceptions or become circular as satisfactions, needs, or drives rapidly multiply to the point where there is one for each reinforcer. In the end, all of these theories have proved to be unsatisfying — at least for any practical purposes.

The one reinforcement theory that has held up under experiment is David Premack's wholly behavioral theory. According to Premack, all possible actions of a given animal may be ranked in order of value.[25] The ranking between any two actions is determined by a choice test in which the animal has free access to both. The activity the animal spends most time doing is ranked higher in value. Then, if a higher ranked activity is made contingent on a lower ranked activity, the lower activity will increase in rate (be reinforced); if a lower ranked activity is made contingent on a higher one, the higher activity will decrease in rate (be punished). For example, a hungry rat, given a free "choice test" among eating, running in a wheel, and pressing a lever, will choose eating over wheel running and wheel running over lever pressing. Thus, eating is more valuable than wheel running, which is more valuable than lever pressing. With this value hierarchy established by the choice test, the effect of

[25] David Premack, "Reinforcement Theory," in David Levine, ed., *Nebraska Symposium on Motivation* (Lincoln: University of Nebraska Press, 1965), 123–79.

contingencies is predictable: higher valued acts will reinforce lower valued acts; lower valued acts will punish higher valued acts. Consequently,
if a lever press serves to release a locked wheel (allowing the rat to run),
wheel running will reinforce lever pressing (will increase its rate), while
if eating a food pellet serves to motorize the wheel (forcing the rat to run),
wheel running will punish eating (will decrease its rate). The degree of
reinforcement or punishment will depend on the difference in choice-test
value. In other words, behavior in one situation (the free choice test) is
used to determine a set of values, which is then used to predict behavior
in another situation. Because the choice test, on the one hand, and the
contingency, on the other, are independent of each other, Premack's theory
is not circular. Value, in Premack's theory, has only a behavioral meaning,
not a physiological or introspective one. However unsatisfying it may
have seemed initially, this theory has held up under experimental testing
and has become quite satisfying to those of us who work with it.[26]

X. Conclusion

From the viewpoint of teleological behaviorism, the autonomy of an act
is the degree to which the act is part of a pattern of acts, each done not for
its own sake, but for the sake of the pattern as a whole. Autonomy, thus
conceived, is not a property of the individual act or a feeling within the
actor. It is, rather, a matter of perception—not the actor's perception, but
rather the perception made by an observer. But we make such a perception for a reason. Why should we want to discriminate between a person's autonomous acts and those that are compelled? The answer, I believe,
is that such a distinction is useful to society in attributing responsibility
and in distributing rewards and punishments. I am not saying that there
is, or should be, any one-to-one correspondence between autonomy and
responsibility on the one hand, or between responsibility and reward and
punishment on the other. But I am saying that whether a given act is or
is not an autonomous act must be decided on the basis of the needs of an
efficient social and political system, and not on the basis of either some
property of the particular act or on some state of the actor—spiritual,
volitional, cognitive, or physiological—unobservable to other people.

Philosophers are attracted to the concept of internal autonomy because
they think that it is a good thing for people to be free to choose their
behavior, or free to act without internal compulsion, or free to set moral

---

[26] Premack's method of determining value is a primitive version of the economist's
"revealed-preference" method of determining utility functions; the economist observes choices
under two or three sets of constraints, then uses these observations to derive a utility
function. The utility function is then used to predict choice under a new set of constraints.
If the prediction turns out to be wrong, the economist reexamines the constraints or rede-
termines the utility function. The method is wholly behavioral. The utility function is just a
summary of behavioral observations. It may have no coherent internal representation.

laws for themselves. But why are philosophers attracted to such a concept, and in what sense is autonomous behavior a good thing? Is it good because it just feels good to act freely, or because one internal mechanism rather than another underlies the act? Or is autonomy a good thing because it is useful to society to classify a person's actions as autonomous or not? To argue for the latter is not to imply that autonomy is a wholly arbitrary social classification, having nothing to do with individual behavior. Moreover, autonomous acts are not always good; first-degree murder, after all, implies autonomy. Nor are nonautonomous acts always bad. People may act impulsively (do what they prefer at the moment) and still act well. Nevertheless, as in the case of first-degree murder, it is useful for society to distinguish between discrete acts done for their own sake, or for the sake of immediate rewards, and acts done for the sake of more abstract values and distant rewards. In other words, it is useful for society to distinguish between virtuous or vicious acts that, on the one hand, are performed because they are immediately rewarded (or high in immediate value) and virtuous or vicious acts that, on the other hand, are performed because they are part of a highly valued, temporally extended pattern of acts.

Psychology, State University of New York at Stony Brook

THE PARADOX OF GROUP AUTONOMY*

By Christopher Heath Wellman

Introduction

This essay explores the prospects of developing a satisfying account of group autonomy without rejecting value-individualism. That is, I will examine whether one can adequately explain the moral reasons to respect a group's claim to self-determination while insisting that only individual persons are of ultimate moral value.

I divide this essay into three main sections. First, I explain my understanding of the value of individual autonomy and the implications this has for group autonomy. Next, I review three possible accounts of group autonomy, featuring value-collectivism, individual autonomy, and individual well-being. In the end I find none of these approaches to be fully adequate; thus, I conclude the third and final section by introducing what I label the "Paradox of Group Autonomy."

I. The Value of Autonomy

There is widespread agreement that individuals enjoy a privileged position of moral dominion over their self-regarding affairs. It is not always clear when any given action is purely self-regarding, of course, but many people believe that we should be allowed to choose freely when our behavior is not harmful to others. One justification given for this view of individual self-determination is that it fosters overall well-being. This justification rests upon three plausible observations: each person is likely to be (1) the most knowledgeable about, (2) the most interested in, and (3) the best positioned to promote her own welfare.[1] In light of these three considerations, it seems reasonable to conclude that, in the absence of extenuating circumstances, each agent is likely to fare best when she is given authority over her self-regarding affairs. Thus, if we wish to promote overall or aggregate well-being, a sensible strategy would be to design the criminal law and other institutions so that each person is treated as sovereign over her own affairs. In short, considerations like

* I benefited greatly in writing this essay from a discussion at the Social Philosophy and Policy Center, Bowling Green State University. I am also grateful for the written comments that I received from Andrew Altman, David Copp, Jonathan Malino, Russ Shafer-Landau, James Stacey Taylor, Carl Wellman, and especially Ellen Frankel Paul.
[1] These observations are noted and discussed by John Stuart Mill in *On Liberty* (1859; reprint, Indianapolis, IN: Hackett, 1978).

these explain why we should treat each person as enjoying what we might call a "right to autonomy."[2]

Although I disagree with neither the premises nor the conclusion of this consequentialist defense of individual dominion, I do not think that this approach provides the only, or even the primary, reasons to respect a person's autonomy. I ultimately favor a nonconsequentialist account of the value of autonomy, for two reasons. First, I am convinced that individuals retain their positions of dominion even when their decision-making clearly does not maximize overall happiness. If we derive the value of autonomy exclusively from consequences, however, then it remains valuable only when and to the extent that it produces those consequences. Imagine, for example, that Jezebel, if left to her own devices, would quit her job and move to Santa Fe, where she would spend her time (and life savings) trying to pen "the Great American novel." Suppose also that anyone who even casually knows Jezebel and her limited literary talents would recognize that such a move is a recipe for disaster. (Or, for a more pedestrian example, suppose that Jezebel is making these huge sacrifices to move to Santa Fe to be with a man for whom she is profoundly ill suited.) My view is that no one may rightfully interfere with Jezebel's plans, even if it is abundantly clear that this interference would produce better consequences. That is to say, even if all of the evidence suggests that Jezebel's move would be horribly detrimental to her well-being, she remains at liberty to make this move because it is *her life*. Of course, there is nothing wrong with trying to persuade Jezebel of the folly of such a move, but one may not forcibly interfere if one's best efforts at persuasion fail to convince her.

The second reason that I am dissatisfied with consequentialist explanations of the value of autonomy is that they seem ill equipped to capture the sense in which our duties concerning autonomy are owed *to* the individual whose autonomy is in question. As Tom L. Beauchamp and LeRoy Walters put it: "To respect the autonomy of . . . self-determining agents is to recognize them as *entitled* to determine their own destiny."[3] According to the consequentialist, the reason that a government, for example, ought not to force me to practice a certain religion is because a policy of religious coercion is unlikely to produce the best overall results. The real objection to such a policy, however, seems to me to be that this interference with my religious self-determination treats *me* wrongly. The chief problem with such an intrusion into individual autonomy is not that

---

[2] Given that *autonomy* can mean very different things to different authors (including those in this volume), it is important for me to make clear that when I write of a person enjoying autonomy, I mean that she has a right to act without external interference. Thus, in this essay, "group autonomy" refers to a group's right to be free from interference in determining its own affairs.

[3] Tom L. Beauchamp and LeRoy Walters, *Contemporary Issues in Bioethics*, 4th ed. (Belmont, CA: Wadsworth, 1994), 23 (emphasis in original).

it leads to a world containing less happiness; it is that a person's privileged position of moral dominion would be violated. Thus, I believe that no matter how the calculations ultimately come out, the balance of consequences is, at best, beside the most important moral point. If happiness would be maximized by disrespecting autonomy, then I would typically favor respecting autonomy to the detriment of overall well-being. If happiness would be maximized by respecting autonomy, then this strikes me as a lovely coincidence, or perhaps even a buttressing consideration, but not the core argument in favor of respecting autonomy.

In fairness to advocates of the consequentialist approach, I should acknowledge that some theorists, including R. M. Hare and Russell Hardin, have designed sophisticated arguments to counter objections like the two that I expressed above.[4] For example, in response to my first concern, Hare suggests that, ironically, those who wish to maximize overall happiness should, most of the time, not aim to do so. Rather, because of both our limited information and our tendencies toward personal bias, we are better off, Hare reasons, when we adhere to a strict set of rules. Applying this general line of reasoning to the particular issue of autonomy, Hare might say that, even though there clearly would be cases in which we could maximize happiness by interfering with the self-regarding behavior of others, the best strategy for maximizing total welfare over the long haul would be to endorse a blanket prohibition against paternalistic meddling. Put in terms of Jezebel's move, for example, Hare's logic suggests that, while one might in fact produce more good than harm by interfering with Jezebel's move, it is better if one never even considers interfering because, more often than not, one would wrongly interfere. Thus, because allowing the discretion to interfere would predictably lead to numerous cases of harmful meddling (and because the harms from meddling would outweigh the gains that we could reasonably expect to result from any instances of beneficial interference), sophisticated consequentialists would favor prohibiting all interference. With such a prohibition, consequentialists can address my first worry that the autonomy of people such as Jezebel ought to be respected even in instances when disrespect for autonomy would apparently maximize overall well-being.

As for my second concern, that consequentialism cannot accommodate the conviction that our duties regarding autonomy are owed *to* those whose autonomy is in question, theorists such as Hardin have developed an account of rights that explains why we should behave *as if* our duties correlate to the rights of others. Hardin proposes a conception of rights derived from consequentialism, which he believes accords well with our convictions about the strength of rights. Emphasizing the limits of human reasoning, Hardin follows Hare in suggesting that enlightened conse-

---

[4] See R. M. Hare, *Moral Thinking* (Oxford: Oxford University Press, 1981); and Russell Hardin, *Morality Within the Limits of Reason* (Chicago, IL: University of Chicago Press, 1988).

quentialists would regularly *not* aim to maximize happiness when deliberating about how to act. Owing to both the inefficiencies of performing
the calculations and the likelihood that we would often reach the wrong
conclusion, Hardin holds that we would better realize good consequences
if we followed certain rules. In particular, Hardin thinks that we should
act as if people have certain rights to self-determination.

Of course, any consequentialist who recommends an allegiance to rules
faces a familiar problem. Exceptional cases inevitably arise in which de-
viating from the rules will obviously and dramatically increase overall
happiness (for example, in a case where one could save many lives
by stealing medicine from a pharmacist). These glaring exceptions are
thought to be dilemmatic for rule-consequentialists for two reasons. First,
if they advocate breaking the rules, then they are really just closet act-
consequentialists who appear, once again, saddled with the unpalatable
conclusions that so often drive them to embrace the rules initially.[5] Second, if they express an unwavering allegiance to the rules, then it is hard
to see how they are genuinely consequentialists (as opposed to, say, "rule-
worshippers"). Translating this dilemma into the language of rights, it
appears that consequentialists cannot fully embrace rights while remaining consequentialists. Ultimately, even if only in exceptionally rare cases,
anyone whose appreciation for rights stems solely from the consequences
must choose between either abandoning her defense of rights or turning
her back on consequentialism. Consider, for example, the rights of the
pharmacist whom I mentioned above. If a theorist recommends stealing
from the pharmacist, then she appears to give short shrift to the pharmacist's property rights; but if the theorist prohibits such stealing, then it
is not clear to what extent she remains a consequentialist.

Interestingly, Hardin acknowledges that consequentialists face such a
choice, but he denies that this choice is dilemmatic. Hardin argues that
there need be no regrets about remaining true to consequentialism because our convictions regarding rights do not entail that they trump all
consequential considerations, no matter how grave or weighty. Instead,
Hardin argues that unbiased reflection on our pretheoretic convictions
reveals that, while we certainly do not believe that our rights are vulnerable to the everyday ebb and flow of utility maximization, neither do we
think that they are so powerful as to trump all conceivable consequences.
(Indeed, even Robert Nozick, for many people the "poster-theorist" of
nonconsequentialist accounts of rights, stops short of insisting that these

---

[5] I should explain my use, here, of the term *rule-consequentialism*. As I understand it, there
are (at least) two ways of being a rule-consequentialist, depending upon whether one
focuses upon standards of rightness of acts or maxims for action-guidance. R. M. Hare, for
instance, is an act-consequentialist with respect to his standard of the rightness of acts, but
a rule-consequentialist regarding the maxims that he recommends for action. For the purposes of this discussion, I understand rule-consequentialists to be all those who (regardless
of their standards of right action) recommend following rules as a matter of action-guidance.

side constraints [that is, rights] are perfectly general and absolute. In his famous footnote in *Anarchy, State, and Utopia*, he acknowledges: "The question of whether these side constraints are absolute, or whether they may be violated in order to avoid catastrophic moral horror . . . is one I hope largely to avoid.")[6] In other words, most of us believe that rights are extremely valuable normative advantages, which protect our important interests from the vagaries of group efficiency and other forms of consequential maximization, but few think that rights provide perfectly general and absolute protection even in the most extreme circumstances.

Hardin's characterization of rights is crucial because it matches perfectly the type of account that a suitably sophisticated consequentialism is able to generate. To see this, notice that Hardin breaks from Hare by recommending that we be prepared to deviate from the standard rules in extraordinary circumstances. Hardin does not recommend breaking the rules whenever the agent thinks that it might maximize happiness, nor does he suggest (as Hare seems to) that the best way to maximize utility is by flatly refusing to ever consider the consequences. Instead, Hardin advocates cultivating a general but defeasible disposition to follow the rules. As he puts it:

> [T]he reason for not violating relevant institutional rules in practice in particular cases is related to the reasons for having them in the first place: the costs of setting up the devices for deciding on when to violate the rules are too great to be justified by the gains from violation. When this conclusion seems not to follow in a particular case, then we may institutionally, as we do individually, resolve the case against the rules.[7]

Transcribing to rights this prescription of fidelity to rules, we see that the account of rights that Hardin recommends provides individuals with general, but not absolute, protection against the concerns of utility. This is significant, of course, because it frees Hardin from the awkward counterexamples that have so often dogged consequentialists.[8] Indeed, if Hardin is right about our pretheoretic intuitions concerning rights, then the shoe is now on the other foot: Whereas those who champion our inviolable rights have traditionally concocted thought experiments to show that consequentialists cannot fully respect our fundamental rights, these same rights advocates are now put on the defensive for their untenable assertion that our rights are invulnerable to even the most extreme po-

---

[6] Robert Nozick, *Anarchy, State, and Utopia* (New York: Basic Books, 1974), 30 n.

[7] Hardin, *Morality Within the Limits of Reason*, 79.

[8] A standard counterexample invoked against consequentialists is that they would have to condone punishing the innocent whenever doing so would benefit the overall community. See, for example, H. J. McCloskey, "A Non-Utilitarian Approach to Punishment," *Inquiry* 8 (1965): 239–55.

tential consequences.[9] (Yet, if they are willing to admit that rights do not necessarily trump all conceivable appeals to consequences, then it is hard to see how their account differs from Hardin's.)

Returning to autonomy, we can see how the preceding analysis sets the stage for a substantially improved consequentialist account. Sophisticated consequentialists are now in a position to make two claims. First, they can suggest that we should allow others to choose their own courses of action even when there is ample evidence to suggest that their choices will not bring about the best consequences. And, second, in all but the most extraordinary circumstances, consequentialism directs us to act as if we owe duties of forbearance to various individuals, because it instructs us to behave as if people have rights that give them discretion over their own affairs. In other words, consequentialists can consistently recommend that we should act as if the moral rights that are falsely posited by commonsense morality were genuine.

Although I consider these revisions to be marked improvements, they are not enough to convert me to consequentialism. Put briefly, I remain uncomfortable with all approaches that derive the value of autonomy from consequences, because such approaches can, at best, suggest that autonomy should be regarded *as if* it were a basic value; they can never value autonomy for its own sake. This type of indirect approach strikes me as problematic because, as Bernard Williams famously observed, it involves "one thought too many."[10] To see why a version of Williams's objection is applicable here, notice that the sophisticated consequentialist's position on autonomy essentially reduces to the following: (1) The goal of maximizing well-being, when combined with (2) the limits of human reasoning, generates (3) a recipe for action-guidance that matches our convictions about when autonomy should be respected. The problem that lingers, even if one grants that (3) follows from the combination of (1) and (2), is that we should not have to invoke (2) to get (3). The importance of individual autonomy does not depend upon this incidental consideration, and consequentialism can be criticized (indeed, rejected, I think) because it must rely upon this unrelated consideration in order to generate a plausible version of action-guidance.

To appreciate my distaste for the indirect approach utilized by consequentialists such as Hare and Hardin, imagine that humans developed in ways that made us both much more knowledgeable and much less biased about the affairs of others. In short, suppose that our reasoning capacity were not so limited. Under these admittedly counterfactual conditions,

[9] Given how routinely consequentialists are criticized for not treating rights as absolute, it is striking how few rights theorists commit themselves to any absolute rights. One rights theorist who does treat (some) rights as perfectly absolute is Alan Gewirth, "Are There Any Absolute Rights?" *Philosophical Quarterly* 31, no. 122 (1981): 1–16.

[10] Bernard Williams, "Persons, Character, and Morality," in Bernard Williams, *Moral Luck: Philosophical Papers, 1973–1980* (Cambridge: Cambridge University Press, 1981), 18.

consequentialists would apparently have no reason to recommend acting as if others are entitled to direct their self-regarding affairs. In my view, however, expanding the limits of human reasoning would in no way jeopardize our privileged position of dominion over our own lives, because *our* personal sovereignty has nothing to do with the cognitive capacities of *others*. Rather, autonomy strikes me as a fundamental value. Irrespective of the results, we are entitled to be the authors of our own lives because they are our own—we own them, so to speak.

Now, one might object to the foregoing thought experiment for its use of radically counterfactual conditions. That their theory generates awkward conclusions for imaginary beings who are unlike us is no problem for consequentialists, because theories of morality should be evaluated strictly in terms of their application to existing moral agents. As Hardin notes: "If we get a moral theory that is compelling for our own world, we should be delighted at the success and not worry whether it would be compelling in some fanciful alternative world."[11] It only stands to reason, this objection continues, that the content of morality would vary in accordance with the features of those who are bound by it. (Indeed, to propose an extreme example, perhaps there would be no morality whatsoever if humans were changed so that we no longer had any interests.) Thus, why criticize consequentialism for its implication that autonomy's value would diminish if humans were different?

While I certainly appreciate the general admonition that we ought to be wary of misusing counterfactual thought experiments, I do not think that this objection is applicable in this particular case. The counterfactual thought experiment that I concoct here strikes me as apt and illuminating because the human feature that I imagine to be altered (i.e., our reasoning capacity) is unrelated to autonomy. I concede that some of the dictates of morality might change if the limits of human reason were eliminated, but it is hard to see why we should be any less entitled to determine the course of our own lives. Thus, I hold that the counterfactual that I have utilized in this particular thought experiment is not misleading. On the contrary, it reveals why consequentialism's account of the value of autonomy is misguided.

Before concluding this critique of the consequentialist account of the value of autonomy, I need to acknowledge how restricted in scope my critique has been. Throughout this section, I have assumed that the consequentialist is interested in maximizing only well-being, where well-being is not understood to include autonomy. Consequentialists come in many shapes and sizes, however, and some (partly in response to the types of objections that we have been reviewing here) stress that a person's well-being is partly constituted by her autonomy, or even that autonomy is among the intrinsic goods that must be considered when

---

[11] Hardin, *Morality Within the Limits of Reason*, 25.

determining the right action. Although I think that these attempts to appreciate more fully the value of autonomy are important improvements, they are not enough because they still cannot explain relational duties. In other words, while I think that sophisticated consequentialists are to be applauded for the pluralism that they embrace, their pluralism does not go far enough. We need a pluralism not just within but extending beyond consequentialism.

The chief reason why no autonomy-related amendments within consequentialism will ultimately suffice is because agents are *entitled* to their self-determination, and *entitlement* is a fundamentally deontological notion that cannot be fully cashed out in consequentialist terms. Thus, no matter how much one tinkers with either the action-guidance or the roster of intrinsic values within consequentialism, it will remain ill equipped to capture an essential feature of autonomy. In other words, even if a consequentialist can explain why we ought not interfere with Jezebel's self-regarding behavior (either because one should adopt a general rule against such interference or because autonomy is among the goods to be maximized), a consequentialist cannot adequately explain that we owe it *to* Jezebel not to interfere because she is *entitled* to live her own life.[12]

Although I insist that the full story of autonomy cannot be told without invoking deontology, I do not mean to suggest that consequences are morally irrelevant, or that the deontological reasons that we have to respect an agent's self-determination can never be outweighed by competing reasons generated by consequential considerations. In this regard, I join Hardin in arguing that autonomy is not an unrestricted sovereign. By agreeing with Hardin that autonomy does not necessarily trump all appeals to consequences, and yet, by maintaining that autonomy is a basic source of moral reasons, I regard myself as positing a pluralistic account reminiscent of the approach to ethics advanced by W. D. Ross.[13] That is, I conceive of autonomy as a basic moral value, which provides others with deontological moral reasons not to interfere with one's self-regarding behavior, irrespective of the expected consequences of such interference. Of course, nothing about insisting upon the deontological nature of autonomy requires one to deny that consequences also matter. Thus, it is always possible that the potential consequences of (non)interference generate sufficient moral reasons to outweigh the reasons against interference that stem from autonomy. Finally, I must confess that, like

---

[12] To appreciate the essentially deontological nature of autonomy, consider the analogous case of promise-keeping. Consequentialists can give very sophisticated explanations for why we should keep our promises. Indeed, they can even explain why we should keep our promises in cases where we could maximize well-being by breaking them. But consequentialists cannot fully capture the sense in which the promisor owes it *to* the promisee to keep the promise, because consequentialism can adequately explain neither why the promisor owes something *to* the promisee nor how the promisee would be *wronged* by the broken promise.

[13] W. D. Ross, *The Right and the Good* (Oxford: Oxford University Press, 1930).

Ross, I have no fully codified algorithm that specifies precisely when moral reasons springing from autonomy prevail over competing reasons.

Having explained consequentialism's inability to capture accurately the value of individual autonomy, let us now turn to group autonomy. The first thing we must do in developing our account is to distinguish between two possible concepts of group autonomy. To appreciate the difference between these two concepts, first consider a country that does not allow women to vote in national elections or a municipality that prohibits blacks from living on a given side of the railroad tracks. I can understand why someone might say that such a country disrespects the group autonomy of women or that such a city disrespects the group autonomy of blacks. After all, individuals are discriminated against on the basis of their membership in a given group, and it seems plausible to suggest that all members of the group suffer, even those women who do not care to vote and those blacks who are not interested in living on the prohibited side of the tracks. However, without diminishing the importance of these types of discrimination, I want to stress that these cases do not constitute restrictions on *group autonomy* as I understand the term here.

For the purposes of this essay, I conceive group autonomy to be something that can be exercised by a collective *as a whole*, rather than individually by persons in a group. Thus, on my understanding of group autonomy, examples might include the right of a corporation to choose its retirement policies, the right of a chess club to set its membership dues, the right of a condominium association to accept or reject the sale of a unit to a prospective buyer, the right of a Native American Indian tribe to choose which language will be spoken in its schools, the right of a country to accept or reject an offer to merge with another country, and the right of a territorially concentrated group to secede from its country. All of these examples are potential cases of group autonomy as I use the term here, insofar as they involve groups *qua* groups determining their own affairs. Group autonomy exists when the group as a whole, rather than the individuals within the group, stands in the privileged position of dominion over the affairs of the group.

Having specified what I mean by group autonomy, we can now apply the lesson of the preceding discussion to groups in particular. The fundamental point, thus far, has been that we have deontological moral reasons to respect an agent's autonomy. The moral duty that we have not to interfere in Jezebel's affairs is a duty we owe *to Jezebel*, rather than some general, freestanding duty (owed to humanity? to no one? to the cosmos?) to maximize overall well-being. Extending this insight to groups, it seems as though any autonomy-based duties regarding collectives will be owed either to the group or perhaps to the members of the group. If we have a duty not to interfere with a chess club's plan to increase its membership dues, for example, then this duty is *owed to* the group. That is to say, the group's autonomy has a basic value, from which two things follow: (1) we might have a duty not to interfere with the group's self-determination, even if interfering would maximize overall well-being; and (2) even if it turns out that not interfering would maximize aggregate welfare, the chief problem with interfering would be that it violates the dominion of the group. These conclusions cohere with my pretheoretic intuitions. After all, the principal reason why the United States may not forcibly annex Canada, for instance, would seemingly have to be that such aggrandizement would treat Canada and/or Canadians wrongly. I will spend the remainder of this essay showing that it is remarkably difficult to offer theoretical support for these pretheoretic convictions.

II. Theoretical Explanations of Group Autonomy

As I see it, there are three salient, potential avenues open to someone who seeks to explain group autonomy. These possibilities invoke value-collectivism, individual autonomy, or individual well-being. In this section I will argue that none of these options is able to generate an account of group autonomy that coheres with all of our core convictions.

Let us begin by considering value-collectivism. The easiest and most seamless way to establish that group autonomy is perfectly analogous to individual autonomy is to suggest that groups are normatively analogous to individuals. That is, perhaps groups and individual persons enjoy the same positions of dominion over their own affairs simply because there is no morally relevant difference between the two. Although I am attracted to this position for the convenient way in which it supplies the theoretical building blocks for a satisfying account of group autonomy, I must confess that I find this position to be, prima facie, implausible. Indeed, I think that Michael Hartney puts the point nicely when he suggests the following:

> [P]eople generally believe that communities are important because of their contribution to the well-being of individuals. Such a view is part of what might be called value-individualism: only the lives of individual human beings have ultimate value, and collective entities derive their value from their contribution to the lives of individual human beings. The opposite view we might call 'value collectivism': the view that a collective entity can have value independently of its contribution to the well-being of individual human beings. Such a position is counter-intuitive, and the burden of proof rests upon anyone who wishes to defend it.[14]

Thus, unless I can supply a compelling explanation as to why groups, like individuals, have ultimate value, it strikes me as inappropriate to suggest

[14] Michael Hartney, "Some Confusions Concerning Collective Rights," *Canadian Journal of Law and Jurisprudence* 4, no. 2 (1991): 297.

that group autonomy is morally equivalent to individual autonomy. Of course, there has been no lack of theorists who argue on behalf of value-collectivism, but I know of no one who does so successfully. For instance, Michael McDonald defends the intrinsic value of groups on the ground that they possess all of the requisite properties. "Individuals are regarded as valuable because they are choosers and have interests," he writes. "But so also do communities make choices and have values. Why not then treat communities as fundamental units of value as well?" [15]

To answer McDonald's (ostensibly rhetorical) question, my reservations about regarding groups as valuable in themselves stem from my interpretation of the sense in which groups can be said to have interests. I recognize that groups can meaningfully be said to have interests insofar as groups can flourish or founder depending upon their circumstances, and it makes sense to say that anything that contributes to the health of a group is in its interests. For example, it is perfectly intelligible to say that the emergence of the Internet might prove to be detrimental to the interests of many community-based chess clubs because the incentive to maintain membership in these clubs may diminish markedly with the newfound convenience of playing "virtual" chess with people all over the world without ever leaving one's house. But, while there is nothing awkward about speaking of a chess club having interests, it is important to appreciate that these interests are not, in and of themselves, fundamentally morally significant in the way that an individual person's are. The key, here, is that a person has a vantage point from which she experiences the world; thus, her lived experience is better or worse depending upon the degree to which she flourishes or founders. It is this experience that makes her interests fundamentally morally significant.

The problem with value-collectivism, then, is that, while there is a sense in which groups might be said to have interests, groups themselves (that is, apart from the individuals who comprise them) have no vantage point from which they experience either the realization or the thwarting of their interests. Put another way, whereas people care intensely whether they flourish or founder, it does not matter to a group itself whether or not its interests are promoted. Given this, it seems that we have no alternative but to conclude that group interests are not of fundamental moral value. As a consequence, there is, in fact, a morally important difference between groups and individual persons, which explains why only the latter are of nonderivative moral value. And finally, the fact that groups are not valuable in themselves seems to me to entail that group autonomy cannot be valuable in the same way as individual autonomy. As Charles Beitz puts it, given "that states, unlike persons, lack the unity of consciousness and the rational will that constitute the identity of persons . . . [and are

---

[15] Michael McDonald, "Should Communities Have Rights? Reflections on Liberal Individualism," *Canadian Journal of Law and Jurisprudence* 4, no. 2 (1991): 237.

not] organic wholes with the unity and integrity that attaches to persons qua persons . . . [i]t should come as no surprise that this lack of analogy leads to a lack of analogy on the matter of autonomy."[16]

Regarding my insistence that an entity's interests are morally relevant only if these interests matter to the entity itself, one might object on the grounds that such a claim unduly restricts the set of things that can have ultimate value. Among the unfashionable implications that follow from this stance, for example, are the conclusions that ecosystems, great works of art, and various objects in nature can have no value apart from their contribution to the lives of sentient beings. Some people will find this unpalatable insofar as it implies that there would be nothing wrong with burning the Mona Lisa, destroying the Great Barrier Reef, or chopping down all of the world's trees if one were the last sentient being alive. Although I have some reservations about these conclusions, I do not regard them as reductiones ad absurdum of my stance. Inconvenient or not, my considered conviction is that, although it is perfectly intelligible to say that various nonsentient things have interests, these interests are not morally significant in themselves. Thus, despite the difficulties that it might pose for developing a satisfactory account of group autonomy, I must confess that I know of no adequate defense of value-collectivism. As a result, whatever account of group autonomy I can generate must be consistent with value-individualism.[17]

Having rejected value-collectivism, it seems natural to explore the possibility of deriving group autonomy from the individual autonomy of the members of the group. On this view, group autonomy creates duties that are owed to the members of the group. For example, while the duty to allow the Augusta National Golf Club to choose its new members is not owed to the club itself, it may be owed to the club's members, which is to say that the members would be the ones wronged if someone unjustifiably interfered with the club's self-determination. Given my belief that, unlike groups themselves, the individuals who make up these groups are of ultimate moral importance, I find this way of understanding group autonomy to be very attractive. The question remains, however, whether there is sufficient theoretical support for such a conception of group autonomy. In short, what justifies the view that we owe it to individuals to respect the autonomy of the groups to which they belong?

---

[16] Charles R. Beitz, *Political Theory and International Relations* (Princeton, NJ: Princeton University Press, 1979), 81.

[17] I should emphasize that, while I take the morally significant differences between groups and individual persons to show that our account of group autonomy cannot be perfectly analogous to our account of individual autonomy, I am *not* suggesting that this disanalogy shows that group autonomy need not be respected. Rather, I claim only that it is incumbent upon us to provide some explanation (compatible with value-individualism) why we have moral reasons not to interfere with the self-determination of groups. In short, the implausibility of value-collectivism requires us to offer an explanation for the importance of group autonomy, which we need not give in the case of individual persons.

The most salient answer to this last question, I think, is that respect for group autonomy is owed to the members of these groups because group autonomy is an extension of the autonomy of individuals. Stated another way, group autonomy often matters morally because individual autonomy matters morally, and individuals sometimes exercise their autonomy in concert with others. Perhaps the best way to understand the view that group autonomy is an extension of the autonomy of its members is to think of the group as something akin to a proxy for its constituents. Suppose, for example, that I send my friend as a proxy to an important department meeting. If my colleagues refuse to count this proxy vote, then they wrong *me*, not the person whom I have appointed as my proxy. I think that when our participation within a group enables the group to act on our behalf, the group can play a role analogous to that of an appointed proxy. And if an external party wrongly interferes with the group's activity, then this interference wrongs the members of the group, those for whom the group is a proxy.

To see why this construal of group autonomy makes sense, let us return to the example of the Augusta National Golf Club. The position under consideration is that whatever autonomy-based moral reasons we have to refrain from forcing the club either to accept or to reject certain new members exist in virtue of the value of the autonomy of the club's individual members. On this view, what is wrong with forcing Augusta to accept, say, Annika Sorenstam is neither that such forcible interference decreases overall well-being, nor that such interference diminishes the welfare of any individuals who currently make up the club (it may do neither). The real problem is that it disrespects the autonomy of the club members.

Because this account depends upon the plausibility of regarding group autonomy as an extension of the autonomy of individuals, it is worth reflecting upon how groups like Augusta are formed. Initially, a number of charter members get together to form a club. Often there are disagreements regarding what rules should govern the club, but no one has a gun held to her head during the ensuing debate, and, most often, people are able to work through these disagreements (although, occasionally, when the disagreements are significant enough, one or more of the potential members will abandon the project of forming the club). Once the club is created, new members may or may not be added. A prospective member might not be thrilled with every aspect of the existing arrangement, but, again, no gun is held to her head, and anyone who is sufficiently concerned about the club's constitution is free to not join. Often, the rules or composition of a club will change over time (sometimes gradually, other times abruptly), and it is always possible that existing members will become so unhappy with these changes (or perhaps the club's resistance to change) that they will want to leave. If so, they are free to exit. Finally, consider an individual member's control over adding new members. If these decisions are made collectively, then no one has complete control over this process. (Even if each member has veto power over new members, this gives each existing member only the unilateral power to exclude others, not the unilateral ability to include them. Conversely, if anyone has the unilateral power to invite a certain number of new members, then other existing members have a correlative lack of power to exclude them.) Some might think that this lack of individual control within the group undermines the understanding of group autonomy as an extension of individual autonomy. In the imaginary case of Augusta and Annika Sorenstam, for example, how can we conceive of interference with the group's decision as disrespecting the individual's autonomy when the individual did not have control over the process to begin with? Here, I think that the individual's history with the group is crucial. While it is true that any given member of Augusta may not have unilateral freedom to accept or reject Annika Sorenstam, each member was free to not join the club. And since each member freely joined the club with its rules about membership (as well as its secondary rules about how the primary rules regarding membership might be changed), it strikes me as plausible to regard interference with the group's self-determination as interference with each member's autonomy. Moreover, let me be explicit that I think that one's autonomy is infringed regardless of one's personal position on inviting Sorenstam to be a member. Thus, even if I were among the outvoted minority who thought that Annika Sorenstam *should have been invited to join*, my autonomy would be violated by some party outside of the group *forcing* Augusta to accept Sorenstam as a member. In short, the autonomy of each member of Augusta would be equally disrespected by a third party's interference with the club's self-determination.

Along these same lines, consider a real-world example involving group autonomy that was recently adjudicated by the U.S. Supreme Court. The United States Professional Golf Association (PGA) is a voluntary group that does a number of things, including hosting various golf tournaments. Naturally, these tournaments are governed by very elaborate rules, so one of the chores of the PGA is to set, promulgate, and adjudicate these rules. One rule is that competitors must walk rather than ride in a golf cart. Casey Martin is a talented golfer who asked for an exemption from this rule because his medical condition makes it extremely difficult and painful to walk 72 holes over the course of four days. The PGA denied Martin an exemption. The association's position is that an essential element of the sport of golf is the endurance involved in walking the course. Martin subsequently sued the PGA, and the Supreme Court ultimately ordered the PGA to grant Martin an exemption.[18] Regardless of whether or not the

[18] *PGA Tour, Inc. v. Martin*, 532 U.S. 661 (2001). *Boy Scouts Of America v. Dale*, 530 U.S. 640 (2000), is another recent case in which the U.S. Supreme Court had to decide whether to respect a group's self-determination. In this case, the Court held that forcing the Boy Scouts

Court's decision was correct, it involved limiting the PGA's group autonomy. (Very roughly, the Court's decision was the right one if the moral reasons in favor of forcing the PGA to grant Martin the exemption were sufficiently compelling to outweigh the moral reasons generated by the PGA's right to self-determination. I personally have no strong sense of whether the Court's decision was correct; here, I want to emphasize only that, even if interference was justified, the moral reasons against interfering with the PGA's affairs remained.)

Not everyone will accept my portrayal of group autonomy. Nevertheless, I think that understanding group autonomy as an extension of the autonomy of the individuals who comprise the group captures nicely my pretheoretic convictions regarding cases like the Supreme Court's actual interference with the PGA, as well as the hypothetical interference with the Augusta National Golf Club. I continue to have reservations about this account, however, because it does not appear broad enough to include all cases of group autonomy. In particular, just political states (and perhaps some "cultural nations")[19] strike me as paradigm candidates for group autonomy, and yet it is not clear how either can be accommodated on this account. Imagine, for instance, that citizens in the United States become frustrated at being second-rate in hockey, and thus seek to rectify their team's inferiority by uniting to form one country with Canada. It seems to me that Canada has the right to accept or reject this merger, and if the United States forcibly annexed Canada after it rejected the offer, then this annexation would be a violation of Canada's autonomy. Although the following example is more controversial, I also believe that the Quebecois might have the right to choose whether to remain in Canada or to secede and form their own country, and Canada would be disrespecting Quebec's group autonomy if it forced the Quebecois to remain in the union.[20] The problem with explaining group autonomy as an extension of individual autonomy is that it appears ill equipped to explain either of these cases.

---

to retain a homosexual scoutmaster violated the group's First Amendment right to expressive association. As the decisions in both the PGA and Boy Scouts cases indicate, the Court tries to balance a group's right to self-determination against competing interests. And since (like me) the Court has no fully codified algorithm with which it adjudicates these cases, it is not altogether clear when the Court will find a state interest to be sufficiently compelling to outweigh a group's claim to expressive association (that is, in my terminology, a claim to group autonomy).

[19] By a *cultural nation*, I mean a group of people who either have or seek some form of political self-determination, and who identify with one another because of their shared cultural characteristics, such as a common language, religion, territory, set of norms, etc. Cultural nations seldom coincide perfectly with the constituencies of political states, thus, cultural nations often claim various rights to political self-determination against their political states. Examples of cultural nations include the Basques, the Catalans, the Croatians, the Kurds, and the Quebecois.

[20] Obviously I do not think that the Quebecois have an unconditional right to secede no matter what, but for a defense of their qualified right, see Christopher H. Wellman, "A Defense of Secession and Political Self-Determination," *Philosophy & Public Affairs* 24, no. 2 (1995): 142–71.

The worry, of course, is that, unlike the Augusta National Golf Club and the PGA, the United States and the nation of Quebec do not owe their respective memberships exclusively to the autonomous choices of their constituents. Crucial to regarding group autonomy as an extension of individual autonomy is that the group's actions derive at some basic level from the autonomous actions of the group's members. (This is why I emphasized that the members of Augusta freely chose to join the golf club and are equally free to withdraw if they become sufficiently dissatisfied with the rules, including those that govern the selection of new members.) Indeed, to see the importance of this condition, imagine that I believe myself to be a messianic figure whose calling is to start a religious community in Arizona. Because my considerable efforts to recruit a devoted flock garner no followers, I ultimately kidnap hundreds of people and transport them to Arizona where I force them to set up a religious community. Under these circumstances, it strikes me as ludicrous to suggest that third parties have autonomy-based moral reasons to respect the group's self-determination. The key is that, because the individual members are not exercising their autonomy in concert with one another, it is unreasonable to construe the group's autonomy as an extension of the individual autonomy of the group's members. And if interfering with this group's self-determination is not tantamount to interfering with its members' autonomy, then it is hard to see how this interference wrongs anyone. As a result, there appear to be no autonomy-based moral reasons against interfering with such a group.

The problem for political states is that they are more like this imaginary religious community than the Augusta National Golf Club, insofar as they are not comprised of constituents who have freely agreed to join them. In order to perform the functions that justify their existence, states are, by necessity, defined territorially, and voluntary compliance is a luxury that they can ill afford to extend to individuals within their geographical boundaries.[21] And, given that states nonconsensually coerce all those over whom they exercise sovereignty, it is not clear how we can, with intellectual integrity, regard any state's group autonomy as an extension of the individual autonomy of its citizens.

Of course, in pointing out that states are not constructed entirely from the autonomous choices of their constituents, I do not mean to suggest that they are, therefore, necessarily illegitimate. To my mind, despite being nonconsensual, political coercion is often justified by vitally important benefits that could not be secured in its absence.[22] And, given that

---

[21] Most theorists concede that political states have not garnered the explicit consent of their constituents, but many theorists suggest that citizens can be interpreted as having tacitly consented. The landmark rebuttal of this view is A. John Simmons's article, "Tacit Consent and Political Obligation," *Philosophy & Public Affairs* 5, no. 3 (1976): 274–91.

[22] I argue that states may legitimately coerce their constituents even in the absence of consent in Christopher H. Wellman, "Liberalism, Samaritanism, and Political Legitimacy," *Philosophy & Public Affairs* 25, no. 3 (1996): 211–37.

states join consensual groups like Augusta in not illegitimately disrespecting the autonomy of their members, this suggests the possibility that a
group's autonomy might be derived from the individual autonomy of its
members only in those cases in which the group does not unjustly restrict
the autonomy of its members.[23] I must admit that I am mightily attracted
to this view for its ability to generate precisely the conclusions that I favor.
(Augusta and just political states would be entitled to group autonomy,
whereas our imaginary religious community and unjust states would
not.) Nonetheless, I resist the considerable temptation to accept this view
because I do not see how a group's autonomy is an extension of an
individual's autonomy merely because the group never unjustly restricts
that individual's self-determination.

The distinction between "extension of" and "permissible restriction of"
autonomy can perhaps best be illustrated by returning to the analogy of
a proxy. It seems plausible to understand group autonomy as an extension of an individual's autonomy if it is reasonable to regard the group's
actions as a proxy for the individual. A group acts as a proxy when an
individual autonomously embraces that group as something of a proxy.
When a group merely refrains from impermissibly infringing upon an
individual's autonomy, however, this does not, in itself, make the group
a proxy for the individual; thus, there is not the same reason to regard the
group's autonomy as an extension of the individual's. In the absence of
some other account that bridges the gap between an "extension of" and
"the permissible restriction of" autonomy, it strikes me as unwarranted to
assert that a group's autonomy is derived from the individual autonomy
of its members as long as the group does not unjustly restrict the autonomy of its members.[24] As a result, while the more general approach of
understanding group autonomy as derived from individual autonomy
seems to work wonderfully for some types of groups, it cannot explain

---

[23] Charles R. Beitz considers the view that all just states have a right to autonomy in
Political Theory and International Relations. He does not necessarily endorse this view; his
primary concern is to show that, even if it is true that all just states have a right to autonomy,
this does not explain why we should not interfere with the self-determination of unjust
states.

[24] I should acknowledge that several people have pressed me on this point. Two common
suggestions have been that either the right to self-determination of a just state must be
grounded in whatever gives the group sovereignty over its members, or interfering with the
self-determination of a just state violates the autonomy of those citizens who identify with
their state, where identification involves regarding the state as acting on one's behalf.
Although each suggested view is tempting, I fear that neither is ultimately satisfactory. The
problem with the first is that, because a state's justification for its sovereignty over its
constituents depends in no way upon any autonomous actions or omissions by these constituents, it is unclear how invoking sovereignty can help supply the missing link between
the state's autonomy and the autonomy of its citizens. Regarding the second option, it
strikes me that considering personal identification as an extension of autonomy leads to
unpalatable conclusions. If, for example, professional tennis player Martina Hingis does not
disrespect my autonomy when she defeats the player with whom I most identify, then why
would the United States disrespect my autonomy if it were to disrespect the self-determination
of the country with which I most identify?

the importance of autonomy for all the groups that we would like. In particular, it does not explain the moral reasons that we have to respect the self-determination of just states and suitably organized cultural nations.

The third potential account of group autonomy derives the value of group autonomy from the welfare of the members of the group in question. This approach is also value-individualist, and it promises to explain the value of autonomy for a broader set of groups, so it appears better equipped to accommodate our convictions regarding just political states and cultural nations. Indeed, one of the chief lessons that contemporary liberals have (belatedly) learned from communitarians is the profound extent to which individual well-being depends upon the health of the various noncontractual groups to which individuals belong. Thus, while social contract theorists have long emphasized the crucial benefits that political institutions supply by subduing the harmful chaos that would inevitably occur in their absence, only recently have writers (following Will Kymlicka) begun to stress that healthy cultures are pivotal to the life-prospects of their members.[25] Moreover, it seems only natural that groups like political states and cultural nations are more likely to flourish when they are left to organize their own affairs, free from the interference of others. Thus, perhaps the best way to account for the importance of group autonomy is in terms of the value of group autonomy to the well-being of the individuals within those groups.

Although this type of explanation appears capable of casting a net wide enough to include political states and cultural nations, I fear that it cannot generate a satisfying theory of group autonomy. In particular, because it ultimately derives the value of group autonomy from the promotion of welfare, it is vulnerable to the problems that we discussed above in connection with Jezebel. To review, I offered the example of Jezebel to illustrate my dissatisfaction with explaining the value of (individual) autonomy in terms of its promotion of well-being. The problem with such an instrumental, consequentialist account is that it instructs one to respect autonomy only when and to the extent that such respect will maximize well-being. As I tried to show with Jezebel's ill-advised plan to move to Santa Fe, however, our convictions suggest that Jezebel retains her privileged position of dominion over her own affairs even when she is inclined to act in ways that are likely to cause her great unhappiness. Put plainly, we dismissed the consequentialist approach for its inability to capture our conviction that we may not permissibly interfere with Jezebel's move to Santa Fe simply because it is Jezebel's life, and she is entitled to run the risk of ruining it if she wants.

The case of Jezebel is pertinent again, here, because analogous problems emerge if we conceive of group autonomy as valuable only to the

[25] Will Kymlicka, *Liberalism, Community, and Culture* (Oxford: Oxford University Press, 1989).

extent that it promotes the well-being of the individuals within the group. To see this, let us return to the case of Canada's group autonomy, again assuming that the United States wants to merge with Canada in order to achieve world supremacy in hockey. The appeal of interpreting the value of group autonomy as a function of individual well-being is that it allows us to explain Canada's group autonomy without importing the fiction of political consent. The problem, however, is that it leaves us with an anemic account of Canada's right to self-determination. To see this, imagine how the United States should act if Canada were to refuse the invitation to merge. In particular, notice how this approach counsels the United States as to whether or not it may forcibly annex Canada. Because the value of Canada's group autonomy derives from its tendency to promote the welfare of Canadians, its autonomy is valuable only to the extent that it does so. Thus, just as we saw in the case of Jezebel, this approach does not require us to respect Canada's group autonomy when Canada exercises its autonomy in a way that fails to maximize the welfare of its constituents. With this in mind, imagine that Canada rejects the United States' merger offer because it recognizes that it can remain the preeminent hockey power all on its own. However, a strong case can be made that Canadians would, on balance, dramatically benefit from the merger; after all, uniting with the United States would instantly elevate Canada to world dominance in baseball, football, and basketball. Under these circumstances, it appears that the United States has no moral reason not to forcibly annex Canada. Given that Canada's group autonomy is valuable only to the extent that it is conducive to promoting the welfare of Canadians, there appear to be no moral reasons to respect Canada's self-determination when Canada prefers to act in a way contrary to that welfare. In short, this approach recommends that the United States may forcibly annex Canada whenever it reasonably expects this annexation to promote the well-being of Canadians.

Now, a sophisticated consequentialist might invoke a long list of considerations as to why, *in the real world*, we could almost never reasonably expect that an annexation would produce the best results for those who are annexed. I am inclined to accept this stance, but—as in the case of Jezebel—these types of considerations strike me as beside the most important moral point. No matter how seldom it would turn out to be the case that well-being would be maximized by disrespecting a country's wishes to remain independent, the consequentialist account of group autonomy seems to miss the mark. The real reason why the United States may not permissibly forcibly annex Canada is simply because doing so would wrongly deny Canada the self-determination to which it is entitled. In my view, Canada has a right to order its internal affairs in a variety of nonoptimal ways, and, as long as it treats neither its constituents nor foreigners unjustly, others have a duty to respect its right to self-determination. Thus, while others are not required to stand by idly if

Canada should engage in unjust activities like ethnic-cleansing or apart-heid, Canada does have a right to make choices such as whether or not to sign the North American Free Trade Agreement (NAFTA), regardless of what we might reasonably expect would maximize Canadians' well-being. And finally, it is important to emphasize that if someone unjusti-fiably forces Canada to sign NAFTA or to merge with the United States, for example, the principal problem with this coercion is not that it fails to maximize overall well-being. Rather, the real crime is that it wrongs the Canadians, it wrongly disrespects their right to order their own affairs. Because an account that derives the value of group autonomy from its tendency to promote the welfare of the individuals within the group cannot capture this fact, it (like the individual well-being approach) is ultimately unsatisfactory.

In the end, then, none of the three possible accounts of group autonomy is entirely satisfying. Espousing value-collectivism requires us to turn a blind eye to the significant differences between groups and individual persons; viewing group autonomy as an extension of individual auton-omy leaves us unable to explain the right to self-determination of just states and cultural nations; and deriving the value of group autonomy from its contribution to the well-being of a group's constituents fails to explain the deontological reasons to respect group self-determination.

III. Conclusion: The Paradox of Group Autonomy

Given my inability to construct an adequate account of group auton-omy that satisfies all of my pretheoretic convictions, I am left in a quan-dary, which I label the "Paradox of Group Autonomy." This paradox arises because of the apparent incompatibility of three separate claims, all of which seem to be true. To review, these claims are as follows:

(1) *There are deontological reasons to respect an agent's autonomy.* The moral reasons to respect an agent's autonomy depend for their existence upon neither the good consequences of the particular instance of respect nor the good consequences of a general policy of such respect.

(2) *Value-collectivism is false.* Although certain groups may be ex-tremely important, their importance depends entirely upon their value to individuals.

(3) *Just political states, and perhaps some cultural nations, are among those groups whose autonomy we have deontological reasons to respect.* They are among the agents who would be wronged if their self-determination were disrespected.

Because this paradox arises from three mutually incompatible state-ments, obviously I could dissolve the problem by denying any one of these three claims. If (1) were false, then I could easily construct a consequentialist account of group autonomy broad enough to include political states and suitably organized nations. If (2) were false, then I would have no difficulty explaining the deontological reasons to respect the autonomy of all suitably valuable groups. And if (3) were false, then deriving the importance of group autonomy from the autonomy of the group's members would be broad enough to capture all genuinely autonomous groups. Because all three of these claims seem no less true despite their mutual incompatibility, I am prepared to reject none of them. Thus, I know of no way out of the paradox.

Philosophy, Blumenfeld Center for Ethics, Georgia State University

ABORTION, AUTONOMY, AND CONTROL OVER ONE'S BODY*

By John Martin Fischer

I. Introduction

It is often thought that if a developing human being is considered a "person" from the beginning, then it would follow that abortion (at any time) would be impermissible. For, after all, a person has a stringent right to life, and because life is a prerequisite for enjoying any other goods, it is plausible that the right to life is a "basic" or "fundamental" one, not easily overridden by other considerations. The right to life, it would seem, could not be outweighed by another individual's preferences, even preferences about what should happen in or to her body.

Judith Jarvis Thomson, in her remarkable 1971 essay, "A Defense of Abortion," argues that even if we assume that a human fetus is a person, it does not follow that abortion is always impermissible.[1] Part of her argument is that, in some contexts, an individual's right to determine what happens in or to her body overrides another individual's right to life. To support this contention, Thomson offers her (now famous) "violinist example," which I shall describe in detail in the next section of this essay. The example raises subtle and difficult questions about the relationship between the right to life and the cluster of rights that constitute one's right to control over one's body. Furthermore, the example and its analysis raise important questions about the nature of autonomy.

In this essay I shall seek to show how certain ways of invoking autonomy cannot aid in a defense of Thomson's strategy of argumentation on behalf of the "pro-choice" position (according to which abortion is in some cases permissible). Ultimately, however, I shall argue that considerations of autonomy (and control of one's body) can be employed to

* I am grateful to Gideon Yaffe for various helpful conversations about the issues discussed in this essay. I have also benefited from the extremely knowledgeable and useful advice of David Boonin-Vail. David Hershenov has given me generous and useful comments. I have read versions of this essay to the philosophy departments at the University of Southern California and Utah State University; on both occasions I benefited from the discussions.

[1] Judith Jarvis Thomson, "A Defense of Abortion," *Philosophy and Public Affairs* 1, no. 1 (1971): 47–66. Reprinted in William Parent, ed., *Rights, Restitution, and Risk: Essays in Moral Theory* (Cambridge, MA: Harvard University Press, 1986), 1–19. (Subsequent references will be to the essay reprinted in Parent, ed.) Thomson's essay has been widely reprinted and discussed in a voluminous literature. A good recent discussion is David Boonin-Vail, "A Defense of 'A Defense of Abortion': On the Responsibility Objection to Thomson's Argument," *Ethics* 107, no. 2 (1997): 286–313.

support the pro-choice position. I shall argue that Thomson's violinist example is inadequate as it stands, but that it (together with Thomson's analysis) points us toward a more compelling defense of the pro-choice position.

II. A Puzzle

There are many cases in which it seems clear that we have to change our plans, or even allow our property to be used, in order to assist another person who needs help. If someone leaves a baby on my doorstep, or if I see a baby crawling toward a swimming pool, then I must (from a moral point of view) stop what I am doing and offer assistance. Of course, there are limits to what I am required to do; for example, I am not morally required to adopt the baby who has been dropped off on my doorstep. But I do have to help, and I think that there are cases in which most people would say that I can be morally required to change my plans considerably and to allow my property to be used in significant ways.

Consider an example given by Joel Feinberg:

> Suppose that you are on a backpacking trip in the high mountain country when an unanticipated blizzard strikes the area with such ferocity that your life is imperiled. Fortunately, you stumble onto an unoccupied cabin, locked and boarded up for the winter, clearly somebody else's private property. You smash in a window, enter, and huddle in a corner for three days until the storm abates. During this period you help yourself to your unknown benefactor's food supply and burn his wooden furniture in the fireplace to keep warm. Surely you are justified in doing all these things. . . .[2]

Of course, if you do these things, you acquire various obligations: you must explain to the owner what has happened, apologize for the intrusion and damage that you have caused, and make amends financially. But it would be a hard-hearted extremist who would deny that it is permissible for you to enter and use the cabin. If it is indeed permissible, then surely the owner could not legitimately prevent you from doing so. If members of the owner's security team were monitoring the cabin and could prevent you from entering, and if they actually took such steps, then their conduct would be outrageous and clearly unacceptable. Indeed, Thomson accepts such a conclusion about Feinberg's case.[3]

I think that it is not a significant step from the above judgment to the contention that the owner would have to allow you to enter, even if he (or

---

[2] Joel Feinberg, "Voluntary Euthanasia and the Inalienable Right to Life," *Philosophy and Public Affairs* 7, no. 2 (1978): 102.

[3] Judith Jarvis Thomson, "Rights and Compensation," *Nous* 14, no. 1 (1980): 3–15.

she) were actually in the cabin. Here, presumably, you would not need to smash a window to get in, nor to burn the furniture, and so forth. But it is also presumably true that you could be rescued soon, and you would only cause inconvenience to the owner briefly. Of course, here too, you would have to offer an explanation and an apology, and you would need to make amends.

Consider, now, a more extreme version of Feinberg's example. I originally presented this case a decade ago in a discussion of Thomson's argument for the pro-choice position:

> Suppose you have planned for many years to take a trip to a very remote place in the Himalaya mountains. You have secured a cabin in an extremely remote and inaccessible place in the mountains. You wish to be alone; you have enough supplies for yourself, and also some extras in case of an emergency. Unfortunately, a very evil man has kidnapped an innocent person and brought him to die in the desolate mountain country near your cabin. The innocent person wanders for hours and finally happens upon your cabin.
>
> You have the following problem. You can radio for help, but because of the remoteness and inaccessibility of your cabin and the relatively primitive technology of the country in which it is located, the rescue party will require nine months to reach your cabin. Thus, you are faced with a choice. You can let the innocent stranger into your cabin and provide food and shelter until the rescue party arrives in nine months, or you can forcibly prevent him from entering your cabin (or staying there) and thus cause his death (or perhaps allow him to die). It is evident that he will die unless you allow him to stay in the cabin.[4]

Let us call this example the "cabin case." In this case it seems clear to me that it would be outrageous and unacceptable for you to prevent the innocent stranger from coming into or remaining in your cabin. After all, the stranger did not violate any of his duties in arriving at your doorstep. He was kidnapped. You do own the cabin, and it would cause you considerable inconvenience to allow the stranger to stay. But you must change or adjust your plans, put up with the significant inconvenience, and provide shelter and sustenance to a complete stranger. Or so it appears to me.

But now consider Thomson's well-known example:

> You wake up in the morning and find yourself back to back in bed with an unconscious violinist. A famous unconscious violinist. He

    [4] John Martin Fischer, "Abortion and Self-Determination," *Journal of Social Philosophy* 22, no. 2 (1991): 5–13, esp. 6.

has been found to have a fatal kidney ailment, and the Society of Music Lovers has canvassed all the available medical records and found that you alone have the right blood type to help. They have therefore kidnapped you, and last night the violinist's circulatory system was plugged into yours, so that your kidneys can be used to extract poisons from his blood as well as your own. The director of the hospital now tells you, "Look, we're sorry the Society of Music Lovers did this to you—we would never have permitted it if we had known. But still, they did it, and the violinist now is plugged into you. To unplug you would be to kill him. But never mind, it's only for nine months. By then he will have recovered from his ailment, and can safely be unplugged from you." Is it morally incumbent on you to accede to this situation? No doubt it would be very nice of you if you did, a great kindness. But do you *have* to accede to it?[5]

Thomson thinks that it would be outrageous to suppose that you had to stay in a hospital room for nine months plugged into the violinist. (In contrast to the cabin case, where it seems impermissible to cast off the suddenly appearing stranger, here the outrage seems to be "on the other side," as it were.) Thomson thinks that it is clear that you need not continue to be plugged into the violinist, and thus you may unplug yourself or consent to having someone else unplug you, thereby bringing about the death of the violinist.

Of course, the violinist is an innocent person with a stringent right to life. But, according to Thomson, your right to determine what happens in or to your body outweighs the violinist's right to life in this situation. In general, the idea that an individual has a right to life does not entail that anyone else is required to give him or her whatever is needed to sustain life. And this is a context, on Thomson's view, in which you need not provide the violinist with what he needs in order to continue living. By analogy, she wishes to argue that even if we assume that a human fetus is a person (and thus has a stringent right to life) from the moment of conception, it does *not* follow that abortion is never permissible. The violinist example shows, according to Thomson, that abortion would be permissible in cases of rape; the pregnant woman's lack of consent to the sexual intercourse is parallel to your lack of consent to having the violinist connected to your kidneys. (Thomson also defends the permissibility of abortion in contexts other than rape, such as the context of voluntary intercourse when there is contraceptive failure; but she employs other examples and considerations in these contexts.)

When I first thought about Thomson's violinist case, I agreed with her intuition that it would be perfectly permissible for you to unplug yourself. As she points out, we have duties to be what she calls "Minimally

---

[5] Thomson, "A Defense of Abortion," 2–3.

Decent Samaritans"; thus we have a duty to perform easy rescues, such as saving a baby who is heading toward a swimming pool. But we do not have a duty to be "Good Samaritans," and remaining plugged into the violinist would seem to be an act of Good Samaritanship (and, thus, above and beyond the call of duty). I also accepted Thomson's suggestion that the violinist example is analogous to that of pregnancy due to rape. The problem, however, is that I also find it plausible in the cabin case that I must allow the stranger to stay for the nine months, as I stated above.

Here, then, is a puzzle: Why is it permissible in the violinist example but not the cabin case to act so that the innocent person dies? And here is a related puzzle: If indeed the examples are morally different in the way that I have suggested, which is more closely analogous to the context of pregnancy due to rape?

III. THE RIGHT TO CONTROL ONE'S BODY

Someone might think that there is a pretty clear difference between the violinist example and the cabin case that, in fact, makes the moral difference. In the violinist case, you are being asked to allow the violinist to remain in direct contact with your body. Additionally, parts of your body—your kidneys—are being used by the violinist to filter toxins out of his body. So there is direct contact with parts of your body, and parts of your body are being used by another, all without your consent. In contrast, in the cabin case you are asked to sacrifice your plans and your property, but not your body. There is no direct contact with your body, and your body or parts of it are not being used to provide assistance to someone else.

I think that the notion that we all have the right to control our bodies—that is, to determine what happens in or to our bodies—is a deeply important idea. Presumably, it is part of a cluster of rights that constitute the more abstract right to personal autonomy. It is not, however, a straightforward task to interpret or give content to the right to control one's body in the relevant way—namely, the right to determine what should happen in or to one's body. I shall begin by pointing out that on certain natural ways of understanding this right, it is not useful to our project of distinguishing between the cabin and violinist examples, because it is not plausible that the right, so understood, outweighs another person's right to life.

So, let us suppose that the right to determine what happens in or to our bodies is the right that someone else not be in contact with our bodies and use them without our permission. This formulation is very rough; we obviously need further specifications of the notions of "contact" and "use." For example, the violinist's contact with my kidneys is mediated by a set of tubes and a medical device, but this still is supposed to count as the relevant sort of contact. I think that it would not be easy to specify just the sorts of contact and use that are to be ruled out, but I shall leave these matters aside.

To see the problem with this suggested interpretation of the right to control one's body, consider the following variant on Thomson's violinist case.[6] In the "surgery variant," you are in a terrible accident, and you must have major surgery. Because of the nature and extent of the surgery, you must stay in a hospital bed (hooked into a complicated medical apparatus) for nine months. Now the story proceeds just as in Thomson's violinist case: a representative of the Society of Music Lovers introduces himself one morning, saying that they have connected a great violinist to your kidneys. . . . In this thought experiment it was easy to connect the violinist up to you, as the apparatus had a ready-made kidney hookup.

My intuition in this variant on Thomson's original case is very different from my initial intuition about her violinist example. I am inclined to think that it would be impermissible for you to detach yourself from the violinist in this variant and thereby cause his death. And yet, here, the violinist would be in contact with and using your body in just the same way in which he used your body in the original violinist example.

We could imagine another version of the surgery case. Suppose, as above, that you have had surgery and must stay in a hospital bed for nine months. But now imagine that for some reason the violinist must be connected to an exotic medical device that, in turn, must be connected to a patch of your skin. The device scans the skin and uses the information to keep the violinist alive. The information from your skin is the only way that the violinist can be kept alive for nine months. Here, again, I think it would be impermissible for you to cause yourself to be unplugged from the violinist. So, under certain circumstances (such as if you are confined to the hospital already), it seems to me that you can be required to remain in contact with another person and allow that other person to use your body in order to stay alive.

In an intriguing article, David B. Hershenov has presented a set of examples by means of which he also contends that it is evident that sometimes one must allow another individual to be in contact with and use one's body (and in Hershenov's examples the duration of the assistance is extensive).[7] Here is one of his examples:

> The . . . scenario . . . involves two people on a birdwatching trip who become entangled in ropes on an elevated platform that contains a trap door. If the door should open, they will fall twelve feet to the ground. Neither person is in any way responsible for his own or the other person's predicament. The cause of their bad luck is a sadist

---

[6] I presented this example in Fischer, "Abortion and Self-Determination," 7. The example was originally suggested to me by Alexander Rosenberg.

[7] David B. Hershenov, "Abortions and Distortions: An Analysis of Morally Irrelevant Factors in Thomson's Violinist Thought Experiment," *Social Theory and Practice* 27, no. 1 (2001): 129–48.

who has put his ropes above a hole he has dug in the forest floor just to torment strangers.

Their luck is about to worsen, for they each know that in about fifteen minutes the trap door will indeed open and they will fall to the ground. Let's just assume that the two unfortunates can predict with the utmost certainty what will happen to them when they fall. Because of the way they are positioned, the much larger person will hit the ground first and his body will shield the smaller person from all injuries. The larger person knows that due to the way he will hit the ground, he will suffer nine months of intermittent back pain, nausea, and abdominal swelling comparable to what a pregnant woman bears. But if the larger person is released from the ropes, which can be done only with the help of a third party, then he will be free from harm. The larger man will not fall at all since he has been disentangled from the ropes, while the smaller man, instead of being cushioned and shielded by the former, will die upon impact due to the position his body will be in when he hits the ground.[8]

About this example, Hershenov says:

I would be utterly aghast at the actions of any third party who, without even the pain-avoidance motivation of the larger person on the platform, enables the latter to escape some discomfort, which results in the death of the smaller person. My attitude is that it would also be very wrong for the larger person to deliberately maneuver out of the ropes and thus bring about the death of the other innocent person. . . . [T]he larger person doesn't seem to have the right to opt out of the burden that Thomson believes women who don't wish to continue a pregnancy are entitled to opt out of. Thomson obviously considers it horribly unfair that an abortion-seeking woman who insists, "This body is *my* body," will find her protests to be as futile as "shouting into the wind." Yet when these same words that Thomson puts in the mouth of the pregnant woman are uttered by the larger person entangled in ropes, they have little appeal. That such protests fall on deaf ears does not seem at all objectionable.[9]

Now I am inclined to agree with Hershenov that the larger person may not permissibly detach himself. I believe that this case buttresses the moral that I drew from the surgery cases discussed above: that the right to control one's body, interpreted as the right that another individual not be in contact with and use one's body, does not always outweigh an innocent person's right to life. Thus, this right cannot help to resolve the

---

[8] Ibid., 134.
[9] Ibid., 134–35.

puzzle of how to distinguish between the cabin and violinist cases. I should point out, however, that there is a further set of questions about how all of the above cases relate to abortion. As I shall argue below, Hershenov's suggestion that his case is relevantly similar to a case of a pregnancy due to rape is seriously misguided.

IV. Autonomy

In my previous essay, "Abortion and Self-Determination," I argued that the cabin case and the violinist case are crucially different because they involve different sorts of infringement of self-determination or autonomy. (I shall henceforth use the term "autonomy" to refer to the sorts of self-determination in question.) My argument was basically as follows.

Begin by noting that there is a "nonabsolute," as well as an "absolute," conception of autonomy. On the absolute conception, all cases in which one's plans or projects cannot be pursued, or one's preferences are not met, count as equally severe violations of the right to autonomy. I do not think that our ordinary notion of the right to autonomy, or the set of constraints that protect this right, is absolute in this sense. Or perhaps we have such an absolute conception, but also a nonabsolute conception, which play important roles in our moral views. On the nonabsolute view, autonomy admits of degrees, and there can be degrees of severity of violations of the right of autonomy.

The nonabsolute conception of autonomy needs some kind of relatively "objective" specification of "central" or "important" activities or choices. On this approach, one's actual preferences (and their degrees of strength) need not correspond to the objective ordering of centrality or importance of activities, and interferences with more central or important activities constitute more significant violations of the right to autonomy. By an "objective" account I mean an account that does not take as decisive the individual's point of view. The relatively objective account may be specified by the "reflective equilibrium" of the relevant community.

For example, on the one hand, we would take it as a significant restriction of our autonomy if the government prohibited individuals from driving cars with internal combustion engines. On the other hand, a requirement that cars be inspected regularly to make sure that they meet emissions standards would be a less significant restriction of one's autonomy, as would a requirement to install catalytic converters to reduce undesirable emissions. Also, the rule that prohibits driving faster than sixty-five miles per hour on a freeway in California may thwart one's preferences from time to time, but it is not a significant restriction of one's autonomy (especially as compared to a blanket prohibition on driving).

Rules prohibiting freedom to express oneself or to read what one wishes would significantly restrict our autonomy. But rules that regulate (in a reasonable way) the contexts in which expression is allowed need not be significant restrictions on autonomy (quite apart from some individuals' preferences). So, for example, a rule that proscribes the use of bullhorns in a residential neighborhood late at night is not nearly as significant a restriction on autonomy as a rule that, say, prohibits private reading of certain newspapers, magazines, or literature.

Given this admittedly rough and vague characterization of the non-absolute conception of autonomy, my contention in my earlier essay was that there is a significantly greater violation of the right to autonomy in the violinist example than in the cabin case. In the violinist example, if you are indeed required to stay in bed hooked into the violinist, then this may well interrupt plans and projects that are important to you. Let us say that you are a lawyer in the middle of a major trial, or a professor in the middle of a semester of teaching, or a psychotherapist who is giving therapy to many patients, and so forth. In all of these cases your sudden unavailability would be a major problem for you (as well as for others). Also, it would be a significant imposition on you if you were a parent in charge of a family. Being required to stay hooked into the violinist involves a significant disruption of your plans, projects, and commitments, and it is a disruption about which you had no prior warning. Here, it is helpful to contrast the original violinist example with the surgery variant: in the surgery variant the requirement to stay plugged into the violinist takes place against a different "baseline," one by reference to which there are already few opportunities to pursue your normal activities. As a result of the surgery your central projects and plans already have had to be adjusted.

I argued, further, that the cabin case is more similar to the surgery variant than to the original violinist example. I put the point as follows:

> In the cabin case you have planned a certain sort of "retreat" in the Himalayas, and the insertion of the innocent stranger does indeed disrupt your plans. After all, you had planned to be alone, and you had wanted your solitude. But nevertheless the presence of the stranger is compatible with your pursuing the fundamentals of your plan: you can still stay in your mountain cabin, take long contemplative walks, study and read, and so forth.[10]

I concluded that the violinist example posits a more significant violation of your right of autonomy than does the cabin case, and thus the two cases are fundamentally different.

Upon further reflection I am now disinclined to think that the notion of autonomy can be invoked in this way to solve the puzzle of distinguishing the cabin case from the violinist example. To begin, note that (quite apart from any intentions of the Society of Music Lovers) you might

---

[10] Fischer, "Abortion and Self-Determination," 8.

well have decided to take a "sabbatical" and to live a simple, meditative existence for nine months, not leaving your room (except to take care of certain necessities). You might have planned to read and reflect quietly for nine months. Even so, I doubt that anyone who believes that you do not have a duty to stay hooked up to the violinist in Thomson's original case will say that you do, in fact, have such a duty in my new version of the case. Thus, I am skeptical that what is doing the work in the original violinist case is the significant violation of autonomy to which I pointed in my earlier essay.

Further, one can also adjust the cabin case as follows. Suppose that the trip to the Himalayas is no "mere retreat." You are a writer, and given your (admittedly somewhat eccentric) character, you simply cannot write if there is anyone in your vicinity, especially a stranger literally living with you. Your ideas are finally ready to be written out, and you have devoted a good part of your professional life to preparing for this year of writing; you doubt whether you will ever have such an opportunity again.

In this revised version of the cabin case, it seems to me that you *still* need to take in the innocent person and allow him to live with you for nine months. And note that this would involve a significant violation of your autonomy insofar as your pursuit of your long-planned professional project would be stymied. Thus, it does not seem that we can invoke the notion of autonomy in the way that I sketched in my earlier work in order to solve the puzzle about the original violinist example and the cabin case.

Further support for this conclusion comes from another example presented by Hershenov:

> [The example] involves a dedicated marine biologist anchored on a research raft many miles from shore. He has made arrangements for a boat to pick him up in a number of months. His raft is crowded with necessities such as food, water, and medicine, as well as expensive equipment. The hundreds of thousands of dollars of equipment, which he spent years saving for, then assembling and modifying, as well as the preparatory data he has collected, are irreplaceable. He has spent most of his adult life saving and preparing for this project. It is fair to say that this project gives his life meaning.
>
> A cruise ship sails by the researcher, the passengers wave to him, and he hollers greetings in return. Suddenly the ship explodes and debris from the accident destroys the researcher's radar reading, preventing him from sending an SOS. No one on board the ship had any time to radio for help. Everyone on the ship died in the explosion or drowned, except for one small child who will soon succumb to the frigid waters if not pulled from the sea. But there is no room on the raft for the child unless all of the irreplaceable expensive equipment

and data are thrown overboard and forever lost. Even then, the raft will still be so crowded that either the child will have to sit on the lap of the biologist, or the latter will have to sit and sleep in an awkward position pressed against the child. Either arrangement will cause the researcher months of discomfort equivalent to that of pregnancy or the predicament of the person supporting the violinist.[11]

This case seems to me parallel in relevant respects to the revised cabin case. Also, Hershenov goes on to say about his case:

> My intuition, and that of nearly all of those I have informally polled, is that the marine biologist *must* save the child even though it means abandoning his life's work, taking on months of physical discomfort, and facing a future in which his life's project goes unfulfilled since he doesn't have the time or resources to plan a second expedition.[12]

Hershenov's example of the researcher and the cruise ship involves both a significant violation of the researcher's autonomy and also direct contact with the researcher's body. Hershenov concludes from his examples and supporting analysis that you must stay hooked up to the violinist in Thomson's example.

In contrast to my view in my previous article, I am now inclined to agree with Hershenov. It seems to me that you must stay hooked up to the violinist. I start with a very strong and clear intuition that the owner of the cabin in Feinberg's example may not prevent you from entering the cabin (and using its contents). Further, I do not think that the owner's duties would be any different, if he were in the cabin and you could not be rescued for nine months. Additionally, it would make no difference to me if this constituted a significant violation of the owner's autonomy (if, for example, the owner could not pursue a central project because of your presence). Finally, I am not convinced that what distinguishes Thomson's violinist example from such cases is the fact that in Thomson's example you would be in direct contact with the violinist's body, and he would be using part of your body. After all, you must sacrifice some autonomy in the surgery variant and in Hershenov's two cases. Thus, I am inclined to conclude that my initial intuition about Thomson's violinist example was wrong, and that it is impermissible to unplug yourself from the violinist.

V. Rape, Abortion, and the Special Status of Pregnancy

I now want to turn to the second puzzle that I mentioned above at the end of Section II, that is: What is the relationship between cases such as

---

[11] Hershenov, "Abortions and Distortions," 133.
[12] Ibid.

the violinist example and the cabin case (and, for that matter, Hershenov's cases of the birdwatchers caught in ropes and the researcher and the cruise ship), on the one hand, and pregnancy and the permissibility of abortion, on the other? Most critics of Thomson have argued that although it is permissible to unplug yourself in the violinist example, it is *not* permissible to have an abortion. Thus, they have argued that there are important disanalogies between the violinist example and the context of pregnancy. As Hershenov puts it, "Rarely found is a critic of Thomson who argues that since one *must* support the violinist, one therefore must support the fetus."[13] Hershenov goes on to say, "However, in this paper I shall defend just such an unpopular view. I will try to convince the reader that to disconnect the violinist would be an injustice."[14] What is striking about this passage is Hershenov's contention that it is obvious that, if it is an injustice to disconnect the violinist, then it would similarly be an injustice to have an abortion (given that a human fetus is assumed to be a person).[15] I shall argue that Hershenov's contention is problematic. Thus, although I now believe that one must not unplug oneself from Thomson's violinist, I do not think that this implies that abortion would always be impermissible, even on the assumption that the fetus is a person. So I will join some of Thomson's critics in contending that there are disanalogies between the violinist case and the context of pregnancy, but the disanalogies that I identify will point in precisely the opposite direction: they show that even if one must remain plugged into the violinist, it need not follow that abortion is impermissible.[16]

I want to emphasize at this point that I am not here presenting what I take to be an argument for the permissibility, all things considered, of abortion; I am simply pointing to various factors in virtue of which I contend that the context of pregnancy due to rape differs from the violinist case. Further, I do not claim that all of these factors are of equal moral significance. My contention here is simply that *it does not follow* from the necessity of remaining plugged into the violinist that abortion is impermissible.

Thomson's violinist example is plausibly thought to be analogous to a case of pregnancy due to rape. But there are differences between the two contexts. As Rosalind Hursthouse has emphasized, rape is almost always a violent, brutal, and physically and psychologically painful experience

---

[13] Ibid., 131.

[14] Ibid.

[15] Hershenov is not arguing for the pro-life position. Rather, his view is that abortion cannot be defended by the sorts of considerations that are invoked by Thomson, on her assumption (which Hershenov elsewhere denies) that a human fetus is a person from conception. Hershenov, 148.

[16] Rosalind Hursthouse develops many of the same disanalogies. See Rosalind Hursthouse, *Beginning Lives* (Oxford: Blackwell Publishers, 1987), 178–216. Although we identify some similar disanalogies, Hursthouse focuses primarily on what I shall call "standard" cases of rape. Also, I shall point out in the text that our analyses of their significance differ.

for the woman who is raped. Let us begin with a typical rape, in which there is violent and painful nonconsensual imposition of sex on the woman. If pregnancy results, the woman now has in her body a developing human being with her genetic material conjoined with that of the rapist. Thus, to force the woman to carry this pregnancy to term would be to force her to bring into the world a child with her genes; this may well be something to which she deeply and legitimately objects, especially given that she may not want to keep the baby. Even if a mother plans to put a baby up for adoption, she may well object to being forced to bring into being a child with her genes—a child whom she cannot or will not care for, but about whom she would naturally have deep concerns.

Worse yet, to force the mother to carry this fetus to term would be to force her to bring into the world a child who has both her genes and those of the man who brutally victimized her. Again, she may object to having to bring into being a child that is in this way partly hers and partly his. I believe that she has a right that her genetic material not be fused with his in this way. The entire process of nurturing the fetus in pregnancy could not help but remind the mother of the brutal and painful rape. Further, if she should come into contact with or hear about the child (or adult) in the future, this would typically remind her of the pain and violation to which she was subjected. The mere knowledge that this individual exists, quite apart from any contact with him or her, would be likely to produce such feelings. And yet there would also be natural feelings of affection and identification with the developing fetus and then the child (and adult), should the mother be forced to carry the pregnancy to term. These ambivalent feelings would likely create a kind of mental torture that would be inflicted upon a mother, if she is not allowed to have an abortion.

I agree with Hursthouse, then, that in a case of pregnancy due to rape, typically there are features that are not present in the violinist case or the other cases discussed above. In the rape case, there is a distinctively brutal kind of sexual violation that then issues in a fetus with the genetic material of the mother fused with that of the rapist. If an abortion is not permitted, then the mother will have to nurture inside her—in the distinctive ways that a mother biologically supports a developing human organism—a being with her own genetic material and that of the rapist. Further, she will be forced to bring into the world such a being. Of course, there is nothing like this in the cases discussed above: the violinist does not have your genetic material (and your genes are not fused with those of a brutal victimizer). Although in the violinist case you are seriously inconvenienced, you are not painfully assaulted sexually. Future awareness of the violinist (perhaps attending his concerts or hearing his music on a compact disc) would certainly remind you of a period of some discomfort and inconvenience, but it would not evoke memories of the distinctively horrible kind of pain and victimization involved in rape.

I suppose someone might say that in a case such as Hershenov's example of the researcher and the cruise ship, the researcher might be significantly traumatized by the explosion of the ship and the subsequent deaths of many innocent people (which he might have witnessed). The child might always remind him of these terrible events. Perhaps this sort of trauma could be as horrible as the distinctively personal and sexual brutality of rape, but I am not sure of this. In any case, Hershenov's example would lack the feature of a being coming into existence with the mother's genetic material fused with that of her victimizer.

Indeed, Hershenov constructs his examples in such a way as to focus on what he takes to be parallel levels of sacrifice, pain, or burden between a pregnant woman and the relevant individuals in his thought experiments. Recall that he says about the researcher and the child:

> Even then, the raft will still be so crowded that either the child will have to sit on the lap of the biologist, or the latter will have to sit and sleep in an awkward position pressed against the child. Either arrangement will cause the researcher months of discomfort equivalent to that of pregnancy or the predicament of the person supporting the violinist.[17]

And Hershenov says about the birdwatchers entangled in ropes:

> Because of the way they are positioned, the much larger person will hit the ground first and his body will shield the smaller person from all injuries. The larger person knows that due to the way he will hit the ground, he will suffer nine months of intermittent back pain, nausea, and abdominal swelling comparable to what a pregnant woman bears.[18]

It is striking in these passages that Hershenov focuses on alleged parallels between the levels of pain, discomfort, and inconvenience that are suffered by the individuals in his examples and by pregnant women. I think that he may too easily assume that such parallels exist, especially when pregnancy is due to rape. Whereas a parallel of this sort may in fact be present in some elaborate examples, an exclusive focus on this set of dimensions leaves out crucial *differences* between the examples and pregnancy due to rape. Hershenov, thus, loses sight of the special problems stemming from the existence of a fetus who has the mother's genetic material together with that of her rapist.

My previous discussion of these issues was mistaken in a similar way. In "Abortion and Self-Determination" I wrote:

[17] Hershenov, "Abortions and Distortions," 133.
[18] Ibid., 134.

Clearly, there are extremely easy, uncomplicated pregnancies, and extremely difficult, complicated pregnancies, and a range of cases in between. Intuitively, the very easy pregnancies are in the relevant respects rather like the surgery and cabin cases, whereas the difficult pregnancies are more like the violinist case. Because of the variation in the difficulty (and thus intrusive and disruptive nature) of pregnancy, it is difficult to say whether it is, on balance, more like the violinist case or the surgery and cabin cases.[19]

Again, the focus on the "difficulty" of the pregnancy hides other relevant differences between *all* of the cases (violinist, surgery, and cabin) and pregnancy due to rape.

There may be other cases of rape that are a bit different from what might be called the "standard" kind of case. I am now thinking of the phenomenon of "date rape," in which someone surreptitiously, say, slips into a woman's drink a drug that renders her unconscious and thus vulnerable to sexual exploitation. The drug may induce subsequent amnesia or only partial memory of the episode. Let us suppose that a woman becomes pregnant as a result of date rape of roughly the kind that I have just described. It might now be suggested that she would not have the same sort of traumatic associations that would be present in a woman who was forced to carry a pregnancy to term in a standard case of rape. But this suggestion is too facile.

Although the resonances would no doubt be different, they still would be significant and disturbing. The woman would still know that she had been exploited and victimized, even if she had been unaware of this victimization as it happened. Further, she now knows that her genetic material is fused with that of her victimizer. If she is prevented from terminating the pregnancy, then she would be forced to bring into the world a baby who is in this way both hers and that of her victimizer. No one should be forced to do this, in my view. Her inevitable awareness of the child (and the adult) in the future could not help but remind her of her victimization, and I believe that she has the right to decide whether or not she wishes such a being to come into the world.

VI. AUTONOMY AND THE RIGHT TO CONTROL ONE'S BODY REVISITED

As far as I know, Rosalind Hursthouse is the only other philosopher who has defended the claim that whereas it may well be unacceptable to detach oneself from the violinist in Thomson's original example, it does not follow that it would be impermissible to have an abortion in the case

---

[19] Fischer, "Abortion and Self-Determination," 10.

of rape.[20] I have considerable admiration for Hursthouse's description of the ways in which the context of pregnancy due to rape differs from the violinist example, a description that focuses on many of the same features that I have identified above. We do, however, have a difference of opinion about how ultimately to interpret the relevant phenomena.

Hursthouse criticizes Thomson for what Hursthouse takes to be an exclusive focus on moral rights; she believes that the conceptual scheme of rights is insufficiently nuanced to capture all the relevant facts about abortion. Hursthouse says:

> [Thomson's article discusses] abortion in terms of the right to determine what happens in or to one's own body. No other real case of killing involves the exercise of this right; abortion does and is thereby unique. However, that abortion, as a case of killing, uniquely involves the exercise of the right is far from being its only special feature, and I would maintain that the fundamental flaw in Thomson's article is that this is the only special feature she clearly recognizes. This flaw underlies her singular concentration on rights. . . .[21]

In a later passage, Hursthouse says:

> That pregnancy is utterly unlike the violinist situation in these different ways is, of course, perfectly obvious, though all too easily forgotten in the context of abstract philosophy. What is not so obvious is why they are morally relevant. They are relevant because abortions are sought for reasons which connect with these facts.
>
> It is a notable aspect of Thomson's article that very little is said about women's reasons for wanting abortions. . . . Now this is once again the result of the preoccupation with rights and hence with acts which are unjust; for the injustice of an act is largely determined by whether or not it violates rights, independently of the agent's reasons for acting so.[22]

Hursthouse then takes it that an "abstract philosophy" that focuses on rights cannot account for the subtle and complex reasons why women would want abortions. She is thus inclined away from a rights-based moral philosophy and toward some sort of Neo-Aristotelian, virtue-based approach.[23]

In contrast to Hursthouse, I am not inclined to think that the disanalogies between such cases as the violinist example and pregnancy due to

[20] Hursthouse, *Beginning Lives*.
[21] Ibid., 204–5.
[22] Ibid., 207–8.
[23] Ibid., esp. 218–37.

rape can only be captured by moving away from a rights-based morality. Actually, I think that they point us back toward the ideas of autonomy and the right to control one's body—the right to determine what happens in or to one's body. Perhaps above interpretations or uses of the notions of autonomy or the right to control one's body were too crude, and a more refined analysis of these ideas is called for. Although I cannot give a systematic or detailed refinement, I shall sketch the direction in which such an approach might go.

Start with the basic idea that persons have a right to autonomy. Now this right is an abstract right, composed of a bundle of more specific rights. One of these rights, presumably, is the right to control one's body: the right (as Thomson puts it) to determine what happens in or to one's body. One interpretation of this right is the right that someone else not be in contact with one's body, thereby using some part of it. The discussion above suggests that this is not the correct interpretation of this right, insofar as this right is supposed to outweigh another individual's right to life. An alternative interpretation, suggested by the above discussion, includes the right not to be forced to carry to term—to nourish and biologically sustain in the distinctively human way—an entity in which one's genetic material is fused with that of someone who has victimized one in certain ways. I think that it is plausible that a woman has the right to control her body, interpreted in this way. So understood, we do not yet have any example in which another's right to life outweighs this right.

I have suggested what I have called an interpretation of the content of the right to control one's body. Alternatively, the proposal could be that we need properly to specify the members of the bundle of more specific rights that compose the right to control one's body. Presumably there is a hierarchy of rights, with the right to autonomy being relatively abstract or general. It is composed of a bundle of more concrete or specific rights, including the right to control one's body. This right, in turn, is composed of a bundle of more specific rights, including the right not to be forced to have one's genetic essence fused with that of one's victimizer and allowed to become the blueprint of a being that is nurtured and brought into the world in the distinctive way in which a mother nurtures a developing fetus and brings it into the world.

By refining one's analysis or interpretation of autonomy, Thomson's basic idea can be defended, and one need not depart from a rights-based approach in order to capture her fundamental, intuitive ideas. She started with the idea that even if a fetus has a stringent right to life from conception, there are certain circumstances (such as rape) in which abortion would be permissible. Further, she explained the permissibility of abortion in those circumstances in terms of a woman's right to determine what happens in or to her body. I think that this points us in exactly the right direction. It may be that the violinist case does not capture the specific way in which it is unacceptable to use or violate another's body, but it does not follow that human beings do not have the right, suitably interpreted, to determine what happens in and to our bodies. More specifically, it does not follow that a woman does not have a right to determine whether she brings to term—nourishes and biologically sustains—an entity whose genetic material is fused with that of someone who has victimized her in certain ways, a right that is arguably stronger than the fetus's right to life.

VII. AN OBJECTION

I believe that something like the above rudimentary sketch of an autonomy- and rights-based account can adequately support Thomson's basic intuition about the permissibility of abortion in cases of rape. One might, however, feel a residual dissatisfaction with my account. Let us suppose that we could involuntarily render a woman unconscious (perhaps using the "date rape" drug that I referred to above) and then implant in her a fertilized egg, which, in this case, is someone else's. Now it would surely be just as objectionable to require this woman to carry the pregnancy to term here as it would be in the two previous rape cases. And yet the woman's right to control her DNA—that is, the right that she not be forced to allow her DNA to be fused with that of her victimizer and to bring the new being into the world—does not apply here.

I still would want to say that abortion is permissible in a context such as this. Recall what I said above about a previous case: "If an abortion is not permitted, then the mother will have to nurture inside her—in the distinctive ways that a mother biologically and emotionally supports the developing human organism—a being with her own genetic material and that of the rapist." The case now under consideration shows how the various elements of this quotation can pull apart: a woman could (hypothetically at least) be forced to nurture inside her—in the distinctive ways that a mother biologically supports the developing organism—a being who does not possess her genetic material. And a woman may find this also unacceptable.

I think that this case shows that another more concrete right in the cluster of rights that constitutes the right to control one's body must include the right not to have one's body used against one's will to nurture a developing organism in the distinctive way that a mother biologically supports the developing human organism. Even if the genetic material is not the mother's own, there is a natural tendency to develop feelings of identification with the organism developing inside her. These feelings and emotional identifications are deep. A woman who was forced to be subject to these feelings, knowing that she was exploited and victimized in the implantation of a fertilized egg from which an organism developed, would typically have feelings of ambivalence and resentment not unlike those that I sketched above. I believe that it is unacceptable to require a woman to be tortured in this way. Note that, as above, the torture would not stop once the child was born, for the memories of exploitation in this particularly personal and "biologically deep" way would likely persist throughout her life. Again, I believe that the proper analysis of this admittedly somewhat far-fetched and difficult kind of case will start with the notions of autonomy and the right to control one's body. Here, as with the other cases of rape, what emerges is the need for a more refined interpretation of the right to control one's body. The problems stem from the distinct sort of victimization that is involved in rape (or, more broadly, the involuntary causation of pregnancy).

In exploring whether there is a moral difference between Thomson's violinist example and his birdwatchers case, Hershenov says:

> Could the difference be due to the distinction between being dependent on the inside rather than the outside of someone's body? I don't think this distinction is psychologically or morally pertinent. The irrelevance of any inner-outer distinction can be highlighted by the fact that the burdens that the larger person suffers from the impact turn out to be internal in nature—nausea, spinal problems, and abdominal swelling—though the latter can also be classified as an external effect. So while an internal organ is not used in the way the kidney is, it is internal organs, tissues, and bones that are adversely affected by the fall.[24]

But the morally relevant factors are not *simply* "internal." I have suggested that they pertain to one's biological essence and also the distinctively human process of biological development—the way in which a mother biologically supports the developing organism and is deeply emotionally affected by this process. Internal organs, tissues, and bones may be adversely affected by the larger birdwatcher's fall, and this may result in serious pain and suffering. But I would contend that this suffering is of an importantly different nature than the specific form of suffering that is endured by a woman who is forced to carry to term a pregnancy induced in the ways that we have envisaged—by brutal victimization or even insidious victimization. The "internal/external" distinction is not sufficiently refined to capture this difference. What is at stake, at the most fundamental level, is the woman's right to control her reproductive capacity.

VIII. A Further Clarification

Consider the following modification of the researcher and raft scenario proposed by Hershenov (who, now, substitutes a female for the original male researcher):

---

[24] Hershenov, "Abortions and Distortions," 136.

Years earlier, the researcher had one of her eggs involuntarily taken from her body. She was aware of and horrified by this invasion. Then the egg was fertilized by the man responsible for the invasion of the woman's body. Assume that a second woman voluntarily carried the fetus to term. The resulting child, genetically tied to the wronged woman researcher and the man who wronged her, is on the cruise ship. The tremendous blast of the cruise ship sends the child onto the research raft, where it imposes on the woman's body. (The researcher knows that this child is genetically her own.) The researcher must push into the water either the child or her irreplaceable equipment since there isn't room on the raft for both.[25]

Hershenov asks whether my intuition is that the woman does not have to support the child. As Hershenov points out, the researcher is faced with providing nine months of bodily support to the child of the man who violated her bodily integrity. The child, unlike the fetus, may even look like the evil man. One can similarly ask whether one's intuitions about the cabin case would change, if the individual who arrives at one's doorstep had been created as the result of the sort of process described above, or, say, the theft of one's sperm.

I reply that my view is not that one has some sort of right to destroy—or to fail to assist—any person who was created as a result of one's genetic material having been involuntarily taken, whether egg or sperm. Surely, even if a man's sperm has been stolen from a sperm bank and used, without his consent, to fertilize an egg, the man has no right to kill the resulting child. Rather, my view is that a woman has the right to control her reproductive capacity: she has the right not to be forced to nourish and sustain and bring into the world a baby who was conceived as a result of rape. Because of the intimate and distinctive nature and meaning of this biological process, and the typical physical and emotional changes that it induces in a woman, she has the right to control it. But once such a child has been brought into the world, the structure of one's rights and obligations changes.[26]

---

[25] Hershenov, personal correspondence to the author, August 23, 2001.

[26] It might be thought that if a woman has the right to control her reproductive capacity in the way that I have suggested in the text, then it should not matter whether the pregnancy was due to rape. Even if the pregnancy were due to voluntary intercourse without the use of contraception, it would seem that the mother's right to control her reproductive capacity would imply the permissibility of abortion. After all, the fact of rape does not in any way diminish the fetus's rights or status.

I am not in fact committed to the contention that the fact of rape makes the sort of difference that I have indicated above in the text. But I would point out that, although rape does not in any way diminish the fetus's status or right to life, it may well change how we weigh the totality of factors that go into our all-things-considered judgment about the permissibility of abortion. Given that the fetus is assumed to be a person, it may be that a woman's right to control her reproductive capacity does not imply the permissibility of abortion, given that she has not used contraceptive measures and has had voluntary intercourse. This is a delicate and difficult issue.

IX. Conclusion

Some critics have contended that Thomson's well-known violinist example is disanalogous in an important way to the context of pregnancy. They have typically thought that, whereas it is permissible to unplug yourself from Thomson's violinist, it is *not* permissible to have an abortion. They have suggested that abortion is a case of killing, whereas unplugging yourself would merely be a case of letting die, or that abortion is intentional killing, whereas unplugging yourself is merely unintended but foreseeable killing, and so forth. Many other alleged asymmetries have been suggested by Thomson's critics. I too have highlighted asymmetries, but they have been in service of precisely the opposite conclusion: Although it is not permissible to unplug yourself from the violinist, it is permissible to have an abortion in certain circumstances, in particular, in the context of rape.

I have contended that other critiques either fail to take note of the distinctive wrongness of forcing a woman to bring into the world a baby conceived as a result of rape, or they too quickly conclude that this distinctive wrongness cannot be understood in terms of the right to autonomy and, thus, the right to control one's body. Thomson's violinist example may be crude in certain ways, but it points us in the right direction. Surely it *is* outrageous to force a woman to acquiesce to her most essential biological feature—her DNA—being used in the way in which it is used in a case of pregnancy due to rape. It is, surely, equally outrageous to force a woman to allow her reproductive capacity to be used against her will. So, even if a fetus is assumed to be a person from conception (an assumption that I am not inclined to make), and even if it is unacceptable to unplug yourself from the violinist, it would *not* follow that abortion is in all contexts impermissible.

Philosophy, University of California, Riverside

FREEDOM AS A POLITICAL IDEAL*

By Steven Wall

I. Introduction

I shall assume that a well-ordered state is one that promotes the freedom of its subjects. My question is what is the kind of freedom that the state ought to promote? This question is different from the question of what freedom is. It might be thought, for example, that freedom consists in the autonomous pursuit of valuable goals and projects, but that the state cannot directly promote this freedom. On this view, the state would not be able to make its citizens free. However, it might be able to do things that make it easier or more likely for them to be free. The freedom that the state promotes might be merely an aspect of or a condition for the freedom that really matters.

A political ideal of freedom tells us what kind of freedom the state ought to promote. If the ideal is sound, and if a state successfully promotes the kind of freedom that this political ideal identifies, then the state will have done all that it can do to promote the freedom of its subjects, even if some of its subjects remain substantially unfree. My purpose in this essay is to articulate and defend a particular ideal of political freedom. This ideal holds that the state ought to promote and sustain an environment in which its subjects are best able to carry out their plans and to form new ones. The freedom-supportive state, on the ideal that I shall offer, is the state that best enables its subjects to plan their lives, whatever their plans might be.

II. Political Freedom and Personal Autonomy

Political freedom is valuable because of its contribution to the freedom of individual persons. Here I shall assume, but will not defend, the claim that individual freedom is best understood in terms of personal autonomy.[1] I shall also assume a particular understanding of autonomy. An autonomous life is one in which a person charts his own course through

---

* I would like to thank Ellen Frankel Paul and fellow contributors to this volume for their helpful comments and suggestions.

[1] Many writers distinguish freedom from autonomy. They hold that freedom applies to particular options, whereas autonomy refers to the way in which a person leads his life over time. See, for example, Joel Feinberg, *Harm to Self* (Oxford: Oxford University Press, 1986), 62–68. I do not deny that this distinction can serve some theoretical purposes. But, because my concern in this essay is with what a state should do to assist persons in leading free lives, I shall not insist on the distinction here.

307

life, fashioning his character by self-consciously choosing projects and assuming commitments from a wide range of eligible alternatives, and making something out of his life according to his own understanding of what is valuable and worth doing. So described, autonomy is a distinctive ideal. It applies to a person's whole life or to large stretches of it.

To realize autonomy, one needs several things. One needs at least (1) the capacity to form complex intentions and to sustain commitments, (2) the independence necessary to chart one's own course through life and to develop one's own understanding of what is valuable and worth doing, (3) the self-consciousness and vigor necessary to take control of one's affairs, and (4) access to an environment that provides one with a wide range of valuable options.[2] Elements (1) and (3) refer to mental capacities and virtues. Element (2) refers to one's relations with other persons who could exercise power over one. Element (4) refers to the environment in which one lives.

I shall argue that the state should be primarily concerned with the second and fourth elements. A freedom-supportive state is one that protects the independence of its subjects and ensures that they have access to a wide range of valuable options. The reason for limiting the concern of the state to elements (2) and (4) is that the state is generally not an effective instrument for cultivating mental capacities and virtues.[3] When the state attempts to improve individuals' psychologies or remove intrapersonal barriers, it is likely to do more harm than good. The state that attempts to make its subjects masters of themselves will likely just end up oppressing them.[4] This is not to say that the lack of certain psychological capacities or the presence of certain internal constraints do not diminish or undermine autonomy. They clearly do. My argument here simply recognizes the limits of the state's power to promote freedom.

This is why a political ideal of freedom should not be identified with freedom itself. The freedom that the state should promote and protect is valuable and important, but it is a only part of and a condition for the freedom that really matters.[5] It should now be clear why a state that does

---

[2] I discuss each of these requirements in greater detail in Steven Wall, *Liberalism, Perfectionism, and Restraint* (Cambridge: Cambridge University Press, 1998), 127–61.

[3] There are a few things that the state can effectively do in this regard. For example, it can do its best to ensure that all children receive an adequate education. But even here there are serious limits to what the state can do. Whether a child receives the kind of education that he needs to live an autonomous life depends more on what his parents do than what his state does.

[4] Here I follow Isaiah Berlin, *Four Essays on Liberty* (Oxford: Oxford University Press, 1969), 131–34; and Philip Pettit, *A Theory of Freedom: From the Psychology to the Politics of Agency* (Oxford: Oxford University Press, 2001), 127. As Berlin notes, "many of the nationalist, communist, authoritarian and totalitarian creeds of our day" have been informed by a view of freedom as self-mastery (144).

[5] The freedom that the state promotes may be valuable for its own sake, in addition to its contribution toward what I have been calling "the freedom that really matters"; but I shall not consider this possibility in this essay. I shall assume that the primary reason why political freedom is valuable is that it contributes to the autonomy of those who enjoy it.

all that it can and should do in promoting freedom may exercise authority over some individuals who remain substantially unfree. Their failure to be free is not *its* failure.

III. Three Problems

What kind of freedom should the state promote? What kind of freedom-supportive environment should it strive to create and sustain? A political ideal of freedom provides answers to these questions. But, of course, there are rival ideals of political freedom. How should we decide between them?

I suggest that any satisfactory political ideal of freedom must respond well to three problems. I shall refer to these problems as *the problem of integrity, the problem of pluralism,* and *the problem of unacceptable implications.* We may be able to decide between rival political ideals of freedom by assessing how well each responds to these problems. This, at any rate, is the approach that I shall take in this essay.[6]

The three problems require explanation. *The problem of integrity* is the problem of showing how political freedom is a distinct ideal, one that is not reducible to some other ideal and one that is capable of conflicting with other values. There is a temptation in political philosophy to make freedom compatible with all that is valuable. When this temptation is not resisted, freedom becomes a master value that subsumes all that is thought to be valuable. Likewise, there is a temptation to reduce freedom to some other value or ideal, since doing so provides a ready explanation for why freedom is valuable. For example, it is sometimes claimed that a freedom-supportive state is a state that treats its subjects with equal concern and respect.[7] Such a claim threatens to reduce political freedom to equality.

An adequate account of political freedom must not succumb to these temptations. Political freedom is one ideal that a state should be concerned with. Promoting political freedom may conflict with other values that the state should also be concerned with, such as security, equality, or excellence. The best state is not necessarily the state that best promotes and sustains political freedom.[8] The problem of integrity, then, is to explain the value of political freedom without claiming too much or too little for it. If too much is claimed for it, then it will not give us a clear target at which the state could aim. If too little is claimed for it, then

---

[6] Naturally, I believe that these three problems are especially important ones, even if they are not the only ones that confront an account of political freedom.

[7] See Ronald M. Dworkin, "What Is Equality? Part 3: The Place of Liberty," *Iowa Law Review* 73 (1987): 1–54.

[8] I shall make no attempt in this essay to assess how important political freedom is compared to other values that the state can promote or protect, such as security, equality, or excellence.

political freedom will direct us toward some other ideal or value to which it is reducible.

The second problem, *the problem of pluralism*, refers to the fact that political freedom can be reduced or diminished by different factors. Sometimes theorists attempt to show that there is only one freedom-reducing factor—such as physical obstruction—and that all other (purported) freedom-reducing factors are really just instances of this one factor. Below I shall argue that this is a mistake. And if it is a mistake, then an important problem must be faced. Assuming that there exists a plurality of freedom-reducing factors, each of which is not reducible to the others, then how should these factors be combined or aggregated into one overall measure of political freedom? If one state does a good job of minimizing one freedom-reducing factor, and another state does a worse job of minimizing this factor, but a better job of minimizing others, then how are we to decide which state is better in terms of promoting political freedom? The need to find satisfactory answers to these questions is the problem of pluralism.

The problem of unacceptable implications is the most straightforward of the three problems. Theoretical discussions of individual freedom notoriously give rise to troubling paradoxes.[9] The same is true of political freedom. The problem of unacceptable implications concerns how to avoid or at least diminish the force of these paradoxes. An account of political freedom that has strongly counterintuitive implications is one that should not be accepted. For example, if an account of political freedom yields the judgment that a state that engages in an enormous amount of coercive interference in the lives of its subjects is one that scores well in terms of political freedom, then we should reject this account. The difficulty is that each account of political freedom will give rise to its own set of counterintuitive implications.

The ideal of political freedom that I shall propose and defend in Section VI relates judgments of freedom to the opportunities that persons have to plan their lives. As such, this ideal is vulnerable to the objection that a state can make its subjects "more free" by getting them to change or simplify their plans. Thus, on this objection, subjects of *Brave New World* might paradoxically turn out to be living in a free state.[10] Obviously, this would be an unacceptable implication. For my ideal of political freedom to be at all plausible, I shall need to explain why it does not have this implication.

---

[9] These paradoxes result from the fact that there exists a range of highly plausible, but mutually inconsistent, judgments about freedom. For example, the judgment that a person who hands over his money at gunpoint does not perform a free act conflicts with the judgment that a person cannot be unfree to perform an act that he actually does. For discussion of a number of these paradoxes see Christine Swanton, *Freedom: A Coherence Theory* (Indianapolis, IN: Hackett, 1992).

[10] See Berlin, introduction to *Four Essays on Liberty*, lii.

There are likely other problems that are relevant to assessing rival ideals of political freedom. But the problems of integrity, pluralism, and unacceptable implications are central problems. A satisfactory ideal of political freedom must be able to present freedom as a distinct value, show how different freedom-reducing factors can be combined in overall judgments of a free state, and show how the account of political freedom that it offers can avoid grossly unacceptable implications.

IV. RIVAL IDEALS

Keeping these problems in mind, I now consider two important ideals of political freedom that rival the one that I shall be defending. I refer to these rival ideals as *freedom as noninterference* and *freedom as nondomination*.[11] The selection of these two ideals for discussion is motivated in part by their importance and in part by what can be learned from them. As we shall begin to see in the next section, a better ideal of political freedom is one that builds upon the insights of both of these rival ideals while avoiding the problems that they encounter.[12]

Let us start with freedom as noninterference, an ideal that has deep roots in the liberal tradition of political thought. Adherents of this ideal view interference as the primary threat to freedom. A freedom-supportive state, they hold, will be one that does a good job of reducing interference. However, to understand exactly what this means, we must clarify the concept of interference. If a state offers its citizens a subsidy to visit natural parks, then in one sense this subsidy may be an act of interference, but not in a sense relevant to freedom as noninterference.[13] Likewise, if a person offers me unwanted advice, then he may be interfering with my affairs; but, here too, not in a sense relevant to freedom as noninterference. Thus, judgments of interference taken from ordinary language are not identical to judgments of interference as this phrase relates to political freedom. We therefore need to analyze the sense of interference in question.[14] I propose the following account: *A interferes with B if A hinders B*

---

[11] For discussions of freedom as noninterference, see Berlin, *Four Essays on Liberty*; David Miller, "Constraints on Freedom," *Ethics* 94 (1984): 66–86; and Jan Narveson, *The Libertarian Idea* (Philadelphia: Temple University Press, 1988), chaps. 2, 4. For discussions of freedom as nondomination see Philip Pettit, *Republicanism: A Theory of Freedom and Government* (Oxford: Oxford University Press, 1997), chaps. 2–3; and Pettit, *A Theory of Freedom*, chaps. 6–7.

[12] A third important and influential ideal of political freedom, one that I shall not discuss here, identifies a freedom-supportive state with the state that best promotes civic participation. I criticize this radical democratic view of political freedom in detail in Steven Wall, "Radical Democracy, Personal Freedom, and the Transformative Potential of Politics," *Social Philosophy and Policy* 17, no. 1 (2000): 225–54.

[13] But in this example will not the subsidy itself have been raised by coercive interference? Not necessarily. If we like, we can stipulate that the subsidy is raised from revenues from the state's voluntary lottery.

[14] I draw here on my discussion in Steven Wall, "Freedom, Interference, and Domination," *Political Studies* 49, no. 2 (2001): 216–30.

from doing what B would have done in the absence of A's action. And I propose that we say that to hinder someone from doing something is either to prevent him from doing it or to make it more costly for him to do it. According to this definition, acts of interference either remove options from people or increase the costs to them of choosing the options that remain open.

This construal of interference is formulated with certain threats to freedom in mind. Coercive directives are the primary means by which agents of the state (but not only agents of the state) interfere with the lives of others. An ideal of political freedom should accordingly put the focus on coercive directives. Offering bribes or giving advice may in some circumstances plausibly be said to reduce the freedom of those who are targeted by such efforts,[15] but for the purpose of assessing political freedom, we can put such cases to one side.

A more difficult issue concerns whether interference must be intentional. If *A* hinders *B* by mistake, has *A* interfered with *B*? The focus on coercion suggests that interference is the result of intentional action. But perhaps this is too restrictive.[16] If I am unable to carry out some plan because an obstacle has been put in my path, then I may have been interfered with, irrespective of whether the obstacle was deliberately placed in my path or whether its placement was an unintended consequence of human action. Let us say, then, that *A* hinders *B* if *A* either does so intentionally or does so in a way for which it makes sense for *B* to ask *A* for a justification for his action. If this is correct, then not every obstacle placed in my path will be an interference, but sometimes I will be interfered with even when no one intended to do so.

Many other difficult issues remain. Manipulation is a freedom-reducing form of interference, but it does not remove options or increase the cost of pursuing them. Instead, it distorts the way in which persons decide which options they want to pursue. Nevertheless, we can say that, in common with coercive directives, manipulation hinders a person from doing what he would have done in the absence of such interference. A more difficult problem concerns how property rights relate to or condition acts of interference. If the police prevent me from trespassing on your land, then the state has interfered with me. But it surely matters whether or not you have legitimate property rights to the land in question.[17] A full account of interference must address this matter, but I shall pass over it here.

---

[15] For discussion see Harry G. Frankfurt, "Coercion and Responsibility," in Ted Honderich, ed., *Essays on Freedom of Action* (London: Routledge and Kegan Paul, 1973); and J. P. Day, "Threats, Offers, Law, Opinion, and Liberty," *American Philosophical Quarterly* 14, no. 4 (1977): 257–72.

[16] David Miller, "Constraints on Freedom," *Ethics* 92, no. 4 (1983): 66–86.

[17] When you talk with the police, you might say that I am interfering with you because I am trespassing on your land. This suggests that in order to identify acts of interference we need first to have specified who has rights to what. I return to this point in Section VII below.

As sketchy as these remarks are, they go some way toward giving content to the ideal of freedom as noninterference. According to this ideal, a freedom-supportive state will reduce or minimize interference. It will strive to establish an environment in which its subjects are able to pursue their plans free from interference and coercion by others. Those who adhere to the ideal of freedom as noninterference need not think that the state should never interfere in order to promote other values. They might think that other values should sometimes take precedence over political freedom, but when this occurs they will view it as imposing a cost, even if they think that it is a cost worth paying.[18]

So described, freedom as noninterference captures some of the truth about political freedom, but it is not a sound ideal. Before discussing the problems that it encounters, I want to introduce the second ideal that I mentioned above—freedom as nondomination.[19] Domination can take the form of interference, but, importantly, it is not reducible to it. A can dominate B without interfering with him, and A can interfere with B without dominating him. So the goal of reducing domination can diverge from the goal of reducing interference. Freedom as nondomination holds that the former goal is the one that a freedom-supportive state should pursue.

But what exactly is domination? In the sense relevant to political freedom, it refers to the condition or status of living at the mercy of another. Consider the case of a slave. A slave is distinguished from a nonslave by the slave's complete lack of independence. He lives his life utterly subject to the arbitrary will of his master. Importantly, the slave remains a slave even if his master allows him, for the most part, to do as he pleases. A slave is still a slave even when he has a liberal master.

Slavery, of course, is an extreme instance of domination. Less extreme instances abound in everyday life. A woman lives under the dominating eye of her husband. A junior member of a firm does not speak his mind to his senior colleagues. And a small business owner is paralyzed by the fact that his government may, at any moment, arbitrarily confiscate his economic assets. Each of these subjects lives, to a lesser or greater extent, under the arbitrary control of others. Notice, moreover, that in each of these examples, the dominated person need not be "interfered with" by those who dominate him. The woman may never be interfered with by her husband because she realizes how to please him. The junior member of the firm may learn to hold his tongue and the business owner may never be interfered with because his government does not confiscate his

---

[18] See Berlin, introduction to *Four Essays on Liberty*, liii–liv.

[19] The leading contemporary proponent of freedom as nondomination is Pettit. My discussion of domination draws on, but does not perfectly follow, his account of this concept. See Pettit, *Republicanism*; and Pettit, *A Theory of Freedom*. Pettit follows Quentin Skinner, *Liberty Before Liberalism* (Cambridge: Cambridge University Press, 1998), in holding that this ideal of political freedom has deep roots in the civic republican tradition of political thought.

assets. Thus, domination does not require actual interference. This is why domination can occur in the absence of interference.[20]

Reflection on these examples suggests the following general account. Domination is a condition that exists within a social relationship when one party is subject to the arbitrary power of another. We can measure the intensity of domination along four main dimensions: (1) How extensive is the power that is exercised within the relationship? (2) How predictable is its exercise? (3) To what extent is this power subject to checks? And (4) how easy is it for the dominated party to exit the relationship?

The first and fourth dimensions are reasonably clear, but the second and third require comment. When someone rules in an arbitrary manner, he often does so capriciously. For instance, we call a government arbitrary when it rules by decree and not according to the rule of law. One important element of arbitrary power, then, is unpredictable rule.[21] But this cannot be the whole story about such power. To see why, consider this example: an abusive husband rules over his wife in strict accordance with a set of rules that he has formulated. Here we have a case of domination that does not involve submission to the capricious will of another. The husband's behavior is predictable and consistent.[22] So, if the wife in this example is dominated, and if domination is to be understood in terms of being subject to the arbitrary will of another, then there must be more to arbitrary rule than capricious rule.

What then is the additional element? The answer is to be found in the kind of vulnerability involved in being subject to domination. The dominated person's ability to make her own decisions about her life depends crucially on the will of another. In our example, the dominated wife lives her life under the watchful eye of her husband. Even if she is able to predict his behavior, she remains subject to his rules, not her own. Moreover, she is not in a position to force him to change his rules so that they are more acceptable to her. The power that he exercises over her is arbitrary in the sense that she has no way to make it track her interests.[23] Much power that is arbitrary in this sense is also capricious and unpre-

---

[20] Domination can occur in the absence of interference, but might it be reducible to expected interference? The idea that it can be is defended by Ian Carter in his *A Measure of Freedom* (Oxford: Oxford University Press, 1999), 237–45. On Carter's view, the dominated agent is unfree because there is a high probability that he will be interfered with if he acts or attempts to act in a number of ways that are open to him. But this reduction of domination to expected interference fails to explain why unpredictable interference is worse (from the standpoint of freedom) than predictable interference. Two agents who confront the same amount of expected interference might differ in their freedom if one is able to predict the interference, whereas the other is not. This is true, at least, on the view of political freedom that I shall defend below in the text, a view that understands freedom in terms of the nonobstruction of planning.

[21] See Jeremy Waldron, "The Rule of Law in Contemporary Liberal Theory," *Ratio Juris* 2, no. 1 (1989): 79–96.

[22] I am assuming here that the husband does not frequently and unpredictably change the set of rules that he strictly adheres to in dominating his wife.

[23] See Pettit, *A Theory of Freedom*, 134.

dictable. But power can be arbitrary, even if it is not exercised capriciously, so long as those who are subject to it have no way to check it or to force it to take account of their interests.[24]

A fully adequate account of domination would need to provide some way to integrate or balance the four different dimensions that I listed above (the extent of power exercised, its degree of predictability, the extent of checks upon it, and its degree of avoidability). But I shall not attempt this integration here. I hope that these brief remarks on domination suffice to give us a reasonably clear picture of the ideal of freedom as nondomination. This ideal rightly views the state as a (potentially) very dangerous, dominating agent. After all, states claim the authority to rule every aspect of our lives. States often rule in unpredictable and arbitrary ways, and the costs of exiting our relationship with them are extremely high. Accordingly, proponents of freedom as nondomination typically view a freedom-supportive state as one that exercises a minimum of arbitrary power. If you are to be politically free, they insist, you "must not fall into a condition of political subjection or dependence, thereby leaving yourself open to the danger of being forcibly or coercively deprived by your government of your life, liberty, and estates."[25]

Beyond the goal of reducing the arbitrary power of the state, and in some tension with this end, freedom as nondomination directs the state to combat domination within civil society. As the above examples suggested, many forms of domination exist within nonpolitical, social relationships. Thus, on the nondomination view of political freedom, a freedom-supportive state not only must minimize its own arbitrary power, but also must seek to create and sustain an environment in which the arbitrary power of others is also minimized.

V. POLITICAL FREEDOM AND ITS VALUE

I have been discussing two rival ideals of political freedom, freedom as noninterference and freedom as nondomination. I now want to argue that, despite their genuine attractions, neither ideal is adequate. One reason for this is that each ideal exposes inadequacies in the other. To see this, consider the following two archetypal governments.[26]

The Arbitrary Liberal Government: This is a government that interferes in the lives of its subjects much less often and with much less

---

[24] Ibid. Pettit describes arbitrary rule as rule that is "not forced to track the interferee's avowable interests and that typically reflects the interests or perceptions of the interferer." But this does not capture the other element of arbitrariness—namely, subjection to the unpredictable or capricious will of another. And this other element is, as we shall see, important to assessing political freedom.

[25] Skinner, *Liberty Before Liberalism*, 69–70.

[26] I have discussed slightly different versions of these examples elsewhere. See Wall, "Freedom, Interference, and Domination," 220–24.

intensity than the governments of almost all modern states. For the most part, its massive regulatory powers remain underutilized. But this government is not freedom-supportive. It rules by administrative fiat, and its regulations are not rationally consistent or predictable. As a result, its subjects have great difficulty planning their lives. They never know what their government is going to do next.

The Nonarbitrary Illiberal Government: This is a government that is constrained by well-designed constitutional checks and balances. It governs in strict accordance with the rule of law. And it governs in a manner that does a reasonably good job of tracking the interests of those who are subject to its power. Nonetheless, the government is illiberal in the sense that it interferes with its subjects to a much greater degree than do the governments of almost all modern states. It regulates a wide range of activities, for example, prohibiting smoking and drinking, enforcing dietary restrictions and exercise requirements, and nationalizing schools and hospitals.

These examples represent ideal types. Most arbitrary governments are not liberal, and most nonarbitrary governments do not interfere with their subjects to such an extreme extent. But the examples, while not fully realistic, raise an important question. From the standpoint of political freedom, which is worse, the arbitrary liberal government or the nonarbitrary illiberal government?

To answer this question confidently we would need to know much more about the details of these two governments. But this should not distract us here. The point of the question is that an adequate ideal of political freedom should give us some way of thinking about how to answer it. It should help us to think about which is worse from the standpoint of political freedom, arbitrary power or illiberal interference. Neither freedom as noninterference nor freedom as nondomination help us to approach this question. Or, to put the point more precisely, each does so in a way that is too easy. If proponents of freedom as noninterference judge the arbitrary liberal government to be freedom-supportive simply because it seldom interferes, then they are clearly missing something important. Such a judgment would be an unacceptable implication of their view. Likewise, if proponents of freedom as nondomination judge the nonarbitrary illiberal government to be freedom-supportive, simply because it does not act arbitrarily, then they too are missing something important. Such a judgment would be an unacceptable implication of their view.

Can these self-indicting judgments be resisted? Do proponents of these ideals have the resources to account for the archetypical governments that I have presented?[27] If the answer is no, then we have good reason to look for a third ideal of political freedom. Before drawing this conclusion, however, I shall discuss an important reply available to proponents of these ideals.[28] The reply attempts to take the sting out of the examples.

Not infrequently writers draw a distinction between freedom and its value. They sometimes ask rhetorically, What is the value of freedom if one lives in conditions in which one cannot exercise it or enjoy it?[29] If I live in a state that has an ideal set of rules for governing the free transfer of property, but I own nothing myself, then what is the value of this freedom to me? Drawing on this distinction, a proponent of freedom as noninterference might argue that the arbitrary liberal government is deficient not because it reduces political freedom, but because it diminishes its value. In the same spirit, the proponent of freedom as nondomination might say the same thing about the nonarbitrary illiberal government. Both types of proponents might then conclude that a freedom-supportive state is the state that promotes *both* political freedom and its value.

This reply has the effect of dramatically reducing the distance between the two rival ideals of freedom as noninterference and freedom as nondomination. The two camps will converge in their judgments if the following occurs: (1) it is agreed that the freedom-supportive state should be as concerned with promoting the value of political freedom as it is concerned with promoting political freedom itself; and (2) the proponent of freedom as noninterference concedes that being subject to arbitrary power reduces the value of freedom, while the proponent of freedom as nondomination admits that even nonarbitrary interference reduces the value of freedom. The difference between the two sides will reduce to a disagreement over how to distinguish between actual freedom-reducing factors and factors that merely condition freedom's value. But proponents of

[27] Some might be tempted to view these two governments not over time, but at particular points in time. When asked which government is worse from the standpoint of political freedom, some might interpret this as a series of questions about the two governments at different time-slices. If one does this, then at many points in time one will have to conclude that the arbitrary liberal government is a model government in terms of political freedom. Indeed, on the time-slice view, one will not be able to discriminate between arbitrary and nonarbitrary governments that engage in the same amount of interference at a given point in time. This is to miss something important. A plausible ideal of political freedom should be able to explain both why interference reduces freedom and why arbitrary interference is more freedom-reducing than nonarbitrary interference.

[28] I shall not attempt to anticipate every possible reply that proponents of these ideals could make to my archetypal governments. By discussing (what I consider to be) the strongest reply that is available to such proponents, I hope to cast some doubt on the plausibility of these ideals. This will fall short of a decisive refutation, but it should provide some motivation for the search for an alternative, and I hope better, ideal of political freedom.

[29] See Berlin, introduction to *Four Essays on Liberty*, xlv–xlvi.

both sets of ideals will converge on what is important, namely, what a freedom-supportive state should be promoting.

However, in all likelihood, proponents of these rival ideals would want to insist on some priority rule for ranking the promotion of freedom above the promotion of its value. Depending on the priority rule proposed, this ranking would enable proponents of the respective ideals to arrive at different judgments about the freedom-supportive state. The difference between freedom as noninterference and freedom as nondomination would then boil down to a difference in emphasis. Proponents of the former would insist that reducing interference is more important than reducing domination, while the latter would insist on the opposite.

Drawing a distinction between freedom and its value does indeed appear to take the sting out of the examples that I have presented. Does it overcome the problem of unacceptable implications, however, and uphold the integrity of political freedom as a distinct ideal? Notice that if both political freedom and its value are to be promoted, then a freedom-supportive state has two goals, not one. This is a problem. Recall that in investigating the ideal of political freedom, we are not attempting to identify the full range of justified state action. Perhaps a good state will promote both political freedom and its enjoyment, as well as other valuable goals. We are now, however, seeking to understand only what a freedom-supportive state ought to promote. It should promote political freedom. It need have no other goal. Indeed, the pursuit of other goals— such as the goal of increasing the value of political freedom—may compete against or conflict with the goal of promoting political freedom. We do well, then, to keep these two goals distinct. In seeking to avoid the counterintuitive judgments of my two example governments, the reply that a freedom-supportive state promotes both political freedom and its value obscures this important point.

Those who would press the reply might now object that my representation here mischaracterizes what they are saying. They might say that noninterference and the value of noninterference, or, alternatively, nondomination and the value of nondomination, are constituent parts of a single value. This value is what political freedom is. Accordingly, the freedom-supportive state has only one goal, which is the promotion of political freedom so understood.

This rejoinder, however, generates its own problems. To begin with, it threatens to compromise the integrity of freedom as a political ideal. Interference and domination are not the only factors that condition the enjoyment of freedom. A number of other factors, such as residing in a country with a clean environment, plausibly condition the value or enjoyment of freedom. Should such factors be counted as constituent elements of freedom as a political ideal? If we say yes, then political freedom starts to resemble a master value encompassing all or most of what a state might reasonably be in the business of promoting.[30] This would amount to, or come close to, denying that political freedom is a distinct ideal, thus succumbing to the problem of integrity. While laws that protect clean air may be a good thing (and may enhance the enjoyment of political freedom), we should not say that the state promotes political freedom when it passes these laws.

Of course, proponents of freedom as noninterference and freedom as nondomination might insist that only interference or domination count as constituent elements of political freedom. Other factors that condition its value, they might say, are not included within it. This would rescue their respective ideals from the problem of integrity, but it would do so at the price of being ad hoc. Once factors that condition the value of freedom are included within the value itself, then we are owed an explanation for why some factors get included and others do not. Proponents of the two ideals have not provided any such explanation, and it is unclear how they might do so. But even if they can offer the needed explanation, a second problem lies in wait. If political freedom includes two components—noninterference and nondomination—then how should we decide which component is more important? Should we say, for example, that one component takes lexical priority over the other? This seems doubtful. If the state has a choice between greatly reducing interference or slightly reducing exposure to domination, then even a proponent of freedom as nondomination should allow that the state should reduce the interference.

This suggests that on any plausible view of political freedom, the two components must be balanced against one another. But to explain how this should be done we need a priority rule or a standard to guide us. Without such a rule or standard, we will not be able to make reasonably determinate judgments about the promotion of political freedom. When confronted with a choice between an arbitrary liberal government or a nonarbitrary illiberal government, we will not be able to say which is worse from the standpoint of political freedom. Working from within either freedom as noninterference or freedom as nondomination, we may be able to say which of these governments does worse in compromising freedom and which does worse in reducing its value, but we will not be able to say which government is worse overall.

The problem, here, is what I earlier termed the problem of pluralism. If political freedom consists of different components, then we need to know how to establish a proper measure for the components in arriving at overall judgments of political freedom. It is important to see that this problem is a theoretical problem. We may be able to avoid the problem in some practical contexts. For example, if a state in a given set of circum-

---

[30] Pettit argues for a wide range of public policies by appealing to the value or enjoyment of nondomination. In his eyes, a freedom-supportive state should be in the business of doing most of what a state might reasonably do. See Pettit, *Republicanism*, chap. 5.

stances cannot do much to reduce interference, but can do very much to reduce domination, then the problem that I am now calling attention to would not be particularly troubling. A freedom-supportive state in these circumstances should act to reduce domination rather than attempt to reduce interference, and this judgment holds true whether we view freedom as nondomination or as noninterference.

Notwithstanding this point, the problem of pluralism is not, first and foremost, a problem of applied political theory. It is a problem that concerns the theoretical structure of our judgments about political freedom. An account of political freedom that identifies a plurality of freedom-reducing factors, but offers no guidance as to how they should be integrated into overall judgments of political freedom is, other things being equal, less satisfactory than one that can guide us.

I contend that neither proponents of freedom as noninterference nor proponents of freedom as nondomination have the resources to overcome the problem of pluralism. When seeking to avoid the counterintuitive implications that are forced upon them by the examples of an arbitrary liberal government and a nonarbitrary illiberal government, proponents may be tempted to appeal to the distinction between political freedom and its value. However, if they do this, then their accounts of political freedom will fare poorly with respect to the problem of integrity, or the problem of pluralism, or both. We have ample reason, therefore, to investigate whether a third ideal of political freedom might be able to incorporate the good insights of both freedom as noninterference and freedom as nondomination, while avoiding the difficulties that these rival ideals encounter. Let us turn now to this task.

VI. FREEDOM AND PLANNING

I have already intimated that the ideal of political freedom that I wish to defend centers on the ability of persons to plan their lives. Lacking a concise name for this ideal, I shall employ the somewhat cumbersome appellation *freedom as the nonobstruction of planning*. According to this ideal, a freedom-supportive state promotes and sustains an environment in which its subjects are best able to carry out their plans and to form new ones.

I need to explain what I mean, here, by planning, and why it is reasonable to think that there is an intimate connection between planning and political freedom. Planning is one kind of practical activity. It can be contrasted with other kinds of practical activity, such as the kind of activity that we engage in when we act from impulse.[31] Typically, planning

---

[31] Practical activity terminates in intentional action, but not all intentional action is well described in terms of forming plans and carrying them out. For a more detailed discussion of practical activity, see Christine Swanton, *Freedom: A Coherence Theory*, 49–60.

is a process that involves setting for oneself a goal (or goals), deliberating about which actions to take in order to achieve the goal(s), reaching a judgment that certain actions should be undertaken in the pursuit of the goal(s), and forming intentions to carry out those actions. So described, planning involves committing oneself to undertake future actions. Planning is the way we actively control and shape our lives.

Plans and the process of forming them can be simple or complex, limited or comprehensive. (Some plans might affect the freedom of others, but I shall address that concern in Section VII.) I might plan to take a walk this afternoon. This plan is simple and limited. The steps that I need to take in order to fulfill it are relatively few, and the impact that it will have on my life as a whole will be very modest. Alternatively, I might plan to become a physician. This plan is complex and comprehensive. The steps that I need to take in order to fulfill it will be many and will require a good deal of ongoing deliberation on my part. The impact of this plan on my life will be substantial. If I seriously adopt and pursue a comprehensive plan and fail to achieve it, then, other things being equal, my life will be significantly affected for the worse. The reason for this is that comprehensive plans, like the plan of pursuing a career in medicine, have a hierarchical structure. They embed a plurality of simpler and more limited plans. In planning to become a physician, I might plan to pursue one line of study rather than another, or I might plan to start a family later rather than sooner. Failure to achieve one's comprehensive plan often casts a shadow over the simpler and more limited plans that were embedded within it.

Much more could be said about plans and the role that they play in our lives;[32] but these brief remarks should suffice for present purposes. It should be clear that persons are planning agents. Even those persons who lead relatively spontaneous lives are distinguished not by the absence of plans, but by the lack of enduring, stable, comprehensive plans in their lives. It should also be clear that planning is integral to autonomy. We take charge of our affairs and chart our own course through life by adopting and pursuing plans.[33] This, in turn, suggests why it is reasonable to think that there is an intimate connection between planning and freedom. To lead a free life, we must be able to form plans and to take steps to carry them out.

---

[32] See Michael E. Bratman, *Intention, Plans, and Practical Reason* (Cambridge, MA: Harvard University Press, 1987).

[33] Could one live an autonomous life without any plans? I doubt it. One might resolve never to commit oneself to any future course of action, preferring instead to always "live in the present." But this would itself be a kind of plan. Even if one could somehow avoid making plans altogether, I suspect that one's life would be so lacking in narrative structure that it would be wrong to call it autonomous. This is one reason why I characterized autonomy (see Section II above) in terms of the manner in which, and circumstances under which, we form complex intentions and sustain commitments.

Building on this idea, the ideal of political freedom that I am now recommending holds that a freedom-supportive state should sustain and promote an environment in which its subjects are best able to plan their lives. But now, it may be asked, why emphasize the obstruction of planning when assessing political freedom? After all, as we have seen, interference and domination also reduce political freedom. Moreover, a person can be interfered with or subjected to domination even if he is not forming or pursuing any plan at all.

The response to the question comes in two parts. First, the main reason why interference and domination reduce political freedom is that they both obstruct the ability of persons to plan their lives. Interference diminishes our freedom by closing off or raising the costs of options that are relevant to our plans. Domination diminishes our freedom by subjecting us to the arbitrary will of another, which in turn hinders our ability to plan our lives by leaving us vulnerable to the often unpredictable power of the dominator. The root explanation, then, for why both interference and domination are freedom-reducing factors is that they both are important and effective means by which agents can and do obstruct the plans of others. For this reason, an ideal of political freedom should put the focus on the obstruction of planning rather than on interference or domination. The former idea subsumes the latter two.

Second, while it remains true that it is possible to interfere with or dominate a person without obstructing his plans (think, for example, of the person who forcibly prevents me in a given situation from acting on an impulse), this possibility is not particularly important for judgments of political freedom. The reason for this is that if a state sustains and promotes an environment in which its subjects are best able to plan their lives, then this will also be an environment in which interference and domination are minimized. For, at least generally speaking, the state is not in a position to know when acts of interference or domination impede the plans of persons and when they do not do so. A law that criminalizes gambling may hinder some individuals from giving in to the impulse to gamble, but the law will also almost certainly hinder some who have made gambling a part of their plans. Since the state cannot effectively target the former group while excluding the latter group, then a state that wishes to promote freedom will not pass the law.

This is true, as I just allowed, only generally speaking. There are exceptions. But consideration of the exceptions strengthens, rather than weakens, the plausibility of freedom as the nonobstruction of planning. To see this, consider laws that require a short waiting period before one is allowed to purchase a firearm. It is not unreasonable to think that these laws do a good job of interfering with those who are moved to buy firearms on impulse, without significantly obstructing those whose plans include owning a firearm. Such laws are good examples of how a state can engage in interference without obstructing the plans of those who are interfered with. But laws that only restrict those who are acting on impulse, and do not obstruct the plans of anyone, are not plausible candidates for being judged as laws that reduce freedom. Indeed, a strong case can be made that such laws can actually increase freedom by preventing people from acting in ways that they would not act if they were not in the grip of an impulse. The extent to which this is true is not something that I shall explore here. My point is that even when the state interferes with or dominates its subjects, but does not obstruct their plans (and it can only do this in exceptional cases), its action does not plausibly reduce their freedom.[34]

It is worth pausing now to consider an important objection. Some will claim that freedom as the nonobstruction of planning fails to account adequately for the freedom associated with spontaneous intentional action.[35] Consider, for instance, a character whom we can call "the spontaneous man." This is a person who believes that he acts most authentically when he acts without deliberation or planning of any sort. The spontaneous man might concede that his ability to engage in the kind of spontaneous activity that he prizes is best protected by a state that sustains an environment in which persons are best able to form and execute their plans. But he might object that an ideal of political freedom that is characterized in terms of the nonobstruction of planning would fail to give the freedom that he prizes its due.

Several replies can be made to the spontaneous man. First, as I mentioned above, even those individuals who lead relatively spontaneous lives must engage in some planning to lead the lives that they want to lead. A spontaneous decision to paint in the afternoon typically requires either that one plan to get materials that are needed to paint, or that one previously had planned to have materials around in case one spontaneously decides to paint. As I have stressed, it is a mistake to identify all plans with highly structured, long-term commitments. Second, if the spontaneous man values his spontaneous activity, then if he is rational he should take steps to ensure that he can successfully engage in it. For example, he should avoid assuming long-term responsibilities. This, ironically, requires a good deal of planning.

These replies go some distance toward responding to the objection raised by the spontaneous man. However, a determined proponent of this objection will insist that the obstruction of purposive, spontaneous activity still is not fully accounted for by the ideal of political freedom that I am defending. Does this objection give us good reason to revise my

---

[34] Recall here the assumption in Section II above that freedom is best understood in terms of personal autonomy. On alternative understandings of freedom the point in the text might not be plausible. For example, if freedom were best understood in terms of the satisfaction of desire, then such laws would plausibly reduce freedom.

[35] I thank Keith Lehrer and James Stacey Taylor for helping me to see the force of this objection.

account? At this point it is necessary to recall some of the assumptions that I made earlier in this essay. I assumed that freedom is best understood in terms of personal autonomy. I also assumed a particular understanding of personal autonomy, one that identifies the autonomous life with a life of freely chosen projects and commitments. If this understanding of autonomy is essentially correct, then it is appropriate to give planning agency the kind of prominence that I have given it here. Autonomous persons are planning agents, and their plans are integral to their autonomy. A full response to the spontaneous man, accordingly, requires a defense of this understanding of autonomy.

I shall not attempt to provide this defense here.[36] But if it can be given, then freedom as the nonobstruction of planning will emerge as a highly plausible ideal of political freedom. This ideal not only explains why and how interference and domination reduce freedom, but also implies that neither interference nor domination, per se, reduce freedom. They reduce freedom only to the extent that they obstruct planning.[37] Yet, as important as these points are, they do not exhaust the case for freedom as the nonobstruction of planning over its rival ideals. An important issue remains to be discussed.

As we saw in Section V, the ideals of freedom as noninterference and freedom as nondomination run into the problem of pluralism once they attempt to respond to my two examples of the arbitrary liberal government and the nonarbitrary illiberal government. By introducing the distinction between freedom and its value, proponents of these ideals of freedom can explain why both of these governments are not freedom-supportive, but in doing so, these proponents incur the problem of balancing freedom and its value. To achieve this balance in a non ad hoc way, proponents of both ideals need to appeal to some rule or standard to provide guidance on how the balancing should be done. Neither group of proponents, I suggested, has the resources to provide such a standard.

It should now be fairly clear that freedom as the nonobstruction of planning does not confront this problem. Since the ideal recognizes that both interference and domination are freedom-reducing factors, it does not have any difficulty accounting for the examples of arbitrary liberal government and nonarbitrary illiberal government. Nor do I need to invoke the suspect distinction between freedom and its value in order to judge either sort of government. Finally, the ideal does not lack a standard for balancing the relative importance of interference and domination in making judgments about political freedom. The standard it uses is the degree or extent to which these freedom-reducing factors obstruct the ability of persons to plan their lives. Indeed, reference to this standard

---

[36] For some defense, see Wall, *Liberalism, Perfectionism, and Restraint*, 127–61.
[37] This is not to say that they are objectionable only when they obstruct planning. Freedom is just one value. Interference and domination may be bad for reasons other than the role that they play in reducing freedom.

enables us to address the question that neither freedom as noninterference nor freedom as nondomination is able to approach satisfactorily: What is worse from the standpoint of political freedom, the arbitrary liberal government or the nonarbitrary illiberal government?

I do not mean to say that proponents of freedom as the nonobstruction of planning can answer this question without exercising judgment or without knowing more about the concrete details of these respective governments. The point is simply that this ideal provides us with a way of thinking about how to answer this question. We should compare these two governments in terms of the extent to which they frustrate the plans of those who are subject to them. The government that produces the greater amount of frustration is the one that is worse from the standpoint of political freedom. By referring to this standard, we can gauge, even if only roughly, the significance of different categories of state action, such as:

1. that which subjects citizens to both interference and domination
2. that which subjects citizens to domination, but not interference
3. that which subjects citizens to interference, but not domination

In principle, an instance of state action that falls under any one of these categories can be worse (in terms of reducing political freedom) than an instance that falls under any of the other two. But, in practice, state actions that fall under the first category are likely to be the greatest threats to political freedom. The reason for this is that when state action dominates as well as interferes, it is much harder for those who are subject to this action to plan around it. This is why many writers in the liberal tradition have stressed the importance of the rule of law to a free society.[38] If we can know in advance the laws and rules that will constrain us, then we can take into account this knowledge when we formulate our plans and deliberate about how best to pursue them. But if we are subject to a state that arbitrarily and unpredictably interferes with us, then its actions are likely to be far more disruptive to our plans.

I doubt that much of anything useful can be said in the abstract about state action that falls under categories (2) and (3). We need to look at the concrete consequences of such types of action to determine their impact on political freedom. But an example might shed some light on the matter. Consider compulsory military service. Suppose that State A announces that it plans to institute a mandatory five-year service requirement for approximately one-fourth of all male citizens between the ages of eigh-

---

[38] See John Locke, *Two Treatises of Government*, ed. Peter Laslett (Cambridge: Cambridge University Press, 1988); F. A. Hayek, *The Constitution of Liberty* (Chicago: University of Chicago Press, 1960); and John Rawls, *A Theory of Justice* (Cambridge, MA: Harvard University Press, 1971), 206–13.

teen and forty-five, but the state does not specify how it will select them or when the requirement will take effect. This announcement would, in all likelihood, substantially disrupt the plans of many citizens, and it would do so even if the state eventually drops the idea. Here domination would occur in the absence of interference. Now, contrast State A with State B, which enacts the same five-year service requirement but does so according to fair and publicly known rules. On the assumption that there is a genuine public need for military service, this state action plausibly could be described as interference without domination. Since the requirement would be administered according to known rules, it would not substantially disrupt the lives of those who are not selected to serve; those who are selected to serve will at least know when their service will begin and end, and they can take some steps to plan around it.

Nevertheless, even when State B's interference is predictable, nonarbitrary, and, thus, does not constitute domination, it still compromises freedom. The men who are selected to serve in State B will have to spend five years in the military. For many of them, the disruption that this will cause to their plans will be substantial. It will likely be much more substantial than the disruption that is caused to one's plans when one is merely vulnerable to being conscripted into military service at some unspecified time. So, in comparing State B's action with the noninterfering domination by State A, which merely announces an arbitrary plan to begin conscription, we would need to weigh the greater degree of frustration that State B would cause a smaller number of people against the lesser degree of frustration that State A would cause a larger number of people. In short, when assessing political freedom, we must consider both the intensity of the frustration that is caused by a state action and the number of people who are adversely affected.

Of course, a good deal more work needs to be done in order to make this kind of comparison even tolerably precise. I have said nothing, for example, about how we should measure the intensity of frustration that a given state action causes to a given person's plans. But my ambition, here, is not to work out a metric for measuring political freedom.[39] I have simply aimed to give some idea of how freedom as the nonobstruction of planning would approach the task of comparing and aggregating instances of interference and domination. My claim is not that this task will be easy or straightforward, but only that this ideal of political freedom at least provides us with a standard for doing it. In this respect, the ideal of political freedom as nonobstruction of planning fares better than both freedom as noninterference and freedom as nondomination in responding to the problem of pluralism.

[39] Perhaps no such metric is possible. The best we may be able to do is to make reasonable rough-and-ready judgments about what state actions (or what kinds of governments) cause more obstruction to planning than others.

Moreover, as we have seen, in responding to this problem, freedom as the nonobstruction of planning does not blur the distinction between political freedom and its value. According to this ideal, some citizens may be free, but not in a position to enjoy their freedom. Others may be free to pursue their plans, but their plans may be worthless or ill advised. Indeed, for some citizens, it will be true that they would be better off if they had much less political freedom. This is as it should be. The freedom-supportive state is not necessarily the best state. Political freedom is one value among others. And in this essay I have said nothing about its importance as compared to other values with which it may come into conflict.

VII. Refining the Ideal

In presenting the case for freedom as the nonobstruction of planning over its rivals, I have emphasized a number of key points. The ideal does well in assessing which is worse from the standpoint of political freedom, arbitrary liberal government or nonarbitrary illiberal government, as described in Section V. The ideal responds well to the problem of pluralism, and it preserves the integrity of political freedom by not conflating it with the value or the enjoyment that freedom might bring. But even if these points are sound, the ideal still might be unacceptable. It may succumb to the problem of unacceptable implications.

I cannot respond here to every possible objection that might be pressed against the ideal of freedom as the nonobstruction of planning. Instead, in this section, I shall consider two important problems that threaten its plausibility. The first problem concerns the dependence of plans on the institutional environments in which they are formed. The second problem concerns the *Brave New World* scenario that I mentioned at the beginning of this essay. Unfortunately, even with respect to these two problems, I shall not be able to respond to them in a fully satisfactory way. My more modest objective will be to suggest how these problems should be addressed. This, in turn, will lead to further refinement of the ideal of political freedom as the nonobstruction of planning.

The first problem I shall address calls attention to the fact that the plans of persons are dependent on the institutional contexts in which they live. This raises some difficult issues that we have not confronted. To view freedom as the nonobstruction of planning is to hold that a person's political freedom is reduced whenever his plans are obstructed by another agent, whatever those plans may be. But this leads to some counterintuitive implications. For some agents, while acting fully within their rights, obstruct the plans of other agents; other agents have plans that involve the deliberate violation of the rights of other persons. Do these possibilities not suggest that talk about the obstruction of plans must presuppose, at a fundamental level, a shared understanding of legitimate rights and entitlements? If so, it is not clear what the relationship is between this background understanding and political freedom.

To bring out the problem here, consider a simple example. If I own a tract of land and I erect a fence to keep you from walking across it, which you had planned to do, then I thereby obstruct your plans. If, however, I am prevented from erecting the fence, then my plans are obstructed. Whose plans should a freedom-supportive state favor? It might be said that, in answering this question, we should just abstract from ownership issues and compare the intensity of the obstruction of plans that occurs (or would occur) in this kind of case. But doing this would miss an important point. My plans are legitimate, whereas yours are not. Your plans, after all, involve violating my rights.[40]

To take account of this example, it is tempting to say that political freedom involves the nonobstruction of *legitimate* plans. But if we say this, then we need a background account of rights and entitlements in order to make sense of what counts as a legitimate plan. This is something that I have not provided. Moreover, it is hard to see how I could provide it simply by reflecting on the idea of nonobstruction of planning. The worry, then, is that freedom as the nonobstruction of planning, as I have so far described the ideal, is seriously incomplete as an account of political freedom.

In response to this worry one might note that the same problem confronts both of the rival ideals that we have considered. Proponents of freedom as noninterference and freedom as nondomination must explain the connection, if any, that exists between the freedom-reducing factors that they recognize and the rights and entitlements of citizens. So the problem that we are now considering is not a special one for freedom as the nonobstruction of planning. Still, it is a problem. It presents us with a dilemma. Either we embrace a moralized account of freedom as the nonobstruction of (legitimate) planning, in which case judgments of political freedom are parasitic on an undefended background account of rights and entitlements, or we say that judgments of political freedom are insensitive to such rights and entitlements, in which case we must embrace the counterintuitive implications that I mentioned above.

Fortunately, the dilemma is not as formidable as it appears. Even if freedom as the nonobstruction of planning does not give us a full account of political freedom because it depends on, but does not provide, a background account of rights and entitlements, it does not follow that the ideal is empty or unimportant. An adequate justification of rights and entitlements will need to draw on a wide range of considerations. Some of these considerations will refer to values other than political freedom. This is why freedom as the nonobstruction of planning cannot generate, all by itself, a complete account of justified rights and entitlements. How-

---

[40] I am assuming here that I have justly acquired the land and have (legitimate) property rights in it.

ever, on the assumption that the state should promote freedom, the justification of the rights and entitlements of citizens should be sensitive to considerations that bear on political freedom. For example, some assignments of rights and entitlements may fare very poorly in contributing to an environment that enables people to form plans and carry them out. Other assignments may fare much better in this regard. If so, freedom as the nonobstruction of planning would provide reasons for favoring the latter over the former.

Once again, an example may help to make this point clearer. In order to be successful, planning agents need to be able to coordinate their activities efficiently. Some institutional structures, such as competitive markets with well-defined property rights, foster coordination and efficiency much better than do other institutional structures, such as command economies or systems without well-defined private property rights. For this reason, freedom as the nonobstruction of planning should favor the former institutional structures over the latter.[41] There are, of course, numerous ways of specifying property rights in market societies. Reference to this ideal of political freedom may provide some guidance as to how those rights should be specified, but other considerations will bear on the matter as well. Indeed, there will likely be a plurality of different ways of reasonably specifying property rights, ways that are compatible with the goal of achieving an economic environment in which agents can efficiently coordinate their activities.[42] If so, then freedom as the nonobstruction of planning will not tell us which specification(s) we should adopt. But the ideal will tell us that a freedom-supportive state would uphold one of these reasonable specifications. Judgments of interference and domination, therefore, can be understood against the background of the existing system of property rights, so long as it falls within the range of the reasonable specifications.[43]

---

[41] It is true that some institutional structures that are not plausibly freedom-supportive nonetheless might do well in terms of the nonobstruction of plans. Feudal societies provided stable and predictable environments for those who lived in them, but they did not provide their members with a wide range of options. According to the ideal of political freedom that I am proposing, a freedom-supportive state is one that sustains a planning-friendly environment while providing its members with a wide range of opportunities.

[42] In his groundbreaking paper "The Problem of Social Cost," *Journal of Law and Economics* 3 (1960): 1–44, Ronald Coase argues that so long as transaction costs are negligible and property rights are well-defined, economic agents will bargain their way to an efficient outcome, irrespective of the initial assignment of property rights. Assuming this theorem to be correct, it would have some bearing on the claims advanced here. Coase's argument suggests that in specifying property rights one important consideration is to do so in a manner that will minimize transaction costs between different agents. This, in turn, will enable them to coordinate their activities and pursue their plans more efficiently.

[43] But, it may be asked, what if I live in a political society that does not have a system of property rights that is reasonable in this sense? Then freedom as the nonobstruction of planning will direct the state to reform its system of property law so that it becomes reasonable. There are numerous complications raised by this, however, that I shall pass over here.

The suggestion, then, is that we can avoid being caught between the two horns of the dilemma. To avoid counterintuitive implications, judgments of interference and domination must be sensitive to existing assignments of rights and entitlements. Indeed, persons form their plans against the background of a shared understanding of these rights and entitlements. So, in a sense, we first need this shared understanding before we can talk sensibly about the freedom to pursue plans. But, at the same time, the main idea behind the ideal—that people should live in an environment in which they can best form and pursue plans—favors some assignments of rights and entitlements over others, even if this idea does not specify a uniquely correct assignment. This means that judgments of political freedom are not simply parasitic on a background institutional structure.

Much more could be said about the complex relationship between institutions, rights, and freedom-reducing factors, but these brief remarks should, at least, allay the worry that freedom as the nonobstruction of planning is either deeply implausible or an empty ideal.

Let me turn, next, to the second problem that threatens the plausibility of this ideal. An ideal of political freedom that ties judgments of political freedom to the plans of those who are subject to the state's authority must address the following question. Can a person have his freedom reduced even when his plans have not been obstructed in any way? Suppose, for example, that my government prohibits foxhunting and that the option to go foxhunting is not one that I need to pursue for any of my present plans. Then does not my government restrict my freedom even though it does not obstruct my plans?[44] It is tempting to respond that while the option to go foxhunting is not relevant to my present plans, it may, for all I know, be relevant to my future plans. As a planning agent, I have a freedom-based interest not only in pursuing my present plans, but also in living in an environment that does not restrict my options in the future. So, when my government prohibits foxhunting, it limits my freedom by closing off a possible future option.

There is surely something credible to this response at first. After all, people do take up new plans, and sometimes the plans that they take up are ones that they never would have guessed they would take up. Nonetheless, the response rings hollow. With respect to at least *some* options (call them nonserviceable options), I can know with great confidence that I will not need them for any of my current or future plans. I can also know with great confidence that even if I had access to such options, I would not acquire any need for them. Yet, when I am prohibited from pursuing these options, is not my freedom still limited?

---

[44] Alternatively, if my plans include the option to go foxhunting, and my government prohibits this option, do I become freer simply by abandoning the plan that includes this option? This is the classic problem of the contented slave.

This question poses a version of the *Brave New World* problem. In *Brave New World*, the plans of the subjects of the state have been adjusted so that they do not conflict with the restrictions that are imposed on them. But it would be crazy to characterize this state as freedom-supportive. Of course, in *Brave New World* the state has manipulated its subjects. This manipulation is a form of freedom-reducing interference. But we can easily vary the example. Suppose that the subjects in this world have voluntarily adjusted their plans so that they do not conflict with the restrictions that are imposed on them.[45] Here it seems that freedom as the nonobstruction of planning will not be able to account for the subjects' lack of political freedom.

Any account of political freedom that relates options to the subjective mental states of persons will run into this kind of problem.[46] To overcome it, we need to introduce an objective condition. Given the characterization of personal autonomy in Section II above, such a condition is readily available: *For a person to be politically free, he must have access to an environment that provides him with a wide range of valuable options.*[47] Since this condition does not depend on the subjective mental states of persons, it will not be satisfied in *Brave New World* scenarios. Thus, by calling attention to this objective condition, we can avoid the unacceptable implication that persons in such worlds could be politically free. But now an obvious objection comes into view. If we are going to insist on the objective condition, then all of the emphasis on the subjective plans of persons becomes strangely otiose, does it not? In seeking to overcome the problem of *Brave New World*, has freedom as the nonobstruction of planning effaced itself?

Fortunately, the answer is "no." The satisfaction of the objective condition is plainly insufficient for a freedom-supportive environment. The reason for this is that the importance of a given option for a person depends on the role that it plays (or would play) in his current (or future)

---

[45] See Elster's discussion of character planning in Jon Elster, *Sour Grapes: Studies in the Subversion of Rationality* (Cambridge: Cambridge University Press, 1983), 117–19.

[46] See the discussion in Richard Arneson, "Freedom and Desire," *Canadian Journal of Philosophy* 15, no. 3 (1985): 425–48.

[47] This condition raises a number of difficult questions: How should options be individuated? What counts as a sufficiently wide range of options? What constitutes "access" to an option? And what functions does the state have in ensuring that this condition is met? I shall not attempt to provide answers to these questions here, but a few remarks are necessary to prevent misunderstanding. For the most part, valuable options can be provided by civil society. State action is not needed to create them. However, without state action, some citizens may find themselves in a situation in which they lack the resources needed to have access to these options. Does this show that the freedom-supportive state must also be (at least to some extent) a welfare state? Perhaps, but perhaps not. It is possible that civil society, through charitable and intermediate associations, could ensure that all citizens have adequate access to the options that they need in order to be politically free. But whether such welfare provision would be sufficient and whether it would increase or diminish interference and domination relative to state welfare provision are matters that cannot be pursued here.

plans. A state that provides its subjects with a wide range of valuable options, but systematically thwarts their plans either through interference or through domination would not be a freedom-supportive state. Thus, while satisfaction of the objective condition is important, it fails to explain the ways in which the freedom of persons can be curtailed even when they remain free to pursue a wide range of alternative plans.

Return now to the foxhunting example. Assume that the following is true for a given person: (a) the option to go foxhunting is not relevant to any of his current plans; (b) the option to go foxhunting would not be relevant to any of his future plans even if it were available to him; (c) the fact that this option is not relevant to his current plans and would not be relevant to his future plans is not the result of being manipulated by another person; and (d) he lives in an environment that provides him with a wide range of valuable options. Given these demanding conditions, freedom as the nonobstruction of planning yields the result that when the state prohibits this person from pursuing the option of foxhunting, it does not reduce his freedom. This is, I think, the right judgment to reach in this kind of example. The best case for thinking that the restriction of nonserviceable options does reduce the freedom of persons rests on the worry that if we do not affirm this view, then we will not be able to account for *Brave New World* scenarios. But conditions (c) and (d) rule out such scenarios.

Moreover, at this point, it is worth reminding ourselves that freedom as the nonobstruction of planning is an ideal of political freedom. It does not purport to offer a full account of the free person or the autonomous life. Its focus is on what the state should do if it wishes to promote freedom. Seen from this perspective, if the state prohibits an option that is not relevant to my plans, there is every reason to think that it will be relevant to the plans of others.[48] This is why, first and foremost, the prohibition would reduce freedom. Now, it might be objected that the state *could* prohibit me from pursuing the option without prohibiting others from doing so, and in this way diminish my freedom without denying the option to anyone who needs it to pursue his plans. But, if this were to happen, freedom as the nonobstruction of planning can still explain why this state action would be freedom-reducing. A state that aimed to reduce my options, but not the options of my fellow citizens, would be an arbitrary state. By singling me out, and by subjecting me to arbitrary interference, it would be dominating me. This would remain true even if its dominating interference foreclosed an option for which I had no use,

---

[48] It is logically possible, even if it is something that would scarcely ever happen, that a state might prohibit an option—such as the option to eat glass—that none of its citizens would ever have any need for in pursuing their plans. On the account of political freedom that I am defending, it would not be possible to account for why this would be a reduction in freedom—if it is indeed a reduction in freedom! I leave it to the reader to consider whether this is a troubling objection to this ideal.

given my current and future plans. This is true because, as we have seen, merely being subject to domination reduces freedom. In this case, it would be reasonable for me to believe that if my government singles me out with respect to this option, then it could do so in the future for other options that I do or would care about. And this reasonable worry itself would obstruct my ability to plan my life.[49]

Bringing together the points developed in this section, I can now state more completely the demands that freedom as the nonobstruction of planning imposes on a state. According to this ideal, the freedom-supportive state must (1) sustain a legal and economic structure that allows its subjects to coordinate their activities and plans efficiently; (2) ensure that all of its subjects have access to a wide range of valuable options; and (3) minimize the interference and domination that frustrate the plans of those who are subject to its authority. The first and second of these demands are, in a sense, prior to the third; in the freedom-supportive state, persons will form and pursue their plans against the background of a shared understanding of their institutional rights, entitlements, and available options.

VIII. CONCLUSION

It is time to take stock. I began this essay by stressing the distinction between political freedom and the freedom that really matters. I asserted, but did not defend, the claim that the freedom that really matters is best understood in terms of personal autonomy. Assuming that this claim is correct, it is implausible to think that a state can make its subjects free. At best, it can assist them in becoming free or provide facilitative conditions for their freedom. An ideal of political freedom tells us what the state should do in this respect.

I have tried to show that freedom as the nonobstruction of planning is the best ideal of political freedom on offer. It does a better job of responding to the problem of integrity, the problem of pluralism, and the problem of unacceptable implications than do its main rivals, and it explains in a satisfying way why both interference and domination reduce freedom. It also explains why certain institutional structures, such as the rule of law and the market economy, are (plausibly) supportive of political freedom.

Notwithstanding its attractions, political freedom, as I have stressed throughout this essay, is but one ideal. It can conflict with other values. For this reason, we are not entitled to conclude that a state that best promotes freedom is the best state, all things considered. The freedom-supportive state, according to the ideal of political freedom that I have

---

[49] In this case I am like the slave who has a liberal master. I am free to pursue my plans, but I stand under the shadow of a dominating presence that may intervene at any time to obstruct them.

defended, is neither egalitarian nor perfectionist.[50] It need not ensure that all subjects have an equal set of opportunities, nor does it need to take steps to help people form and pursue valuable or worthwhile plans. This naturally raises the question of whether, and to what extent, political freedom should be compromised for the sake of these other values. But this is a question to be taken up on another occasion.

Philosophy, Bowling Green State University

---

[50] This requires an important qualification. To the extent that freedom as the nonobstruction of planning rests on the ideal of personal autonomy, and to the extent that this ideal itself is a perfectionist ideal, then the freedom-supportive state, as I have characterized it, is perfectionist. The point in the text is that the freedom-supportive state need not favor some plans over others because of their intrinsic value or their contribution to human flourishing.

INDEX

Abortion, 238; impermissibility of, 292, 297, 306; permissibility of, 289, 297, 300–305; and rape, 286, 289–90, 293, 296–300, 303–6

Accountability, 25, 89–90, 112, 232–36. *See also* Responsibility

Activity, 34–42, 44, 47, 49–54, 68–69, 83–90

Addiction, 101, 102, 122, 211, 247–48, 256–57; negative, 252–54; positive, 252–54, 257; and relative addiction theory, 253

Affections (*affectus*). *See* Emotions

Age of Reason, 8–11, 22–23, 204

Agency, 32, 34, 39, 49–50, 52; and psychological functioning, 157, 158, 168–76; rational, 221–26, 243–44

Agential direction, 156–57, 168–70. *See also* Autonomy, as self-direction

Agential governance, 156–58, 168–70, 172–75. *See also* Autonomy, as self-governance

Alienation, 217, 233–34, 236, 240. *See also* Desires, repudiation of

Alzheimer's disease, 103

Anarchy, State, and Utopia (Nozick), 269

Animals (nonrational creatures), 18, 21 n. 34, 22–23, 227

Antigone, (Sophocles), 2

Appetite, 36, 38

Aquinas, Thomas, 226

Aretaic appraisal, 232–36, 241. *See also* Accountability; Attributability

Aristotle, 43, 50, 221, 226, 227–28, 229, 230, 257

Arpaly, Nomy, 205–6

Assumption of the Transitivity of Autonomy, 133–38, 140–41, 150, 154–55. *See also* Autonomy, and coercion

Athens, 1 n. 1, 3, 6

Attributability, 232–33. *See also* Accountability; Aretaic appraisal

Augusta National Golf Club, 277–78, 279, 280, 281. *See also* Autonomy, group

Autarky (*autarchia*). *See* self-sufficiency

Authority: agential, 168–69, 209, 226, 265

Autonomy: arational, 197–98; and coercion, 5, 101, 102–3, 131–35; conditional, 245, 256–58, 293–94; defined, 32, 70, 101, 307–8; and democracy, 54–56, 107–8; deontological view of, 272–74, 284–85; developed over time, 80, 91–98, 102; and duress, 127–28, 130–33, 135–55;

etymology of the term, 1, 2–3, 4–5, 26, 30, 90 n. 7; "global" sense of, 100–101, 109; group, 265, 273–85; hierarchical analyses of (*see* Hierarchical analyses); impaired, 127–28, 130–38, 141–55; "local" sense of, 100, 109; and moral philosophy, 30–32; political, 1, 4, 6, 7; and politics, 31–33, 51–69; preservation of, 89, 121–26; psychological arguments for, 81–86; psychological impediments to, 102–3, 109–10, 115 n. 33; as a right (or class of rights), 32, 109, 114, 117–18, 265–66, 268, 286, 290, 293–96, 301–2, 306; as self-control, 101–2, 201–2, 256; as self-determination, 108–12, 220; as self-direction, 26, 34–42, 101–2, 199, 204, 206, 218; as self-governance, 26, 34, 71–80, 83–85, 101–2, 221, 226–29, 231–32, 241, 243–44; as self-regulation, 84, 87, 199–204; unconditional, 245, 254–57, 293–94; value of, 6, 34, 81–90, 99–100, 106–7, 112–26, 265–74

Autonomy-Hierarchy (AH) thesis, 156–58, 167, 169–71, 172, 175–76. *See also* Hierarchical analyses

Autonomy-Transparency (AT) thesis, 171–73

Beauchamp, Tom L., 266

Behavior, 30; patterns of, 245, 251–52, 253, 257–59, 263–64; voluntary, 20, 249, 257, 305 n. 26

Behaviorism: and behavioral psychology, 245–47 (*see also* Skinner, B. F.); teleological, 245–47, 249–52, 254–64

Beitz, Charles, 275–76, 281 n. 23

Benson, Paul, 148

Berlin, Isaiah, 111 n. 25, 114, 116, 118–19, 121

Blessedness: Spinoza's concept of, 43, 45, 49, 56, 57, 58. *See also* Self-perfection

Bondage, 33, 37, 177. *See also* Slavery

Braino (example of the). *See* Manipulation

Bratman, Michael E., 182, 209–10, 211

Brave New World (Huxley), 310, 327, 331, 332

Capacity: for autonomy, 67, 68, 101–4, 120–21, 241; for moral decision, 222, 224, 225–26, 237

For EU product safety concerns, contact us at Calle de José Abascal, 56–1°,
28003 Madrid, Spain or eugpsr@cambridge.org.

www.ingramcontent.com/pod-product-compliance
Ingram Content Group UK Ltd.
Pitfield, Milton Keynes, MK11 3LW, UK
UKHW020341140625
459647UK00018B/2257